Toward a Society under Law

Toward a Society under Law
Citizens and Their Police in Latin America

Edited by

Joseph S. Tulchin and Meg Ruthenburg

Woodrow Wilson Center Press
Washington, D.C.

The Johns Hopkins University Press
Baltimore, Maryland

EDITORIAL OFFICES

Woodrow Wilson Center Press
One Woodrow Wilson Plaza
1300 Pennsylvania Avenue, N.W.
Washington, D.C. 20004-3027
Telephone: 202-691-4029
www.wilsoncenter.org

ORDER FROM

The Johns Hopkins University Press
Hampden Station
P.O. Box 50370
Baltimore, Maryland 21211
Telephone: 1-800-537-5487
www.press.jhu.edu/books/

Cartography on pages 106, 292, 293 by Matt Kania

© 2006 by the Woodrow Wilson International Center for Scholars
All rights reserved
Printed in the United States of America on acid-free paper ∞

2 4 6 8 9 7 5 3 1

Library of Congress Cataloging-in-Publication Data

Toward a society under law : citizens and their police in Latin America /
edited by Joseph S. Tulchin and Meg Ruthenburg.
  p. cm.
  Includes bibliographical references and index.
  ISBN 0-8018-8559-0 (pbk. : alk. paper) — ISBN 0-8018-8558-2 (cloth : alk. paper)
  1. Community policing—Latin America. 2. Police—Latin America. 3.
Crime prevention—Latin America. 4. Rule of law—Latin America. I.
Tulchin, Joseph S., 1939– II. Ruthenburg, Meg.
  HV7936.C83T69 2006
  363.2098—dc22   2006033496

**Woodrow Wilson
Center Press**
Washington, D.C.

The Woodrow Wilson International Center for Scholars, established by Congress in 1968 and headquartered in Washington, D.C., is a living national memorial to President Wilson. The Center's mission is to commemorate the ideals and concerns of Woodrow Wilson by providing a link between the worlds of ideas and policy, while fostering research, study, discussion, and collaboration among a broad spectrum of individuals concerned with policy and scholarship in national and international affairs. Supported by public and private funds, the Center is a nonpartisan institution. It establishes and maintains a neutral forum for free, open, and informed dialogue. Conclusions or opinions express in Center publications and programs are those of the authors and speakers and do not necessarily reflect the views of the Center staff, fellows, trustees, advisory groups, or any individuals or organizations that provide financial support to the Center.

The Center is the publisher of *The Wilson Quarterly* and home of Woodrow Wilson Center Press, *dialogue* radio and television, and the monthly newsletter "Centerpoint." For more information about the Center's activities and publications, please visit us on the web at www.wilsoncenter.org.

Lee H. Hamilton, President and Director

Board of Trustees
Joseph B. Gildenhorn, Chair
David A. Metzner, Vice Chair

Public Members: James H. Billington, Librarian of Congress; Bruce Cole, Chairman, National Endowment for the Humanities; Michael O. Leavitt, Secretary of Health and Human Services; Condoleezza Rice, Secretary of State; Lawrence M. Small, Secretary of the Smithsonian Institution; Margaret Spellings, Secretary of Education; Allen Weinstein, Archivist of the United States; Designated appointee of the president from within the federal government: Tami Longaberger

Private Citizen Members: Robin Cook, Donald E. Garcia, Bruce S. Gelb, Sander R. Gerber, Charles L. Glazer, Susan Hutchison, Ignacio E. Sanchez

Contents

List of Tables and Figures ix

Preface xi

1 Introduction: Toward a Society under Law
  Joseph S. Tulchin and Meg Ruthenburg 1

Part I Issues and Themes

2 The Impact of Community Policing and Police Reform
  in Latin America *Hugo Frühling* 15

3 Advocacy Networks and Police Reform: Assessing
  Their Impact *Claudio A. Fuentes* 55

4 Crime and Social Policies in Latin American Urban Centers
  Claudio C. Beato F. 90

5 Measuring the Costs of Crime and Violence as an
  Input to Public Policy: Evidence from Mexico City
  *Graciela Teruel, Renata Villoro, Andrew Morrison,
  and James K. Hammitt* 126

Part II Case Studies

6 Paths toward Police and Judicial Reform in Latin America
  Paulo de Mesquita Neto 153

7 Police Reform in Latin America: Brazil, Argentina, and Chile
  Heather H. Ward 171

8 Citizen Participation and Public Security in Argentina,
   Brazil, and Chile: Lessons from an Initial Experience
   Catalina Smulovitz   206

9 Citizen Security Policy in Argentina: The National
   Crime Prevention Plan *Alberto Föhrig,
   Julia S. Pomares, and Cecilia Gortari*   243

10 Civilian Oversight of Security in Peru: The Testimony
   of a Participant *Carlos Basombrío Iglesias*   261

11 Elements for a Study of Crime in Mexico City
   Arturo Alvarado Mendoza   280

Part III Conclusions and Recommendations

12 Conclusion: Security and the Rule of Law in a Democratic
   Society *Joseph S. Tulchin and Meg Ruthenburg*   319

About the Contributors   325
Index   329

Tables and Figures

Tables

4.1.	Homicide rates for Latin American countries, selected years, 1989–2000	91
4.2.	IDB-supported violence control programs in Latin America, 2002	94
4.3.	Cost-benefit comparisons of selected intervention strategies in childhood and adolescence, Rand study, 1996	97
4.4.	Cost-benefit comparison of eight Brazilian crime prevention programs	98
4.5.	Economic costs of violent crime in six Latin American countries (expressed as percentage of GDP in 1997)	100
4.6.	Comparing areas with and without homicide clusters in Belo Horizonte, 1995–2002	107
5.1.	Economic costs of violence using an accounting framework (percent of GDP)	129
5.2.	Variable definitions	136
5.3.	Descriptive statistics	137
5.4.	Hedonic estimates of price-attribute relationship	138
5.5.	Computed elasticities of housing rents vis-à-vis explanatory variables	139
5.A1.	"Specification results," Box-Cox transformation	143
5.A2.	"Specification results"	144

5.A3.	"Specification results"	145
8.1.	Selected general crime statistics for Saavedra area, October 1999–May 2000	216
11.1	Percentage of crimes reported in the Federal District and metropolitan municipalities of México State, 1999	286
11.2	Organized criminal activity by type of offense, 1994–1998	299
11.3.	Estimates of unreported crimes, 1996–2002	305

Figures

4.1.	Homicide distribution in Belo Horizonte, 1995–1998	106
4.2.	Interpersonal violence, robbery, and armed robbery	110
5.A1.	Box-Cox transformation	143
5.A2.	Box-Cox transformation	144
5.A3.	Box-Cox transformation	145
11.1.	Crime trends throughout Mexico and the capital metropolitan area, 1988–2001	284
11.2.	Crime rates in Mexico City metropolitan area, 1995–1999	285
11.3.	Crime incidence by borough and municipality, 1997	292
11.4.	Crime incidence by borough in the Federal District, 2002	293
11.5.	Proportion of adults reporting being the victim of a crime in the past three months in annual surveys, 1996 to January–May 2002	301
11.6.	Proportion of adults victimized by crime: incidence of crimes reported versus not reported to authorities, 1996 to January–May 2002	302
11.7.	Victimization and crime rates (per 100,000 inhabitants), Federal District, 1996–2002	303
11.8.	Comparison of crimes reported to authorities and crime incidence reported in victimization surveys, 1996–2002	304
11.9.	Estimates of unreported crimes	305
11.10.	Ratio of reported crimes and estimated crime incidence from surveys, 1996–2002	306
11.11.	Evolution of crime and population growth in Mexico City, 1989–2002	307

Preface

The Woodrow Wilson Center's Latin American Program has been engaged in studying citizen security for several years. In 2003, we published *Crime and Violence in Latin America: Citizen Security, Democracy, and the State,* edited by Hugo Frühling and Joseph S. Tulchin with Heather A. Golding. This volume represented the first phase of our inquiry into citizen security, compiling a broad set of papers from diverse authors to assess the state of crime and violence in Latin America.

The present volume is born of our second phase of work, in which we convoked forums throughout Latin America to bring together the stakeholders in reform processes including the police, the judiciary, and government officials. Based on this experience, we decided to commission a new set of papers analyzing more profoundly different kinds of police reform and various aspects of crime reduction policies.

Through these first two projects, we discovered that soaring crime rates are not the only problem facing countries in Latin America. Due to poor relations with police, citizens have a tendency to exaggerate levels of crime. This inflated perception of insecurity presents a real threat to Latin America's democracies, as citizens call for more repressive policing and wax nostalgic for the kind of heavy-handed social control they experienced under dictatorships. To combat the perception of insecurity, the distance between the police and the citizenry must be closed; citizen participation is key to achieving this. With this in mind, we formulated our latest project on citizen security: an action-research project aimed at reducing the distance between the forces of law and order and the community they serve.

The Latin American Program's work on citizen security has been generously supported by the William and Flora Hewlett Foundation. The editors would also like to extend our appreciation to Latin American Program interns Allison Werner, Alana Parker, and Lisa Kraus. Tamara Taraciuk was an indispensable support person for the citizen security project. Cristina Jimenez, Jessica Varat, and Allison Garland also helped shape the final manuscript. Finally, the editors would like to thank Cindy Arnson and Joe Brinley, who oversaw the final stages of publication.

Toward a Society under Law

Chapter 1

Introduction: Toward a Society under Law

Joseph S. Tulchin and Meg Ruthenburg

Nearly a decade ago, the Latin American Program of the Woodrow Wilson Center convened a group of experts from around the hemisphere to talk about the rising rates of crime that seemed to affect nearly every country in the region. There were two concerns that led to convoking the meeting. The first was that crime rates, especially for violent crimes, were soaring, even in some countries, such as Argentina or Costa Rica, which were long considered relatively peaceful. In some places, most notably Colombia and cities such as São Paulo, more murders were being committed than in other regions of the world and more than at any time since data on such matters had been collected. Indeed, Latin America became considered one of the most violent regions in the world. This kind of violence and lack of security affects social confidence in the democratic system, an element central to the social compact, without which political stability is impossible. At the same time, crime and citizen insecurity undermine sustainable development by wasting resources and corroding the confidence necessary to engage in economic activity. For these reasons, it was critical to gain an understanding of the crime problem in Latin America.

The second concern that prompted our meeting was more complex. The media seemed to be obsessed with crime and there was considerable evidence from public opinion polls in several countries that, in large measure as a result of word of mouth communication with friends and family and the sensationalism of the media, the public's sense of how often crimes were committed actually exceeded the known data about crime rates by significant margins. The public reaction to this sense of insecurity was to call upon their elected representatives to crack down on crime, even if that meant resorting to measures that undermined democratic governance and the rule of law. In a region where democracy still was "new" or "unconsolidated" in most countries, calls for greater use of force to clamp down on crime, for the use of the armed forces where the police were considered too weak for the challenge, and for other measures associated with authoritarian regimes were disquieting. In addition, it became apparent that an inflated sense of insecurity leads to the alienation of the individual from his or her society and, consequently, diminishes the quality of citizenship in Latin America. In this way, the psychosocial perception of insecurity seemed as significant as crime itself in undermining democratic governance, which suggests that reducing the perception of insecurity may be easier to achieve in the short run than lowering rates of crime.

The question posed at the first meeting, then, was what could be done to deal with citizen insecurity that would strengthen, not undermine, democratic governance. We began with a survey of conditions in the region and a general assessment of the important lines of inquiry. This effort resulted in the publication of the book *Crime and Violence in Latin America: Citizen Security, Democracy, and the State* (2003), edited by Hugo Frühling and Joseph S. Tulchin with Heather A. Golding (Woodrow Wilson Center Press and John Hopkins University Press).

Several key issues emerged in this volume leading the editors to formulate seven policy recommendations to increase citizen security and strengthen the rule of law in Latin America. These recommendations call for policing strategies that reduce the distance between the forces of law and order and the citizens they serve; the development of clear indicators of police effectiveness, particularly metrics that could be compared across countries and time; better external and internal oversight of police forces; addressing crime through preventive action and strengthening democratic institutions; professionalizing police forces, including equipping them with appropriate technology; sensitivity to the legacies of past authoritarian governments when addressing questions of the public's relationship with security forces; and, finally, the development of partnerships among international organizations, civil society organizations, and the state.

These conclusions all indicated that it was necessary to reduce the sense of space between the police and the population and make dealing with the community an integral part of the work of a professional police force. As a result, we decided to carry out a second phase of research focusing on applying aspects of these recommendations to police reform and the relationship between citizens and police in Latin America. We also decided to become proactive in the effort to achieve our objectives and approached the governments of several countries and offered to partner with them in organizing forums aimed at convincing both the police and the community that police reform was possible and useful. In these forums, we brought together the police, the judiciary, and other state officials in a nonpartisan setting to share the conclusions reached in our first phase of research and promote dialogue among the stakeholders in the reform process. These forums were successful, in part, due to the facilitation of the Wilson Center. On the one hand, the center was able to serve as a neutral intermediary in highly charged national dialogues among actors who often did not trust one another. On the other hand, because of the Wilson Center's long experience with comparative research, we were able to forward a comparative approach to citizen security research and reform. This comparative approach was successful in defusing the claim—made variously by the police, ministries of the interior, and community groups—that their country was unique, their problems more complex than those of other countries, and that, as a result, police reform was impossible. In each of the four experiences—in Argentina, Brazil, Chile, and Peru—we succeeded in advancing the dialogue and in speeding the policy process. To complement these practical interventions in national debates, we commissioned papers to evaluate the reform process in six countries in light of the policy recommendations resulting from our first phase of research. The present volume is the result of these endeavors.

Toward the Rule of Law

While our work at times may focus on murder rates or the technology available to the region's police forces, the overarching purpose of our studies and interventions is to strengthen the rule of law. We believe that it is impossible to maintain the rule of law without a professional police force. Nevertheless, the context in which that police is professionalized is crucial. Improving the quality of the police must be accompanied by an increasing sense of accountability among the police. Accountability, in this case, means both compliance with rules and laws and a better sense of how to serve their communities. The rule of law requires the constructive interaction of the police, judiciary, and population. Each of the three elements bear responsibility for the rule of law, and all three must learn to interact. This is a particularly difficult problem in countries, such as Argentina or Mexico, where democratic citizenship is of very recent origin and is still imperfectly developed, the judiciary has no tradition of autonomy or of professionalism, and where the police were traditionally instruments of authoritarian repression. Even twenty years after the transition to democracy in Argentina, for example, the police of the province of Buenos Aires are still regarded as thoroughly corrupt, as riddled with ties to organized crime, and as a force that has little respect for citizen rights and due process. Reform in such extreme cases is akin to cleaning the Augean stables.

At the international level, creating a community of democracies is a powerful buttress for national and even local efforts at judicial and police reform. In the quest for greater accountability, in the struggle against corruption, in the demand for standards of law and order, the most advanced lead the less advanced. International civil society organizations, especially those concerned with protecting human rights or due process, have shown remarkable persistence in their efforts to defend individuals from abuse or to defend due process and have scored impressive successes over the past decade. They also have taken the lead in pushing international organizations to codify these positions. While the unilateralism of the administration of George W. Bush and its hostility to multilateral codes of conduct have slowed the pace of the advance of international civil society, they have not stopped the process. It is optimistic—although not quixotic or Pollyannaish—to expect that the central tendency in global society is toward the rule of law.

An Overview of the Book

This book addresses a wide variety of issues affecting police reform efforts and the prevention and reduction of crime. The first part of the book addresses some of the major issues and themes in police reform, including types of reform, the role of different actors in reform efforts, and the function and importance of accurate crime indicators and indicators of police effectiveness. The second part of the book consists of case studies. In the third part, the editors offer suggestions for future research and intervention.

In moving toward the rule of law, it is essential to get the citizenry involved not just to reduce crime but to ensure democratic solutions are sought instead of repressive policies. The key is to lead the citizenry closer to a more constructive relationship with the forces of law and order. This inflated perception of insecurity is inextricably tied to the poor relationship between the forces of law and order and the citizenry. Contributing factors that make it difficult to generate trust amongst citizens themselves, and between the community and police forces, include the stigmatization by police of youth and the poor; the perception in society that the police forces are inefficient and corrupt; the community's reluctance to denounce crimes; the increasing demand for private security; and changes in citizens' behavior, such as adding security bars to windows and doors and not going out alone at night. In practice, this situation and the exaggerated perception of insecurity lead to increased demands for repressive policies and to citizens being more willing to sacrifice certain liberties in order to feel more secure; for example, anxious citizens have demanded longer jail sentences, lower ages of criminal responsibility, and the use of the death penalty in reaction to their sense of insecurity. The dilemma, then, for policymakers in democratic societies is to create policies that can increase security while maintaining respect for the rule of law.

One way to bring the police closer to the community is through community policing programs. In Chapter 2, Hugo Frühling examines the origins of police reform and analyzes four community policing projects in Colombia, Guatemala, and Brazil. Frühling argues that police reform has become a necessity as the relationship between the police and the citizenry has changed. Whereas police forces in Latin America's nondemocratic regimes tended to be militarized, centralized, and isolated from society, the region's newly democratic states call for a different kind of police. A dramatic increase in crime rates since the return to democracy further exacerbates the need for an effective, responsive, and open police force. Indeed, Frühling's analysis suggests that the police have in fact been a part of the problem. The lack of effective communication between the police and the citizenry combined with high rates of police abuse have led to a situation where citizens avoid contact with police; they may not report crimes and may be uncooperative with investigations. Given this situation, the community policing model, a model emphasizing preventive policing and strong community relations, has emerged as a solution to Latin America's policing problems.

Frühling reviews the North American community policing model and the ways in which this model has been implemented in Latin America. In Chile, the military-type police force, the Carabineros, instituted the Quadrant Plan, a plan designed to address high crime rates in urban areas. Frühling also examines four other cases of community policing programs that have been evaluated by the Inter-American Development Bank. These programs exist in São Paulo, Brazil; Villa Nueva, Guatemala; Bogotá, Colombia; and Belo Horizonte, Brazil. In his analysis, Frühling concludes that in general these community policing programs do lead to a better relationship between the police and the community; it is unclear, however, whether they have a significant impact on reducing crime and violence. In any case, these programs by themselves do not necessarily correct the problems of police abuse and corruption. Cities utilizing community policing programs may need to incorporate other measures, including officer retraining, in their reform efforts in order to deal with abuse in police forces.

It could be argued that there are two different kinds of reform that Latin American police organizations must undergo: one type of reform would allow the police to deal with crime and violence more effectively, the second type would make police forces more accountable to the citizens they serve. In Chapter 3, Claudio Fuentes addresses this second aspect of police reform by assessing the impact of advocacy networks on police accountability. Fuentes utilizes the advocacy coalition approach to analyze how advocacy networks in contemporary Argentina and Chile can influence public policy and the factors that impede these networks from having an enduring impact on policy processes. Based on this analysis, Fuentes offers a series of recommendations concerning the role of organized civil society in police reform efforts. He demonstrates that civil society organizations can play an essential role in police reform by monitoring police practices and policy implementation and scrutinizing legal procedures.

The dramatic growth of crime and violence in Latin America is not well understood. In Chapter 4, Claudio Beato emphasizes how this lack of comprehension may point police reform down the wrong path. Beato demonstrates that with only a cursory understanding of the phenomena of crime and violence, policymakers often put forward counterproductive strategies. The sensationalistic coverage of crime and violence in the media often lead people to conclude that crime is such a pressing problem there is no time to waste on studies and evaluations. Policymakers often believe that shoring up police forces with better equipment and higher wages will lead to a reduction in crime. Beato argues, however, that police organizations may be in more need of updated managerial models and better data about crime than better arms. Beato views the lack of reliable data and broad-based information on crime and violence as a major hindrance to police reform programs. He advocates analyzing the spatial distribution of crime in major urban centers as a way for police forces to target specific kinds of criminal activity in the areas where they are likely to occur; this kind of analysis also allows police to design effective prevention programs based on reliable data. This way of understanding crime and violence moves us away from a socioeconomic understanding of criminal behavior toward one that implicates social and environmental policies.

Toward this same goal of creating data and indicators for better understanding crime and violence, Graciela Teruel, Renata Volloro, Andrew Morrison, and James Hammit use the new approach of hedonic and contingent valuation methodologies to estimate the socioeconomic costs of violence in Mexico City. Reducing crime and violence is a task that involves both police and the citizenry; the authors of Chapter 5 focus on society's understanding of crime and, specifically, on the ways in which society is willing to participate in combating crime. The hedonic model and the contingent valuation methodology the authors use are known as "willingness-to-pay" methodologies. Here, the authors measure how willing the population of Mexico City is to pay for reductions in crime. By understanding the concerns and desires of the community, as well as its willingness to contribute to solutions, policymakers may tailor crime-reduction strategies to address the particular kinds of crime that concern a specific neighborhood. This strategy would not only contribute to citizen security through a reduction in the actual crime rate but would also boost the community's perception of security, which may be as important as crime rates for strengthening democratic governance.

The second part of the book uses case studies to illustrate different kinds of police reform processes. In Chapter 6, Paulo de Mesquita Neto characterizes three paths to police reform depending on whether the reform effort was driven by international actors, the government, or civil society. International actors interceded in the reform efforts in Haiti and Guatemala. In Haiti, however, police and judicial reform followed an international intervention; in Guatemala reform came about following a peace process.

Colombia, Peru, and Chile represent cases where reform has come from inside the government. The kind of reform undertaken, though, depends greatly on what part of the government proposes the reform. In both Colombia and Peru, reform came about in the context of severe public insecurity. These reform efforts were led by the government with the support of the military. In Chile, on the other hand, the police and the judiciary—not the government—led the reforms.

Lastly, police and judicial reform may come about as a result of pressure from civil society. In Argentina and Brazil, where police are not only distrusted by nongovernmental organizations and citizens but where they are known actors in cases of horrendous human rights violations, civil society organizations played a crucial role in reforming the institutions of law and order.

In Chapter 7, Heather Ward reviews recent police reform projects in Argentina, Brazil, and Chile. Ward concurs with Mesquita Neto in that the type of reform undertaken and the results of the reform process depend heavily on which actor or actors drove the reform effort. After her analysis of reform in the three countries, she concludes that reform processes may be strengthened with the involvement of multiple actors. In addition, Ward suggests ways in which three principal actors—the police, the state, and civil society—can best participate in the reform process. For police forces, for example, it is important that the reform process include something positive for the police and engage the active participation of police officials of different ranks. However, police reform must also involve the state and civil society in order to be considered legitimate by society. Ward warns against politician-led police reform using the Buenos Aires example as a cautionary tale. In Buenos Aires, as in other cases, politicians opted for overly ambitious reforms that could not be completed in the short period of time in which a politician fills a particular post. These reforms also alienated the police from the process, thereby condemning the efforts to failure. The greatest challenge for civil society, on the other hand, is getting the police to accept civil society groups as overseers and collaborators. The case of Minas Gerais is a useful example of civil society–police collaboration; the Center for Studies of Crime and Public Safety has actually helped the police collect and interpret data, which allows for more effective policing. Finally, while Ward emphasizes that there is no set model for police reform, she suggests that more evaluations of reform experiments are necessary in order to help shape more effective reform programs.

Catalina Smulovitz also calls for further evaluation of police reform experiences. In Chapter 8, she examines community policing projects in Argentina, Brazil, and Chile in terms of the levels and kinds of citizen participation they involve. While the experiments she analyzes cannot all properly be called community policing, each of them invokes citizen participation in some way. In Argentina, Smulovitz concludes, public concern about insecurity has led to contradictory and undependable policies. In Chile, on the other hand, the community policing policies have been more constant due to a greater government presence. Finally, in Brazil both public authorities and civil society groups have been able to shape the security agenda.

Like Frühling, Smulovitz concludes that community policing programs in themselves are not sufficient to correct systemic problems in police agencies.

Specifically, she identifies four principal problems in implementing community policing programs: trust, restructuring police agencies, relations with nonpolice bureaucratic agencies, and citizen participation. Community policing initiatives presuppose a certain level of trust between the public and the police. Smulovitz finds that this level of trust rarely exists. Furthermore, building trust is a long-term process, which does not bode well for the short-term success of these community policing initiatives. Restructuring police agencies in order make community policing successful is no less difficult. It is necessary to work with police agencies so that police do not feel threatened by the changes and, therefore, may be more receptive to them. Another problem undermining the effectiveness of community policing programs is the lack of coordination between state agencies, polices forces, and community organizations. Community policing should serve the needs of the community; when there is little coordination or collaboration with the community, it is difficult for police to respond to the community's concerns and wishes. Finally, because citizen participation is integral to community policing, it is important that participation be sustained over time. Steps must be taken to promote and maintain community participation in these initiatives.

In Chapter 9, Alberto Föhrig, Julia Pomares, and Cecilia Gortari undertake a close analysis of the National Crime Prevention Plan, which was a nationwide urban security plan for Argentina designed in 2000. The plan is important in that it brings together different state agencies and departments and other actors in an unprecedented way. While the authors concede that the plan is an important step in addressing the complex issue of security, they recognize problems with the will to change the decision-making process on security issues and a lack of statistical and qualitative data, a hindrance to designing and evaluating security policies. Furthermore, better coordination of the different aspects of law and order, such as police, the judiciary, and the penal systems, is needed. Lastly, the authors lament the failure to fully incorporate the Argentine Federal Police into the plan.

In Chapter 10, Carlos Basombrío describes the situation reformers faced at the beginning of President Toledo's administration, by sharing his personal experience as vice minister of the interior during the recent police reform process in Peru. When Basombrío and his team entered the ministry with newly elected democratic president Alejandro Toledo, they encountered a security situation in need of modernization and oversight. Under the government of Alberto Fujimori, public security was under the direct control of the armed forces. Because of the excesses and abuses of power that occurred under Fujimori, civilian oversight of police and military activity was an important priority for Toledo and his administration. The task of Toledo's Ministry of the Interior, therefore, was to put security under civilian control. In addition to appointing a civilian minister of the interior, Toledo selected a civilian minister of defense. The minister of the interior undertook an ambitious reform of the National Police, which called for restructuring the National Police force, creating better oversight of police activity, and modernizing the force. The Special Commission for Restructuring the National Police concluded that the police should contribute to the democratization of the country and improve relations with the community by encouraging citizen participation. The commission also argued that the quality of life for the National Police must be improved, corruption must be confronted, and a modern police training system must be developed.

Basombrío's experience at the Ministry of Interior also provides important lessons on the importance of strengthening democratic institutions. Citizen security had not been a priority for Fujimori, who was engaged in a military struggle with the Shining Path movement. In fact, Fujimori used Shining Path and the citizenry's sense of insecurity to gain support for his repressive policies. While he was eventually able to quell the threat of Shining Path, this victory came at the expense of Peru's democratic institutions. When Fujimori was finally forced to leave power and seek exile in Japan, he had devastated Peru's democracy. Because of this, Toledo's administration was determined to fight insecurity through democratic means and by shoring up Peru's institutions of democracy.

In Chapter 11, Arturo Alvarado develops a snapshot of crime in Mexico City. His goal is twofold: to define and describe crime and to build a set of data to understand and address the phenomenon.

In the third part of the book, the editors outline recommendations for future research and intervention, focusing more specifically on the role of the public because, in the final analysis, the rule of law depends as much on an engaged citizenry and on a transparent judiciary as on a professional police force. The challenge for the future is to get the community involved as the ultimate guarantee of the rule of law. The editors propose a type of community intervention in order to bolster citizen participation and positive relations between the citizenry and the forces of law and order. The approach needed would specifically focus on strengthening democratic governance and increasing citizen participation in forums of discussion of citizen security issues. In addition to efforts to improve policing and judicial effectiveness, improving citizen security requires measures that enhance accountability and citizen participation. This type of approach presupposes three basic assumptions. The first is that capacity building and empowerment will increase citizens' interest in citizen security issues and that will derive in a greater participation in forums of discussion on these issues. The second assumption is that bringing the community and the police forces together will counteract the public's exaggerated perception of insecurity. The last assumption is that citizen participation in security issues is vital to obtain the desired results, that is, a series of policies at the local level that will lead to a decrease in crime rates without undermining democracy and the rule of law.

What is clear is that increasing rates of crime and the public's escalating anxiety over crime and insecurity pose real threats to the health of democracies in Latin America. It is also obvious that while police reform and judicial reform are necessary, they are not sufficient to resolve the problem of insecurity. In order to meaningfully and effectively address citizen insecurity, the citizenry must be involved in a way that promotes a cohesive and inclusive society capable of being coagents in their security without resorting to violence or vigilantism and without demanding that the state use repressive tactics that weaken the foundation of a democratic society.

Part I

Issues and Themes

Chapter 2

The Impact of Community Policing and Police Reform in Latin America

Hugo Frühling

Introduction

The 1991 peace agreement between the government of El Salvador and representatives of the armed opposition, as well as the similar 1996 agreement in Guatemala, paved the way for two of the most comprehensive recent efforts to reform police institutions in Latin America. Both agreements called for new civilian police to replace the old police, which were controlled by the armed forces and known for repressive, politicized action that rendered them untenable in a democratic system. The reforms involved a range of international actors and occurred in parallel with institutional changes that introduced oral trials and an adversarial criminal justice system based on the U.S. and German models (Stanley 1999; Neild 2002).

There were also attempts to transform police forces elsewhere in the region. During the 1990s, the military police in various Brazilian states launched community policing programs. The announced goal was to improve relationships with the community, reduce police violence, and gain greater public acceptance. The first formally evaluated experiment took place in Copacabana, Rio de Janeiro, in 1994. It was brief, but was followed by similar experiments in many other Brazilian cities (Muniz et al. 1997). A more systematic recent reform effort has taken place in Peru, following the exit of President Alberto Fujimori in 2001. The Argentine province of Mendoza launched in 2005 a community policing project aimed at increasing responsibilities and resources of chiefs of precincts, as well as improving the quality of the service provided to the communities. The Chilean police force, the Carabineros, is also moving forward with a strategic plan that involves preventive strategies focused on small geographic areas called quadrants. The purpose of this approach is to increase the level of contact with the populace.

Given the differing levels of professionalism among the various police forces involved in these processes of change, and the different political and social contexts in which the forces operate, it may well be asked whether these reforms can properly be analyzed as if they were similar in nature. The catalysts for reform differ in different countries. In Argentina, for instance, most of the reforms have been promoted and implemented by provincial governments dismayed with the scandals provoked by police corruption. In Guatemala and El Salvador, the transformation of the police was prompted by the United Nations as well as bilateral technical assistance in the process of building new and democratic police forces. In Colombia it was the police itself that decided to initiate internal reforms given that the government was predisposed to impose major changes on its structure and strategies. At a certain level of generality, however, similar driving forces are at work; these include the process of democratization that has been underway in the region in recent years, which has reinforced demands for institutional change to reduce police violence, open channels of communication with the community, and encourage the concept that the police should serve the community; an increase in crime, which has created pressure to professionalize police strategy and personnel; and, finally, dissemination of models of public administration and management that emphasize a flexible response by public institutions, focus primarily on results rather than on compliance with norms, and encourage decentralized decision making and an orientation emphasizing the public service aspect of the police.

Although the problems faced by Latin America's numerous police forces vary significantly, there are underlying similarities that justify a common approach to analyzing the challenges they are dealing with today. One similarity is the complex relationship between the police and the government, which for extended periods of time has been undemocratic. Latin American police forces have tended to be political tools, so that in many countries they have been manipulated by the government in power. This has seriously undermined professionalism and respect for the rule of law, since it creates incentives for the application of individualistic criteria in the selection and promotion of police personnel; partly as a reaction to this, there has been a trend in Chile toward isolating police institutions from political influence.

Latin American police forces today are still based on a model that is hierarchical, centralized, and military in nature. This is most evident in the region's militarized police services, such as the Brazilian Military Police, the Chilean Carabineros, and the Peruvian National Police, but may also be seen in forces that define themselves as civilian. The hierarchical organizational model facilitates discipline within the force, but reform is required if progress is to be made toward more flexible management models that create incentives for cooperation with the community.

Police training systems and the content taught tend to reinforce the existing organizational model by emphasizing obedience, discipline, and theory and knowledge of legal norms, rather than teaching results-based management methods. With the possible exception of Chile, surveys indicate that the public has a low opinion of this type of policing. Hence, citizens report a relatively low percentage of the actual crimes committed, because of their feeling that the police will do little by way of response (United Nations 1999, 36–38).

Of particular note among efforts to solve these problems are projects that emphasize the local component of the police's role, and efforts to establish a closer relationship with the community. This chapter examines some of the origins of the reform process underway in many of the region's police forces. It considers the role of community policing and its connection with underlying changes in policing models, and looks at four community policing projects—in Bogotá, Colombia, in Villa Nueva, Guatemala, and in São Paulo and Belo Horizonte, Brazil. An analysis of these cases, along with an assessment conducted by the Inter-American Development Bank (IDB), highlights the essential components of any police reform capable of achieving the desired results.

The Origins of Police Reform

The general nature and specific content of the reform efforts described here are shaped by three general factors. The first is the process of democratization that occurred in many of the region's countries during the 1980s and 1990s, which made it clear that existing police forces and actions were incompatible with democratic norms and human rights. The second is a sharp rise in common crime in almost all of the region's countries, leading to urgent demands for increased police presence and for government solutions. This demand, reflected in surveys, has led to the creation, or increased prominence, of think tanks involved in studying policing issues, as well as to the leadership role assumed by government (and, in some cases, by police forces themselves) in addressing the issue. A final factor is the discussion of changes in policing taking place against a global (and, specifically, Latin American) background of an evolving state. The size of government is diminishing, public enterprises are being privatized, central government functions are being decentralized and assigned to local or regional levels of government, and mechanisms are being sought to hold government accountable for its effectiveness and efficiency (Bresser Pereira 1999). The concepts that shape the reform of the state frequently affect proposals relating to policing. In particular, it is often suggested that business management criteria be applied to police management. It is clear that the problems facing police forces are shared by Latin American public sectors generally, although the problems are more serious in the case of police forces because of the coercive power they wield.

The confluence of these three historical factors explains why current police reform proposals face the problems and challenges of institutional change that are so different from what they previously were. First, demands to control crime, while at the same time drastically reducing police abuse, may be perceived as contradictory by large segments of the public. This makes consistent and long term reform difficult in many cases.[1] Second, increased crime and fear of crime create pressure for police to show short-term results, when the organizational problems that they face require long-term measures. Finally, the large numbers of individuals in the region's police forces, serious funding problems, and a centralized and highly regulated management model create major obstacles to the transformation and modernization of police institutions.[2]

The Police and the Citizen in Latin America

The establishment of new democratic regimes in Latin America during the 1980s and 1990s opened the door to criticism of the police abuses that had spread extensively under previous authoritarian regimes. An analysis of complaints of violence, at the hands of the civilian police, to the Internal Affairs Unit of the Civil Police of Bahia (Pernambuco state, Brazil) gives cause for serious concern: 24.12 percent of a total of 1,140 complaints during the period 1993–1997 concerned torture, 5.61 percent beatings, 2.8 percent homicide, and 6.84 percent death threats. In total, these categories represented 40 percent of all complaints. The majority of these were merely filed, or led to recommendations for administrative sanctions, without ever reaching the judicial system (Lemos-Nelson 2001). The data reflect both the seriousness of the violations allegedly committed by the police and a lack of internal administrative control over police conduct.

The police of the state of São Paulo suffered from similar problems. Incidents of violence by the force frequently received wide coverage in the media. In 1991, 1,056 civilians were killed by the Military Police; in 1992, the number rose to 1,421. Although the toll dropped to 592 in 1995, 368 in 1996, and 405 in 1997,[3] victimization surveys showed that only 33 percent of crime was reported to the police, out of fear or due to a belief that the police were inefficient (Mesquita Neto and Affonso 1998). The persistence of this situation led to the criticism of the force by human rights organizations and academics. The Nucleus for the Study of Violence of the University of São Paulo began a joint project with the Human Rights Center of the University of Ottawa aimed at increasing contacts between São Paulo military police officers and Canadian police officers that might eventually lead to the adoption of community policing strategies by the São Paulo police.

A survey of low-income sectors in Chile's three largest cities, in 1992, early in the democratic regime, revealed strongly critical attitudes toward the police, which was perceived as abusing its authority (Correa Sutil and Barros 1993). This led to changes in legislation to protect the rights of arrestees. The legislation did not entirely allay the criticism. In 1998, the so-called Law on the Rights of Arrested Persons was passed, requiring that, when arresting individuals, police must tell them the reason for the arrest and inform them of their rights.[4]

Existing studies suggest at least three reasons for this situation. First, there is an underlying acceptance of institutional violence in the culture, even when it violates legitimately promulgated standards. Thus, policies that advocate the harsh treatment of suspects find strong support in the region, especially when crime is perceived to be increasing, or in periods of authoritarian rule when individual rights are suspended.[5] Second, in societies with sharp social class divisions, police attitudes tend to strongly favor those close to the top of the social scale, and there tends to be greater use of force against citizens of lower socioeconomic status.[6] Finally, internal and external controls on police conduct seem inadequate, even where there is a desire to provide a remedy for illegal action by the police.[7] Individual observations reveal major delays in dealing with cases, a tendency to wait for court rulings when the conduct under investigation is a crime, and a common failure to use information generated by the disciplinary system to modify the selection of police candidates, training systems, and operational procedures (Neild 2002, 9).

Crime and the Police in Latin America

A second factor driving police reform is the rise in crime in almost all Latin American countries in recent years. According to the Pan American Health Organization, the homicide rate for 1998 was 54 per 100,000 inhabitants in Colombia, 20 in Venezuela (rising to 33 in 2000), 15.1 in Ecuador, 26 in Brazil, and 15.7 in Mexico. Particular cities may have much higher rates than the country averages; the rate in Cali, Colombia, for instance, is 94 per 100,000 inhabitants, while Caracas, Venezuela, has a rate of 71 per 100,000.[8] Even countries with low homicide rates have high rates for other violent crime. According to Latinobarómetro figures, for example, 32 percent of Chilean households stated that one of their members was a victim of violent crime in 1996. Police figures for reported crime in Chile show a continuous rise in robbery in recent years, from 75.2 robberies per 100,000 inhabitants in 1999, to 169.5 in 2000.[9] The rising crime rate has led to an increasing lack of confidence in the police and a widespread feeling of insecurity. Lucía Dammert and Mary Fran Malone (2002, 285) argue that lack of confidence in the police is one of the most important factors accounting for the prevailing feeling of insecurity in Argentina.

The Pan American Health Organization's ACTIVA project found that 15.6 percent of the population in Santiago considered police efficiency poor or very poor, while 18.1 percent in San Salvador, 25.1 percent in Cali, 27.6 percent in Caracas, and 28.7 percent in Rio de Janeiro had a similar opinion.[10]

A survey by *El Mercurio* and sixteen other Latin American and U.S. newspapers showed that while 81 percent of the population in the United States expressed high or moderate confidence in the police, the figure for Chile, which was the most positive among Latin American countries, was only 38 percent. In the fifteen participating Latin American countries, average confidence in the police was only 28 percent.[11]

In view of rising crime, the need to professionalize police conduct and introduce changes in strategy has become part of the public debate. There are two positions. One stresses the need to expand police functions and prerogatives of control, while the other focuses on the need to create channels for citizen participation, in order to encourage police accountability vis-à-vis the residents. Supporters of the latter alternative are to be found among human rights activists and progressive academics who believe community policing can introduce major changes in police practices. The IDB has approved a number of loans to Latin American governments to deal with problems of violence and common crimes. Loans to Uruguay and Chile contain components of community policing.

The progressive implementation of community policing programs can be explained as part of a strategy whose principles coincide with those that govern reform of the state in Latin America. Thus, economic and political factors create pressure for changes in the administration of the state, in order to bring it into closer contact with, and make it more accountable to the citizens; create greater decentralization by assigning more of its functions to local government; and increase operational flexibility. When translated to police organizations, these changes tend to be consistent with concepts of community policing.

Decentralization and State Reform

During the 1980s and 1990s, interest in state reform increased in Latin America. This was due, in large part, to the economic crisis, which created pressure to reduce the size of the state, make government accountable to the public, transfer functions to local and regional government in order to reduce costs, bring public services closer to the citizenry, and reduce the size of the organizations providing such services (Bresser Pereira 1999, 2–9).

This process is sometimes propelled by political factors. Thus, decentralization in Venezuela is partly a result of the delegitimization of the alternately ruling political parties. This delegitimization led to the creation of a commission for reform of the state, and to municipal and state elections in 1989. Public education and primary health care in Chile were transferred to municipal governments under the military regime, increasing the functions, budgets, and visibility of municipalities. Once democracy was in place, municipal elections were reinitiated (in 1992), and the new mayors gained considerable political prominence.[12]

Decentralization and reform of the state are not without their effect on the police. Decentralization leads to the emergence of local and regional authorities with an interest in developing citizen security programs in their respective geographic areas, which are sometimes in competition with central government programs. In Chile, for example, the mayor of Las Condes has developed patrolling programs using municipal guards and vehicles, representing something of an alternative to regular police patrols (Sandoval 2001, 66), and municipal police services have been created in a number of cities in Ecuador and Guatemala. All of this encourages the police to pay more attention to local realities and local authorities, which sometimes have a role in financing the police.

Moreover, changes in the organization of the state are reflected in new concepts of public administration. Public entities are placing increased emphasis on serving the consumer, responding to citizens' values and expectations, assessing the quality of services provided, and incorporating consumers or citizens in the process of formulating, implementing, and evaluating their own performance (Mesquita Neto and Affonso 1998, 17).

The door is open to new debate on organizational structure and on how to foster necessary changes in police forces. Thus, the report of the Special Commission on Restructuring the National Police in Peru points to the force's excessive bureaucracy, poor coordination, impoverished information flow and information sharing, inadequate controls, use of military structures as an organizational model, little delegation of authority, and duplication of functions (Comisión Especial 2001).

In those police forces that are taking early steps to bring about organizational changes along the lines indicated here, the official discourse increasingly reflects business management concepts. Thus, a Colombian National Police publication states that "[t]he change in culture requires a substantial shift in how the organization is directed, replacing rigid hierarchical authority by a model based on leadership and management" (Policía Nacional [1998], 25). The publication further details management concepts, posing the question of what constitutes a real manager, and offering the response: "A manager is, without exception, any person who leads human groups within an organization. The management function does not depend on the team's position in the hierarchy, and certainly not on the size or type of the group to which it belongs" (Policía Nacional [1998], 27).

It remains unclear how profound a change in police culture may have been produced as a result of such expressions. The evidence that emerges from the cases of community policing examined below indicates that the cultural change has been less pronounced than might have been expected. Effects on organization are more likely in the case of the region's more professional police forces than in those forces with less solid organizations.

In any event, privatization and administrative decentralization bring new actors onto the stage in regard to citizen security. This, along with increased demands for more democratic policing, leads to community policing programs or to other less systematic efforts to create better relationships with the public.

The North American Community Policing Model

The North American community policing model that has dominated policy debate in recent years has certain essential elements. First, it emphasizes preventive police activity focusing on very small geographic areas (i.e., neighborhoods). Second, it encourages close community relations and ongoing consultation with citizens, in order to ensure that the police take account of the community's perceptions (Sherman 1995). Third, it involves the police in mobilizing the community to take preventive action. Finally, it relies on a consensus-based strategy, in which the police study the conditions and circumstances leading to crime and minor violations that significantly affect people's lives. Other frequently cited elements of this model are a focus on specific security problems that affect residents and on prevention, as opposed to an approach of strictly reactive response to calls from citizens; an emphasis on dealing with people's subjective fears, while revising police priorities and recognizing that the community, however it is defined, plays a fundamental role in solving neighborhood problems; and finally, the recognition that police forces must be restructured to meet the demands of this strategy (Rosenbaum 1998, 7).

The role of the community is a key factor. The community policing model of ongoing consultation with the community has three main functions: (1) it makes the police aware of local interests and needs, which do not always coincide with their prior perceptions; (2) it provides an opportunity for the police to educate citizens about behaviors that help prevent crime; and (3) it provides channels for citizens to directly express their complaints, offering a mechanism by which the public can immediately assess the work of the police (Bayley 1994, 105–20). One factor that contributes strongly to the development of community policing is the perception, by minorities and marginalized groups, of excessive and discriminatory use of force against them by the police. Thus, community policing presents itself as a strategy that emphasizes proper treatment of the public and a reduction in police violence.

Applying the community policing model generally requires major organizational changes. To begin with, a community policing force cannot be a specialized unit within the police organization; on the contrary, all police employees must act consistent with the principles of community policing, and even those working in specialized units must maintain communication and relations with their colleagues in the field in order to respond adequately to problems that arise in the neighborhood (Schafer 2001, 23–24).

Organizational changes associated with community policing include promoting executive risk-taking and selecting executives who can encourage members of the force to improve themselves and adopt new behaviors. Each and every member of the institution must be a professional with initiative, prepared to address security problems from a broad perspective. This means being committed to solving social problems that have an impact on crime and employing strategies that go beyond merely applying the law to specific situations. The shape of such an organization, and the profile of the police officer who is part of it, are not typical products of traditional police training programs.

The changing paradigms of police training are clearly seen in the case of the Canadian province of Ontario. Police in Ontario had always been trained to obey and to act as a single body. The new training program emphasized principles such as justice and access, relevant learning, accountability, cooperation, community participation, investigation, and sensitivity to diversity skills. A new training program for the Canadian Royal Mounted Police focuses on increasing recruits' ability to work with victims and with the community, preventing conflict, resolving and mediating disputes, providing information on crime prevention, and developing interpersonal communication. The initial program for recruits is based on five types of action, summarized by the acronym CAPRA: identifying clients (citizens, communities, public agencies), acquiring and analyzing information, creating partnerships and alliances with citizens' organizations and public entities, response and service through crime prevention and law enforcement, and assessment through constant review of each officer's commitment and of the organization's ongoing commitment to continued learning and to changing old practices (de Lint 1998, 272–74).

Community Policing in Latin America

The community policing training model stresses the role and responsibility of the street officer, who gains a sense of accountability for the results of his work from his identification with the force and its objectives. Rather than emphasizing specific material to be learned, the teaching process attempts to encourage the development of abilities and skills. Although studies show that police organizations are highly resistant to change in all contexts,[13] changing the organizational paradigm is particularly difficult in Latin American police forces in which there are low levels of professionalism and motivation, and significant problems in controlling abuses and corruption.

Police institutions with higher levels of professionalism undoubtedly have a better chance of making the transition to the new organization paradigm presented here. Even they, however, can be expected to experience much greater resistance than in developed countries, given the enormous changes involved. Moreover, change requires budgetary shifts and new social attitudes toward the police, who must garner public recognition as true professionals (Sandoval Quappe 2002).

Based on this assessment of the reasons for the increasing influence of the community policing model in Latin America, and of the consequent institutional and training changes required, several experiences in the region will be examined here, along with existing evaluations of their outcomes. The attempt is to determine both the results of implementation and the impact on the process of institutional change. Current police reform in Latin America takes on various forms. At one end, it attempts greater closeness with the community, without actually calling itself community policing—apparently because the police forces involved do not accept the premises of the community policing model. At the other extreme are community policing reforms designed to transform the police as a whole.

The Quadrant Plan of Chile's Carabineros

Chile's military-type preventive police force, the Carabineros, enjoys popular support because it is seen as disciplined and free of corruption. They have implemented a series of institutional changes over the last three years, most notably the Quadrant Plan, which is designed to address increased crime in urban areas and the imbalance in the allocation of human and logistical resources assigned to the various municipalities within the Metropolitan Region (the administrative division of the country that includes the nation's capital). This imbalance works to the disadvantage of the poorest and most populous municipalities (Frühling 1999; Ward 2001). The plan has not been subject to any public outside evaluation, but it represents a beginning by making community participation a part of crime prevention for the first time.

One objective of the plan is to increase police presence on the street. The small quadrants are designed for this purpose. Each quadrant is assigned to one precinct station, a police unit under the command of an officer with the rank of major, responsible for allocating officers and vehicles according to the specific needs of the quadrant. Needs are assessed in terms of preventive patrols required, number of police procedures to be carried out, and normal law enforcement tasks that the police conduct. In designing the quadrant, a number of factors are taken into consideration, including the linear extent (in kilometers) of the sector to be subdivided, the traffic situation and street conditions, and how much area can be covered by a patrol vehicle during an eight-hour shift.

The responsibility for managing a quadrant is "delegated" and "subdelegated" to two strata of officers, whose jobs are to address and solve problems presented by the quadrant's citizens. The officers are selected according to fixed criteria and are given special training in community relations, public service, and problem solving (Villarroel 2002). A report to the public is made every three months. The report normally consists of statistical information on police activity, and neighborhood leaders and government officials in the area are invited to attend the occasion on which the report is released. The information provided can be aggregated by municipality or disaggregated by smaller sectors (Frühling 1999; Ward 2001).

The Quadrant Plan, first implemented in the Metropolitan Region, clearly favors motorized patrols over foot patrols, which are one of the marks of community policing programs. Although experts see the plan as a first step toward recognizing the community's role in crime prevention, it does not yet constitute a definitive change in orientation from an institution that conceives of itself as enforcing the law to one that views itself as providing a service to the public. The plan does not include changes in such areas as the internal organization of the force, the police subculture, training, or internal controls. This lack of change expresses the fact that the plan is not viewed by the Carabineros as part of a process of institutional transformation.

As a complement to these programs, which were decided upon by the Carabineros itself, the central government moved to create Neighborhood Citizen Security Committees in Santiago during the second half of the 1990s. These committees received assistance and training from the Social Organizations Division of the Ministry of the General Secretariat of Government. The precise number of committees actually formed is unclear. As of late 1998, there were 261, although they varied significantly in the intensity and continuity of their work (Sandoval 2001, 60–61). Recent information indicates that a majority of committee participants (57.1 percent) were women who did not work outside the home and who were generally active in other neighborhood groups. The committees' activities included street patrols, organizing sports events for young people, and lobbying municipal government for better street lighting and garbage removal (Jordan and Sotomayor 2000).

In August 2000, the government launched a new initiative designed to make social participation in crime prevention a part of the country's institutional structure. The new "Community Safety Plan—Promise 100" was designed to create "security councils" in those municipalities defined as vulnerable due to high rates of crime and poverty. The members of the councils include the mayor, a representative of the Carabineros, a representative of the Investigative Police, and delegates from other community organizations. The councils create security policy at the municipal level and decide on funding for projects presented by neighborhood organizations, using funds provided for this purpose by the central government.

Four Cases of Community Policing

Other countries have also made various attempts to bring together the police and the community. Following is an examination of four such projects evaluated by the IDB, with a consideration of their impact on the police institutions involved. An attempt will be made to draw conclusions that could be useful in designing and implementing similar projects in the future. The IDB evaluation process took place during 2001 and 2002, and was performed by five researchers with expertise in police matters. They focused on four projects that were selected because of their duration and the amount of information available on them, which permitted effective evaluation of their impact: the São Paulo (Brazil) Community Policing Program, the Villa Nueva (Guatemala) Community Policing Program, the Bogotá (Colombia) Community Policing Program, and the Belo Horizonte (Brazil) Community Policing Program.[14] Although the amount of information available in the different cases varied, they had all been subject to independent monitoring, there was information on the process as experienced within the police organization during implementation, and information had been gathered on the features of the community organizations that established relations with the police. The conclusions that emerged from the analysis are summarized below, along with comparisons with other international experiences.

São Paulo, Brazil

As in each of Brazil's states, the São Paulo Military Police is an auxiliary arm of the army. Although its role is to carry out preventive policing, its organization and functions are regulated by the Ministry of the Army.

Between 1980 and 1990, the state of São Paulo, like the rest of Brazil, experienced a sharp rise in crime. According to Ministry of Health data (Mesquita Neto and Affonso 1998), the number of deaths from homicide or battery rose from 3,452 in 1980 to 12,350 in 1996, that is, 36.2 homicides per 100,000 inhabitants. The robbery rate also rose dramatically. Police response to this situation was seriously lacking, and the public's confidence in the police was correspondingly low. On 10 December 1997, the commanding general of the Military Police officially adopted community policing as the force's philosophy and operational strategy.

In São Paulo, the main entity responsible for analysis and discussion of the implementation of the community policing program is the Advisory Commission for the Implementation of Community Policing. The commission's membership varies in number and individuals over time; as of August 1998, it included representatives of human rights organizations, community councils, the State Federation of Industries, business councils, the Paulist Association of the Public Prosecutor's Office, the Lawyers' Guild of Brazil, and the United Nations Latin American Institute for the Prevention of Crime and Treatment of Offenders (ILANUD), among others.

The commission discussed the population's security problems, set priorities, and determined solutions to be applied. A set of goals and objectives for the police was defined, including the teaching of democratic values and respect for human rights—concerns never previously part of Military Police doctrine. Among these goals were instituting the community policing model as the organizational strategy of the Military Police; improving police education and training; improving the recruitment and promotion system; integrating the police force with other public bodies; and enhancing the reputation and rights of the police (Mesquita Neto and Affonso 1998, 40–50).

The police chose forty-one areas in which to begin the project, with policy in place to govern patrols, women police officers, traffic police, railroad police, forest police, and fire fighters. Company commanders chose the neighborhoods where the project was to be implemented. The community policing program was implemented between December 1997 and July 2001 in 199 of the 386 companies that make up the state Military Police force;[15] thus, over half of the companies implemented community policing (Mesquita Neto 2004). From September 1997 to May 2000, 239 community-based substations were created, and close to sixteen thousand police officers received training in community policing (Kahn 2003, 2). The new program meant increased preventive patrols in selected areas, the establishment of mobile stations in certain neighborhoods, efforts to increase school security, and drug prevention programs.

Maintaining communications with the police, the Advisory Commission for the Implementation of Community Policing monitored and evaluated the problems that emerged during the implementation of the new model. Although the implementation does represent an achievement, the relationship between the community and the police was a troubled one. In meetings with citizens, the police took note of problems, but there was rarely any rigorous follow-up of the measures adopted to solve them.

On another front, a decree by the state government created Community Security Councils, each composed of individuals from a given police district to meet to discuss problems of public security and work with the police to propose solutions. The councils meet monthly and send minutes of the meetings to the Coordinator of Public Security Councils, an organ of the state's Secretariat of Security. The dialogue in these councils between police and citizens does not appear to have been productive, and they seem to have functioned more as a forum for complaints concerning, and demands from, the police than as a forum to organize collective civil solutions. Nonetheless, they do at least represent the principle of citizen control (Mesquita Neto 2004, 125).

Villa Nueva, Guatemala

Several community policing programs were developed as part of Citizen Security in Central America, an international project run by the Inter-American Institute of Human Rights. The program, a pilot experiment that did not involve changes in the overall organization of the police, took place in Belize, Costa Rica, El Salvador, Guatemala, Honduras, and Nicaragua, and sought to promote an approach that focused on community policing and problem solving.[16] The fact that the organizations involved were financed by international cooperation gave the international funders influence over the program; at the same time, however, it was clear that once the cooperation period was over, the program would face the real test of sustainability.

Meetings with representatives of state entities and civil society to determine where the program would be implemented and which individuals would be responsible for the process. The location was selected by political staff at the Ministry of Government, not by the police. Villa Nueva was a municipality with 192,000 inhabitants in the department of Guatemala that included the nation's capital. Despite the lack of a system of reliable and uniform crime statistics, certain limited data recorded by the National Civil Police of Villa Nueva indicated that the most common crimes before the project began in 1998 were robbery, battery, homicide, and auto theft (Chinchilla 2004, 42).

The project focused on the National Civil Police, which grew out of the peace agreements between the government and guerrilla forces. Although the old security forces were dissolved and replaced by the new police, the composition and level of training of the new force fell far short of expectations. The army continued to play a role in domestic security, and the great majority of the new force came from the ranks of the old security forces, after a period of retraining.

The National Civil Police had already made some efforts to mobilize civilians to be active in security. It encouraged the creation of local Citizen Security Councils to provide information and support for the police and to bring together the police and the community. The councils, coordinated by the head of the force's Public Relations and Information Office, were supported by station and substation chiefs. They included representatives of the different sectors of the local population (government, fire fighters, educational institutions, professional and community associations, neighborhood committees, merchants, businesspeople, the judiciary, and the Public Prosecutor's Office). According to one study, the councils have worked well in middle- and upper-class communities; however, in more economically depressed areas, where crime is a more serious problem or where paramilitary groups were present during the armed conflict, the model fails, due to long-standing distrust between the police and the citizenry (IEPADES 2000).

The Villa Nueva project began with a series of preparatory activities, including an assessment of local crime data. An initial survey was also conducted to register public opinion and provide data from the victims' point of view. The next step was to create a Municipal Citizen Security Council with representatives from all of the institutions and entities involved or interested in the subject. The council's objective was to coordinate the different activities that were to be carried out in Villa Nueva concerning crime prevention and control. Because of the size of the council, the members created an executive committee responsible for carrying out the actions agreed upon. The activities of the police were to emphasize patrols in high-crime areas and reduce the illegal sale of alcoholic beverages by monitoring and penalizing businesses that sold alcohol near schools and parks. Meetings were also organized among police, prosecutors, judges, and defense lawyers in order to coordinate their activities and increase the efficiency of their institutions. Contact with youth gangs was pursued, with the participation of community leaders, teachers, and members of the National Civil Police, in order to promote the social rehabilitation of gang members involved in criminal activity.

Bogotá (Colombia)

In contrast to Villa Nueva, community policing in Bogotá was the result of an internal decision by the police force, although the model adopted and the training provided had a strong international component. The police force suffered greatly from the violence created by drug trafficking and guerrilla activity. In the late 1980s, the attempt to combat drug trafficking seriously affected attitudinal and behavioral standards within the organization. Police were involved in human rights violations (Llorente 2004, 67). In the early 1990s, they came under serious questioning because of their ineffectiveness and their participation in the killing of criminals, prostitutes, and mentally ill persons in various cities. Cases of corruption were also a source of concern.

In response to criticism, a two-phase reform process was begun in 1993. The first phase sought to accentuate the civil nature of the police, even though the force continued to report to the Ministry of Defense. In 1995, an internal purge was initiated. It was driven by the command structure itself, and affected senior officials as well as the rank and file. The results of this type of measures can be seen in surveys such as the one carried out in Bogotá in 1996, dealing with public expectations of the police (Centro Nacional de Consultoría 1996). The survey suggested that community policing was capable of responding to citizens' demands; however, it was not until 1998 that the commander of the city's police department adopted community policing as the jurisdiction's most important program.

The initiative has been supported by the police hierarchy, and has enjoyed the collaboration of the Bogotá Chamber of Commerce, which initially proposed creating the Urban Guard, to be funded by the municipal administration, under the mayor's control (Llorente 2004, 72). The national government, in turn, made community policing throughout the country one of the central tenets of its security policy.

One thousand police officers were chosen and trained for the community policing program. Candidates were chosen on the basis of a profile representing qualities considered relevant to the objectives. These officers form a special branch of the patrol service, which also includes employees carrying out traditional police work. The community police are assigned to work in specific permanent patrol areas.

The main manifestation of community work has been police support for the Local Security Fronts and Citizen Security Schools. The fronts serve as support networks for the police. Organized by blocks or sections of neighborhoods, they conduct informal patrols and work with neighbors when suspicious situations arise. Neighbors exchange telephone numbers and install neighborhood alarm systems. Although there are nearly 5,400 fronts in Bogotá, they cover only 13 percent of the city's blocks (Llorente 2004, 87–90). The Citizen Security Schools focus on local leaders and attempt to produce citizens knowledgeable about security to serve as disseminators. The police provide training on legal issues, as well as information on preventive measures that citizens can take. Since their creation in 1996, these schools have trained 21,000 citizens to become members of the security fronts.

Although the driving force behind the program has principally come from within the country, there has been international support for training the officers who constituted the initial nucleus of the project. Twenty-one Bogotá police officers attended a four-week seminar at the University of Barcelona in 1998 run by specialists in community policing and by Urban Guards. In 1999, ten additional officers participated in a similar course in Toledo, Spain.

Belo Horizonte, Brazil

In Belo Horizonte, capital of the state of Minas Gerais, the immediate predecessor of the current program was a project carried out in some of the city's neighborhoods beginning in 1993. A recent evaluation of that experiment judged it a failure; because the police lacked the necessary training, the program had no indicators that would have made it possible to evaluate its effectiveness, and was perceived as a tool for the police to obtain funding from the community for its own projects (Souza 1999).

In 1999, the Minas Gerais Military Police command implemented a broader program, based on results-based policing. This involved deploying police according to geographic information on crime, and the creation of Community Security Councils whose objective was to formulate, with the police, preventive strategies in response to the area's needs. The driving force behind this program is primarily the Military Police, which has received support from the Federal University of Minas Gerais to develop training, both for the members of the community councils and for the police. As in the case of São Paulo, there is little coordination between civil and military police, and the former, whose role is crime investigation, hardly participates in the program (Beato F. 2004).

The central objective of the councils is to develop preventive programs with community participation. There is one council for each of the twenty-five companies of the police force. The members of the councils are the company commanders, and representatives of the mayor's office and other entities and associations. According to their charters, the councils are to train police for community action, attract new members, disseminate programs that help communities to protect themselves, and gather periodic information on the police services provided to citizens (Beato F. 2004, 142–43).

Emerging from these community councils are anecdotal examples of joint efforts with the police, designed to address acute public security problems, but their activity and the influence they exert on police action vary widely. There is also an inverse relation between the level of functioning of the councils and the level of violent crime; thus, where there is more violent crime, the functioning of these community organizations is relatively poor (Beato F. 2004, 167).

Institutional Obstacles to Change

As explained above, community policing programs in Latin America are trying to confront profound internal and external challenges. Consequently, their impact must be measured not only in terms of their ability to reduce fear and actual crime levels, but also in terms of their ability to produce significant change within the police itself. The comparative literature consistently shows that successful community policing programs create a problem-solving orientation among a majority of the police officers, and they require a decentralization of police functioning, emphasizing close relationships with the community and establishing a more flexible system of shifts and schedules to allow employees time to contact community members during nonworking hours when they are able to attend meetings. Studies in the United States also stress the need for a new management system that supports employee participation and views those at the command level as facilitators rather than as authorities in a hierarchically centralized system (Wyckoff and Skogan 1994). As seen in Canada, this type of philosophy leads to profound changes in police training, the objectives of which are consistent with criteria commonly used in private enterprise.

A central aspect of any community policing program, by definition, is the emphasis on the officers on the street, who are in direct contact with the public. A six-city analysis of community policing states that the majority of departments implementing community policing "are primarily interested in changing the way that police on the street—the initial point of contact with the public—carry out their job in conjunction with the citizens" (Lamm Weisel and Eck 1998, 55). It is imperative that there be more foot patrols, or some other form of ongoing presence and interaction with the public, such as occurs at small neighborhood police stations. To ensure that the police establish frequent contact and close relationships with the community, officers assigned to a given patrol area must be required to remain there for a fixed, and significant, period of time (Frühling 2000).

However, although community policing demands a major use of personnel in order to create significant relationships with residents, funding for personnel is often not available to the extent necessary to meet the requirements of the model. The Villa Nueva substation, for example, had only 117 officers at the beginning of the project—far from sufficient (Chinchilla 2004, 46). Although eighty officers from the old National Police were added, the police-resident ratio remained lower than in the rest of the country. Moreover, once the Inter-American Institute of Human Rights withdrew from the project, the ratio fell almost to where it had been at the start. The lack and instability of staffing led to extending the workday to as much as twelve hours. This, added to the need for more foot patrols, provoked complaints from the police officers (Chinchilla 2004, 49). Moreover, despite the changes, the traditional features of a police organization remained in place, and the structure remained rigid and authoritarian in its treatment of subordinate personnel.

The cost of the Bogotá community policing program represented only 5.7 percent of all investment made in the Metropolitan Police by the national government and municipal administration in the period of time covered by the program (Llorente 2004, 74). Only 6 percent of the police officers in the Bogotá Police Department are assigned to community policing; this is 15 percent of the number of officers involved in preventive patrol activity. It is clear, then, that nontargeted preventive patrolling and reactive response to incidents are still the prevailing modalities. As in the case of Villa Nueva, community service covers a significant proportion of the city—blocks containing 3 million inhabitants, or 42 percent of Bogotá's population. However, the ratio between officers and residents is excessively low, and the result is that, according to surveys, only 13 percent of households and

16 percent of the city's commercial establishments say that their neighborhood is served by the community police (Llorente 2004, 82).

Unlike the Villa Nueva experiment, which was a pilot case, and the Bogotá program, which was not intended for immediate implementation by the police as a whole, the São Paulo program was an attempt to produce profound change in the police organization. The mission and values of the Military Police were redefined, the police participating in the program received special training, specific companies were selected to carry out the program, small stations were established in neighborhoods, and mobile stations were acquired as a way of establishing closer ties with residents (Mesquita Neto 2004, 119–23). In 2001, a total of 7,305 police worked in mobile stations and neighborhood stations. However, both the number of police involved and the funding levels were low. In 1998 and 1999, the Military Police had no officers exclusively assigned to the implementation of community policing at either the state or local level. As a result, officers had to attend meetings or establish contacts with neighborhood residents in their assigned areas on their own time—generally after the end of their shifts. Only in 2000 did the Military Police create a Department of Community Policing and Human Rights, designed to plan and coordinate the program. Although much of its budget has been devoted to training police and neighborhood leaders, a large majority of police personnel still have not participated in the community program at all (Mesquita Neto 2004, 124). In Belo Horizonte, surveys of police indicate that only 24.7 percent performed foot patrols during the last five years (Beato F. 2004, 161).

Related to these constraints is the difficulty that police management has in ensuring the stability of the force in the neighborhoods they patrol. This is due in part to demands for police in other areas, in part to requests from police themselves who wish to be transferred elsewhere, and in part to the process of promotion and transfer, which involves the constant movement of personnel. In Villa Nueva, those interviewed frequently referred to the project's high turnover rates, which required constant training of new community police officers (Chinchilla 2004). Turnover in commanders was also identified as a problem in the Belo Horizonte program (Beato F. 2004, 146).

Yet another institutional difficulty that affects community policing programs is the very culture of police institutions, which is skeptical that programs of this type can adequately deal with crime. As a result, the principles of community policing are not applied wholeheartedly. Although such resistance has been seen in similar programs in the United States, it can be assumed that resistance will be greater in centralized and very hierarchical institutions in societies where democratic beliefs are weak. The idea that strict enforcement of the law, alone, is enough to control crime can easily prevail in such a context.

For example, in a survey of twelve hundred police officers in the city of Belo Horizonte, conducted by the Research Center on Public Security (Centro de Investigação em Seguridade Pública [CRISP], at the Federal University of Minas Gerais), 46.1 percent of respondents thought that the most important measures for controlling crime were increasing material and human police resources and increasing police salaries; 58.7 percent agreed totally or partially with the statement that "the people equipped to evaluate what the police do are their colleagues," which raises questions about the principle of community accountability underlying community policing programs; and 44.7 percent of police pointed to human rights organizations in explaining why the public had difficulty understanding the work that the police do (Beato F. 2004).

An ILANUD (Instituto Latinoamericano de la Organización de las Naciones Unidas para la Prevención del Delito y el Tratamiento del Delincuente) survey of a sample of Military Police officers in São Paulo indicates that they had a generally positive view of community policing; only 16 percent of respondents thought that the project should be discontinued (Kahn 2003, 18). Comparing community policing with traditional police work, 46.7 percent of community police officers surveyed considered community policing more satisfactory from a personal perspective, and 50.6 percent stated that community policing did a better job of serving the community. However, only 21.4 percent thought community policing was more effective in dealing with crime (Kahn 2003, 25).

One final and serious obstacle to implementing community policing programs is the lack of identification that low-ranking officers feel with such programs, as well as the insufficient training officers receive in regard to problem solving. In Belo Horizonte, the street police, unlike senior officers, showed little knowledge about the community program. Evaluations show a vast difference between senior and subordinate personnel in their knowledge of and degree of preparation for participating in the program. Specifically, there is little appreciation for the role of citizen councils; only 10 percent of personnel below the rank of sergeant had a high level of knowledge in this respect (Beato F. 2004, 162–63).

The ILANUD survey of the São Paulo Military Police indicates that the concept of community policing is appreciated at the rank of sergeant and above, while officers at the corporal and private levels show resistance:

34.4 percent of the sample of ranking officers considered community policing more efficient as a means of fighting crime, but only 17.8 percent of the rank and file agreed (Kahn 2003, 25). Indeed, 66.6 percent of the rank and file considered community policing a public relations tactic to improve the image of the police, an opinion shared by 43.5 percent of ranking officers as well. How does one explain this phenomenon?

First, there has almost surely been a failure in the attempts to train and involve subordinate personnel in the program. As Claudio C. Beato F. notes (2004, 163), a high degree of obedience by subordinates is a basic element of centralized, hierarchical organizations; hence, little effort is typically made to creatively involve lower-ranking personnel in institutional changes. Another factor is that such efforts by senior officers may evoke little enthusiasm from subordinates, who prefer to simply meet standards and carry out orders, and who resist more autonomy, since it would mean having personal accountability for results.

These institutional difficulties may partially explain the information suggesting that the bulk of police activity continues to be reactive in nature, rather than utilizing the type of problem solving involved in community policing models (Beato F. 2004). The ILANUD survey in São Paulo appears to suggest something similar. A sample of community police and traditional police were asked about the number of hours they spent on different activities during the course of a week. With the exception of foot patrols, which occupied 22.5 hours per week on average for community police and 15.42 hours for traditional police, the figures for time spent on specific activities, such as vehicle patrols, formal meetings with the community, assistance efforts, and social services, was similar for the two groups. Community police even stated that they devoted more time in an average week to answering emergency calls than did their traditional colleagues (Kahn 2003, 33). This would seem to indicate that there are no substantial differences between the work done by the two groups, calling into question the depth of the transformation occurring in the institutions that have undertaken these programs.

In summary, institutional obstacles prevent community policing programs from being implemented with the thoroughness required. In some cases, human and material resources are far from sufficient to provide the levels of personnel and time required for effective preventive programs. The degree of centralization in the decision-making process, combined with an institutional culture that favors execution of orders over initiative, limits the possibilities of innovative or decentralized action. Thus, the impact is limited by the prevailing institutional culture, and by the fact that, in contrast to similar experiments in North America, community police in Latin America function as specialized units, and are not fully integrated into the overall program being carried out by the institution.

The Relationship between Police and Community

Given a history of conflict between the police and the public, it is hardly surprising that difficulties should arise in implementing community policing programs in Latin America, where citizen participation has not succeeded in defining priorities for police action, and citizens are ill-prepared to interact with the police or to take courses of action designed to solve the security problems affecting them. The relationship between police and citizens may be structured according to three models. The first emphasizes the role of a central commission that is collectively responsible for creating security in a given area. Its members come from different sectors, usually representing institutions and nongovernmental organizations, as well as from the police. The commission's role is advisory or deliberative, though in rare cases it may have decision-making power. In the second, mixed model, the role of the central commission is complemented by the work of neighborhood committees. In the third model, police-community relations are thoroughly decentralized, and it is the police who encourage the creation of preventive committees in the jurisdictional areas of the various police stations.

The Villa Nueva program follows the first of these models. When the project began, the Municipal Citizen Security Council was formed, incorporating representatives of all institutions and organizations involved or interested in the issues. The objective of the council was to coordinate crime prevention and control activities. It formed an executive committee to carry out the actions agreed upon. The executive committee was initially composed of a chairperson (a trial court judge), a woman representing education directors, and a substation chief of the National Civil Police. Shortly thereafter, it was expanded to include representatives of other sectors (religious, business, media, and municipal government). The executive committee met at least once a week through 2000; its members also dedicated time to the activities outlined in the action plan. The executive committee contributed to the process of cooperation among police, governmental institutions, and private enterprises (Chinchilla 2004, 50).

São Paulo's program is based on the mixed model. A central Community Policing Advisory Commission, created by the police, is the main forum for police and community representatives to discuss issues arising in connection with the program. Its members have strictly advisory powers, but their views appear in the official documents dealing with implementation of the new strategy. This consultative structure at the state level is supplemented at the local level by numerous community councils on public security, and by community venues. These groups hold events in which both the police and the community participate. The commission meets regularly every one or two weeks. Studies show that representatives of more conservative groups, along with business groups, have come to dominate the meetings (Mesquita Neto and Affonso 1998). This has led to frequent comments suggesting that neighborhood police stations benefit special groups—such as government officials, politicians, and business people—more than they do the most vulnerable sectors of the population (Mesquita Neto and Affonso 1998, 34).

In 2000, the Military Police restructured the commission, creating seven subcommissions responsible specifically for structure, assessment, relations with government agencies, relations with agencies within the criminal justice system, community relations, social communication, and professional motivation. The Military Police also created a broadly based council including, in addition to the chair, vice-chairs, a secretary general of the Advisory Commission and seven advisors, of which only three are from the Military Police. The purpose of this new structure is to promote participation on the part of more diverse groups and organizations in the community policing process (Mesquita Neto 2004, 134).

The network of local organizations has been mobilized to offer support to the Military Police. One of the most notable expressions of this support is financial contributions; another is volunteers who work in the small neighborhood police stations. Citizens also organize neighborhood security groups to share information regarding suspicious individuals in the area.

Minas Gerais uses the third model. Here, no central advisory commission was created; from the beginning, an effort was made to decentralize police activity and community relations. In each of the areas covered by the twenty-five companies that make up the police force, Community Security Councils were created to work with the police to plan patrols and other preventive activities. The councils' charters state that they are responsible for bringing in new members, training police for community action, gathering and systematizing information on police services in order to assess them, carrying out informational campaigns to help communities protect themselves, and providing programs to address social problems that carry implications for citizen security (Beato F. 2004, 143).

Training for the people participating in the local committees is indispensable if citizen participation is to go beyond voicing complaints about police inaction and actually contribute to designing measures to solve security problems. In the case of Bogotá, the Community Policing Office of the National Police has reported two types of community relations. On the one hand, mechanisms for relationship and participation are created according to the local context, with police and citizens taking flexible roles in determining the mechanisms. On the other hand, more formal programs involve neighborhood organizations in patrol activity. The most important of these are the Citizen Security Schools and Local Security Fronts, which had been developing in the city since 1996 as a National Police initiative (see preceding discussion).

Strictly speaking, a mixed scheme of citizen participation seems to be the most conducive to creating real impact through participatory programs. The reason for this is that the members of these central state or municipal commissions usually have substantial social influence that can affect the police planning process and contribute to the execution of joint programs between the police and other local or regional government agencies. This is not to say that agreements between neighborhood committees and local police cannot also be useful in dealing with crime, but a relationship organized purely at the neighborhood level risks having little impact on police conduct at the command level.

The only evaluation of the community councils that I am aware of was carried out by CRISP. It examined a number of dimensions of the councils' functioning. Values for the variables were nonexistent, low, moderate, and high. According to the evaluation, all of the councils were functioning a year after their creation, the majority at the medium level, and a minority at a high level. The vast majority had low or medium levels of representativeness, despite efforts to attract new members. Councils were less fully representative in locales with high levels of violence, or characterized by great social diversity. The oversight capacity of councils, vis-à-vis the police, is generally low. Although there is some attendance at meetings, participation is moderate or low in most cases. Meetings are generally held on a weekly or monthly basis, with ten to thirty people attending. In the community policing model, participation should become independent of the police command structure, so as to provide oversight of police conduct and effectively promote public priorities; however, the evaluation found that autonomy vis-à-vis local police commands was low or nonexistent in eleven cases, moderate in eight, and high in only one case. This presents a dilemma: What methods should be implemented to make the councils, created by the police, independent? In Belo Horizonte, as in São Paulo, a minority of the social organizations involved in preventive programs apparently use strategic action planning and problem-solving methods to address crime. The level of training among the civilian leadership of the councils seems to have been generally low, although in a minority of cases the opposite was true. Finally, police of officer rank participating in the councils evinced a high level of support for community participation programs, while police of lower rank showed little familiarity with the programs.[17]

One of the main factors affecting the councils' functioning seems to be the crime rate in the particular area; this is understandable, since in areas with high crime rates, the readiness to cooperate with police is, by definition, less pronounced. Moreover, police officials are more supportive of community policing where the crime rates are low, while favoring more coercive methods in areas where there is more violence.

Relations between Police and Other Public Entities

The objective and subjective security of the population does not depend solely on police action. The community policing model assumes that the police will coordinate effectively with other public entities to solve security problems.

In the Villa Nueva project, the creation of the Municipal Citizen Security Council led to a series of initiatives that required coordination among police, municipal government, prosecutors, judges, and public defenders. The presence of the council helped solve specific problems, such as lighting in public places. As a result of institutional cooperation with judges, the judicial system adopted more expeditious procedures for taking statements from people arrested by the police, overcrowding in police lockups was reduced, and pressure on police finances was diminished (Chinchilla 2004, 30, 57). However, the regularity of meetings with various governmental institutions fell off notably when international participation in the project ceased.

In Bogotá, there was an effort by the police and the municipal administration to cooperate in the framework of the Mission Bogotá program, which was one of the pillars of citizen security policy under Mayor Enrique Peñalosa's administration (1998–2000). The program sought to recover public spaces by involving the affected public in assessing the problems and devising solutions. Joint action involving the community police was required. In these cases, however, cooperation failed as a result of institutional jealousies between the staff of Mission Bogotá and the police, competition for leadership in creating security schools and fronts, and the inherent difficulty involved in coordinating highly visible public and political entities with no direct hierarchical relationship (Llorente 2004, 86–87).

The pressure of the public security problem has impelled municipalities in Minas Gerais to provide funds for the police. In one election year, the prefect (mayor) of Belo Horizonte announced that he would provide $2 million for the purchase of police vehicles and arms, and for organizing databases for security councils. However, because of weak organizational coordination between the police and the local government, the funds were used simply to support traditional reactive police strategies (Beato F. 2004, 165). This outcome, probably due to police preferences, also reflects the fact that organizational coordination would require that local government have explicit authority for security matters, and that the police be required to take municipal government's priorities into account when planning activities. The lack of explicit authority for municipal government makes it difficult to coordinate government and police agendas.

In North America, closer relations with the community and with local government agencies are easier for community policing programs because security policy is local and fully decentralized. This is not the case in Latin America, where police report to central or regional governments, and collaboration suffers accordingly. However, the fact that institutional collaboration between police and other public agencies is less systematic than might be hoped is also due to the fact that the police are resistant to assuming responsibility for social demands, which they view as lying beyond their area of authority. At the same time, local government feels that community-based programs, while solving some problems, create new demands for in vestment that are difficult to satisfy.

Results of Community Policing Programs

Measuring, in a reliable manner, the impact of community policing programs on the population's levels of fear and on the frequency of crime is not easy, since none of the cases provides data to compare the situation in the community policing areas with the areas where traditional policing is continuing. Moreover, only in Villa Nueva were victimization surveys conducted before and after the program; hence, in three of the cases, one must rely on figures based on reports to the police.

Two victimization surveys were conducted in Villa Nueva, one before the project in 1998, the other in 2000. The 2000 survey shows a major reduction, compared to 1998, in the percentage of respondents who reported being victims of a crime in recent months (23.8 percent versus 34 percent). According to testimony gathered by the researcher, increased police patrols and cracking down on businesses that sell alcoholic beverages illegally may have contributed to the result.

There are indications that confidence in the police increased somewhat as a result of the program. The percentage of victims who reported crimes to some authority increased slightly, from 30.3 percent in 1998 to 31.5 percent in 2000. At the same time, the feeling among these people that the authorities did nothing to respond to their reports fell from 7 percent in 1998 to 4.8 percent in 2000. Consistent with this, the prevalence of the view that the police had conducted an investigation increased from 0.7 percent in 1998 to 1.8 percent in 2000 (Chinchilla 2004, 52–56).

Asked about the quality of neighborhood police service after the project was implemented, however, the Villa Nueva residents' response was quite negative. Thus, while 44.7 percent considered service adequate or very adequate in 1998, this figure was 18.3 percent in 2000. Similarly, the percentage of respondents who felt that service was somewhat or totally inadequate rose from 51.3 percent to 79.3 percent. The same negative results appeared in relation to police patrols. In 1998, 49.3 percent of respondents stated that the police patrolled their area often or very often, while in 2000 this percentage had fallen to 23.8. The opinion that the police presence was small or nonexistent increased from 27 percent in 1998 to 37.1 percent in 2000. There are two possible explanations for this. First, the implementation of community policing may have created higher expectations for neighborhood police protection, which had clearly not been met. Second, the population may have perceived that greater patrol efforts were channeled to those entities with available resources—such as banks—which received special attention from the police (Chinchilla 2004, 55).

Surveys conducted by the program headed by the Inter-American Institute of Human Rights indicate that the Villa Nueva experiment has had a positive impact on the population's sense of insecurity. The 2000 survey shows crime to be less prominent among citizens' major concerns. There is also a relative improvement in the percentage of people who describe the area as very insecure.[18]

The interviews conducted in March 2000 reflected positive assessments of the community policing project, as well as a desire to continue it. Those interviewed in August 2001, however, unanimously criticized the lack of follow-up and the obvious weakening of the program once the support of the Inter-American Institute of Human Rights ended.

In São Paulo, evaluation of the program's impact took the form of public opinion surveys at the state level, along with studies in certain localities. The former show an improvement in the opinion of the police in the state in general, although the scope of the study and lack of sufficiently disaggregated data make it impossible to determine whether this is a primary consequence of the community policing program. However, the only way of determining whether changes in levels of fear and in public feeling regarding the police are a function of community policing, is to target surveys in areas where community policing is actually in effect. Two such studies have been conducted. The first examined Jardim Ângela, in the southern part of the city, which is one of the most violent areas, according to the Forum in Defense of Life. The forum surveyed 945 residents and businesspeople to assess the impact of community policing. The results showed that residents and individuals working less than one kilometer from the small neighborhood police stations had a more positive perception of community policing, its effect on security, and the treatment of citizens than those living or working farther from the stations. This suggests that the impact is not sufficiently distributed and does not reach all people in the sectors involved. Somewhat similar results were obtained in an ILANUD study in 2000 focused on twenty-three neighborhoods that have neighborhood police stations and twenty-three that do not. Where there is a community policing program and residents are familiar with it, fear levels are lower, opinions of the police are more positive, and there is more support for the program than where the program exists but is less known, or where there is no such program (Kahn 2003, 10).

These two surveys seem to suggest that the impact of community policing on citizens' feelings of insecurity depends on the extent to which police make personal efforts to establish closer relationships with the community, and on the use of the media to publicize the program and its benefits. They also suggest, however, that the impact of the program is highly dependent on physical proximity to the police. Whether because of a lack of personnel or a failure to establish closer contact with the population, the existence of the program is not obvious to all residents of the neighborhoods involved.

Regarding crime control, the results of these two studies are not encouraging. In Jardim Ângela, a majority of the population continues to believe that the police do little to combat drug dealing, and even believe that they are involved. The ILANUD study shows that the presence of small community police stations does not affect victimization rates. These conclusions are supported, to some degree, by police crime statistics. As Paulo de Mesquita Neto (2004, 128) indicates, homicides, robbery, and theft declined in the metropolitan region in 2000, but not in the inner city—the location of the majority of small police stations from which community patrols are dispatched.

Available information suggests some preliminary inferences, although the existing information base does not allow for definitive conclusions. First, community policing programs are strongly supported by the population, which favors their continuation. They improve the public's image of the police and—when the existence of the programs is well known—reduce people's fear. This indicates that community action in itself does not reduce fear, but that intense, recognized police presence is required as well. A pattern of constant interaction and communication with the public is also necessary. The relationship with the community must reflect a concern for establishing close relations with lower-income sectors, bearing in mind the danger that closer relations with the community will produce disproportionate benefits to the most powerful sectors, which already have access to private security. With respect to crime rates, results are inconclusive. The reduction in crime in Villa Nueva could well be due to increased patrols and monitoring rather than to the community strategies themselves.

Conclusions and Proposals

Community policing programs are being implemented increasingly in Latin America, due to the variety of factors discussed above. First, there is a prevailing lack of public confidence in the police in many countries. Second, there is a need to change strategies in order to deal with a massive increase in criminal violence, even in those countries considered most secure. Finally, there is a need for police forces to undertake the decentralization and administrative modernization already underway in other sectors of the state.

The case studies presented here indicate that community policing programs provide a partial answer to the challenges they were designed to address. Public confidence in the police rises in places where such programs are in effect, and the citizenry has an interest in establishing closer relations with the police. It is less clear that these programs, in themselves, tend to reduce police abuses, although they appear to be a step in the right direction. They need to be complemented by retraining programs for police officers with tendencies toward abuse, early warning systems to deal with repeat violators, and other measures (Frühling 2002, 35). In terms of reducing crime and violence, the results are not conclusive, although it is still unclear whether this is due to the community policing model itself or to problems in implementation—particularly insufficient cooperation between police and other regional and local governmental entities.

Community policing does appear to be more than an attempt to produce changes in the external environment. International organizations, governments, and sometimes police forces themselves have put forth various programs promoting closer relations with the community as a first step in transforming the police into a truly modern, democratic organization. The information presented here suggests that skepticism exists as to whether this goal is actually being achieved in the countries whose programs have been described—or, indeed, whether such change is even possible. In developed democratic countries where scientific assessments of community policing are available, profound transformations have been achieved. Community policing has led to new internal values systems, reduced hierarchical distance within police organizations, and produced a drive for innovation and individual responsibility that transcends disciplinary systems and other controls by the command structure. Beyond the problems this can entail—which have been addressed in the literature—it is clear that these changes are fully consistent with current principles and values of public administration (de Lint 1998). Thus, the paradigm behind the community policing model implies that the police, as professionals responsible for public order, must design strategic solutions to meet the demands of citizens, addressing patterns and trends in crime. It is clear that the human, material, and organizational resources in Latin American police forces, and their organizational paradigms, are very different, and that moving toward the so-called "new managerialism" requires conditions that are simply not present in the Latin American environment. A culture-dependent skepticism regarding these programs among subordinate police personnel is part of the reality that must be taken into account, as are the lack of training for strategic problem solving and the financial and logistical problems that limit the expansion of these programs beyond mere pilot experiments.

These programs, while different in minor ways, may all be defined as programs to bring the police into closer contact with the community. Although their benefits may seem clear, they have not yet definitively opened the door to a process of institutional transformation and cultural change, or even to a change in the preventive strategies utilized by the police. Beyond the doubts expressed here, however, a number of important conclusions emerge from these cases. The consequences for the planning and execution of future programs designed to bring the police and the community closer together are summarized below.

The importance of defining a clear course of action for implementation of the program. Not all of the community policing programs described here were preceded by careful planning aimed at maximizing their impact and usefulness. A few issues emerge from the analysis so far. First, community policing programs should make explicit their doctrinal principles, and these principles should be reflected in the internal structures of the organization, as well as in training programs for senior and subordinate officers. Second, the programs should be based on a carefully designed and well-funded plan, and locations for implementation should be chosen on the basis of strategic criteria that include progressive implementation and ongoing independent evaluation. Third, these programs require proper links with local governments, which must have authority to act in specified areas of public security. Links must also be forged with citizens' groups capable of interacting with police and collaborating authoritatively in discussions, actions, and evaluations.

Internal setting of objectives by police. Given the inevitable resistance to this type of program, a clear determination of purpose and of the role of each individual police employee is essential. Along with setting objectives, there must be an overall vision of the police and a redefinition of missions and values, where needed. A document should be produced setting forth these definitions, to be disseminated to all members of the police force. First, however, it should be determined whether there is internal consistency between program objectives and the measures that can actually be implemented. Objectives must be consistent with the means adopted, and with individuals' willingness to support the objectives. A foot patrol cannot be planned if the police who are to conduct it are clearly resistant to the activity. Nor can a national plan be declared if no funds are available to execute it on a national scale.

Part of this effort to communicate the program within the police must include courses on community policing as part of a general curriculum, in addition to specialized courses for ranking officers and subordinate personnel. These training programs are extremely important, since, as the case studies show, most police have no experience with community policing and the prevailing institutional culture in their organizations favors a traditional approach to security problems. The courses must also include a theoretical component dealing with community policing, in addition to components to develop interpersonal skills and familiarize police with resources within a given community that can be drawn upon for support. There also, however, must be a practical component that teaches the actual work involved, familiarizing police with the types of dilemmas they will face under the new model. The curriculum must be designed by police officials, with input from civilian advisors, and exercises with real cases must be included.

It is also essential that, as the new model is implemented, there be discussion groups involving both ranking officers and subordinate personnel participating in the program, so that their observations can be reflected in new training materials.

Careful planning of program implementation. Planning by police management must address multiple issues. In order for the public to become aware that there is a community-based program in progress, there must be a significant foot presence. Police should be provided the time needed to attend public meetings and establish contact at the street level. Funds are needed to design and implement training programs for police and citizens, and to print and distribute information. It is vital that, from the start, funding include resources for ongoing monitoring by an academic institution unconnected with the police and with the program's implementation process, one that is not dependent on the results of the program. Another important design aspect of the program is the need to have human resources allocated to each geographic area for a relatively long period, in order to ensure stable and intense contact with citizens. This may require changes in personnel policy. Finally, the changes involved must apply to all members of the police force in their relations with the public. Information acquired in the community policing process should flow throughout the institution, so that problem solving strategies reach all units.

The selection of locations for programs cannot be capricious. A set of areas should be selected for pilot programs in such a way as to make the program replicable, in a progressive manner, in the rest of the city. This allows a program's weaknesses and strengths to be tested, facilitates impact assessment, and makes it possible to secure the funds needed to carry out the program effectively. Selection should be based on objective criteria defined according to well-designed variables. Socioeconomic criteria and crime rates are the most important considerations. Thus, the areas selected should be representative of high-, medium-, and low-income sectors, in addition to representing high, medium, and low crime rates. This will make it possible to evaluate the program's results in areas with differing social realities and crime environments, and to make comparisons with control areas that have similar characteristics where the program is not being carried out.

Links between the Community Policing Program and Local Organizations

In many cases, there is no real association or coordination among police, local government, and citizen organizations involved in crime prevention. Clearly, no community policing program can be carried out without police participation. But these programs also require participation by the community and on the part of public agencies involved in local government that offer crime prevention programs to complement police activity. It is common in the region for government to take responsibility for community participation, while the police work to increase community relations, but without any coordination between the two efforts (Dammert 2001). This problem is due in part to the fact that municipal government has only recently begun to work in the area of security, and its agenda is not yet clear (Sozzo 1999). Moreover, police are funded by provincial or national governments; thus, mechanisms for reporting to local authorities tend to be either nonexistent or unclear. A means must be found to coordinate the agendas and interests of organizations with differing sources of legitimacy and authority.

For a community policing program to be successful, it must be designed jointly by police and the municipal government, which play important roles in social and urban policy. Citizens invited to meet with police are likely to request services that the police do not provide, such as better lighting for certain areas, fencing of empty lots, or changes in bus stop locations or public transportation routes. Municipal governments have the benefit of a network of relationships with parents and foster parents, neighborhood groups, and sports clubs, all of which are potential resources for helping to solve problems important to residents.

It is not easy to create sustainable community participation programs. The two variables that affect sustainability are whether citizens are properly trained to act alongside the police in a complementary role, and whether their opinions influence the shaping of police action. In this respect, the Belo Horizonte experience, where the same problem-solving training is provided for police and residents, is particularly interesting.

Certain aspects of citizen participation referred to in the case studies are not unlike what emerges from studies in North America and elsewhere. In high-crime areas, participation is low, while citizens' level of training to participate in the programs is also low. In these cases, two types of measures can help. First, massive training of residents in crime prevention is important. Second, there must be strong emphasis on follow-up for problems residents pose to the police and to municipal government. In the absence of such action, citizen participation lacks meaning, both for the public and for the public organizations that wish to use community participation to solve their security problems.

Notes

1. Examples include the Copacabana, Rio de Janeiro, community policing project, which ended with a change of government, and the changes produced by the reform of the Buenos Aires Police with the inauguration of Governor Ruckauf in 1999; see Frühling (2001).

2. Peru's National Police, for example, is composed of approximately one hundred thousand officers, and the 2001 report of the special commission for restructuring the force states that "The police were not a political or budget priority in the 1990s. Infrastructure for citizen security and public order is therefore in a highly deteriorated state" (Comisión Especial 2001).

3. Ouvidoria da Polícia de São Paulo, "Mortos por Políciais, 1990 a 2002" (table), http://www.ouvidoria-policia.sp.gov.br/pages/Tabelas.htm.

4. A study by Claudio Fuentes (2000), however, indicates that complaints of police violence submitted to military prosecutors have continued to rise.

5. This argument is set forth by Lemos-Nelson (2001).

6. An interesting empirical study that has tested this hypothesis appears in Birkbeck and Gabaldón (1998). See also Ramos and Musumeci (2004).

7. A study of the internal control system of the Argentine police is Palmieri, Martínez, Sozzo, and Thomas (2001).

8. The information can be found at Pan-American Health Organization website, http://Paho.org/English/HCP/HCN/VIO/violence-graphs.htm.

9. Official figures are from the Chilean Ministry of the Interior, http://www.interior.gov.

10. This multicenter study was coordinated by the Pan-American Health Organization and carried out in selected cities in Latin America (El Salvador-Bahia and Rio de Janeiro, Brazil; Santiago, Chile; Cali, Colombia; San José, Costa Rica; San Salvador, El Salvador; Caracas, Venezuela) and in Madrid, Spain. Various centers of recognized expertise in the area participated in the study. Its results were published in the *Pan American Journal of Public Health* 5, nos. 4/5 (1999).

11. See "Espejo de las Américas," in *El Mercurio,* Economía y Negocios, 16 April 1998, pp. 8, 9.

12. Executive performance at the local level leads to careers of national scope, as in the case of the mayor of Las Condes in Chile, Joaquín Lavin, who became a leader of the opposition.

13. A study of the impact of a community policing program on the perceptions and

organizational modes of police revealed resistance to the changes that occurred and to how they were implemented, and a certain preference for the traditional model of police action; see Schafer (2001, 139–86).

14. The works produced as a result of this project are Frühling (2004), Mesquita Neto (2004), Chinchilla (2004), Llorente (2004), and Beato F. (2004).

15. The Military Police is organized in commands, battalions, and companies. The latter are the smallest police units. They are headed by a captain and include between one hundred and three hundred individuals.

16. The project spawned several publications by its regional coordinator, José María Rico (1999, 2000a, 2000b).

17. Centro de Investigação em Segurança Pública (CRISP), *Avaliação e acompanhamento dos Conselhos Comunitários de Segurança em Belo Horizonte* (Belo Horizonte: Universidade Federal de Minas Gerais, 2000), cited in Beato F. (2004).

18. Inter-American Institute of Human Rights (IAIHR), *Encuesta de opinión pública, Municipio de Villa Nueva (September 1998 and March 2000)*, cited in Chinchilla (2004).

References

Bayley, David. 1994. *Police for the Future*. New York: Oxford University Press.
Beato F., Claudio C. 2004. "Reinventar la policía: La experiencia de Belo Horizonte. In *Calles más seguras. Estudios de policía comunitaria en América Latina*, edited by Hugo Frühling. Washington, DC: Banco Interamericano de Desarrollo.
Birbeck, Christopher, and Luis Gerardo Gabaldón. 1998. "The Effect of Citizen's Status and Behavior on Venezuelan Police Officers' Decisions to Use Force." *Policing and Society* 8, 315–38.
Bresser Pereira, Luis Carlos. 1999. "Managerial Public Administration: Strategy and Structure for a New State." In *Managerial Public Administration in Latin America*, edited by Luis Carlos Bresser Pereira and Peter Spink. Boulder, CO: Lynne Rienner Publishers.
Centro Nacional de Consultoría. 1996. *La Consulta Ciudadana en Santafé de Bogotá*. Informe No. 36 entregado a la Policía Nacional. Bogotá: Centro Nacional de Consultoría.
Chinchilla., M. Laura. 2004. "El Caso del Municipio de Villa Nueva, Guatemala." In *Calles Más Seguras. Estudios de policía comunitaria en América Latina*, edited by Hugo Frühling. Washington, DC: Banco Interamericano de Desarrollo.
Comisión Especial de Reestructuración de la Policía Nacional del Perú. 2001. *Informe de la Comisión Especial de Reestructuración de la Policía Nacional del Perú*. Lima: Comisión.
Correa Sutil, Jorge, and Luis Barros, eds. 1993. *Justicia y marginalidad. Percepciones de los pobres*. Santiago: Corporación de Promoción Universitaria and Universidad Católica de Chile.
Dammert, Lucía. 2004. "Participación comunitaria en la prevención del delito en América Latina. ¿De qué participación hablamos?" In *Participación ciudadana y reformas a la policía en América del Sur*, edited by Hugo Frühling and Azun Candina. Santiago: Centro de Estudios para el Desarrollo.
Dammert, Lucía, and Mary Fran T. Malone. 2002. "Inseguridad y temor en la Argentina:

El impacto de la confianza en la policía y la corrupción sobre la percepción ciudadana del crimen." *Desarrollo Económico* 42, no. 166 (July–September): 285–301.
De Lint, Willem. 1998. "New Managerialism and Canadian Police Training Reform." *Social and Legal Studies* 7, no. 2: 261–85.
Frühling, Hugo. 1999. "La policía en Chile: Los nuevos desafíos de una coyuntura compleja." *Perspectivas* (Universidad de Chile) 3, no. 1, 63–90.
———. 2000. "La modernización de la policía en América Latina." In *Convivencia y seguridad: Reto a la gobernabilidad*. Alcalá de Henares, Madrid: Banco Interamericano de Desarrollo and Universidad de Alcalá.
———. 2001. *La reforma policial y el proceso de democratización en América Latina*. Santiago de Chile: Centro de Estudio del Desarrollo.
———. 2002. "Policía y sociedad. Tres experiencias sudamericanas." *Renglones* 51 (May–August), 23–35.
———. 2004. "La policía comunitaria en América Latina. Un análisis basado en cuatro estudios de caso." In *Calles más seguras. Estudios de policía comunitaria en América Latina*, edited by Hugo Frühling. Washington, DC: Banco Interamericano de Desarrollo.
Fuentes, Claudio. 2000. *Denuncias por violencia policial en Chile*. Santiago: Facultad Latinoamericana de Ciencias Sociales.
Instituto de Enseñanza para el Desarrollo Sostenible (IEPADES). 2000. "Informe de avance sobre la investigación relaciones policía–comunidad en Guatemala." In *Proyecto Sociedad Civil y Seguridad Ciudadana: Un estudio comparativo de la reforma a la seguridad pública en Centroamérica*. Washington, DC: Washington Office on Latin America, October.
Jordan, M. Mariana, and Cecilia Sotomayor. 2000. "Seguridad ciudadana y comunidad local organizada. Estudio de los Comités Vecinales de Seguridad Ciudadana en tres comunas de Santiago." Santiago: Instituto de Sociología, Universidad Católica de Chile.
Kahn, Túlio. 2003. *Policía comunitaria: Evaluando la experiencia*. Santiago de Chile: Centro de Estudios para el Desarrollo.
Lamm Weisel, Deborah, and John E. Eck. 1994. "Toward a Practical Approach to Organizational Change. Community Policing Initiatives in Six Cities." In *The Challenge of Community Policing*, edited by Dennis P. Rosenbaum. Thousand Oaks, CA: Sage Publications.
Lemos-Nelson, Ana Tereza. 2001. "Police Criminality, Citizenship and the (Un)Rule-of-Law." Paper presented at the Annual Meeting of the Latin American Studies Association. Washington, DC, 6–8 September.
Llorente, María Victoria. 2004. "La experiencia de Bogotá: Contexto y balance." In *Calles más seguras. Estudios de policía comunitaria en América Latina*, edited by Hugo Frühling. Washington, DC: Banco Interamericano de Desarrollo.
Mesquita Neto, Paulo. 2004. "La policía comunitaria en São Paulo: Problemas de implementación y consolidación." In *Calles más seguras. Estudios de policía comunitaria en América Latina*, edited by Hugo Frühling. Washington, DC: Banco Interamericano de Desarrollo.
Mesquita Neto, Paulo, with Beatriz Stella Affonso. 1998. *Policiamento comunitário: A experiência en São Paulo*. São Paulo: Núcleo de Estudos da Violência da Universidade de São Paulo, September.
Muniz, Jacqueline, Sean Patrick Larvie, Leonarda Musumec, and Bianca Freire. 1997.

"Resistencias e dificuldades de um programa de policiamento comunitário." *Tempo Social* 9, no. 1 (May): 197–214.
Neild, Rachel. 2002. *Sustaining Reform: Democratic Policing in Central America.* Washington, DC: Washington Office on Latin America.
Palmieri, Gustavo, Josefina Martínez, Máximo Sozzo, and Hernán Thomas. 2001. "Mecanismos de control interno e iniciativas de reforma en las instituciones policiales argentinas. Los casos de la Policía Federal Argentina, la Policía de la Provincia de Santa Fé y la Policía de la Provincia de Buenos Aires." In *Policía, sociedad y estado: Modernización y reforma policial en América del Sur,* edited by Hugo Frühling and Azun Candina. Santiago: Centro de Estudios para el Desarrollo.
Policía Nacional, República de Colombia. [1998]. *Transformación cultural. La fuerza del cambio.* Bogotá: Policía Nacional.
Ramos, Silvia, and Leonarda Musumeci. 2004. *Elemento suspeito. Abordagem policial e discriminação na Cidade do Rio de Janeiro.* Rio de Janeiro: Centro de Estudos de Segurança e Cidadania.
Rico, José María. 1999. *Seguridad ciudadana en Centroamérica: Aspectos teóricos y metodológicos.* San José: Inter-American Institute of Human Rights.
———. 2000a. *Diagnósticos sobre la situación.* San José, Costa Rica: Inter-American Institute of Human Rights.
———. 2000b. *Informe final de evaluación.* San José: Inter-American Institute of Human Rights, August.
Rosenbaum, Dennis P. 1998. "The Changing Role of the Police: Assessing the Current Transition to Community Policing." In *How to Recognize Good Policing: Problems and Issues,* edited by Jean Paul Brodeaur. Washington, DC: Police Executive Research Forum.
Sandoval, Luis. 2001. "Prevención local de la delincuencia en Santiago de Chile." In *Policía, sociedad y estado: Modernización y reforma policial en América del Sur,* edited by Hugo Frühling and Azun Candina. Santiago: Centro de Estudios para el Desarrollo.
Sandoval Quappe, General Ricardo. 2002. "Los modelos de policía comunitaria, como cambio doctrinario y procesos de modernización de las policías. Sobre qué aspectos trabajar prioritariamente en Latinoamérica?" Presented at the seminar Policía y Comunidad: Los Nuevos Desafíos para Chile, Santiago, 4–5 December.
Schafer, Joseph A. 2001. *Community Policing: The Challenges of Successful Organizational Change.* New York: LFB Scholarly Publishing.
Sherman, Lawrence W. 1995. "The Police." In *Crime,* edited by James Q. Wilson and Joan Petersilia. San Francisco: Center for Self-Governance.
Souza, Elenice. 1999. "Avaliação do policiamento comunitário em Belo Horizonte." Master's thesis, Universidade Federal de Minas Gerais.
Sozzo, Máximo. 1999. "Seguridad urbana y gobierno local. Debate, consenso y racionalidades políticas en la ciudad de Santa Fé." In *Seguridad urbana,* edited by Máximo Sozzo. Santa Fé, Argentina: Universidad Nacional del Litoral.
Stanley, William. 1999. "Building New Police Forces in El Salvador and Guatemala: Learning and Counter-Learning." *International Peace Keeping* 6, no. 4, 113–34.
United Nations, Office for Drug Control and Crime Prevention. 1999. *Global Report on Crime and Justice.* New York: Oxford University Press.
Villarroel, Major Jorge. 2002. *Comunicación de la Dirección de Planificación y Desarrollo de Carabineros de Chile.* Santiago: Carabineros de Chile, December.

Ward, H. Heather. 2001. "Police Reform in Latin America: Current Efforts in Argentina, Brazil, and Chile." Presented to the Working Group on Citizen Security, Woodrow Wilson International Center for Scholars, Washington, DC, April.

Wycoff, Mary Ann, and Wesley G. Skoga. 1994. "Community Policing in Madison. An Analysis of Implementation and Impact." In *The Challenge of Community Policing,* edited by Dennis P. Rosenbaum. Thousand Oaks, CA: Sage Publications.

Chapter 3

Advocacy Networks and Police Reform: Assessing Their Impact

Claudio A. Fuentes

The steady decline of crime in New York City during the 1990s did not come without social costs. Indeed, as crime rates dropped 75 percent, citizen complaints against the New York Police Department increased by more than 100 percent (Chevigny 1995; Human Rights Watch 1998). Comparative studies show that "tough" measures against crime tend to be associated with an increase in police abuses of citizens' basic rights (Neild 2000; Gitlitz and Chevigny 2002; Davis 2002).[1] Given this situation, police reformers have suggested the need to advance reforms in two areas: improving the efficiency of police institutions to prevent crime, and creating mechanisms of internal and external accountability to prevent abuses.

As shown in the chapters by Beato, Smulovitz, and Ward, police reforms in Latin America have put strong emphasis on the first dimension—improving efficiency—but very little has been done in the second area—improving accountability. Advancing these two agendas simultaneously requires three conditions: officers willing to restructure their institutions, politicians willing to enact reforms and restrict police powers, and a society that perceives police institutions as contributors to the problems of public insecurity and urban violence (Merenin 1996). In many Latin American countries, neither police nor politicians are willing to initiate such comprehensive reforms, so organized groups of civil society may play a relevant role by pressuring governments to control police behavior. These organized societal groups—or advocacy networks—can be active in monitoring police activities, influencing legislative passage, and scrutinizing policy compliance (Keck and Sikkink 1998; Neild 2000).

Even though advocacy groups are important within the policy process, few studies have assessed their actual impact in contemporary Latin America

(Smulovitz and Peruzzotti 2000; Neild 2000). We know that advocacy groups matter, but we know little about the conditions under which they matter and the extent of their influence. In this chapter, I attempt to close this gap by analyzing the way human rights advocacy groups have (or have not) influenced domestic policy processes, considering the cases of democratic Argentina (1983–2002) and Chile (1990–2002). Both countries share important features such as high levels of education and socioeconomic status along with a strong tradition of an organized action by human rights activists during and after experiencing military dictatorships. In this context, these two cases may shed some light on the role played by civil society in controlling police institutions.

I argue that advocacy networks can play a central role in getting an issue noticed (agenda setting) and influencing legislative passage. However, the nature of the problem at stake makes this influence transitory or fluctuating. As politicians face a difficult trade-off between protecting citizens' rights and maintaining public order, whether they will enforce laws favorable to the protection of individual rights depends on a set of political and institutional factors that require further analysis.

The first part of this chapter explains the concept of advocacy networks and suggests a general framework—based on the advocacy coalition approach—to understand trends toward restricting and/or increasing police powers in contemporary Latin America. The second part explores the conditions under which advocacy networks can influence the policy process, considering the cases of contemporary Argentina and Chile. The third part introduces the factors that inhibit advocacy networks from having an enduring or permanent influence on the policy process. The last section provides some policy recommendations regarding the role of organized civil society (both local and international) in the context of initiating police reforms in developing countries.

Network Formation and Policy Change

Even though, in principle, democratic governments respect the protection of citizens' rights, policymakers usually face a difficult trade-off between protecting individual rights and maintaining public safety. Individuals want to walk in the streets without fear of being attacked by delinquents or being beaten by police officers. Because citizens want their possessions and personal integrity to be protected, they are willing to give up certain individual rights in order to maintain public safety. However, as citizens give more power to the police, there are greater opportunities for police officers to engage in unlawful practices. This trade-off is particularly acute in developing countries, where police institutions have participated in military regimes that massively violated human rights, where mechanisms of accountability have been historically weak (Chevigny 1995; Frühling 1998; O'Donnell 1998; Neild 2000), and where recurring economic crises have severe social consequences in terms of inequality and social unrest.

Thus, in a conflictive environment, there is likely to be a clear division between those sectors that promote the protection of civil rights from abuse by public authority and those that are willing to give up their individual rights to promote and maintain social order. I mainly focus here on the role played by advocacy networks in the promotion of civil rights. Advocacy networks are "forms of organization characterized by voluntary, reciprocal, and horizontal patterns of communication and exchange" (Keck and Sikkink 1998, 8). Scholars have argued that these networks are relevant because of their influence on issue creation and agenda setting, institutional procedures, the discourses of states and international organizations, policy change in "target states," and state compliance with new rules (Keck and Sikkink 1998, 25; Clark et al. 2001). As rules protecting human rights have become internationally accepted, advocacy networks are likely to coordinate actions at the domestic and international level to advance citizens' rights. Thus, an organization like Amnesty International, the Washington Office on Latin America, or Human Rights Watch is likely to work with local groups in developing countries to pressure governments to fully implement international laws.

However, advocacy networks are not isolated from society. If these groups want to influence the political system, they usually seek domestic and international allies, forming what I call a "civil rights coalition."[2] The goal of this coalition is to improve the de jure as well as de facto status of citizens' rights. Lawyers, local and international human rights organizations, politicians generally identified with liberal and leftist ideas, and some career government officials are likely to support the notion that every citizen has basic inalienable rights, even in cases in which a society is dealing with crime, terrorism, and social disorder. Certainly, the more active groups are human rights advocacy networks attempting to convince other social and political actors of the need to advance people's rights.

But the civil rights coalition is likely to confront those who want to maintain the status quo—what I call the "pro-order coalition." This coalition's primary concern is the maintenance of social order. In many countries, the police, intelligence agencies, some state officials, more conservative political parties, some local and international think tanks, and some sectors of civil society tend to champion this view. These actors will seek to provide police institutions with wide-ranging legal tools to preempt social disorder, terrorism, and crime. Those sectors do not reject the existence of individual rights, but they emphasize that such rights should be circumstantial and that authorities must restrict citizens' rights and widen police powers in order to maintain social peace.

These two coalitions show distinctive structural features. First, the civil rights coalition is likely to be engaged in a collective action problem similar to that encountered by any group seeking to promote a public good.[3] This is because while all citizens want to have their rights protected, only a few citizens actually participate in organizations that promote respect for those rights. Most citizens consider the individual cost of participating in advocacy groups to be greater than the benefits to be accrued. These citizens aim to get a free ride by letting issue-specific, small, voluntary domestic and international organizations provide the public good of protecting them from the abuse of power.[4] Because police violence in general affects the more disadvantaged sectors of society, it is difficult for those citizens to organize in a collective way to defend their physical integrity from the abuse of power.[5] Since coordinated action to demand fair treatment is difficult and costly, one should expect that leaders from the more advantaged sectors of society—human rights groups, political parties, and policymakers committed to civil rights—would take the lead in defending the vulnerable sectors.

In contrast, the pro-order coalition has considerable advantages in terms of resources, coordination, and the ability to respond to individuals' allegations. First, police institutions offer a public service ("public safety") that is highly valued by governments and many citizens, increasing police institutions' leverage vis-à-vis other societal groups. Police institutions may pressure governments to obtain what they consider right for society, that is, tough measures against delinquents, greater institutional resources, and the legal protection of the officers who every day risk their lives in the streets.

Second, coordination for the pro-order coalition is easier than for the civil rights coalition, given the support they have from an established institution—the police. Civil rights groups are less likely to have bureaucratic institutions defending their position.[6] Institutions such as the police have comparative advantages over voluntary organizations because they can direct their financial resources toward effective lobbying. They also benefit from lower costs of mobilization than those incurred by voluntary organizations (Lowery et al. 2002).

Third, in terms of policy implementation, it is always harder to put into practice reforms that address the protection of citizens' rights than to increase police powers. Protecting rights requires creating institutions, transforming institutional practices, and monitoring new rules. Increasing police powers just requires an internal administrative order within the police.

Finally, there is always the problem of proving police abuse. First, evidence of police abuse must be collected within a short period of time; otherwise, it tends to vanish. Additionally, in many developing countries police institutions play the double role of both overseeing public safety and helping judges in the process of collecting evidence, which increases the opportunities for altering evidence. Finally, several comparative studies have shown an intense peer loyalty among officers, building a code of silence regarding illegal practices and misbehavior (for a summary of these arguments, see Waddington 1999).

Thus, if we want to understand certain societies' resistance to improving individual rights (legally or in practical terms), a good point of departure is to observe the power resources and strategies used by these two competing coalitions. In this context, the influence of advocacy networks depends on their ability to overcome problems of collective action to advance their claims in society, and their ability to respond to the challenges posited by competing societal groups (the pro-order coalition) that will likely defend the status quo. Given the nature of the problem at stake, I argue that the pro-order coalition generally has the advantage. To illustrate the argument, the next paragraphs will address the challenges that human rights advocacy networks have faced in Argentina and Chile concerning the issue of police violence after the reestablishment of democracy.

When Advocacy Networks Matter

In a democratic regime, it is expected that if an officer commits an illegal act, he or she will be punished according to a system that provides institutional mechanisms to control such abuses of power. Societies have horizontal and vertical mechanisms of accountability to prevent, control, and punish misbehavior.[7] Thus, if a police officer beats an individual, one should expect that the individual will make an official complaint, that police institutions will make internal investigations, that judges will prosecute the abusive officer, and that police institutions will take measures to prevent future abuses.

What distinguishes developing countries from developed ones is the absence of adequate channels to control this process. One crucial feature that is often missing is an effective mechanism of vertical and horizontal accountability that would protect citizens from the abuse of power and guarantee that rules will be implemented (O'Donnell 1998).

Improving mechanisms of accountability in newly democratized countries necessitates reforms in three areas: (1) restricting police powers to detain individuals and providing citizens with certain basic rights (the equivalent of U.S. *Miranda* rights); (2) creating civilian oversight capabilities over police institutions; and (3) improving the judiciary system to guarantee a fair trial.

The notion of citizens having rights at the moment of their arrest and police institutions being subjected to horizontal and vertical controls is new to Latin America. For instance, the 1901 Chilean penal code established the "detention on suspicion" clause by which police officers could detain individuals based on their physical appearance. This clause was eliminated only in 1998—eight years after the reestablishment of democracy. Moreover, police officers in Chile can still only be prosecuted by military courts, regardless of the crimes that they have committed. In Argentina, the 1868 and 1888 penal codes gave the federal police the power to detain individuals on the grounds of suspicion. In 1944, authorities increased police powers by allowing officers to arrest individuals who failed to prove their identity. Additionally, authorities promulgated police *edictos* (edicts) authorizing security forces to arrest individuals on the basis of minor offenses such as public disorder, "scandal," loafing, begging, and prostitution (Blando 1995). Following the same path, in 1970 Buenos Aires province established a Código de Faltas (code of misdemeanors) cataloguing more than fifty minor offenses that were considered grounds for arrest.

The reestablishment of democracy brought new hopes for reform. Indeed, in both Chile and Argentina some important legal steps have been taken to protect citizens' basic rights. In Chile, the "detention of suspicion" clause was replaced by a "verification of identity" clause and *Miranda*-type rights were introduced for the first time in legal history in 1998. As of early 2003, however, no changes had been made to restrict the wide-ranging powers of military courts or to create internal and external accountability mechanisms over police institutions.[8] In Argentina, reforms came in two waves: a first in the early 1990s that involved restricting police powers to detain individuals and the approval of a penal code at the federal level, and a second wave that involved an in-depth transformation of the Buenos Aires Provincial Police in 1997–1998.[9] As will be described below, human rights advocacy networks have played a significant role in advancing some of the legal reforms. Under certain circumstances, they have been key actors in three ways: framing or making the issue noticeable to the public (agenda setting), collecting relevant information, and establishing alliances with key policymakers to transform the status quo.

Framing Police Violence as a "Social Problem"

In a democratic society, advocacy groups can play a crucial role by controlling state agencies and monitoring police behavior. In Argentina, in the years following the transition to democracy, human rights advocacy groups included police brutality as part of their agenda. For instance, the Coordinadora Contra la Represión Policial (Coordinator Against Police Repression [CORREPI]) was created in 1987 by a group of lawyers and human rights activists to help victims of police violence. They created a nationwide voluntary network of grassroots organizations to provide both legal and social support to victims. By 1997, this network included representatives of thirty-five organizations and approximately seven hundred activists.[10]

CORREPI is probably one of the most effective grassroots social organizations denouncing police violence in Argentina (CORREPI 1998). The death of seventeen-year-old Walter Bulacio on 19 April 1991 constituted a landmark case for human rights activists.[11] Every 19 April, CORREPI, along with several other organizations, stages a protest in Buenos Aires demanding justice and the end of police violence in Argentina. Thousands of people representing a wide range of social organizations come out to show their support. In addition, CORREPI generally organizes protests after some particularly shocking act of police violence has occurred. Most demonstrations are reported by the press, thanks to personal contacts between CORREPI's leaders and journalists.

Another leading organization is the Centro de Estudios Legales y Sociales (Center for Legal and Social Studies [CELS]), a group with a particularly telling history. This center was created in 1978 as an advocacy and legal advice organization for victims of human rights violations. From 1989 to 1991, CELS faced a serious internal crisis regarding its objectives and goals in a democratic context. After the transition to democracy, CELS, like many other human rights organizations in Latin America, was caught in the dilemma of whether to exclusively focus on the past—dealing with the resolution of human rights violations committed during the military regime—or to broaden its agenda to include more contemporary social conflicts.

In 1991, one of the founders of CELS, Emilio Miñones, outlined the center's main problems and challenges. He recognized the need to widen CELS's orientation.[12] Thus, under the lead of a new generation, in 1993 CELS branched out beyond its traditional work on the legacy of past human rights abuses to tackle a range of new issues including police violence, social and economic rights, freedom of expression, indigenous rights, immigration, and international law.[13] By 2000, CELS was considered one of the most relevant human rights organizations in Latin America and its program on police violence included monitoring police activities, providing legal counseling to victims, and working with the government to develop programs to prevent abuse.

The experience of the Argentine human rights groups during the period of transition to democracy is only one of many different paths that can be observed in Latin America. In Chile, the organizations followed a very different path. At the time of the transition to democracy, the human rights movement consisted of a broad range of voluntary, academic, and professional human rights organizations, most of them linked to each other in a dense network of collaboration and reciprocity (Ropp and Sikkink 1999). Under the military regime, the Catholic Church was particularly important in providing financial, institutional, and moral support to the victims of human rights violations through its Vicariate of Solidarity, created in 1976.[14] However, during the transition, the Catholic Church closed the Vicariate of Solidarity, on the assumption that the new democratic authorities would take care of human rights problems in the future.

From a strategic point of view, the transition to democracy in Chile (1990) created new dilemmas for these groups. Many of the organizations were sympathetic to the new center-left government but, at the same time, they wanted to make sure that their demands were addressed. Additionally, these organizations were aware of the institutional constraints the new government faced, particularly in terms of the high level of military and police autonomy. As happened in Argentina and elsewhere, the transition to democracy raised an important strategic question for these organizations: What was the best way to achieve their goals? By the end of 1989, two options were well defined: influencing the government from within, and influencing the government from outside.

Leaders of those groups that had closer ties to the governing Concertación coalition assumed positions in the new administration, with the explicit intention of lobbying authorities from within. Activists from the Vicariate of Solidarity and the Chilean Committee for Human Rights (CHCHR) were politically connected to the Partido Demócrata Cristiano and the Partido Socialista, and several of them actively participated in forming the government's strategy, first in developing the new government's electoral platform, and then in implementing the platform once the transition to democracy took place.[15] Particularly relevant was the decision of the Catholic Church to dissolve the Vicariate of Solidarity and the CHCHR's decision to dissolve a network of more than five thousand volunteers nationwide.[16] As the principal leaders of both organizations were assuming new positions within the state bureaucracy, it was impossible for them to maintain the same level of grassroots activities as before. From being an organization characterized by a dense network of grassroots organizations, the CHCHR transformed itself into a bureaucratic entity with few staff members, fewer resources, and a lower level of interaction with civic organizations.

Insiders, that is, leaders who chose to work within the government structure, had a difficult time trying to influence the government agenda on human rights. First, they confronted a trade-off between their loyalty to the new government and their loyalty to the human rights cause. Second, in the early 1990s, the insiders faced a government that was trying to balance the stability of the country with the human rights agenda: the more the government pushed the human rights agenda, the more political instability the government had to confront, given the strong reaction of the right-wing opposition and the military. In practical terms, the insiders lost contact with old social networks and were unable to address emerging social conflicts from their position within the state apparatus.

Outsider groups, particularly the Corporación por la Defensa de los Derechos del Pueblo (CODEPU), which was created in 1980 to protect victims of human rights violations committed by security forces during the Pinochet regime, and the Corporación por la Defensa de los Derechos Juveniles (CODEJU) adopted a more critical approach, distinguishing themselves from the government. Politically, CODEPU was closer to the leftist sectors that did not form part of the new government (the Communist Party, for instance). As in Argentina, most outsiders faced the dilemma of whether to concentrate their scarce human and material resources on addressing the human rights violations related to the past, or to incorporate a broader definition of human rights and also focus on current social problems, such as police violence, the environment, and social and economic demands.[17] Early in the transition, CODEPU decided to focus most of its resources on addressing the problem of impunity for past human rights violations. Given this decision, in 2002, twelve years after the transition, CODEPU had only one lawyer dealing with allegations of police violence, and the organization lacked the resources to promote citizens' rights or publicize their work.

Collecting Information

A second way in which advocacy groups can become influential is by collecting information on cases of police brutality. This information may help local organizations trace patterns of police abuse (for instance, the victims' age and gender, police methods, and the location where the abuse occurred). As activists trace police behavior, they may be able to focus on certain areas of the country or sectors of the population, monitoring police activities more accurately. The systematization of this information may also help advocacy groups gain a reputation and become more visible and legitimate actors in society. If they release credible information, then international agencies, transnational human rights groups, and other organizations will use the information to pressure governments to comply with international laws. Finally, collecting information may also be helpful during debates on certain legal reforms in Congress, when politicians are translating demands into laws.

In Argentina, early on in the transition process, activists understood that information is power. Since 1989, CORREPI, for instance, has provided a nationwide inventory of police brutality from information culled from a wide network of grassroots organizations. This information has been uploaded to a website, allowing the group to gain visibility domestically and internationally. But probably the most impressive work in terms of data collection is the creation of a database by CELS that lists all cases of police brutality reported by the press since the early 1990s. CELS annual reports include information on trends in police violence, qualitative analysis of police practices, and a profile of the victims. Moreover, after the approval of legal reforms in 1997, CELS monitored these legal changes, providing several policy recommendations for politicians and the government. More recently, CELS has created an online monitoring system of police violence work sponsored by the Federal Direction of Criminal Policy and the Secretary of Justice and Security of the City of Buenos Aires.

In documenting cases of police violence and monitoring police practices, CELS has contributed to agenda setting for police reform in Argentina. By

1996, pro-reformist politicians, policymakers, and journalists were using this data to justify the need for urgent reforms.[18] Moreover, CELS has had some success in monitoring public authorities. For instance, in 1994 a CELS report on police violence was quoted in the annual report on human rights published by the U.S. Department of State. This allowed politicians and human rights activists to join forces and pressure for a change in government policies. As a result of this pressure, the Buenos Aires Province Secretary of Public Safety, Eduardo Pettigiani, resigned (CELS 1994, 21). A year later, CELS and other organizations again successfully pressured the government to dismiss the new secretary of public safety, Luis Patti, who had been involved in human rights violations during the military regime.[19] In 1996, CELS filed a lawsuit requesting police information on detentions and civilian and police deaths, opening a debate on the topic of transparency and accountability.[20] And in 2000, allegations by CELS led authorities from the Federal Council for the Protection of Children to request the organization's help in designing a new policy to prevent police torture of children.[21]

Even though collecting information seems to be an expected task, certain political conditions and internal characteristics of advocacy groups make this objective extremely difficult. In Chile, CODEPU continued to monitor police activities after the 1990 transition to democracy mainly because of the existence of political prisoners who were held in jail after the transition. CODEPU's annual reports on human rights between 1990 and 1994 (CODEPU 1994) led to the 1995 visit to Chile by United Nations Special Rapporteur on Torture, Nigel Rodley, to gather firsthand information on the subject. The final report suggests that although torture is not practiced either systematically or as a result of government policy in Chile, "the cases currently occurring are sufficiently numerous and serious for the authorities to continue looking into the problem and for the State's rejection of torture to be reflected in the adoption of specific measures" (United Nations 1996). The government adopted a defensive position, suggesting that "several cases in the report had not been verified" and that the report actually underscored the government's efforts to protect human rights.[22]

After 1994, CODEPU's reports show a decline in civilian complaints against the police (CODEPU 1999). Because CODEPU focused mainly on the violation of human rights committed during the previous military regime, and because no human rights organization followed the subject of police brutality, it has rarely been considered a problem in Chilean society. However, other quantitative and qualitative evidence suggests a different story. Despite the good public reputation of the Chilean police, the number of civilian complaints against them increased in the 1990s. Indeed, between March 1990 and December 2000, a total of 3,877 legal complaints were filed in courts in the central part of Chile; that is, every day at least one citizen presented a formal complaint against the police.[23] Civilians filed almost two hundred lawsuits against the police in 1990; that figure was more than five hundred by 1998. This trend probably underestimates the number of cases, since not all citizens have the time, money, or willingness to file a complaint against the police.[24] Additionally, only a fraction of the cases presented to a lawyer are actually translated into a formal complaint. Lawyers only tend to file cases in which the victim can provide enough evidence to prove the case in court.[25] Thus, the number of allegations made by citizens against the police is probably higher than the figure given here.

A qualitative analysis of complainants' sociodemographic characteristics[26] shows that they are mostly men (86 percent) from the lower-middle and lower classes. Only half are employed and 30 percent are students. Ninety-five percent of complainants said that police officers beat them with batons. In 20 percent of the cases, they alleged being wounded by gunfire without cause. In 61 percent of the cases, the alleged violence occurred in the streets and in 50 percent of the cases, officers took the victims to the hospital (Fuentes 2001).

Other qualitative sources confirm continued police brutality in Chile during the democratic years. A university study suggests that ill treatment of detainees by the police in the interval between arrest and appearance before a judge or release was fairly common at the beginning of the democratic era (Jiménez 1994). In this study, based on interviews with prisoners in 1992, only 22 percent said they had received good treatment. On the other hand, 71 percent said they had received blows of various kinds, 49 percent said they had received electric shocks, 20 percent said they had been undressed, 6 percent had been hung by their hands or feet, and 5 percent said plastic bags had been placed over their heads (Fuentes 2001, 193–206). A more recent study (1998–1999), based on interviews with teenagers from Santiago's Detention Center, reveals that 81 percent had been subjected to "bad treatment" from police officers at the moment of being arrested: 93 percent said they received blows of various kinds, 36 percent said they had been submerged in water containers, and 21 percent said plastic bags had been placed over their heads to produce asphyxiation (Jiménez 2000).[27]

Thus, even though quantitative and qualitative evidence suggests that the practice of police brutality has continued after the transition to democracy, local advocacy groups have not captured such trends. The advocacy groups' failure to provide systematic data collection and public exposure of the problem along with a well-established pro-order coalition that emphasizes a "zero tolerance" security agenda has made the topic of police accountability practically invisible in Chile. Moreover, all government efforts to improve the relationship between the community and the police focus on how the police can more easily respond to the safety concerns of the population, and how the community can help the police in getting delinquents off the streets (see Chapter 8 by Smulovitz). Policymakers and politicians rarely address issues such as the need to provide citizens with oversight capabilities to control police behavior, the creation of an ombudsman's office, or the reform of the military judicial system.

Local and International Alliances

Advocacy groups can become influential through the establishment of local and international alliances, both with each other and with policy experts and political parties. In Argentina, we observe reinforcing mechanisms of cooperation among activists, policy experts, and political parties. For instance, in 1986, Raúl Alfonsín's government supported the proposal by the influential lawyer Julio Maier that sought a major reform of federal penal code procedures. Two years later, a network of penal lawyers—led by Maier and other Latin American lawyers—established the Iberoamerican Institute of Penal Law in Brazil, to develop a "Model Penal Code for Latin America." Soon, several countries in Latin America began to follow this model and transform the traditional inquisitorial system.[28] These pro–civil rights lawyers—including Julio Maier, Raúl Zaffaroni, León Arslanián, and Alberto Binder—occupied important government positions and provided policy proposals to transform either the judicial system or police institutions. These lawyers maintained close contacts with human rights organizations and pro–civil rights political parties.[29] CELS has been particularly active in incorporating pro–civil rights experts into their activities through the organization of seminars and academic events, thus ensuring that they reach political and social actors on the topic of police institutional reforms.

Another interesting trend in Argentina is that, despite advocacy groups' ideological differences, they have been able to overcome these disputes in order to open a space for collaboration. Although CORREPI rejects a dialogue with public authorities, CELS attempts to influence the policy process. However, this difference has not inhibited the two organizations from sharing experiences and information, and helping each other at critical junctures.

One example is their collaboration in bringing Walter Bulacio's case before the Inter-American Court of Justice. CORREPI documented the case, and CELS provided its international expertise and international links to pressure the Argentine government to solve this case.[30]

Finally, advocacy groups in Argentina have successfully searched for allies abroad. CORREPI, for example, has managed to put information online through the establishment of an alliance with a Spanish human rights network, and it has implemented an e-mail listserv to inform supporters about activities and promote campaigns.[31] CELS has established an extensive network of international alliances to pressure the government from abroad,[32] and copublished a document on police violence with Americas Watch in 1991. By the mid-1990s, CELS had established a key alliance with the Center for Justice and International Law (CEJIL) based in Washington, D.C., to cosponsor lawsuits before the Inter-American Court of Justice. The center has also prepared an alternative report for the United Nations Commission on Human Rights (CELS 2001). Finally, CELS has constantly provided information to embassies and international organizations (e.g., UN Commission on Human Rights, Amnesty International) to maintain pressure on public authorities.

The coordination among advocacy groups and the establishment of alliances with policy experts have not been easy tasks in Chile. As mentioned earlier, during the transition to democracy, Chilean human rights groups experienced tension between insiders, who decided to promote a human rights agenda within the government, and outsiders, who took a more critical view of government policies on human rights issues. With few exceptions, lawyers and activists outside and inside the government do not share information, cases, and strategies to deal with issues of human rights, despite their common interest in improving the status of citizens' rights. Moreover, conflict among human rights groups on how to solve past human rights violations has increased tensions among them.[33] As a general trend, lawyers deal with their specific cases, without sharing ideas and strategies with their colleagues.[34] This reduces the ability of advocacy groups to create a unified front within the human rights movement and to generate a coherent agenda regarding past and present human rights violations.

An example of the lack of collaboration and communication between advocacy groups and policy experts is seen in the issue of the elimination of the "detention on suspicion" clause; by 1992, more than one hundred thousand individuals were being arrested annually by the police using this discriminatory clause, which allowed the police to detain people based on their physical appearance. CODEJU and other groups played an important role in setting the agenda for the debate on this subject. As a result, the president invited these organizations to participate in the commemoration of the third anniversary of the reestablishment of democracy on 11 March 1993. At this event, the president promised executive support for the elimination of the "detention on suspicion" clause.[35] Later on, CODEJU was invited by the director of the police to talk about this issue and, a week later, the president of the Chamber of Deputies announced that he was personally asking the executive to give the bill urgency status, after he had received a visit to his office from the representative of the committee against the "detention on suspicion" clause.[36]

However, after the first proposal on the bill was introduced in Congress in 1993, following a well-coordinated campaign led by CODEJU and several student organizations, social mobilizations to abolish the clause practically stopped. The bill was finally approved in 1998, not because of pressure from "below" but because of the influence of policy experts who, acting independently of human rights advocacy groups, lobbied members of Congress to replace the clause. The reform was made possible thanks to a parallel process that began when a group of pro–civil rights lawyers established a forum for the improvement of the criminal system in 1993. This forum consisted of seventy members, most of them lawyers linked to several left-, center-, and right-wing political parties, and representatives of different universities, professional associations, and policymakers (Vargas 1998). Between 1993 and 1994, they met with key governmental authorities to lobby and promote the major aspects of their proposed reforms, which dealt mainly with the need to abolish the traditional inquisitorial system of justice in which the judge assumed prosecutorial functions.

Moreover, the new system also implied redesigning the relationship between the police and prosecutors. By 1996, most congressional representatives agreed on the need for a substantial modernization of the legal system, including the redefinition of police powers at the moment of arrest. Thus, in May 1996, the Ministry of Justice sent to Congress a new bill, eliminating the "detention on suspicion" clause. According to the government, the goal was to reform police detention procedures "to make them consistent with those reforms proposed in the penal code procedure bill."[37]

The final draft approved by Congress in May 1998 did not reflect the wishes of the Ministry of Justice; rather, it favored the position of a pro-order coalition that influenced the Senate to approve a more conservative reform. Now, police officers could hold without any restrictions individuals who did not carry identification, establishing what is called the "verification of identity detention." In these cases, the police are supposed to use all means possible to facilitate an individual's self-identification. However, individuals can be held in custody for an unlimited period of time. Probably the main victory for civil rights advocates was the approval of *Miranda* rights for detainees. Police officers have to inform individuals about their rights at the moment of the arrest and at the moment of arrival at the police station.[38]

The decision-making process here reveals two interesting features. First, the passage of the legislation was framed by pro–civil rights sectors in the Ministry of Justice as part of a broader debate on the modernization of the judicial system. The pro-order coalition supported the reform because it believed Chile's judicial system needed to be modernized, and the new provisions provided an adequate balance between individuals' guarantees and police powers.[39] In this sense, police abuses were not part of the policy debate.

A second element is related to the existence of a group of professionals who offered technical recommendations to policymakers. These lawyers were part of a professional elite closely linked to government officials and, later on, to leaders of the opposition (Duce 1999). As the issue of police violence was not part of the government agenda, and as traditional human rights groups were not pressuring the government on this particular issue, these professionals did not have incentives to contact human rights advocacy groups.

It is interesting to note that human rights advocacy groups did not react to the new bill once it was promulgated in July 1998. A close look at newspapers from that period shows no reactions from human rights groups or pro–civil rights politicians regarding questionable points of the new law. The press framed the new law as the establishment of *Miranda* rights and the abolition of the "detention on suspicion" clause.[40] No word was mentioned about the establishment of a new and arguably unconstitutional "verification of identity detention" clause.[41]

When Police Violence Continues Despite the Work of Advocacy Networks

The Argentine example shows that advocacy networks become relevant when they are able to overcome collective action problems and make a topic noticeable to the public through mobilizations and public campaigns, when they build a reputation by collecting relevant data, and when they collaborate with each other and establish close alliances with policy experts and other international organizations. However, even in cases in which these conditions favor the work of advocacy networks, policy influence seems elusive. Although important bills restricting police powers were approved between 1991 and 1998 in Argentina, all indicators show that the police continued to engage in illegal practices such as "easy trigger" and torture. According to CELS, civilian killings by police forces in the city and province of Buenos Aires show a relatively constant increase between 1994 and 2000—precisely the years in which Congress enacted important institutional and legal reforms. In 1994, 124 civilians were killed by the police in confrontations, in 1998 this figure was 172, and by 2000 it had risen to 244 (CELS 2001). As a point of reference, civilian deaths by the Buenos Aires Provincial Police represented 10 percent of the homicides reported in the province between 1994 and 1999. Civilian deaths by the Federal Police in the city of Buenos Aires represented approximately 30 percent of the homicides reported in the city for the same period (Fuentes 2003).

What explains the gap between the legal improvement of citizens' rights and police practices? A first intuitive argument blames police institutions. According to this argument, highly autonomous and militarized police institutions may prevent legal reforms from being translated into actual practice. Unchecked security forces with inherited institutional and legal privileges from past military regimes may explain the persistence of police violence (Bayley 1993; Chevigny 1995; Méndez 1999).

Even though this argument is plausible in many developing countries, there is an additional mechanism that explains the resistance to change. Indeed, a particular structure of incentives keeps societies from advancing reforms—and keeps advocacy networks from influencing the policy process. First, citizens want to be safe from police abuse as much as they want to be safe from delinquency; therefore, constituencies can be mobilized to either promote police reforms if violence against citizens is detected or to increase police powers if the perception of crime is rising. Second, governments are likely to rely on increasing police powers to maintain public safety, even when the records show that police practices are contributing to increased levels of violence. Thus, explaining why advocacy networks are sometimes less influential than expected requires an examination of how pro-order groups take advantage of the opportunities provided by the context to advance their claims, and the different strategies used by them to avoid implementing policy reforms. I will illustrate these points in the context of the reform of the Buenos Aires Provincial Police (BAPP) in Argentina and the reform of the "detention on suspicion" clause in Chile.

Reforming the Buenos Aires Provincial Police

The reform of the BAPP is an example of an initially well-coordinated effort by the civil rights coalition to influence the policy process and to enact several reforms restricting police powers. By 1995, several human rights organizations had documented extensive violations of human rights committed by the BAPP (Americas Watch and CELS 1991; CELS 1993–1996). Press reports documented practices of "easy trigger," corruption, and clandestine businesses controlled by police officers.[42] On 19 December 1996, the governor of the province, Eduardo Duhalde, declared the Provincial Police to be in a "state of emergency," which allowed him to reform the structure of the police, reassign material and human resources, and dismiss officers involved in crimes and illegal activities.

Social pressure increased after the assassination of José Luis Cabezas in January 1997. Cabezas was a photographer who was investigating the links between the police and a specific businessman in the province of Buenos Aires (Sdrech and Colominas 1997). Lawyers, specialists on police issues from various parties, deputies of the national and provincial Congress, and human rights groups developed a set of proposals to reform the police.[43] The Alianza, a coalition between the Frente por un País Solidario (Front for the Country in Solidarity [Frepaso]) and the Union Cívica Radical (UCR) parties, incorporated these demands in its electoral platform, making police reform a crucial issue during the 1997 provincial legislative electoral campaign. In April 1997, the CELS organized a seminar on democratic control of the police, inviting key political actors, representatives of police institutions, and human rights organizations. In this event, representatives of Frepaso, UCR, and the Peronist party discussed several proposals to reform the police.[44]

Antireform sectors were also active, however. They were dominated by high- and lower-ranking police officers, provincial government officials, the heads of several *intendencias* (districts) in the province, and "brokers" within the Peronist party who controlled a network of illegal businesses including drugs, prostitution, traffic of stolen cars, and gambling (Dutil and Ragendorfer 1997).[45] As the potential changes threatened their profits and interests, they managed to postpone Duhalde's reforms until after the October elections (Saín 2001), but the electoral triumph of the Alianza at the provincial level made it more difficult for Duhalde to delay these changes any longer. In December 1997, Duhalde promulgated a new police decree (Decree 4508/97), taking over the Provincial Police, and appointing Peronist lawyer León Arslanián as minister of justice and security. Arslanián had previously participated in the reform of the penal code at the federal level, and now executed important changes, such as the dismissal of more than twelve hundred officers involved in illegal practices, the decentralization of the police command structure, the appointment of civilians to key high-ranking positions within the police, the creation of citizen review boards to monitor police practices, and the creation of internal mechanisms to control police practices. The center-left Alianza, human rights organizations, and professional organizations supported these initiatives, and by July 1998, three major bills related to the changes were approved in the provincial legislature.

The provincial government also created the Institute of Criminal Policy and Public Safety. This was a multiparty initiative in which representatives of the three major political parties (Peronist, UCR, and Frepaso) and human rights organizations—particularly CELS—were represented. This institute was conceived as a center to produce empirical studies and policy initiatives to support the governor's reforms.

Pro-Order Coalition: Resisting Change, Reversing Policies

The reform discussed above was strongly resisted by a cohesive alliance among certain sectors of the police, political brokers in several districts, some *intendentes* (the equivalent of mayors), and important representatives of the Peronist party. They used illegal, institutional, and electoral strategies to block and reverse some of the policies that the government was seeking to implement; several of the mechanisms used by these actors to maintain the status quo are given below.

Illegal methods. Soon after the government announced the transformation of the police, the press reported threats from "anonymous sources" against those who were promoting police reforms. In December 1997—one week after the governor's announcement of a second intervention—a group of officers who belonged to the so-called Police Movement (Movimiento Policial [MOPOL]) held a meeting to study measures of pressure against the government. They threatened to produce chaos in the public safety system by not responding to judicial or citizens' requests. As a representative of MOPOL stated, "[T]he best strategy is to do nothing and, if there are problems, this will increase insecurity, and therefore they [the government] will feel more pressure to stop reforms."[46] In March 1998, a police officer who was investigating police agencies received telephone threats.[47] The same month, two legislators who were working on the legislation to reform the police received new threats from "the big family of the Buenos Aires police."[48]

Bureaucratic blockage. Another way to resist the reform was by not implementing policies already approved. Some *intendentes* who had close relationships with antireform officers resisted the implementation of certain policies, and some lobbied the governor to keep in place certain chiefs of police whose positions were threatened. Former policymakers who occupied positions during the reform period admit that they received hundreds of calls from *intendentes* and judges requesting they not dismiss certain police officers.[49] Another way to block the reform was through the manipulation of certain appointments; for instance, a press note suggests that the police and *intendentes* were manipulating the election of civil society representatives to a Citizens' Board of Safety in charge of monitoring policy implementation.[50]

Electoral strategy. Probably the most effective way to undermine the reform was the promotion of an "iron fist" electoral discourse during the 1999 gubernatorial electoral campaign. Until July 1999, Peronist Governor Eduardo Duhalde and his proactive Secretary of Justice Arslanián strongly supported the need to reform the police. However, candidate Carlos Ruckauf—a Peronist as well—was one of the most important representatives of the pro-order coalition. Ruckauf was leading in the public opinion polls and, on 3 August 1999, he reframed the electoral debate by suggesting that "I will not have compassion for delinquents. We need to shoot delinquents, we need to fight them without hesitation."[51] Two days later he insisted on the point, arguing that "we need to shoot those who commit crimes in the head. I want to see these assassins killed."[52] Within a few days, Ruckauf outlined his platform's goals by suggesting the need to approve tougher rules against delinquency, to appoint police officers to top-ranking positions related to public safety, to keep criminals in jail, and to increase the number of police officers in the streets.[53]

The evident inconsistency between Arslanián's program and Ruckauf's proposals created a serious division within the Peronist party. Arslanián resigned one day after Ruckauf's declarations, arguing that he was not willing to change his plan and that a political conflict within the party would not help the country.[54] In the following two months, Governor Duhalde chose to reverse some of the ongoing changes, given the increasing public support for Ruckauf's tough proposals. For instance, Duhalde reinstated one thousand officers previously dismissed for violent or corrupt behavior[55] and appointed several *comisarios* who had links with corrupt police officers.[56]

But the main changes came after Ruckauf won the election in October 1999. His first decision was to appoint former military officer Aldo Rico as secretary of security. In the 1980s, Rico had led a military uprising against the democratic government, and he had a clear hard-line approach to delinquency.[57] Moreover, Ruckauf reinstated most of the officers dismissed by the previous administration and appointed police officers to key positions that had been previously occupied by civilians. He also sent bills to the legislature to recentralize the police, increase police powers, and allow officers to detain suspects on the streets. These reforms were approved by the legislature in February 2000, albeit after long negotiations between the governing party and the Alianza, given its majority in the legislature. Additionally, the government unsuccessfully attempted to restrict live television transmission of crimes.

The civil rights coalition attempted to stop some of these changes. In the legislature, the Alianza approved some of the government's proposals, such as reducing the ability of prisoners to be released before the end of their sentences and allowing the police to interrogate suspects at the moment of their arrest. Given the Alianza's distrust of police procedures, however, it rejected one proposal to create a photo database of suspects, and another to allow police interrogation of detainees to be used as evidence during a trial.[58] Ruckauf agreed to the conditions because of Alianza's majority in the legislature. However, two weeks later he unilaterally broke the agreement, promulgating a decree that allowed police interrogation to be used as evidence.[59]

Human rights advocacy networks also attempted to reduce the impact of these counterreforms. The CELS tried to demonstrate through the press that shooting delinquents was a common practice in Buenos Aires Province before Ruckauf took office, but that this method had not produced good results.[60] The leftist Frepaso and some human rights organizations publicly accused the secretary of public safety of past corruption, which forced Ruckauf to ask his secretary to resign twenty-five days after he was appointed.[61]

Despite all these efforts, the new government was able to impose several pro-order reforms, including the centralization of the police high command and the approval of rules increasing police powers. The new chief of police,

Amadeo D'Angelo, summarized the new orientation in a few words: "We will close down shantytowns so that delinquents will not get out. If they leave, we will arrest them."[62]

In Argentina, although a well-placed network has been important in blocking reform attempts by the provincial government, it was not the only factor. More important was the electoral triumph of a governor who was a promoter of the pro-order approach, which allowed for a reversal of an ongoing process of reform. Thus, a favorable political opportunity, effective strategies, and constant local and international monitoring have not led to a change in legal rights or police practices. What matters in this case is the comparative analysis of the two coalitions in competition and how they have been able, on the one hand, to frame a problem, gaining the support of a critical mass of people who were willing to protect citizens' rights from police abuses (in the mid-1990s) and, on the other hand, to give up rights in exchange for increasing police powers (after 1999).

The "Detention on Suspicion" Clause in Chile

The debate on police powers in the Chilean Congress illustrates the differences between the civil rights and the pro-order coalitions. In 1993 a bill eliminating the "detention on suspicion" clause was introduced in Congress by representatives closely linked to human rights advocacy groups.[63] The proposal sought the establishment of an equivalent of the *Miranda* rights that should be read by the police to detainees at the moment of the arrival to the police station. Additionally, the bill sought the elimination of certain legal justifications for detaining individuals such as "wearing unusual costumes," "being in unusual or suspicious places," "loafing," and "begging." The proposal was still conservative because it allowed the police to detain individuals who fail to authenticate their identity. This proposal was never discussed in Congress mainly because the Aylwin government felt that it did not have a majority in the Senate to restrict police powers.[64]

After the second democratic government sent the penal code reform bill to Congress in 1995, policymakers in the executive branch became interested in reforming police powers to make such powers consistent with the proposed penal code project. In May 1996, the Ministry of Justice proposed a new bill, eliminating the "detention on suspicion" clause. According to the government, the goal was to reform detention procedures of the police "to make them consistent with those reforms proposed in the penal code procedure bill."[65]

The government also proposed that "torture" be made a crime, that individuals held incommunicado be allowed to contact their relatives or a lawyer at the moment of the arrest, and that judges ask individuals whether law enforcement officials told them their rights. If officers failed to do so, police reports must be invalidated as reliable proof during the trial. This proposal also specifically rejected the establishment of a "verification of identity detention" clause, arguing that it was unconstitutional to detain people who do not carry their ID simply because the constitution does not mandate that individuals carry their IDs.[66] In other words, the government's bill went beyond the original proposal, adopting a more progressive position than the most pro–civil rights deputies in Congress.

In May 1996, however, the Chamber's Commission of Constitution and Legislation modified the executive proposal, to include a "verification of identity detention" clause, allowing the police to arrest individuals who could not authenticate their identity into custody for a period of four hours. This proposal was rejected by the chamber at the end of 1996, which then accepted the government's proposal.

As the debate entered the Senate, the pro-order coalition led by the police and conservative representatives in Congress had more opportunities to influence the outcome. In March 1997, the Senate's Constitution and Legislation Commission approved the establishment of the "verification of identity detention" clause, allowing the police to keep people in custody for four hours. Testifying before this commission, the police suggested that imposing a time frame for detentions was not realistic. Additionally, the police rejected the idea of reading detainees' rights twice. The police suggested that reading individuals' rights in the police station was enough.[67] In September 1997, the Senate approved establishing the "verification of identity detention," established no time restriction for such detentions, and agreed that police officers should read detainees' rights only in the police station. Moreover, the Senate restricted the right of individuals held incommunicado to contact their relatives or lawyers. They mandated that police officers should be in charge of contacting detainees' relatives.[68]

Thus, by December 1997, both houses of Congress agreed on approving the incorporation of "torture" as a crime, abolition of the "arrest on suspicion" clause, establishment of the *Miranda*-type bill of rights, and suppression of police reports as valid evidence if the police did not present detainees with their *Miranda* rights. The more conservative Senate and the more pro–civil rights Chamber of Deputies disagreed on whether the police could detain individuals to authenticate identity, whether *Miranda* rights should be read once or twice, and whether individuals held incommunicado should contact their relatives directly or through a law enforcement officer.

These discrepancies were to be resolved by a mixed commission in Congress. An incident that occurred in January 1998 had a partial effect on speeding this process. On 15 January, the press reported the case of a taxi driver, Raúl Palma, who died as a result of police torture. Doctors found clear evidence that Palma had been subject to mistreatment and torture at a police station. On 18 January, two days after the medical report proved the use of torture by the police against Palma, the executive branch asked Congress to include the proposed bill in the extraordinary congressional period, giving it urgent status.[69]

The civil rights coalition reacted in two ways. First, congressional representatives demanded quick approval of the pending bill in Congress. Second, human rights organizations and their allies within the state bureaucracy (i.e., the Corporation of Legal Assistance) announced that mistreatment by the police was more common than generally reported by the media; and over a period of two weeks, human rights groups denounced more than fifty cases of police violence that occurred during 1997.

At the executive branch level, there was interministerial tension. Authorities of the Ministry of Interior rejected claims of police violence, arguing that torture does not exist in a democratic regime, that cases denouncing the police were the exception rather than the rule, and that the police had taken all legal steps to punish those responsible in the Palma case. But the Ministry of Justice announced that the government was requesting that consideration of the bill in Congress be accelerated. After this announcement, politicians stopped complaining about the illegitimate use of force by the police.

In February 1998, Congress created a jointed commission to solve the two houses' differences of opinion. This commission achieved consensus in April 1998,[70] eliminating the "detention on suspicion" clause, but the Senate vote regarding the "verification of identity detention" prevailed; that is, now police officers could arrest individuals who failed to authenticate their identity. In these cases, the police should provide all means possible to facilitate individuals' self-identification. Moreover, the Senate vote regarding the time frame for such detentions also prevailed: individuals could be held in custody for an unlimited period of time. Additionally, the Senate vote regarding incommunicado detentions also prevailed: individuals could only contact their relatives or a lawyer through a law enforcement officer.

Finally, the Chamber's position regarding the need for officers to inform individuals of their rights twice prevailed. The bill was promulgated in July 1998, incorporating most of the initial Senate version. In 2000 and 2001, new reforms were enacted reestablishing some of the powers lost by the police in 1998 such as searching individuals in the street and private places if they suspect them of illegal activities.

The decision-making process reveals three interesting features. First, the passage of the legislation was framed by pro–civil rights sectors in the Ministry of Justice as part of a broader debate regarding the modernization of the judicial system. The pro-order coalition supported the reform because it believed that Chile required modernization of the judicial system, and the new provisions provided an adequate equilibrium between individuals' guarantees and police powers.[71] In this sense, police abuses were not part of the policy debate. The Palma incident in January 1998 contributed to speeding up an ongoing debate, but it did not alter the content of the reform.

A second element is related to the existence of a group of professionals who offered technical recommendations to policymakers. These lawyers were part of an elite group of professionals closely linked to government officials and, later on, to leaders of the opposition (Duce 1999). As the issue of police violence was not part of the government agenda, and as traditional human rights groups were not pressuring the government on this particular issue, these professionals did not have incentives to contact human rights advocacy groups. Finally, another important element was the existence of proactive policymakers in the Ministry of Justice proposing innovative policy initiatives to Congress. These policymakers recognized the need for the modernization of the judicial system and assumed a strong pro–civil rights stand.

The final draft that passed and became law did not reflect the wishes of the Ministry of Justice; rather it favored the position of the pro-order Senate. Now, police officers could hold individuals who do not carry their IDs without any restrictions. Human rights advocacy groups did not react to the new bill once it was promulgated in July 1998. A close look at the newspapers in that period shows no reaction from human rights groups or pro–civil rights politicians regarding questionable points of the new law. The press framed the new law as the establishment of *Miranda* rights and the abolition of the "arrest on suspicion" clause.[72] No word was mentioned about the establishment of a new and arguably unconstitutional "verification of identity detention" clause.

Conclusion

Latin American countries require more far-reaching and in-depth democratic politics. This includes institutional reforms to make the decision-making process more transparent and to empower citizens; that is, to place citizens in control of what government agencies do (or do not do). Regarding public safety, these countries need to develop institutions such as the Citizens' Review Board that can check on and control police procedures and policies. The current trend of police reform in the region provides a unique opportunity to promote effective mechanisms of internal and external accountability over police forces. As mentioned earlier, police reform should consider *both* the improvement of police institutions' efficiency to prevent crime and the generation of mechanisms of accountability to make police procedures transparent and open to public scrutiny.

Given the above, advocacy networks (local and international) can play a crucial role by monitoring police practices, checking legal procedures, and monitoring policy implementation. Advocacy networks are more likely to be influential under conditions discussed below.

When like-minded groups cooperate with each other to overcome ideological and political differences. Despite the existence of ideological differences between CELS and CORREPI and among several other advocacy groups in Argentina, they have been able to cooperate, organizing a common front at key junctures. This has not been the case in Chile, where human rights groups show similar ideological disagreements but less cooperation. Overcoming ideological differences and solving collective action problems help advocacy groups gain visibility and strength vis-à-vis competing groups in society.

When groups gain a positive public reputation. Being recognized as a serious organization may help groups access the political system and gain visibility in the media. This has been the case of CELS in Argentina during the 1990s, where a continuous and serious compilation of data in the various spheres of political, civil, and socioeconomic rights has helped them become a credible source of information for diverse local and international actors.

When groups gain allies domestically and abroad. Effective influence requires establishing alliances within the political system—including the state apparatus—and abroad. The restriction of police powers in detaining individuals in Argentina and Chile has required a coordinated effort among pro–civil rights lawyers, policymakers, politicians, and activists abroad.

When groups are able to mobilize public opinion. Finally, groups need to influence and mobilize public opinion regarding an issue at stake. This has been the case in Argentina, where human rights advocacy groups' influence in agenda setting brought about a growing consensus on the need to initiate police reforms during the 1990s.

Establishing mechanisms of accountability is an extremely difficult task, even in advanced democracies (Walker 1977; Warren 1991; Human Rights Watch 1998). Although police institutions are likely to reject civilian interference in internal affairs, politicians are likely to support police institutions, if the population considers that tough measures against crime should be top priorities or if there are vested interests between politicians and the police. Thus, transforming police practices of brutality does not only depend on proactive activists but on a set of other political factors. In this chapter, I suggest that the nature of the problem at stake—that is, the trade-off between protecting citizens' rights versus maintaining public order—generates a particular structure of incentives that favors those who aim to maintain the status quo. Pro-order views enjoy comparative advantages in terms of access to the political system, institutional resources, and strategies to deal with attempts to reform the status quo. This seems to be the case in Chile, Argentina, and several other countries in Latin America and elsewhere (Johnson 1990; Neild 2002; Ziegler and Neild 2002; Davis 2002).

Consequently, advocacy networks face several challenges. First, strategies that may work well in an authoritarian context may not be adequate in a democratic regime. Democratic authorities have a set of legal and political tools to preempt and respond to domestic and international criticism. In general, democratic authorities have depicted allegations of police violence as the exception rather than the rule. Moreover, authorities are likely to argue that domestic institutional mechanisms will eventually solve allegations of police misbehavior. Advocacy groups—both local and international—have continued to use a strategy that addresses allegations on a case-by-case basis. The experience of CELS in Argentina demonstrates that while denouncing specific cases is an effective strategy to gain legitimacy, this should be combined with proposing institutional reforms, because institutional mechanisms to deal with police abuses in Latin America are weak and lack both transparency and adherence to basic principles of fairness.

Second, gathering reliable information locally and disseminating it internationally is crucial for in "making the case" of police violence. Again, the experience of CELS shows how advocacy groups can become a relevant focal point for civil rights organizations, as proven by their innovative approach to gathering information, their strategies for pressuring the state to access public information, and their dissemination of information abroad. Advocacy groups should not focus exclusively on collecting cases of police violence but should also concentrate on designing methods to monitor police behavior once a reform is (or should be) implemented.

Third, gaining a better understanding of their political and institutional contexts may help advocacy networks to advance their agenda. Especially if these groups face a well-organized pro-order coalition, they should seek to frame the issue of citizens' rights as complementary—rather than detrimental—to the protection of public safety.

Finally, advocacy networks should improve their capacity to monitor legislative debates and develop alliances with policymakers, the academic community, and technical experts to generate a more persistent influence over the policy process. Denouncing police abuse alone is not likely to have an effect on the policy process. Social actors need to offer plausible policy alternatives and monitor the implementation of policy outcomes. As crime is likely to be a central concern in developing countries, and as citizens are likely to be supportive of a "tough on crime" approach, the main challenge for local and international advocacy groups today is how to contest the "iron fist" discourse in new and innovative ways.

Notes

1. It is also worth noting that as police reforms are implemented and there are greater options to file complaints, rising levels of complaints against the police are likely, which does not indicate greater levels of police abuse. I thank an anonymous reviewer for underlining this point to me.

2. My argument relies on the advocacy coalition approach (Sabatier 1988, 1992).

3. A common collective or public good is defined as any good such that, if any person in any group consumes it, it cannot feasibly be withheld from the others in that group. In other words, even those who do not purchase or pay for any of the public or collective good cannot be excluded or kept from sharing in the consumption of the good, as they can where noncollective goods are concerned (Olson 1971, 14–15). For critical discussion of the concept, see Hardin (1993).

4. Two reasons explain this phenomenon: on issues involving common goods, individuals have a strong incentive to get a free ride by allowing others to provide a collective benefit for them without paying a share of the costs. If an individual cannot be excluded from enjoying the benefits of a public good, then an individual's first inclination is not to spend resources and energy in the achievement of such a good. Second, individuals are not willing to contribute to an organization if they perceive that their contribution will not make a great difference in achieving its stated goal (Olson 1971).

5. We should also anticipate that the wealthy sectors of society use their own resources (influence, lawyers, access to powerful elites) to solve their problems with the police in an individual way.

6. In some cases, the church has assumed the role of defender of human rights. However, the transition to democracy in Latin America was followed by a withdrawal of the Catholic Church from engagement in human rights issues.

7. Horizontal accountability refers to legal mechanisms that allow state agencies to take action in relation to possibly unlawful actions or omissions by other agents or agencies of the state. Congressional committees, the judicial system, the ombudsman's office, and executive commissions are examples of this type of accountability. Vertical accountability refers to legal mechanisms that allow citizens to control and take action against unlawful behavior by agents or agencies of the state. This includes mechanisms such as regular elections, free press, a right to public scrutiny, and a right of association, among other aspects (O'Donnell 1998).

8. In Chile, there is a pending bill in Congress creating a Defensor del Ciudadano (Ombudsman's Office).

9. Argentina is a federal state with a federal police, which deals with federal crimes and the public safety of the Ciudad de Buenos Aires (Buenos Aires District Zone). Moreover, each province has a police department ruled by provincial laws. In this chapter, I restrict my analysis to reforms that have taken place at the federal level and in the Buenos Aires province.

10. Interview with María del Carmen Verdú (Coordinadora Contra la Represión Policial e Institucional), Buenos Aires, 9 April 2001.

11. Walter Bulacio was arrested outside of a stadium when he was trying to gain access to a rock concert in Buenos Aires. The police tortured him in the police station and transferred him to a hospital where he died as a result of serious contusions to his head. As of 2002, the police and the criminal justice system continued to fail to bring those responsible to justice. For example, the officer allegedly responsible for this crime kept his job and was even promoted in the police force, despite the fact that he faced charges in court (interview with María del Carmen Verdú). See also "Sobreseyeron al comisario que detuvo al joven Walter Bulacio," *Clarín,* 14 March 1996; "Habrá condena en el caso Walter Bulacio," *Diario Popular,* 24 March 1996.

12. Interview with Martin Abregú, former director of CELS, Santiago, 26 January 2001.

13. Interview with Martín Abregú. See also CELS annual reports on human rights (1993–2001).

14. For instance, between 1983 and 1988, the Vicariate of Solidarity worked with a yearly average of two thousand organizations nationwide, which included the coordination of more than seventy thousand people every year (Lowden 1996).

15. To mention some of them, Alejandro González, Jorge Domínguez, Roberto Garretón, Carlos López, Felipe Portales, José Zalaquett, and several other professionals who used to work in the Vicariate of Solidarity and in the CHCHR, and assumed new government positions related to human rights issues soon after the transition.

16. Interview with the secretary of the CHCHR, Carlos López, Santiago, 19 January 2001.

17. Interview with CODEPU representative Hugo Gutiérrez, Santiago, 22 January 2001.

18. See, for instance, "Dicen que aumentan los casos de violencia policial en el país,"

Clarín, 18 June 1996; "Aumentan las víctimas incidentals, según el CELS," *Página 12,* 1 July 1998; "Para un solo año, demasiadas balas," *Página 12,* 25 March 1999; "Police violence on the rise," *Buenos Aires Herald,* 18 April 2000. In terms of politicians using this report, see Buenos Aires Province Legislature, 34th session, 24 November 1998; 27th session, 11 December 1997; and 22nd session, 15 November 2000.

19. See "Posible sucesor de Patti," *Página 12,* 13 August 1996; "Patti, Manual del buen torturador," *Página 12,* 19 November 1999.

20. See "El CELS quiere saber," *Clarín,* 18 November 1996; and "La Justicia pregunta por qué la policía federal no da información," *Página 12,* 25 October 1996.

21. "Queremos que el CELS nos ayude," *Página 12,* 29 August 2000.

22. Jorge Berguño, chief of the Chilean Delegation to Geneva. "Controvertido Informe sobre la tortura en Chile entregó relator de la ONU," *La Epoca,* 5 April 1996.

23. These statistics reflect Santiago and three other regions, representing 65 percent of the country's population.

24. A 1992 survey shows that 45 percent of people with any kind of legal problem decided not to file a complaint (Correa Sutil 1993).

25. Interview with Nelson Caucoto, Corporation for Legal Assistance, 29 September 2000.

26. Fuentes (2001) took a random sample of 165 cases—all those to which he had access—and analyzed the sociodemographic characteristics of each complaint. These cases represent 4.2 percent of the entire sample. For specific methodological issues, see Fuentes (2001).

27. Between 1990 and 1994, 104 civilians died in confrontations with the police while another 237 were seriously hurt. However, no comparative statistics on police deaths are available at this point; see Ramos and Guzmán (2000, 135).

28. Reforms took place in Ecuador (1991), Peru (1991), Guatemala (1992), Argentina (1992), Costa Rica (1996), El Salvador (1998), Chile (1998), Venezuela (1998), Paraguay (1998), and Bolivia (1998). By 2002 other countries were debating reforms in Congress, including Nicaragua, Honduras, Dominican Republic, and Panama (Domingo 1999; Struensee and Maier 2000).

29. Julio Maier wrote the original draft of the federal penal code reform in 1986. Alberto Binder and León Arslanián proposed and participated in the institutional reforms of the Buenos Aires Provincial Police in 1997–1998. Binder is closely related to the Frente por un País Solidario (Front for the Country in Solidarity, Frepaso) party, and Arslanián is a member of the Permanent Assembly of Human Rights in Argentina. Raúl Zaffaroni wrote the original draft eliminating the "detention on suspicion" clause for the Buenos Aires City Council. All these authorities have participated in activities organized by CELS and have maintained contact with CELS researchers. Interview with Gustavo Palmieri (CELS), Buenos Aires, April 2001, and interview with Martin Abregú (CELS), Santiago, January 2001.

30. Interview with Fernanda Doz Costa, representative of Center for Justice and International Law, Washington, DC, 23 January 2002.

31. CORREPI's listserv address is correpi@fibertel.com.ar; its online reports can be found at http://www.informativos.net.

32. I interviewed six members of CELS, Buenos Aires, between April and August 2001: Gustavo Palmieri, Sofía Tiscornia, Andrea Pochack, Laura Itchart, María Capurro, and Julieta Rossi.

33. An explicit division among human rights lawyers was evident in relation to the best strategies to deal with the Pinochet case in 2000; see "El club de la pelea. Las querellas y contraquerellas de los DD.HH.," *El Mercurio,* 22 October 2000.

34. The Universidad Diego Portales, Centro de Estudios del Desarrollo, and Faculdad Latinoamericana de Ciencias Sociales (FLACSO) have developed academic programs to study reform of the military justice system and police autonomy, but other NGOs know little about these efforts. Moreover, few academic institutions know about the work on human rights undertaken by the Corporation for Legal Assistance.

35. In his speech, President Patricio Aylwin considered that "the amount of arrests on suspicion is excessive and we need to regulate this system in the short term." *La Tercera,* 12 March 1993.

36. *La Nación,* September 10, 1993, and *Las Ultimas Noticias,* 21 September 1993.

37. Minister of Justice Soledad Alvear, Intervention in the Commission of Constitution and Legislation of the Chamber of Deputies, 8 May 1996.

38. Some of these changes underwent new modifications in 2000 and 2002, restricting detentions to four hours, specifying that police only have to read an individual his/her rights once, and allowing the police to take fingerprints of detainees. For a detailed analysis of these reforms, see Fuentes (2003).

39. Appointed Senator Sergio Fernández said, "I support this bill because in this project there is an equilibrium between individual freedom and public safety." Senators Sergio Diez (Renovación Nacional) and Adolfo Zaldivar Larraín (Unión Democrática Independiente) made similar statements. Senate, Session 17, 20 May 1998.

40. "Sobre derechos del detenido: policías están entrenadas para aplicar la nueva ley," *El Mercurio,* 2 July 1998; "Nadie podrá ser detenido por sospecha," *La Tercera,* 2 July 1998.

41. Indeed, during the debate of this bill, the Ministry of Justice argued that it was unconstitutional to detain people who do not carry their ID simply because the Constitution does not mandate citizens to carry their IDs. In this regard, see Second Report of the Commission of Constitution and Legislation, Chamber of Deputies, 8 May 1996, and *Oficio* number 1223, Ministry of the Presidency, 13 August 1996.

42. Without considering the Argentine Israeli Mutual Association (AMIA) incident, more than thirty-two cases of police corruption were denounced by the press in the course of only one year (1996) (Oliveira and Tiscornia 1997).

43. A prestigious pro–civil rights lawyer, Alberto Binder, was the main author of a draft proposal for police reform.

44. Seminario sobre Control Democrático de los Organismos de Seguridad Interior, Buenos Aires, 7–8 April 1997. Marcelo Saín (who was in charge of writing the Frepaso proposal for the reform of the BAPP), and León Arslanián (who was in charge of implementing the BAPP reform) participated in this seminar.

45. In his study on the Peronist party, Steven Levitsky (2001, 41) argues that local brokers or "problem solvers" are informally linked to the Peronist party and access government resources. However, "there is a dark underside to this social embeddedness. Because urban slum zones are frequently centres of illicit activity such as drug trafficking, prostitution, and gambling, Peronist networks are inevitably linked to these forms of organization as well."

46. Anonymous chief of a police station; "Los policías amenazan con huelga de brazos caídos," *Página 12,* 21 December 1997.

47. "Amenazan al comisario que investiga las agencies," *Página 12,* 3 March 1998.
48. "Amenazan a dos legisladores," *Clarín,* 8 March 1998. More cases were denounced during 1998; see, for example, "La policía está presa en su interna," *Página 12,* 20 September 1999.
49. "Plata sucia," *Página 12,* 26 September 1999. Moreover, former Secretary of Justice and Security León Arslanián recognized pressures from several intendentes to maintain the illegal profit system within the police. "Plin Caja," *Página 12,* 19 December 1999.
50. "En Lomas de Zamora al defensor de seguridad lo eligen entre pocos," *Página 12,* 18 March 1998.
51. "Hay que meterle bala a los ladrones," *Clarín,* 4 August 1999.
52. "Renunció Arslanián y comprometió a Duhalde," *Clarín,* 6 August 1999.
53. "Renunció Arslanián," *Clarín,* August 6, 1999; "La peor astilla," *Página 12,* 8 August 1999; and "Una relación es ascenso," *Clarín,* 28 October 1999.
54. Interview with León Arslanián, Buenos Aires, March 2001.
55. "Reincorporarán a mil policías," *Clarín,* 13 August 1999.
56. "La maldita policía, parte II," *Página 12,* 13 August 1999. A political reason may explain Duhalde's drastic change: he was interested in running for president in the next presidential election (1999) and he needed Ruckauf's support within the Peronist party.
57. Constant conflicts with the press and aggressive statements by Rico favoring a hard-line policy against delinquents made Ruckauf request Rico's resignation only a few months after he was appointed.
58. The law implies that judges may take into account police interrogations but they are not allowed to be used as evidence during a trial.
59. "Las dos jugadas de Ruckauf," *Clarín,* 27 February 2000.
60. "Lo de meter bala ya era doctrina antes de Ruckauf," *Página 12,* 13 August 1999.
61. "Duhalde tuvo que despedir a su secretario de seguridad," *Clarín,* 8 September 1999.
62. "Joven y pobre es igual a delincuentc," *Página 12,* 17 May 2001.
63. The representatives included members of the center-left coalition Adriana Muñoz (PPD), Ramón Elizalde (PDC), Juan Pablo Letelier (PS), Carlos Montes (PS), Jaime Naranjo (PS), Andrés Palma (PDC), and Guillermo Yunge (PDC).
64. Interview with former Minister of Justice Francisco Cumplido, Santiago, 13 September 2000.
65. Minister of Justice, Soledad Alvear; Intervention in the Commission of Constitution and Legislation of the Chamber of Deputies, 8 May 1996.
66. Second Report of the Commission of Constitution and Legislation of the Chamber of Deputies, May 8, 1996, and *Oficio* number 1223, Ministry of Presidency, 13 August 1996.
67. See Report of the Commission of Constitution and Legislation of the Senate, 31 March 1996. See http://www.senado.cl.
68. See discrepancies between the Senate and Chamber of deputies in Session 29, Chamber of Deputies, 21 January 1998, 14–24.
69. "Se dará suma urgencia a estatuto del detenido," *El Mercurio,* 18 January 1998.
70. Report of the Mixed Commission, 30 April 1998. See http://www.senado.cl.
71. See note 39 for details.
72. "Sobre derechos del detenido: policías están entrenadas para aplicar la nueva

ley," *El Mercurio,* 2 July 1998; "Nadie podrá ser detenido por sospecha," *La Tercera,* 2 July 1998.

References

Americas Watch, and Centro de Estudios Legales y Sociales (CELS). 1991. *Police Violence in Argentina. Torture and Killing in Buenos Aires.* Buenos Aires: CELS, Americas Watch.
Bayley, David. 1993. "What's in a Uniform? A Comparative View of Police-Military Relations in Latin America." Paper presented at the Conference on Police and Civil-Military Relations in Latin America, Washington, DC, October 1993.
Blando, Oscar. 1995. *Detención policial por averiguación de antecedentes.* Buenos Aires: Editorial Juris.
Centro de Estudios Legales y Sociales (CELS). 1993–2001. *Informe sobre la situación de los derechos humanos en Argentina.* Buenos Aires: CELS, Siglo Veintiuno, Catálogos.
Chevigny, Paul. 1995. *Edge of the Knife: Police Violence in the Americas.* New York: New Press.
Clark, Ann Marie, Elisabeth Friedman, and Kathryn Hochstetler. 1998. "The Sovereign Limits of Global Society: A Comparison of NGO Participation in UN World Conferences on the Environment, Human Rights, and Women. *World Politics* 51, no. 1: 1–35.
Coordinadora Contra la Represión Policial (CORREPI). 1998. *Listado de casos por violencia institucional, 1983–1998.* Buenos Aires: CORREPI.
Corporación de Promoción y Defensa de los Derechos del Pueblo (CODEPU). 1994. *Informe derechos humanos 1990–1994.* Santiago: CODEPU.
———. 1999. *Informe alternativo al Cuarto Informe Periódico de Chile sobre la Aplicación del Pacto Internacional de Derechos Civiles y Políticos.* Santiago: CODEPU.
Correa Sutil, Jorge, ed. 1993. *Justicia y marginalidad. Percepción de los pobres.* Santiago: Universidad Católica de Chile.
Davis, Diane. 2002. "From Democracy to Rule of Law? Police Impunity in Contemporary Latin America." *ReVista, Harvard Review of Latin America* 2, no. 1: 21–25.
Domingo, Pilar. 1999. "Judicial Independence and Judicial Reform in Latin America." In *The Self-Restraining State,* edited by A. Schedler, L. Diamond, and M. Plattner. Boulder, CO: Lynne Rienner Publishers.
Duce, Mauricio. 1999. "Criminal Procedural Reforms and the Ministerio Público: Toward the Construction of a New Criminal Justice System in Latin America." Master's thesis, Stanford University.
Dutil, Carlos, and Ricardo Ragendorfer. 1997. *La Bonaerense. Historia criminal de la policía de la Provincia de Buenos Aires.* Buenos Aires: Planeta.
Fuentes, Claudio. 2001. *Denuncias por violencia policial.* Santiago: FLACSO-Chile.
———. 2003. "Contesting the Iron Fist: Advocacy Networks and Police Violence in Democratic Argentina and Chile." Ph.D. diss., University of North Carolina at Chapel Hill.
Frühling, Hugo, ed. 1998. *Control democrático en el mantenimiento de la seguridad interior.* Santiago: Centro de Estudios del Desarrollo.
Gitlitz, John, and Paul Chevigny. 2002. "Crisis and Reform: The Police in the Dominican Republic." *Citizen Security Monitor* 1, no. 2: 1–24.

Hardin, Russell. 1993. *Collective Action.* Baltimore: Johns Hopkins University Press.
Human Rights Watch. 1998. *Shielded from Justice. Police Brutality and Accountability in the United States.* New York: Human Rights Watch.
Jiménez, María Angélica. 1994. "El proceso penal chileno y los derechos humanos." *Cuadernos de Análisis Jurídico* 4: 1–275.
———. 2000. *Adolescentes provados de libertad y justicia de menores: Informe de investigación.* Santiago: Universidad Diego Portales.
Johnson, Lyman, ed. 1990. *The Problem of Order in Changing Societies: Essays on Crime and Policing in Argentina and Uruguay.* Albuquerque: University of New Mexico Press.
Keck, Margaret E., and Kathryn Sikkink. 1998. *Activists beyond Borders: Advocacy Networks in International Politics.* Ithaca, NY: Cornell University Press.
Levitsky, Steven. 2001. "An 'Organized Disorganization': Informal Organization and the Persistence of Local Party Structures in Argentine Peronism." *Journal of Latin American Studies* 33, 29–61.
Lowden, Pamela. 1996. *Moral Opposition to Authoritarian Rule in Chile, 1973–1990.* London: MacMillan Press, Ltd. and St. Martin's Press, Inc.
Lowery, David, Virginia Gray, and Matthew Fellowes. 2002. "Sisyphus Meets the Borg: Understanding the Diversity of Interest Communities." Paper presented at the American Political Science Association Annual Meeting, Boston, 28 August–1 September.
Méndez, Juan. 1999. "Problems of Lawless Violence: Introduction." In *The (Un)Rule of Law and the Underprivileged in Latin America,* edited by J. Méndez, G. O'Donnell, and P.S. Pinheiro. Notre Dame, IN: University of Notre Dame Press.
Merenin, Otwin, ed. 1996. *Policing Change. Changing Police: International Perspectives.* New York: Garland Publishers.
Neild, Rachel. 2000. *External Controls, Themes, and Debates in Public Security Reforms.* Washington, DC: Washington Office on Latin America.
———. 2002. "Sustaining Reform: Democratic Policing in Central America." *Citizen Security Monitor* 1, no. 1: 1–36.
O'Donnell, Guillermo. 1998. "Horizontal Accountability in New Democracies." *Journal of Democracy* 9, 12–126.
Oliveira, Alicia, and Sofía Tiscornia. 1997. "Estructura y prácticas de las policías en la Argentina. Las redes de ilegalidad." In *Control democrático de los organismos de seguridad interior en la República Argentina.* Buenos Aires: Centro de Estudios Legales y Sociales.
Olson, Mancur. 1971. *The Logic of Collective Action.* 2nd ed. Cambridge, MA: Harvard University Press.
Ramos, Marcela, and Juan Guzmán. 2000. *La guerra y la paz ciudadana.* Santiago: LOM Ediciones.
Ropp, Stephen, and Kathryn Sikkink. 1999. "International Norms and Domestic Politics in Chile and Guatemala." In *The Power of Human Rights. International Norms and Domestic Change,* edited by T. Risse, S. Ropp, and K. Sikkink. Cambridge: Cambridge University Press.
Sabatier, Paul. 1988. "An Advocacy Coalition Framework of Policy Change and the Role of Policy-Oriented Learning Therein." *Policy Sciences* 21, 129–68.
———. 1992. "Interest Group Membership and Organization: Multiple Theories." In *The Politics of Interests: Interest Groups Transformed,* edited by M. Petracca. Boulder, CO: Westview Press.

Saín, Marcelo. 2001. *La ¿reforma? del sistema de seguridad y policial bonaerense.* Buenos Aires: Universidad de Quilmes.

Sdrech, Enrique, and Norberto Colominas. 1997. *Cabezas. Crimen, mafia y poder.* Colección Pistas. Buenos Aires: Atuel.

Smulovitz, Catalina, and Enrique Peruzzotti. 2000. "Societal Accountability in Latin America." *Journal of Democracy* 11, no. 4: 147–58.

Struensee, Eberhard, and Julio Bernardo Maier. 2000. "Introducción." In *Las reformas procesales penales en América Latina,* edited by J.B. Maier, K. Ambos, and J. Woischnick. Buenos Aires: Ad-Hoc S.R.L.

Vargas, Juan Enrique. 1998. "La reforma a la justicia criminal en Chile: El cambio del rol estatal." *Cuadernos de Análisis Jurídico* 38, 55–169.

United Nations. 1996. "Report of the Special Rapporteur, Mr. Nigel Rodley, submitted pursuant to the Comission on Human Rights." Resolution 1995/37. E/CN.4/1996/35/Add.2. Geneva: United Nations.

Waddington, A.P.J. 1999. *Policing Citizens: Authority and Rights.* London: UCL Press.

Walker, Samuel. 1977. *A Critical History of Police Reform.* Lexington, MA: Lexington Books.

Warren, Christopher. 1991. *Report of the Independent Commission on the Los Angeles Police Department.* Los Angeles: Los Angeles Police Department.

Ziegler, Melissa, and Rachel Neild. 2002. *From Peace to Governance: Police Reform and the International Community.* Washington, DC: Washington Office on Latin America.

Chapter 4

Crime and Social Policies in Latin American Urban Centers

Claudio C. Beato F.

Introduction

The growth in crime and violence in the past two decades has been one of the major challenges for development in Latin America. Homicide rates in this region are more than twice the world average (annually, 22.9 per 100,000 inhabitants versus 10.7, respectively [World Bank 1997]), and the figures for some of the major urban centers (such as Medellín, Cali, San Salvador, Rio de Janeiro, Caracas, and São Paulo) place them among the most violent in the world (Table 4.1). Concern is also growing about the effects of crime and violence on economic, human, and social capital (Moser and Shrader 1999): housing deteriorates or is destroyed, public transportation is reduced as bus and taxi drivers refuse to go into heavy crime areas, and access to public health and education services is likewise limited (Beato F. 2001). There are also fewer job opportunities for people who live in stigmatized locations (Moser 1996). Social capital in some urban locations is eroded because of increased fear and mistrust among neighbors, restricted mobility, and the breakup of violence-ridden households (Lederman et al. 1999; Moser and Lister 1999).

At the macroeconomic level, violence jeopardizes the environment for economic investment in many Latin American societies. From a microeconomic standpoint, it even can discourage individuals from investing in education, for instance, by causing them to be afraid to attend night school (IDB 1999b).

Within this framework, large portions of society share a consensus that Latin America's serious social and economic shortcomings are responsible for the high crime rates in its major urban centers; that is, unemployment,

Table 4.1. Homicide rates for Latin American countries, selected years, 1989–2000

Country	Year	Rate (per 100,000 inhabitants)
Argentina	1997	9.9
Brazil	1997	28.1
–Rio de Janeiro	1998	52.8
–São Paulo	1998	55.8
–Belo Horizonte	2000	26.3
Chile	1989	2.9
–Santiago de Chile	1995	2.2
Colombia	1990	74.4
–Bogotá	1997	49.2
–Cáli	1995	112.0
–Medellín	1995	248.0
Costa Rica	1990	4.4
Ecuador	1990	10.1
El Salvador	1995	95.4
Guatemala		
–Department of Guatemala	1996	101.0
Mexico	1995	40.0
–Mexico City	1995	19.6
Nicaragua	1990	4.9
Panama	1989	5.2
Peru		
–Lima	1995	28.2
Uruguay	1990	4.4
Venezuela	1989	121.0
–Caracas	1995	760.0

Sources: Adapted from IDB (1999a). Updated data from Piquet Carneiro (1999), Lederman (1999), Mexican Health Foundation (1999), and Instituto Apoyo (1999).

inequality, and the lack of compensatory social policies are leading to a rise in criminality and violence. On the other hand, some point to problems in the criminal justice system and use economic theory to underpin this perspective. The deterrence theory credits the criminal justice system with the lion's share of crime control, making lawbreaking not pay for those individuals who have chosen unlawful means of action. This is tantamount to defining the crime world as a marketplace wherein criminals and victims interact; thus, the state can intervene in that market through a prepared and efficient police force, adequate legislation, and a prison complex large enough to hold all the criminals.

Meanwhile, however, not enough thought has been given to designing public policies aimed at lowering crime rates. Current thinking holds that the simple improvement in social and economic indicators or the introduction of institutional reforms in the justice system will be enough. I argue, however, that the major problem today in formulating and assessing crime control programs and policies in Latin America is a cognitive one. Two levels are central here: one is theoretical, harking back to causal dimensions and the articulation among proposals of explanatory models; the other is empirical, especially as regards data generation. The issue is how to articulate the links between these two levels. Even though there is theoretical output on this topic, testing propositions is often impossible due to the absence of clear data on crime and violence. Although there is a strong need for data-gathering programs, only a few countries in Latin America have reliable systems to measure crime and violence, leading many scholars to call for the creation of data banks in this regard (FJP 1988; Rubio 1998; Moser and Shrader 1999; Beato F. 2000; Buvinic et al. 1999). This is partially a result of the fact that many Latin American police organizations are still straitjacketed by old managerial models, often military inspired and outdated in terms of the reality of present-day urban crimes (Buvinic et al. 1999; Beato F. 2001).

This chapter suggests that mapping the location of high-crime areas to help establish correlations between crime levels and social inequality could be useful in designing crime prevention policies. It also suggests that local government initiatives have a central role in the design of prevention projects.

The Conceptual Definition of Public Problems and Policies

A key aspect in defining a public problem involves how it is cognitively conceived; that is, conceptual discussions are relevant in outlining a theoretical framework to guide the formulation of policies and programs to control violence and crime. To conceive public safety policies requires formulating cognitive components as inputs in the creation of programs to be implemented and analytical methods to monitor and appraise their performance (Dunn 1981). In conceptual terms, to formulate problems, alternatives, actions, and results is essentially a theoretical matter, while to evaluate, monitor, recommend, and structure is a technical issue, involving the use of cost-benefit ratios, and efficacy, efficiency, and equity models. This means to work in a cognitive realm whose interests are found in the macro- and micro-analytical levels of social interactions. Understanding the processes taking place in this wide-ranging web of connections and complex phenomena is an invitation for different branches of knowledge to make their contribution. Consequently, several levels of approach are needed to elaborate crime prevention and control policies. Ideally, these levels will make up an "integrated intervention structure" that strives to operate at the structural, institutional, interpersonal, and individual levels (Moser and Shrader 1999). Thus, law enforcement as a system of rules applied to facts reported by participants raises problems that must be analyzed at the microlevel, focusing on the nature of penal laws as rules for decision making and behavior, from which the conditions of their use by the social actors may be inferred. In practical terms, this means that interventions aimed at restraining crime and violence will work through reforms in the organization of the judicial system, police, penal legislation, and an increase in the number of prisons as well as in the severity of penalties. On the other side, within the macrosocial theoretical framework of crime and violence, interest is focused on those risk factors that predispose individuals toward crime—such as poverty, opportunity structures available (or not) to an excluded population, decline in social capital, or gender socialization. More recently, interest has turned to environmental and situational factors that may contribute to crime—such as physical infrastructure, society's routine activities, access to weapons, or availability of emergency medical services.[1]

Conceptual discussions of violence reveal the elements that have influenced the formulation of public policies in this area. The Latin American literature has circumscribed the theoretical debate around specific issues, thus centering public policies on some key themes. For analytical purposes, they can be broken down—albeit with extreme simplification—into two major approaches: those based on the concept that violence and crime are public health problems, and those that focus on the social and economic impact of crime on sustained development in Latin American countries. There are several different ways that can be used to approach the crime problem, but I would like to focus on these two approaches because of public policy implications. The next section will deal first with the public health view, examining domestic violence and the involvement of youth in crime, and then with the issue of crime as regards its economic and social costs.

Public Health Problem: Domestic Violence

Domestic violence occurs among individuals in a household; social violence refers to violence in the streets and other public spaces (Buvinic et al. 1999, 8). Domestic violence, whether physical, psychological, or sexual, is usually against women and children. The hidden nature of this type of violence and the multiple problems regarding the validity and reliability of official information sources have made many Latin American researchers call for victimization surveys as a way to expose this problem and to supplement information from the sadly deficient crime statistics systems.[2]

Intrafamily violence is a theme found time and again in most city programs funded by the Inter-American Development Bank (IDB). Sixty-one IDB-supported violence control programs, through government and non-government organizations (NGOs), are now underway in a number of Latin American countries that cover legal, psychological, educational, or social assistance to women, youth, and children (Table 4.2). Most of these programs are found in Chile (39 percent), followed by Nicaragua (18 percent), and Colombia (11 percent). Intrafamily violence, whether against women or children, is the object of 69 percent of these interventions; the remaining 31 percent deal with social violence.[3]

Due to the enormous variety of possible interventions, policies and programs dealing with domestic violence are diffuse, dispersed, and multi-faceted, which makes their evaluation difficult. Prevention programs have been implemented by hundreds of NGOs in Latin America, acting in dif-

Table 4.2. IDB-supported violence control programs in Latin America, 2002

	Type of Violence					
	Domestic		Other		Total	
Project Location	Number of Programs	%	Number of Programs	%	Number of Programs	%
Argentina	1	100			1	2
Bolivia	2	100			2	3
Chile	18	75	6	25	24	39
Colombia			7	100	7	11
Costa Rica	1	50	1	50	2	3
Ecuador	3	100			3	5
El Salvador	1	100			1	2
Honduras	1	100			1	2
Mexico	1	100			1	2
Nicaragua	10	91	1	9	11	18
Panama			1	100	1	2
Peru	2	67	1	33	3	5
Puerto Rico			1	100	1	2
Uruguay	2	100			2	3
Venezuela			1	100	1	2
Total	42	69	19	31	61	100

Source: IDB (2001).

ferent areas and adopting distinct strategies (IDB 1999c). The schools and the media have been chief targets for this type of intervention: curricula have been revised to do away with gender stereotypes and incorporate specific modules for peaceful conflict resolution. One example is the initiative by the Bolivian government, through its Subsecretariat of Gender Affairs, to jointly produce with the Federal Office of Education a document entitled *La equidad de género en la educación,* which attempts to incorporate a gender perspective in the formulation of educational policy; some four hundred officials and teachers have been trained in this regard. Other initiatives include Argentina's Mass Educational Campaign for Violence Prevention by the Instituto Social y Político de la Mujer in 1998, activities involved awareness campaigns in the media, the dissemination of data and facts, the creation of a website (www.ispm.org.ar), and fund-raising campaigns (IDB 1999c).

So far there has been no assessment of the impact or effectiveness of any of these programs. Such assessment is made difficult by at least three factors. First, the programs in this area need a long time horizon before results can materialize, as intervention in childhood may only yield results many years later. Second, many risk factors associated with the problem are often context dependent; what works in some contexts does not work in others. Last, as has been mentioned, it is extremely difficult to measure this type of violence (Sherman et al. 1997, chap. 4).

Public Health: Youth and Crime

Youth are extremely vulnerable to violence, whether as aggressors or victims. In Latin America, most homicide victims are men, 69 percent of them in the age bracket of 15 to 29 (Sanjuan 1999). The involvement of youth in crime has been mostly through gangs. Although each group's structure varies according to its activities, initiation rites, and the prevailing age of its members, all are involved in illegal activities. The degree of these groups' participation in different types of illegal activities also varies; Brazilian *quadrilhas,* for instance, are more involved in drug trafficking and, often, murder (Zaluar 1984, 1997). A study in Belo Horizonte showed that the sharp increase in homicides in recent years is due to increased crack dealing in certain slums, usually by youth and children (Beato F. et al. 2001a).

The explanation for the existence of these gangs has varied along the theoretical spectrum of criminology. The idea used to be that these groups actually played socializing and controlling roles that institutions such as the family and the church were unable to carry out; the "social disorganization" theory of the old Chicago school has been echoed in many intervention projects for children and teenagers. More recently, however, other scholars have begun to regard gangs as economically driven businesses (Jankowsky 1991).

An influential study by the Rand Corporation to analyze the impact of various crime-prevention strategies compared some intervention programs to tough legislation (Greenwood et al. 1996). The intervention programs included (1) home visits by an assistant soon after the birth of children and continuing up to the age of six, (2) training and therapy for families whose children had displayed aggressive behavior in school or were about to be expelled from school, (3) four years of monetary incentives to induce poor youth to graduate from school, and (4) monitoring and supervision of high school youth showing delinquent behavior. These programs were compared to the impact on California crime rates of the introduction of the legislation known as "Three Strikes."[4] The results of cost-benefit ratio calculations for each strategy are shown in Table 4.3.

The strategy with the most impact has been California's tough legislation, which reduced crime by 21.4 percent within a year. It is an expensive strategy, involving the construction of prisons and the maintenance of skilled personnel in them, in addition to increasing the number of prison inmates to astronomical levels. To reduce the number of crimes by 1 percent, US$258 million is spent; sixty-one crimes are prevented for every million dollars spent. A better cost-benefit ratio than tough legislation can be seen in the programs that offer training and therapy to families or incentives to young people to complete schooling. Although their impact on crime rate reduction is less (6.6 and 15.5 percent, respectively), the programs are also much less expensive. The cost to reduce total crime by 1 percent is around US$55 million for family training and US$37 million for graduation incentives. If the number of crimes prevented for each US$1 million is analyzed (family training prevents 157 crimes, and school incentives prevent 258), the differences still favor social intervention programs. It is not even a matter of choosing between social (preventive or rehabilitative) programs and punitive programs, but rather of considering the possibility of an optimal combination of intervention strategies: for instance, tough legislation has a good impact on crime rate reduction (21.4 percent) at a cost of US$5.52 billion; with a modest increase of another US$568 million (for graduation incentives), there could be a total rate reduction of 36.9 percent.

The same methodology was used to evaluate prevention programs in Brazil for similar results. The World Bank compared programs of primary, secondary, and tertiary intervention in Brazil. The first one is a primary pro-

Table 4.3. Cost-benefit comparison of selected intervention strategies in childhood and adolescence, Rand study, 1996

Item	Three Strikes	Home Visits	Family Therapy	Incentives to Graduate	Supervision of Juvenile Delinquents
Percentage of crimes prevented	21.4	5.5	6.6	15.5	1.8
Annual program cost (in millions of dollars)	$5,520	$3,155	$361	$568	$241
Cost to reduce crime by 1% (in millions of dollars)	$258	$573	$55	$37	$131
Number of crimes prevented for every million dollars	61	11	157	258	72

Source: Greenwood et al. (1996).

gram, called "Bolsa Família," a wide-ranging program aimed at assisting low-income families. At the secondary level, the "Programa Uerê" was developed for an NGO to rehabilitate youth and teenagers who live in the streets in Rio de Janeiro. Another secondary-level program is "Paz nas Escolas," located in selected poor communities in São Paulo. The third-level program, "Fica Vivo,"[5] uses a multidisciplinary approach to help youth avoid becoming involved in crime in general, and specifically homicides. This program targets youth at risk for involvement in gangs. A program similar to D.A.R.E. (Drug Abuse Resistance Education) that police organizations called PROERD focuses on preventing students from becoming involved with violence and drugs. Finally, there are programs targeting people already involved with crime and violence, such as the Associação de Proteção e Assistência ao Condenado (APAC), an alternative imprisonment strategy, or the "Liberdade Assistida," that focuses on teenagers involved in minor crimes. Finally, "Prevenção Ativa" is a prevention program by police that consists of patrols in crime "hot spots." These programs are compared in Table 4.4.

Fica Vivo presents the best cost-benefit ratio, with prevention of 1,549 violent crimes on a budget of 1 million reais (US$1 = ~R$2.1). It is thirty-three times more cost effective than APAC (comparing spending per serious crime prevented), an intervention focused on people already involved in crime.

Table 4.4. Cost-benefit comparison of eight Brazilian crime prevention programs

Programs	Program Cost per Beneficiary (Reais)	Number of Serious Crimes Prevented per Beneficiary	Cost per Serious Crime Prevented (Reais)	Serious Crimes Prevented per 1 Million Reais
APAC	18,417.99	0.87	21,109.75	47.37
Patrulha de Prevenção Ativa	—	—	6916.42	—
Liberdade Assistida	1,323.68	0.91	1,459.94	684.96
UERÊ	8,184.84	0.45	18,290.73	54.67
Paz nas Escolas	192.23	0.16	1,174.45	851.46
Fica Vivo	1,065.70	1.65	645.69	1,548.73
Bolsa Família	2,594.88	0.23	11,256.15	88.84
PROERD	35.43	0.02	1,682.33	594.42
CEAPA	145.40	—	—	—

An examination of several successful prevention programs for at-risk youth revealed some ingredients in common (Moser and Bronkhorst 1999): the management of such programs should be entrusted to multidisciplinary teams; and the mobilization of an interinstitutional network of agencies, including the private sector, is important to ensure that the programs keep pace and continue over time. Another ingredient is the inclusion of the youth themselves in the design, implementation, and evaluation of the programs, facilitating their own involvement with the program's objectives, dialogue, and continuity. Indeed, continuity is critical in this kind of intervention, and toward this end funding must be both public and private, with the participation of businesspeople and community leaders.

Colombia offers a good example in this area. Given that it is mostly youth who become involved in crime, drug trafficking gangs, and guerrilla and paramilitary groups, the strategy developed by the vice minister of youth was to invest massively in reducing school dropout rates. This strategy has proven to be promising in preventing crime. Indeed, it is the basis of some World Bank–developed programs aimed at testing and implementing integrated packages of government and nongovernment services for low-income youth. One of the programs developed in Colombia aims at increasing productivity and earnings for young people in poor communities by reducing school dropout rates, promoting healthy lifestyles, and improving job opportunities. At the project's core are youth development centers, which provide diverse types of assistance to the young and operate from accessible points in the community.[6] Young people in high-risk situations can access a wide range of services and activities, including vocational training, tutoring, health services, educational assistance, cultural and recreational services, and counseling. These services are implemented at the municipal level.

Service Volunteered for All (SERVOL) is an NGO in Port of Spain, Trinidad and Tobago, which works with children and youth in poor neighborhoods who do not attend school. One of the program's components is to develop self-esteem in children, many of whom are victims of physical abuse and aggression. Courses are offered in self-awareness and self-knowledge, how to deal with anger and frustration, nutrition, personal hygiene, and family planning, among others. The Ministry of Social Development and Education has expanded the program to the country as a whole (Moser and Bronkhorst 1999). Another program is being offered by the Psychology Department of Brazil's Universidade Federal de Minas Gerais, involving psychology students who have developed psychosocial intervention strategies in one of the more violent slums in Belo Horizonte. In addition to helping to develop self-esteem, this program is designed to teach children nonviolent ways to solve conflicts.

Economic and Social Costs of Crime and Violence

Table 4.5 shows the economic costs of violence expressed as a percentage of the gross domestic product (GDP) in several Latin American countries. Included in this calculation are costs related to health, such as spending on medical services or years lost through premature incapacitation or death; material costs resulting in spending for police, security systems, and court system services; intangible costs, reflected in how much citizens are willing to pay in order to be rid of violence; and costs from the transfer of assets lost in robberies and theft, in addition to payments in kidnapping and extortion cases (IDB 1999b). These calculations are conservative, in that they do not take into account spending on private security or the effects of violence on private investment. Other indicators of the costs of violent crime would include declines in property values, out-migration of local populations in response to crime, or tourism lost due to crime (Glaeser et al. 1995).

Other costs of violence are expressed in the erosion of social capital. Social capital refers to the set of norms, values, obligations, rules of reciprocity, and bonds of trust established among individuals, making it possible for them to reach common objectives (Coleman 1990). Violence erodes

Table 4.5. Economic costs of violent crime in six Latin American countries (expressed as percentage of GDP in 1997)

	Brazil	Colombia	El Salvador	Mexico	Peru	Venezuela
Healthcare costs	1.9	5.0	4.3	1.3	1.5	0.3
Material costs	3.6	8.4	5.1	4.9	2.0	9.0
Intangible costs	3.4	6.9	11.5	3.3	1.0	2.2
Costs from transfer of assets	1.6	4.4	4.0	2.8	0.6	0.3

Note: Other studies show different results when analyzed at a municipal level. For instance, Rondon (2002) estimates the costs of violence in Belo Horizonte at 4% of the city's GDP.
Source: Londoño (1998).

social capital to the extent that it deteriorates trust relationships in a community and restricts people's mobility in violent areas, thus contributing to less personal interaction. All of this reduces the capacity for communities to self-regulate and organize themselves to combat crime. Moreover, the decrease in social capital weakens the capacity to peacefully resolve conflicts (Lederman et al. 1999).

The reconstruction of solidarity is at the core of programs that seek to restore social capital, attempting to strengthen the feeling of belonging to a group—variously described as "civic life," "social fabric," or "sense of community" (Kubisch 1999). This is the focus used in ten countries by the Pan American Health Organization in fighting domestic violence through pilot projects that entail improving the institutional capacity to respond to and support battered women through reinforcement of vigilance, the creation of a multisector community network, training of police, and increasing public awareness of this kind of problem (Hartigan 1999).

The (Non)Relationship of Crime and Unemployment

In recent years much importance has been attributed to the relationship between the unemployment caused by economic recession on the one hand and crime on the other (Gunn 1998). This a major issue in criminology due to its theoretical implications and for the definition of public policies (Land et al. 1995). But the relation between unemployment and crime can be shown to be weak, inconsistent, or insignificant; at best, we might say that there is a "consensus in doubt" (Chiricos 1987), because results vary due to the analytical techniques and strategies employed (Land et al. 1995).

Much of the discrepancy lies in the difficulty of making explicit the causal mechanisms whereby unemployment leads to crime. On the one hand are a variety of models and theories, such as neoclassic economic models that deal with rational choice (Becker 1977), neomarxist models (Quinney 1977), and traditional crime theories (Merton 1968), according to which an increase in the unemployment rate leads to increased crime motivation. Embarking on a criminal career is seen as the result of an inevitable choice for the fulfillment of ideals and values that cannot be reached via legitimate means. However, the same rational choice might be used to explain the inverse causal mechanism: "One's natural instinct would be to interpret this [positive relationship] as meaning that rising unemployment causes rising crime. But rising crime might as easily cause rising unemployment. If young men examining the world about them conclude that crime pays more than work . . . they may leave their jobs in favor of crime" (Wilson 1983, 80). Unemployment could also be considered a factor in decreasing crime opportunities, to the extent that it might increase the number of people "on the watch" against crime or the degree of alertness in society (Cohen and Felson 1979). Such contradictions may lead to inconsistent results in the studies on this topic. For example, some studies have shown (Beato F. and Reis 2000) that there is no significant correlation between crime rates and unemployment rates. This is a conceptual deficiency: the phenomena with which criminology deals are much more complex than those of economics. The effects of unemployment on the lives of people should perhaps rather be viewed in terms of the welfare and survival of the workers rather than the danger they may present to those who are better off in times of economic recession.

The Importance of Information Systems

Crime information systems must provide both social indicators that can serve the research community to help answer questions about hypothesis testing, theories of criminal behavior, and causes of violence, and they must provide data that will be operationally useful in planning and orientation of specific programs. The major problem today in criminology studies in Latin America is the lack of information systems that can advance the reach of empirical propositions. The implications of this inadequacy for the design and evaluation of crime control policies are obvious. Public policies affecting the criminal justice system in Latin America are often created blindly because the need for them is so urgent that any results are considered successful. But what impacts do these policies have on violence and criminality rates? How much time is needed before they produce positive effects? What combinations will produce the most promising results? How can spending resources on useless approaches be avoided? These analyses are becoming increasingly necessary because of the interest of governments and other funders in identifying and allocating resources based on cost-benefit models (Welsh et al. 2001).

A World Bank report on the impact of violence and criminality on sustained development and in combating poverty in Latin America indicated that the most immediate problem is that "the data are grossly inadequate. The reasons include severe underreporting by victims, lack of systematic survey data, and deficiencies of statistical agencies reporting on incidences of crime and violence. Thus, [the] first priority on an emerging agenda to deal with crime and violence in the region is the need to enhance the knowledge-base about the nature, extent, and evolution of these pathologies" (Ayres 1998, 3).

Given serious underreporting of crimes against property, some researchers have used the homicide rate as a criminality indicator for cities, regions, countries, or even comparisons between countries. However, the simple homicide rate can hide some important differences (Lynch 1995). For example, in 1996, the homicide rate in Rio de Janeiro's metropolitan area was 59.35 per 100,000 inhabitants; São Paulo's metropolitan area had a similar rate of 55.58. However, in Rio de Janeiro, the homicide rate among youths aged 15 to 29 years was 34 percent higher than for the same age group in São Paulo; in addition, homicide with guns represented 87 percent of the deaths in Rio de Janeiro, while in São Paulo they accounted for only 47 percent (Batittuci 1998).

Using the homicide rate as a comparative parameter of violence may not be valid for other reasons, such as (1) "although underreporting of homicides is . . . lower than it is for many other crimes, underreporting and inconsistencies between different sources of information on homicide are serious problems"; (2) many types of serious violence do not always end in homicide (e.g., domestic violence); and (3) "when homicide is used as a principal measure of violence, it tends to overlook the importance of nonphysical violence, such as intimidation" (IDB 1999a, 2). We could also argue that using the homicide rate as a measure of crime or violence is problematic in that it has a specific dynamic that is very different from what occurs with other crimes, such as property crime; for control and prevention programs, this qualification must be made.

Due to the countless deficiencies attributed to official databases, there has been an increased demand for accurate data, especially via victimization surveys. But these are not good instruments for revealing other types of crime, such as white-collar crimes, or for guiding specific policies at the neighborhood level; neither would they contribute to any understanding of organized crime. However, several recent experiments may prove helpful here. The first is from the United States: the National Institute of Justice's program of Community Mapping, Planning, and Analysis for Safety Strategies. Although still under development, the goal is to implement crime and community measurement systems to be used in planning and analysis; such systems could turn any available database into a data warehouse that could aggregate criminal, community, and mapping information and opinion and behavioral research. Cali's experience with DESEPAZ (see below) and the creation of geoarchives (the electronic database needed to make maps) in Belo Horizonte are also illustrations of this trend. Bogotá has invested in creating geocoded databases for crime prevention in recent years. Santiago and Buenos Aires are examples of the use of mapping techniques to manage public security programs.

Although timely data and information on the geographic locations of crime are increasing in information-gathering programs for specific targets and populations, they demand technological and intellectual resources that do not yet exist among the agencies in charge of producing this information, or in the academic community that will deal with the analysis of this information. For example, few police organizations have computer databases or departments assigned to collect and analyze information, or even the necessary statistical software to accomplish these tasks. Even fewer organizations employ any type of technology to map crime locations or use that information for planning and operational purposes. As with all technological matters, this involves forming and training specific task groups.

Another Approach: Analyzing the Spatial Distribution of Crime in Major Urban Centers

Studies of crime and violence tend to focus on socioeconomic or sociodemographic features as good predictors, crediting the criminal with acts of aggression toward society's moral and normative consensus. Since a low degree of moral integration is what produces crime, it follows that the criminal must be punished in order to reestablish the normative nucleus's core values (Durkheim 1978; Clarke 1966; Kraut 1976; Sherman and Berk 1984). A similar approach is to examine not the individuals but the groups to which they belong. Thus, the poor would be the focus of analysis, to the extent that they breed both the agents and the victims of violent crime (Colvin and Pauly 1983; Greenberg 1985).

In contrast to these approaches, I propose an analysis that deals with the context of opportunities for criminal action by examining the spatial distribution of crimes. In this sense, since urban communities (certain slums are cases in point) can continue to show high crime rates despite substantial changes in the social and cultural characteristics of their residents (Reiss 1986), the emphasis is instead on the features of the community and the urban spaces where crimes occur. The first step in this direction is to analytically separate crime incidence from the social characteristics of criminals. In theoretical terms, this implies that criminals are no different from noncriminals: both are equally predisposed to crime (Newman et al. 1997). The motivation for crime is then seen as the result of an immediate environment or opportunity for action, which may be oriented toward a specific type of criminal act (Opp 1997).

There is no denying the importance of socioeconomic background factors as elements that may predispose some individuals to crime. But there are other elements, which are part of a macrostructural socioeconomic context, that make targets available, such as the absence or weakness of control and vigilance mechanisms that tend to inhibit criminal action (Cohen and Felson 1979). The specific environment for action, in addition to being a major determinant of motivation, also creates a predisposition to delinquency in specific cohorts of a population. The concept of "bounded rationality" (Simon 1982), for instance, acknowledges that delinquents are actors who do not always have all the facts or are not fully aware of the situations with which they are dealing (Clarke 1983). At the microlevel, we can analyze the immediate environments for action; at the macrolevel, we can analyze how situational availability relates to the development of a socioeconomic structure that supplies the context of opportunities for criminal action. Hence, the importance of simultaneously analyzing the geographic breakdown of infractions and the socioeconomic context in which they occur becomes clear.

Interpersonal Crime

The crime *explosion* in major urban centers might better be described as an *implosion*, for it occurs more often within communities where both the victims and the perpetrators reside and share the same living space. Belo Horizonte, capital of the Brazilian state of Minas Gerais, has a population of roughly two and a half million inhabitants. Not unlike other major Latin American urban centers, violent crime rates have risen sharply, particularly in the 1990s; in absolute terms, the number of homicides more than doubled over five years, from 326 in 1995 to 685 in 2000. The fact that this sharp increase seems to be associated with drug-related activities, mainly crack (Beato F. et al. 2001), does not explain the concentration of homicides and drug traffic–related activities in some slums and not in others.

Several forms of association between predatory crimes and drugs have been studied in the literature. Most common are topics such as an affinity between drug use and a propensity to commit crime to finance drug dependency, to solve extralegal conflicts, and to acquire expensive weapons for such purposes (Johnson et al. 1991). Goldstein (1985) identified three ways in which homicides in New York State were associated with drugs: psychopharmacological homicides, committed under heavy alcohol or drug intoxication; systemic homicides, perpetrated among people involved in drug selling; and economic compulsion during robbery and thefts against common citizens. The systemic variety of violence associated with drugs usually involves turf wars among rival dealers, aggression and homicide perpetrated within the hierarchy of drug sellers as a way to reinforce and enforce normative codes, drug theft leading to violent retaliation by the dealers and their bosses, the elimination of informers, and punishment for the sale of adulterated drugs or for failing to pay debts owed to drug sellers (Goldstein 1985, cited in Hunt 1990). Some studies stress that homicides are more associated with selling drugs than with using them (Chaiken and Chaiken 1991; Zaluar 1984).

Figure 4.1 identifies some homicide "hot spots" in Belo Horizonte recorded by the police for the 1995–1998 period.[7] The common-sense perception that slums are, per se, a condition for the existence of violent crime is not true. The analysis shows in fact that homicide clusters were found in only six of the eighty urban conglomerates containing slums. These are slums whose population hovers around 30,000 inhabitants, located in the midst of several middle-class neighborhoods. Most of the crimes take place on weekends and at night and occur in places with a high number of bars and drug points of sale, accessible to local residents and to people from neighboring areas alike. In this case, two rival gangs had a turf dispute over points of sale. According to the Homicide Department of the Minas Gerais Civil Police, 62 percent of the homicides in this area were drug related. However,

Figure 4.1. Homicide distribution in Belo Horizonte, 1995–1998

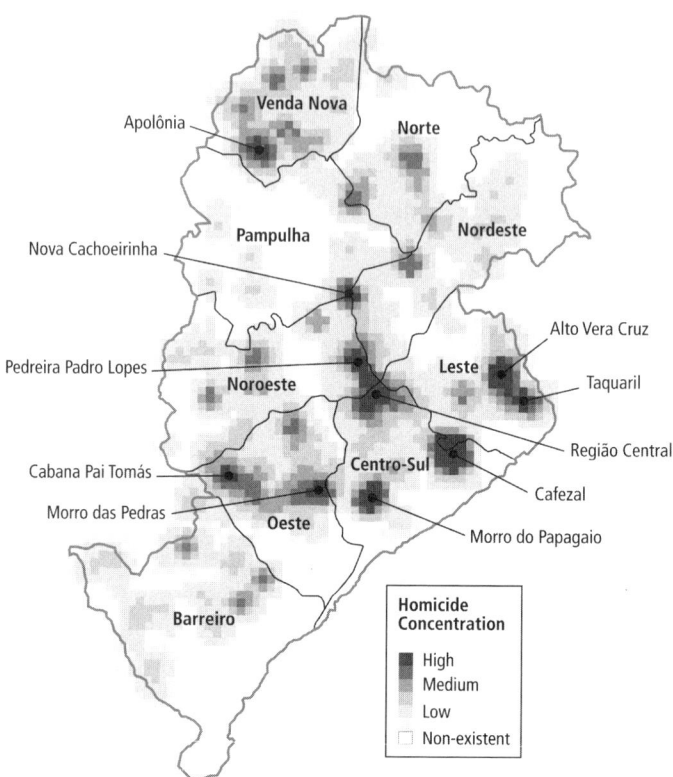

Source: Beato F. 2001b.

of the remaining 38 percent, 17.6 percent were related to revenge, 8 percent to crimes of passion, and 12.4 percent to other causes (ACADEPOL 2000). Thus, it is important to note that although narcotics-related activities caused a major share of the homicides, a sizable portion still related to other types of conflicts that might have been avoided if there were mediation mechanisms available.

Table 4.6 compares selected socioeconomic variables in locales with a high concentration of homicides and locales with an average or low concentration of homicides. Only statistically significant variables are presented. Slums containing homicide clusters clearly had several social welfare and quality-of-life indicators that were considerably inferior: quality of residential construction materials in these locales is nearly eight times inferior to that of the other locales in the city; average schooling is three years lower (5.53 versus 8.51 years of formal schooling); the population is younger, with an average age of twenty-five compared to the citywide average of twenty-nine. In the homicide-ridden locales, child mortality and illiteracy rates are higher. The urban infrastructure index is significantly more deficient in these locations (a five-fold difference). Generally speaking, the social protection buffer index is roughly one-third compared with other regions in the city. Some variables whose results were not significant are of interest precisely for that reason. For instance, comparative analysis of the percentage of formal versus informal sector employment was not significant. This may be another way of corroborating the (non)relationship between unemployment and crime, which was discussed above.

The homicides in the cluster areas occurred in the most public spaces—streets, bars, and other drug-selling spots. It should be noted that these particular urban configurations make it difficult for the police to access these locations and easy for criminals to get away. Streets are narrow and short and there are many dead-end streets; such a labyrinth makes police work

Table 4.6. Comparing areas with and without homicide clusters in Belo Horizonte, 1995–2002

Feature (p value)	Homicide Clusters ($n = 6$)	Absence of Homicide Clusters ($n = 75$)	Total Clusters ($n = 81$)
Residential material finishing ($p = 0.001$)	Mean = 6.59 SD = 3.96	Mean = 0.77 SD = 0.84	Mean = 6.17 SD = 4.11
Years of schooling ($p = 0.006$)	Mean = 8.51 SD = 2.57	Mean = 5.53 SD = 0.61	Mean = 8.29 SD = 2.60
Age ($p = 0.010$)	Mean = 28.96 SD = 3.71	Mean = 24.92 SD = 1.41	Mean = 28.66 SD = 3.74
Formal and informal employment rate ($p = 0.021$)	Mean = 3.39 SD = 1.10	Mean = 2.32 SD = 0.36	Mean = 3.31 SD = 1.10
Child mortality rate per 1,000 ($p = 0.035$)	Mean = 0.28 SD = 0.13	Mean = 0.40 SD = 0	Mean = 0.29 SD = 0.13
Illiteracy rate ($p = 0.000$)	Mean = 11.80 SD = 6.83	Mean = 23.04 SD = 6.06	Mean = 12.63 SD = 7.36
Urban infrastructure index ($p = 0.003$)	Mean = –0.24 SD = 0.66	Mean = –1.10 SD = 0.72	Mean = –0.30 SD = 0.70

Source: Beato F. (2001b).
SD, standard deviation.

difficult, inefficient, and, at times, the police are aggressive toward the local residents. This suggests that drug activities are an important component, but are only a part of a more complex process that results from the lack of social controls in some urban communities. This weakness of social control is similar to Sampson's concept of "collective efficacy":

> Personal ties notwithstanding, it is the linkage of mutual trust and shared expectations for intervening on behalf of the common good that defines the neighborhood context of what we call '*collective efficacy*.' Just as self-efficacy is situated rather than global (one has self-efficacy relative to a particular task), a neighborhood's efficacy exists relative to specific tasks such as maintaining public order.
>
> Moving away from a focus on private ties, the term collective efficacy is meant to signify an emphasis on shared beliefs in a neighborhood's conjoint capability for action to achieve an intended effect, and hence an active sense of engagement on the part of residents. The meaning of efficacy is captured in expectations about the exercise of control, elevating the 'agentic' aspect of social life over a perspective centered on the accumulation of 'stocks' of social resources (or what some call 'social capital'). This conception of collective efficacy is consistent with a redefinition of social capital in terms of expectation for action within a collectivity. Distinguishing between the resource potential represented by personal ties, on the one hand, and the shared expectation for action among neighbors represented by collective efficacy, on the other, helps clarify the dense ties paradox. Namely, social networks foster the conditions under which collective efficacy may flourish, but they are not sufficient for the exercise of control (Sampson 2003, 6).

Crimes against Property

If homicides are the more dramatic face of urban violence, offenses and wrongdoings against property are daily phenomena for much of the urban population. The difficulty in measuring the incidence of property crimes, plus the large number that are un- or under-documented, has led many experts and policymakers to neglect their incidence altogether. Muggings or holdups on the streets of large urban centers are perhaps the most common expression of violence. A Peruvian victimization survey found that such occurrences accounted for 62 percent of reported incidents of violence (Instituto Apoyo 1999). In San Salvador, research data show that nearly 20 percent of the population had been robbed at gunpoint at least once at some point in their lives (Cruz et al. 1998). Victimization surveys in Rio de Janeiro and São Paulo placed the same figure at 52 percent (Piquet Carneiro 1999). In Mexico City armed robbery is the principal type of crime, reaching 70,000 incidents in 1996; the important datum is that violent holdups and robberies increased from 32 to 50 percent of all crimes reported (MHF 1999).

According to the Military Police, in the city of Belo Horizonte offenses against property have increased sharply, with rates jumping from 50 to 60 percent a year since 1995 (Beato F. 2001b). Even more important than their increase is their growing association with the use of violence. As shown in Figure 4.2, armed robbery has been increasing in absolute terms, with the majority of cases involving weapons.

Crimes against property have a dynamic wholly different from that of crimes against persons. Unlike homicides, these offenses tend to occur in the city's wealthier and more developed areas where there is a heavy concentration of commercial activities and an abundant supply of available targets. Analyses of the clusters found in Belo Horizonte make this association even clearer; the chief hot spot for crimes against property is the city's downtown area. Although modest in size (0.9 km^2), this area differs from the others not only in terms of crime indicators but also in the incidence of certain types of economic activity. There is a significant amount of formal and informal trading, with many shops (wholesale and retail), banks, street vendors, and vendors of all kinds, not to mention red-light areas. Particularly favorable to offenders is that so many people come and go, many of whom do not know the area very well. There are also bus and rail stations in this area. When the city of Belo Horizonte was planned, these target areas were inadvertently concentrated in the same geographic locale. Additionally, it should be mentioned that it is easy for perpetrators to escape along any of the many streets and boulevards.

One segment of this downtown area marked by a high crime rate is also the site of a large concentration of the so-called street population, namely, beggars, garbage and paper pickers, drunks, street children, the poorest of the poor, and prostitutes from the surrounding areas. Judging from the high number of offenses around the square, there seems to be good evidence of the "broken windows" theory (Wilson 1983). It is worthwhile noting that there is a security island around the municipal market complex, where many vendors and shopkeepers and shoppers congregate. An effective self-

Figure 4.2. Interpersonal violence, robbery, and armed robbery

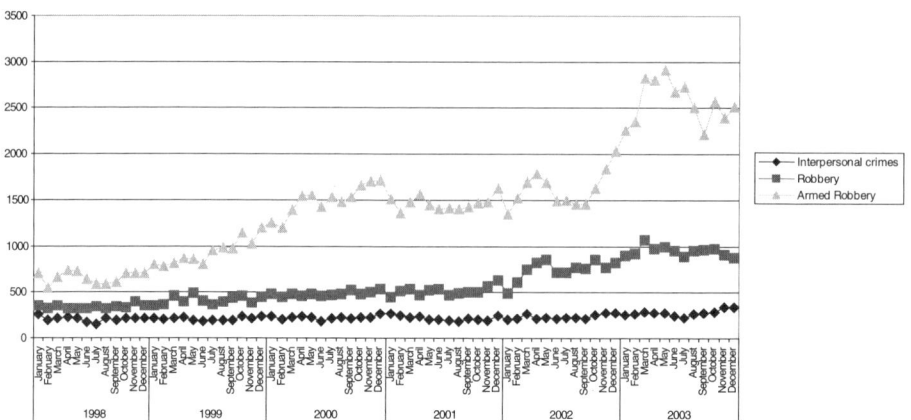

Source: Beato F. et al. 2001, updated.

protection scheme was apparently developed by the local vendors and store owners, so that at least in this city block customers can feel safe.

The large number of people circulating downtown in the daytime makes it easy for thefts against pedestrians to take place, when the crowd is transformed into anonymous and easy "targets" and it is more difficult for the police to act. In the daytime, minors and adults alike display a wide variety of offenses against careless or distracted passers-by. On the other hand, this same concentration makes other offenses more difficult to perpetrate; thus, armed holdups tend to occur more often at night, when fewer people are on the streets. Thefts in commercial buildings are also more likely to occur when there are fewer people about. It is difficult to say which factor might be the more relevant, but certainly both are responsible for the high crime rate in the downtown area.

Some of the offenses are perpetrated by children and youth who live on the streets, where they find many opportunities to practice certain types of crime. It is important to keep in mind, however, that crimes perpetrated by delinquent minors are mostly committed by those who roam the streets at night. The fact that they are on the streets is less relevant than their presence on the streets at night, when there is more involvement with adult criminals and drug dealing is more common (Soares 1999). One strategy for dealing with such crimes looks at "situational prevention" (Clarke 1997). This involves increasing the effort needed for criminals to reach their goals, and likewise increasing the risks of carrying out these activities; reducing anticipated rewards; and removing the excuses and moral justifications used by criminals (Sykes and Matza 1993). This type of strategy has been identified as a way to reduce crime in Lima's urban spaces. Given the high degree of inefficiency of the Peruvian police, the Lima city government created *serenazgos,* urban patrol and vigilance units that make use of sports events, school assistance, youth training, and recreational activities to secure a minimum of crime control (Instituto Apoyo 1999).

The specific composition of crime in each urban space should be taken into account when policies are designed because strategies for prevention and control must be different according to composition. Downtown there is a predominance of crimes against property. Areas with a heavy concentration of commercial activities, such as shopping centers and malls, have an abundant supply of "targets" and many motivated delinquents. These areas are difficult for the police to patrol, due to their demographic density. In the poorer neighborhoods and districts, especially in the slums, there is a higher incidence of homicide, the nature of and motivation for which seem to be to some extent—although not exclusively—related to drug traffic and use.

DESEPAZ: Example of a Promising Urban Crime Prevention Program

The Development, Security, and Peace Program (DESEPAZ) in Cali, Colombia, is a city-level program comprised of various components. Although there is some evidence that it has had an impact on homicide rates, it has been more notable for the scope of its proposals, the originality of which lies in placing city management at the core of the process to implement crime control policies.

Colombia eloquently displays the complexity of the violence phenomenon in Latin America. Despite the fact that common sense associates violence with the drug dealing that started in the 1980s, violence in this country has deeper historical roots. Colombia has suffered a major wave of political violence; over a twenty-year period, about two hundred thousand Colombians were killed or injured in an undeclared civil war (Posada 1999). Indeed, drug dealing is only one ingredient in a complex mix of political violence associated with guerrilla organizations and paramilitary groups. In addition to its influence on urban violence, *narcotráfico* has altered the parameters of Colombian politics by channeling new financial and military resources to old historical foes (Chernick 1999). According to data gathered by Guerrero (1999), the influence of *narcotráfico* on urban violence, although indirect, seems equally devastating, to the extent that it destroys urban communities' social capital, particularly trust in the justice system and the police, which are jeopardized by drug-dealing corruption.[8]

In the 1980s and 1990s, homicide rates increased sharply in the city, from 23 per 100,000 inhabitants in 1983 to 90 in 1993. This made violence the lead topic in the 1992 city mayoral elections. The winner, Rodrigo Guerrero, an epidemiologist, named a group of advisors of diverse political and ideological orientations to study the issue and make proposals. They defined the following program principles: (1) multicausality, recognizing that violence is the result of several complex social processes, (2) research to systematically survey information that may provide support to violence reduction programs, (3) priority on prevention rather than repression, (4) the participation of society, not just government, in the process about which it will be fully informed, (5) tolerance and respect for others' opinions and rights, and (6) active promotion of equity principles.

Given his own professional background, Guerrero also adopted some conceptual principles and procedures from epidemiology. Thus, the strategy was to deal with risk factors identified within the specific context of the program, including alcohol, firearms, a culture of violent response to conflict, impunity and inefficiency of the court system and police, and poverty, social inequality, and marginality.

Once the principles and risk factors to be tackled were defined, DESEPAZ was structured around five major strategic areas: (1) systematic investigation and study of violence, (2) institutional strengthening of citizenship, (3) citizen education and communication toward peace, (4) equity promotion, and (5) youth programs.

The first area, systematic production of information on violence, was to be the foundation for elaborating action plans. Two strategies were adopted: (1) inasmuch as there were significant differences in the data on crime in the city, a permanent working group was formed—comprised of the Metropolitan Police, district attorney, Institute of Legal Medicine, municipal staff, and City Offices of Traffic and Public Health—to meet weekly and prepare a report for the City Security Council (IDB 1999d); and (2) an opinion survey was to be used to evaluate the quality of justice and police services, which were to be assessed every six months.

The second area—assembling an institutional network of support activities—emphasizes articulation, or linkages, among several institutions that deal with security problems. Five aspects were addressed. First, the Municipal Security Council was created, comprised of the city mayor (according to the Colombian Constitution, he is also the chief of police); the army commander; the commanders of the metropolitan and state police; the heads of finance, legal medicine, and the office of human rights; the secretaries of government, traffic, and city health; and the directors of the DESEPAZ program. The council met weekly to evaluate what had happened in the previous week. Second, improvements were made in police quality, requiring a higher level of schooling for recruitment and the development of joint university programs that contained modules on community development, human rights, and constitutional principles. Third, physical improvements were made to police stations, many of which were often seedy, run down, or ill equipped. Fourth, one of the project's more interesting ideas was the creation of Casas de Paz (Peace Houses) in the precinct stations. A wide range of services was offered, such as conflict mediation before legal procedures, legal aid provided by law students, and family commissions that included professionals who specialized in dealing with violence against women. This project was later extended to the whole country. Fifth, university personnel were hired to develop software to systematize and streamline court procedures in the city.

The third area refers to several strategies that were adopted for citizenship and peace education. First, Community Councils were created to establish mechanisms to bring the city administration closer to society. One night a week, the mayor and his staff met with members of each of the twenty *comunas* into which the city was divided to discuss action plans and carry out projects. On average, some two hundred people participated in these weekly meetings. The Niños Amigos de Paz (Children Friends of Peace) program tried to make the children of Cali aware of the dangers of firearms. One of the events was for children to drop their toy weapons into special plastic containers; in exchange they were given a badge identifying them as "amigos de paz" that gave them access to a series of public shows and recreation parks in the city.

The City Social Communication Office organized local media campaigns on the topics of citizenship and respect for other people's rights. Particularly important was the creation of a TV character representing a typical citizen who has no respect for community rules and ends up being ridiculed for that. A plan was also developed to foster community leaders capable of peacefully resolving conflicts. Entrusted to NGOs and local universities, the EDUPAR course focuses on strengthening family and parent-child relations, and mediating conflicts between neighbors. More than seven hundred community leaders attended the course.

The fourth strategic area, equity promotion, related to activities expected from the city government, such as programs to improve education, offer more public service jobs to the population, and create low-income housing.

Finally, based on data from the Fund for Vigilance and Security, which estimated that some 8,500 youth were members of juvenile gangs practicing criminal acts of various kinds, youth programs were created in an attempt to provide resocialization mechanisms for them. Through PARCES, a program in partnership with the private sector, several entities were created: (1) youth houses—social spaces where the young could meet, listen to music, and work out—were set up in seventeen city neighborhoods; (2) the National Sports School trained 330 youth, who have become sports promoters, and this eventually led to intercommunity olympics in which more than a hundred thousand people participated; and (3) jointly with NGOs and the United Nations Development Programme, microbusinesses were organized for young people, many of whom were former guerrilla fighters who had been granted amnesty by the Colombian government; they were hired by the Cali city government for chores such as street cleaning, garbage collection, and maintenance of parks and green areas.

Specific programs were also designed to address some other risk factors. First, since homicides occurred mostly at night and were often associated with alcohol consumption, a decision was made to ban alcohol sales at public events after 1 a.m. Second, since 80 percent of homicides involved firearms, a program was started to have the population turn in their weapons, particularly on special occasions or during feasts and celebrations (this has had the greatest impact on homicide rates). Third, based on a map of locations of high accident incidence, specific interventions were designed including infrastructure projects and alcohol control.

DESEPAZ's experience has become a source of innovative ideas for other Latin American cities, such as Rio de Janeiro and Brasília, and for countries like Jamaica and Uruguay. The program's major contribution has been to illustrate unequivocally the role of city government in crime prevention social programs, thus removing the conservative focus often found in traditional crime control policies, namely, to place the responsibility in the hands of the police and the legal system.

One of the most important characteristics of DESEPAZ was that, from the very beginning, it attempted to develop an information and survey system as the basis for the actions and guidelines it adopted. More than just collecting monthly data on crime, it has assembled a qualitative dynamic system that (although not yet a data bank) has allowed program managers to receive constant feedback. Another positive aspect was the removal of politics from the project. Although it had been widely discussed in the election campaign, from the program's inception people from diverse ideologies were brought in so as to make the issue nonpolitical and to provide a climate for friendly cooperation among different agencies. The program also embraces a wide range of different initiatives. It is public policy aimed at a complex problem, and shows the power and resources available to local governments to solve the problem of crime when it is defined as a public problem or a public health issue.

However, despite efforts to generate information that might serve operational and appraisal purposes, it was not very clear what results the program has had. Partly this was due to the absence of adequate techniques to evaluate results, such as the use of control groups. On the other hand, there were no data to allow for an independent evaluation to be undertaken. Because there has been no adequate recording of successes or failures, we do not know clearly which parts of the policy fared better. It shall never be known whether some of the programs had particularly noticeable results while others failed; indeed, some of the literature on evaluating crime control in other countries regards many of the actions adopted in Cali as ineffective.

Another problem has to do with the plan's continuity. This is particularly acute regarding some of the more unpopular actions taken by the city government, especially the semiprohibition on alcohol. Maintaining guidelines for plans and projects becomes more difficult when they are identified with particular parties or political leaders; thus, policies can be changed when a new government takes over.

This good practice is not unique in Latin America at the municipal level. There are other important policies and programs that have been developed in cities such as in Bogotá and Medellín in Colombia, and Diadema in Brazil. The components of these policies are basically the same of the DESEPAZ, and involve strong leadership by mayors plus several different kinds of social programs and crime opportunity reduction programs. The idea that local governments are essential to crime control is growing in many Latin American countries.

Conclusions

The examples presented here of the impact of social policies on crime come from different geopolitical unit levels. Colombia, Brazil, Chile, San Salvador, and Peru provide results achieved by municipalities combined with better police management and other kinds of interventions at various levels. It is difficult to evaluate which components are more or less effective in each case. The current status of evidence and evaluation studies of social programs does not allow any conclusive assessments. Diverse perspectives on research and intervention to prevent crime have been incorporated, and economists and epidemiologists have raised the level of empirical studies and techniques used to understand crime phenomena; however, it is important to stress limitations of these approaches.

First, there is a noticeable absence of any strategies or programs specifically aimed at urban crime, particularly crimes against property. Here you have to begin to implement crime prevention through environmental strategies. The idea of opportunity reduction programs is a new one in the major cities of the region, but is rapidly gaining acceptance, specifically closed circuit television systems.

Second, experts are developing econometric models to corroborate classical economics theses. In practical terms, however, results have not been encouraging. How and within which specific contexts can opportunity variables be used to elaborate prevention and control programs? How do incentive structures vary among socioeconomic groups? Can we think about "bounded rationality" (Simon 1982; Opp 1993) in such a way as to consider education and professionalization programs as elements of crime prevention? After all is said and done, does the emphasis given to the theory of dissuasion or to crime-related socioeconomic elements lead to macroeconomic solutions and institutional reforms that many Latin American countries are unable to implement in the short run and whose results are not as evident as they are assumed to be?

Third, one of the more obscure points in the incipient analysis of implementing crime control policies in Latin America is found at the organizational level—namely, relations among the social agencies involved. The elegant theoretical justification for the need for a holistic, integrated, interagency approach has not been able to inspire researchers or development agencies to become interested in how to integrate organizations whose missions and objectives are distinct, so that they could act together in specific security-related programs.

What should be done, at least ideally, to solve this deficiency? Among many possibilities, three points seem key to this discussion: (1) the need to establish a solid tradition of empirical and theoretical studies of crime in Latin America; (2) the urgent task of building databases for operational purposes and for the construction of crime indicators; and (3) constructing bridges between universities and research centers on the one hand, and criminal justice organizations on the other, particularly (although not exclusively) the police.

There is little to be gained from the provincial attitude that prevails in the current output of theoretical and empirical studies in Latin America. Obviously there are honorable exceptions, but as a rule there is no systematic tradition to produce studies in this area. Policymakers and researchers are not theoretically and methodologically trained to produce studies of implementation evaluation or cost-effectiveness of public policy programs. There is scarcely any reference to U.S., Canadian, English, French, German, or even other Latin American literature. Even more rare is the use of sophisticated analytical techniques, whether in studies or in evaluations. As has already been discussed, most of this deficiency is due to the lack of databases. There are several reasons for such low production, one of which has to do with the fact that criminology is often treated as a discipline in legal studies, in keeping with the Latin American tradition of crime and violence being relegated to the police and court systems.

The discussion on determining factors in homicide shows how this phenomenon's complexity resides in its many associations, some of which barely receive any theoretical treatment. For instance, the geographic concentration of homicide is an important factor in understanding its socioeconomic dimensions—when drug dealing in these locations arrives, homicide rates sharply increase. There are both practical and theoretical problems. In practical terms, the issue is why some neighborhoods and areas in a city have high crime rates; in theoretical terms, the social disaggregation hypothesis blames higher homicide incidence on socioeconomic features (Bursik 1986). In fact, this causal mechanism does not occur directly but as a result of increasing population mobility and heterogeneity (in absolute and relative terms) in lower-income areas, which weakens traditional bonds of social control and, consequently, leads to a higher number of crimes. However, empirical evidence shows that socioeconomic factors are not clearly linked to (explain) high crime rates in certain locations in cities; environmental features might also favor criminal activities (Stark 1987). Both sets of factors must be taken into account.

Finally, there is the divorce of academics and policymakers. In the 1998 plenary meeting of the American Society of Criminology, the director of the National Institute of Justice imagines a hypothetical and undesirable world in which the academic community would be wholly divorced from the practical interests of criminal justice organizations:

> I suppose we could imagine a world in which the academic community and the practice community did not communicate, except to criticize each other. We could imagine a world in which the academic community goes about its research, maintaining appropriate distance from the nitty-gritty world of practice, publishing in academic journals, and criticizing the crime policies of the country. In this same world, we could envision a community of practitioners who go about their business, doing what they thought best, criticizing the aloofness of academe, and ignoring the findings of research. Yet we clearly do not want to live in this world—we want to see some interaction between research and practice (Travis 1998).

The director inadvertently painted an accurate picture of the current situation in Latin America. Academia and the world of public policy implementation in the arena of criminal justice in Latin America are not only separate, but tension and conflict characterize their interaction. In contrast to the fields of economics, health care, and education, the opposition and open confrontation between universities and research centers, on the one hand, and criminal justice organizations on the other (particularly the police) are historical and deep-rooted.

However, today's perverse reality has bred a growing discussion about the need for change. More than ever before, it is necessary now to build a bridge between policymakers and academic researchers. This is no easy task, inasmuch as government organizations regard researchers as people wholly alienated from real life. In the specific case of criminal justice, members of the police, public ministries, prosecutors, and judges believe that they have nothing to learn from academic researchers. On the other hand, researchers view the universe of applied research with misgivings, as a cheapening of their lofty activity. The establishment of mechanisms to interact with justice organizations may mean an unacceptable loss of autonomy for some researchers. In fact, this feeling ultimately obscures the fact that researchers often do not have much to say to agencies and organizations about practical matters.

There is little possibility of establishing effective urban crime control mechanisms or social assistance policies unless these regions are rescued and revitalized economically. But it is not just a matter of setting macroeconomic policy; rather, it is a question of supplying microinterventions involving public policies carried out by the city administration, the police, and the legal system. The examples of Bogotá, Cali, Medellín, and Diadema are illustrative. The legal system must institute conflict-mediating tools, which are important for cases unrelated to drug trafficking. City government ought to act in the treatment of drug users and in the implementation of cultural and occupational programs for youth. Integrated efforts to reduce crime and enhance public safety should involve joint actions among the police, community leaders, religious institutions, and businesses willing to employ youth from the area (Kennedy 1998). The real key to such interventions is to articulate actions among agencies that are completely distinct from each other and often compete among themselves.

Notes

1. Approaches rooted in social psychology and biology (such as neuroscience, and even genetics) have focused on individual characteristics as predisposing factors; thus, attention is paid to moods, learned social responses, perceptions of reward and punishment, violent sexual preferences, cognitive and communication skills, self-definition of identity, genetic traces, or the chronic use of medication.

2. Domestic violence is an area in which the impact of gender studies has been rather successful, judging from legislation changes in Latin America, the creation of special police units, and the existence of countless organizations offering crisis services—such as telephone hot lines, psychological and social welfare assistance, medical services, and the like (Larrain 1997).

3. This is not a unique approach to the problem of violence. The IDB uses it to deal with a comprehensive and multisectoral strategy targeting specific risk factors (IDB 1999d).

4. Three strikes is an extremely harsh sentencing policy. After a third incidence, the delinquent is sentenced to 25 years in prison, regardless of the seriousness of the offense.

5. This is a program with a methodology developed by the Center for Crime and Public Security Studies (CRISP), Federal University of Minas Gerais, that is being used by the government of Minas Gerais State.

6. This is similar to the strategy adopted in Cali in the DESEPAZ program (see below).

7. The technique used to identify these hot spots is the kernel density approach (*CrimeStat* Manual [Houston, TX: Ned Levine & Associates, 2001]).

8. The following report is based on Guerrero (1999).

References

Academia de Polícia Civil (ACADEPOL). 2000. *Relatório anual de atividades.* Delegacia de Crimes Contra a Vida. Belo Horizonte: Polícia Civil de Minas Gerais.

Ayres, Robert. 1998. *Crime and Violence as Development Issues in Latin American and the Caribbean.* Washington, DC: World Bank.

Batittuci, Eduardo. 1998. "Análise descritiva da criminalidade violenta no Brasil: O caso do homicídio em quatro regiões metropolitanas." *Anais do Grupo de Trabalho 21 do XXII Encontro da ANPOCS.* Caxambu, Minas Gerais, October.

Bayley, William C. 1984. "Poverty, Inequality, and City Homicide Rates: Some Not So Unexpected Findings." *Criminology* 22: 531–50.

Beato F., Claudio C. 1995. "Indexicalidade e literalidade nas descrições sociais." *Dados: Revista de Ciências Sociais* (IUPERJ) 38: 309–28.

———. 2000a. *Fontes de dados policiais em estudos criminológicos: Limites e potenciais.* Rio de Janeiro: Instituto de Pesquisa Econômica Aplicada/Universidade Candido Mendes.

———. 2000b. "Determining Factors of Criminality in Minas Gerais." *Brazilian Review of Social Sciences* (São Paulo) 1: 159–73.

———. 2001a. "Acción y estrategia de las organizaciones policiales." In *Policía, sociedad y estado: Modernización y reforma policial en America del Sul,* edited by Hugo Frühling, 39–56. Santiago: Centro de Estudios del Desarrollo.

———. 2001b. *Crime e políticas sociais na América Latina.* Belo Horizonte: CRISP-Centro de Estudos em Criminalidade e Segurança Pública, Universidade Federal de Minas Gerais.

Beato F., Claudio C., and Ilka A. Reis. 2000. "Desigualdade, desenvolvimento sócio-econômico e crime." In *Desigualdade e pobreza no Brasil,* edited by Ricardo Henriques, 385–405. Rio de Janeiro: Instituto de Pesquisa Econômica Aplicada.

Beato Filho, Cláudio Chaves, Renato Martins Assunção, Bráulio Figueiredo Alves da Silva, Frederico Couto Marinho, Ilka Afonso Reis, and Maria Cristina de Mattos Almeida. 2000. "Conglomerados de homicídios e o tráfico de drogas em Belo Horizonte, Minas Gerais, Brasil, de 1995 a 1999." *Cadernos de Saúde Pública* (Rio de Janeiro) 17, no. 5: 1163–71.

Beato F., Claudio C., Marcelo Ottoni, and Bráulio Figueiredo. 2001. *Atlas da criminalidade em Belo Horizonte.* Belo Horizonte, Minas Gerais: Centro de Estudos em Criminalidade e Segurança Pública, Universidade Federal de Minas Gerais.

Beato, Cláudio C., Mônica Viegas, and Betania T. Peixoto. 2004. "Crime, oportunidade e vitimização." *Revista Brasileira de Ciências Sociais* 19, no. 55: 73–89.

Beato, Cláudio, and Betania T. Peixoto. 2005. "Há nada certo. Políticas sociais, crimes e espaço urbano. In *Prevenção da Violência.*" Edited by João Trajano Sento-Sé. São Paulo: Civilização Brasileira.

Becker, Gary S. 1977. "Crime and Punishment." *Journal of Political Economy* 76, no. 2 (March/April): 169–217.

Blau, Judith R., and Peter M. Blau. 1982. "The Cost of Inequality: Metropolitan Structure and Violent Crime." *American Sociological Review* 47: 114–29.

Bursik, Robert J., Jr. 1986. "Ecological Stability and the Dynamics of Delinquency." *Crime and Justice* 8: 35–66.

Buvinic, Mayra, Andrew Morrison, and Michael Shifter. 1999. *Violence in Latin America and the Caribbean: A Framework for Action.* Working Paper. Washington, DC:

Inter-American Development Bank, Social Development Division, Sustainable Development Department.
Chaiken, J.M., and M.R. Chaiken. 1991. "Drugs and Predatory Crime." *Crime and Justice* 13: 203–40.
Chernick, Marc. 1999. "Changing Perceptions of Violence in Colombia and Implications for Policy." *Violence and Social Capital: Proceedings of the LCSES Seminar Series, 1997–98,* edited by Caroline Moser and Sarah Lister. Latin America and Caribbean Region, Sustainable Development Working Papers, No. 5. Washington, DC: World Bank.
Chiricos, Theodore. 1987. "Rates of Crime and Unemployment: An Analysis of Aggregate Research Evidence." *Social Problems* 34, no. 2 (April).
Clarke, Ronald V. 1966. "Approved School Boy Absconders and Corporal Punishment." *British Journal of Criminology* 6: 364–75.
———. 1983. "Situational Crime Prevention: Its Theoretical Basis and Practice." *Crime and Justice* 4: 225–56.
———, ed. 1997. *Situational Crime Prevention: Successful Case Studies.* 2nd ed. Guilderland, NY: Harrow and Heston.
Clarke, Ronald V., and Derek B. Cornish. 1985. "Modeling Offenders' Decisions: A Framework for Research and Policy." *Crime and Justice* 6: 147–86.
Cohen, Lawrence, and Marcus Felson. 1979. "Social Change and Crime Rate Trends: A Routine Approach." *American Sociological Review* 44: 588–608.
Coleman, James. 1990. *Foundations of Social Theory.* Cambridge, MA: Harvard University Press.
Collins, Randall. 1994. "Why the Social Sciences Won't become High-Consensus, Rapid-Discovery Science." *Sociological Forum* 9, no. 2.
Colvin, Mark, and John Pauly. 1983. "A Critique of Criminology: Toward an Integrated Structural Marxist Theory of Delinquency Production." *American Journal of Sociology* 89: 513–51.
Cook, Philip J. 1986. "The Demand and Supply of Criminal Opportunities." *Crime and Justice* 7: 1–28.
Cruz, José Miguel, Álvaro Trigueros Arguello, and Francisco Gonzáles. 1998. "The Social and Economic Factors Associated with Violent Crimes in San Salvador." In *Determinants of Crime Rates in Latin America and the World: An Empirical Assessment,* edited by Pablo Fajnzylber, Daniel Lederman, and Norman Loayza. Washington, DC: World Bank.
van Dijk, Jan J.M. 1997. "Towards Effective Public-Private Partnerships in Crime Control: Experiences in Netherlands." In *Business in Crime Prevention,* edited by Marcus Felson and Ronald V. Clarke. Monsey, NY: Criminal Justice Press.
Dunn, Willian N. 1981. *Public Policy Analysis.* Englewood Cliffs, NJ: Prentice-Hall.
Durkheim, Emile. 1978. *A divisão do trabalho social.* São Paulo: Abril Cultural.
Fajnzylber, Pablo, Daniel Lederman, and Norman Loayzar, eds. *Determinants of Crime Rates in Latin America and the World: An Empirical Assessment,* edited by Pablo Fajnzylber, Daniel Lederman, and Norman Loayza. Washington, DC: World Bank.
Felson, Marcus. 1994. *Crime and Everyday Life.* Thousand Oaks, CA: Pine Forge Press.
Fundação João Pinheiro (FJP). 1988. *Indicadores sociais de criminalidade.* Belo Horizonte, Minas Gerais: FJP, Ministério da Justiça, Programa Ruas em Paz.
Garofalo, James, and Maureen McLeod. 1986. *Improving the Effectiveness and Utilization*

of Neighborhood Watch Programs. Albany: National Institute of Justice from the State of New York at Albany, Hingenland Criminal Justice Research Center.

Glaeser, Edward L., Bruce Sacerdote, and José A. Scheinkman. 1996. "Crime and Social Interactions." *The Quarterly Journal of Economics,* May.

Goldstein, P.J. 1985. "The Drugs/Violence Nexus." *Journal of Drug Issues* 15, no. 4: 493–503.

Greenberg, David. 1985. "Age, Crime, and Social Explanation." *American Journal of Sociology* 89: 552–84.

Greenwood, Peter W., Karin E. Model, and Peter Rydell. 1996. *Diverting Children from a Life of Crime: Measuring Costs and Benefits.* Santa Monica, CA: Rand Corporation.

Guerrero, Rodrigo. 1999. *Programa desarrollo, seguridad y paz, DESEPAZ, de la Ciudad de Cali.* Programas Municipales para la Prevención y Atención de la Violencia. Rio de Janeiro: Banco Interamericano de Desarrollo, Prefeitura do Rio de Janeiro, 29–30 July.

Gunn, Phillip. 1998. "Uma geografia da violência na região metropolitana de S. Paulo nos anos 80." In *São Paulo sem medo: Um diagnóstico da violência urbana,* edited by P.S. Pinheiro. São Paulo: Garamond.

Hartigan, Pamela. 1999. "Building Community Networks to Address Violence: Pan American Health Organization's Ten Country Programs." In *Violence and Social Capital: Proceedings of the LCSES Seminar Series, 1997–98,* edited by Caroline Moser and Sarah Lister. Latin America and Caribbean Region, Sustainable Development Working Papers, No. 5. Washington, DC: World Bank.

Hindess, Barry. 1973. *The Use of Official Statistics in Sociology.* London: MacMillan.

Hunt, D.E. 1990. "Drugs and Consensual Crime: Drug Dealing and Prostitution." *Crime and Justice* 13: 159–202.

Instituto Apoyo. 1997. *La violencia intencional en Lima Metropolitana. Magnitud, impacto económico y evaluación de políticas de control, 1985–1995.* Prepared for The Magnitude of Violence in Latin America and the Caribbean: Dimensions and Control Policies project. Washington, DC: Inter-American Development Bank.

———. 1999. *Criminal Violence: Studies in Latin American Cities—The Case of Peru.* Latin America and Caribbean Region, Environmentally and Socially Sustainable Development Working Papers. Washington, DC: World Bank.

Inter-American Development Bank (IDB). 1999a. *Magnitude of Violence.* Technical Notes: Violence Prevention. Washington, DC: IDB, Sustainable Development Department, Social Development Division.

———. 1999b. *Economic and Social Consequences of Violence.* Technical Notes: Violence Prevention. Washington, DC: IDB, Sustainable Development Department, Social Development Division.

———. 1999c. *Domestic Violence against Women.* Technical Notes: Violence Prevention. Washington, DC: IDB, Sustainable Development Department, Social Development Division.

———. 1999d. *Control at the Municipal Level.* Technical Notes: Violence Prevention. Washington, DC: IDB, Sustainable Development Department, Social Development Division.

———. 1999e. *Combating Violence in the Americas: IDB Projects and Initiatives.* Washington, DC: IDB, Social Development Division, Sustainable Development Department.

———. 2001. *Inventário de programas municipales en prevención y atención de la violencia.* Washington, DC: IDB.

Jankowsky, M. Sanchez. 1991. *Islands in the Street: Gangs and American Urban Society.* Berkeley: University of California Press.

Johnson, B.D., T. Williams, Kojo A. Dei, and H. Sanabria. 1991. "Drug Abuse and the Inner City: Impact on Hard-Drug Users in the Community." *Crime and Justice* 13.

Kennedy, David. 1998. "Pulling Levers: Getting Deterrence Right." *National Institute of Justice Journal* July.

Kitsuse, J.I, and A.V. Cicourel. 1963. "A Note on the Uses of Official Statistics." *Social Problems* 11: 131–9.

Kraut, Robert E. 1976. "Deterrent and Definitional Influences on Shoplifting." *Social Problems* 23: 358–68.

Kubisch, Anne. 1999. "How Social Capital Is Defined and Operationalized in Social Policy and Antipoverty Programs in the United States." *Violence and Social Capital: Proceedings of the LCSES Seminar Series, 1997–98,* edited by Caroline Moser and Sarah Lister. Latin America and Caribbean Region, Sustainable Development Working Papers, No. 5. Washington, DC: World Bank.

Land, Kenneth C., Patricia L. McCall, and Lawrence E. Conhen. 1990. "Structural Covariates of Homicide Rates: Are There Any Invariances across Time and Social Space?" *American Sociological Review* 95: 922–63.

Land, Kenneth C., David Cantor, and Stephen T. Russell. 1995. "Unemployment and Crime Rate Fluctuations in the Post–World War II United States." In *Crime and Inequality,* edited by John Hagan. Stanford, CA: Stanford University Press.

Larrain, Soledad. 1997. *Curbing Domestic Violence: Two Decades of Action.* Washington, DC: World Bank.

Lederman, Daniel. 1999. *Crime in Argentina: A Preliminary Assessment.* Washington, DC: World Bank.

Lederman, Daniel, Norman Loayza, and Ana Maria Menéndez. 1999. *Violent Crime: Does Social Capital Matter?* Washington, DC: World Bank.

Londoño, Juan Luis 1998. "Epidemiologia económica de la violencia urbana." Presentation at Trigésima novena reunión anual de la Asamblea de Gobernadores del BID, Cartagena de Indias, 16–18 March.

Lynch, James. 1995. "Crime in International Perspective." In *Crime,* edited by James Q. Wilson and Joan Persilia. San Francisco: Institute for Contemporary Studies Press.

McGahey, Richard M. 1986. "Economic Conditions, Organizations, and Urban Crime." *Crime and Justice* 8: 231–71.

Merton, Robert K. 1968. *Sociologia: Teoria e estrutura.* São Paulo: Editora Mestre Jou.

Mexican Health Foundation (MHF). 1999. *Trends and Empirical Causes of Violent Crimes in Mexico.* Washington, DC: World Bank, October.

Moran, Ricardo, and Claudio de Moura Castro. 1997. *Street Children and the Inter-American Development Bank: Lessons from Brazil.* Washington, DC: Inter-American Development Bank, Social Development Division, Sustainable Development Department.

Moser, Caroline. 1996. *Confronting Crisis: A Summary of Household Responses to Poverty and Vulnerability in Four Poor Urban Communities.* Environmentally Sustainable Development Studies and Monographs Series No. 7. Washington, DC: World Bank.

Moser, Caroline, and Sarah Lister, eds.1999. *Violence and Social Capital: Proceedings of the LCSES Seminar Series, 1997–98.* Latin America and Caribbean Region, Sustainable Development Working Papers, No. 5. Washington, DC.

Moser, Caroline, and Elizabeth Shrader. 1999. *Criminalidade, violência e pobreza urbana na América Latina: Rumo a uma estrutura integrada.* LCSES Seminar Series. Washington, DC: World Bank.

Moser, Caroline, and Bernice van Bronkhorst. 1999. *Youth Violence in Latin America and the Caribbean: Costs, Causes, and Interventions.* LCR Sustainable Development Working Paper No. 3, Urban Peace Program Series. Washington, DC: World Bank.

Newman, Graeme, ed. 1999. *Global Report on Crime and Justice.* New York: United Nations Office for Drug Control and Crime Prevention; Oxford: Oxford University Press.

Newman, Graeme, Ronald V. Clarke, and S. Giora Shoham, eds. 1997. *Rational Choice and Situational Crime Prevention: Theoretical Foundations.* Aldershot, England: Dartmouth; Brookfield, VT: Ashgate.

Opp, Karl-Dieter. 1997. "Limited Rationality and Crime." In *Rational Choice and Situational Crime Prevention: Theoretical Foundations,* edited by Graeme Newman, Ronald V. Clarke, and S. Giora Shoham. Aldershot, England: Dartmouth; Brookfield, VT: Ashgate.

Piquet Carneiro, Leandro. 1999. *Determinantes do crime na América Latina: Rio de Janeiro e São Paulo.* Washington, DC: World Bank.

Posada, Alejandro Reyes. 1999. "Rural Violence in Colombia." In *Violence and Social Capital: Proceedings of the LCSES Seminar Series, 1997–98,* edited by Caroline Moser and Sarah Lister. Latin America and Caribbean Region, Sustainable Development Working Papers, No. 5. Washington, DC.

Quinney, Richard. 1980. "O controle do crime na sociedade capitalista: Uma filosofia crítica da ordem legal." In *Criminologia crítica,* edited by Ian Taylor, Paul Walton, and Jock Young, 221–49. Rio de Janeiro: Ed. Graal.

Reiss, Albert. 1986. "Why Are Communities Important in Understanding Crime?" *Crime and Justice* 8: 1–34.

Rondon, Vinicius Velasco. 2002. "Custos da criminalidade em Belo Horizonte." Master's thesis, Universidade Federal de Minas Gerais.

Sampson, Robert. 2003. "Urban Disorder, Crime, and Collective Efficacy." Paper presented at the Seminário Seguridad Ciudadana, Bogotá, Colombia, April.

Sanjuan, Ana María. 1999. *Notas técnicas sobre la violencia.* Washington, DC: Inter-American Development Bank.

Schuerman, Leo, and Solomon Kobrin. 1986. "Community Careers in Crime." *Crime and Justice* 8: 67–100.

Sherman, Lawrence W., and Richard A. Berk. 1984. "The Specific Deterrent Effects of Arrests for Domestic Assault." *American Sociological Review* 84: 261–72.

Sherman, Lawrence, Denise Gottfredson, Doris MacKenzie, John Eck, Peter Reuter, and Shawn Bushway. 1997. *Preventing Crime: What Works, What Doesn't, What's Promising. A Report to the United States Congress.* Washington, DC: National Institute of Justice.

Simon, Herbert A. 1982. *Models of Bounded Rationality.* Cambridge, MA: MIT Press.

Skogan, Wesley G. 1987. "Community Organizations and Crime." *Crime and Justice* 10: 39–78.

Soares, Gláucio Ary Dillon. 1999. *Self-Reported Arrests of Streetchildren in Brasília.* Brasilia: Universidade de Brasília.

Stark, Rodney. 1987. "Deviant Places: A Theory of the Ecology of Crime." *Criminology* 25, no. 4: 893–909.

Sykes, Gresham M., and David Matza. 1993. "Techniques of Neutralization: A Theory of Delinquency." In *Social Deviance: Reading in Theory and Research,* edited by Henry M. Pontell, 180–4. Englewood Cliffs, NJ: Prentice-Hall.
Travis, Jeremy. 1998. "Plenary Presentation to the American Society of Criminology." U.S. Department of Justice. http://www.ojp.usdoj.gov/nij/speeches/asc.htm.
Welsh, Brandon C., David P. Farrington, and Lawrence W. Sherman, eds. 2001. *Costs and Benefits of Preventing Crime.* Boulder, CO: Westview Press.
World Bank. 1997. *Crime and Violence as Development Issues in Latin America and the Caribbean.* Washington, DC: World Bank.
Wilson, James Q. 1983. *Thinking about Crime.* New York: Vintage Books, Random House.
Zaluar, Alba. 1984. *Condomínio do diabo.* Rio de Janeiro: Ed. Revan/Universidade Federal de Rio de Janeiro.
———. 1997. "Gangues, galeras e quadrilhas: Globalização, juventude e violência." In *Galeras cariocas: Territórios de conflitos e encontros culturais,* edited by H. Vianna. Rio de Janeiro: Editora Universidade Federal de Rio de Janeiro.

Chapter 5

Measuring the Costs of Crime and Violence as an Input to Public Policy: Evidence from Mexico City

Graciela Teruel, Renata Villoro, Andrew Morrison, and James K. Hammit

Introduction

Crime and violence have surged in many countries in Latin America in recent years, placing Latin America in the unenviable position of being classified as the world's second most violent region after sub-Saharan Africa (Buvinic et al. 1999). Violence and crime are clearly center stage on the public policy agenda of the region, as country after country struggles to enact public policies for their control and prevention.

This chapter presents estimates of the socioeconomic cost of violence for Mexico City using a methodology that has not been previously used to estimate these costs—a hedonic housing model. It also suggests coupling this model with contingent valuation analysis, as both methodologies allow the estimation of social costs with much greater precision than others that have been used to date.

Before entering into the details of the hedonic and contingent valuation methodologies, and before justifying the argument that they provide greater precision, a more basic question must be addressed: Why is it useful to estimate the socioeconomic costs of violence at all? First, estimating the costs of violence to society provides a measure of the problem's importance that is easily understood both by policymakers and the general public. Putting a monetary figure on the losses generated by violence allows for interesting counterfactual exercises, such as asking, "How much faster would have been the growth of GDP in the absence of violence?" or "If homicide rates were reduced to their historical levels of ten years ago, how much would GDP rise?" Second, estimates of the costs of violence allow policymakers to compare the costs generated by violence with those generated by other social ills. Other things being equal, those ills generating higher social costs will be deserving of having more resources allocated to their prevention.

In the near future when data are available, violence researchers will be able to calculate the social costs of different types of violence, such as murder, rape, armed robbery, and so on. Much like public health experts use disability-adjusted life years lost as a metric to inform the allocation of health system resources among different diseases, information on the social costs associated with different types of violence will be able to be used to help orient expenditures in violence prevention.

The next section describes the methodologies available to estimate the social costs of violence, including the accounting methodology, disability-adjusted life year calculations, and two approaches to measuring willingness to pay. The third section presents empirical results from one of the willingness-to-pay approaches—a hedonic housing model—estimated for Mexico City, and the fourth section offers some conclusions and suggestions for future research on the socioeconomic costs of violence.

Methodological Issues

Estimating the socioeconomic cost generated by various social ills would be a simple exercise if there were markets in which these ills—pollution, traffic congestion, and crime, for example—were bought and sold; if this were the case, one could simply use the market price as a measure of the value that society attaches to reducing a particular ill. In the absence of such markets, researchers are obliged to use other means to estimate the damages to society of nonmarket "bads."[1] In the case of violent crime, three types of methodologies are available to measure its cost to society: an accounting methodology, disability-adjusted life year calculations, and estimates of willingness to pay. This last category is subdivided into what economists term "stated preference" approaches and "revealed preference" approaches. Stated preference means that individuals are queried directly about the amount that they are willing to pay to avoid a nonmarket bad, or what is the minimum amount they are willing to accept to continue to live with the bad; contingent valuation analysis is the most popular form of stated preference methodology. Revealed preference approaches, on the other hand, attempt to extract willingness-to-pay estimates from the demand for other goods into which willingness to pay for the nonmarket good in question may be capitalized; hedonic housing and land models are the most popular form of revealed preference methodology for nonmarket bads.

The Accounting Methodology

The vast majority of the authors that have measured the social costs that arise from crime and violence have used an accounting methodology (Bourguignon 1998; Buvinic et al. 1999; Cohen et al. 1996; Londoño and Guerrero 1999; Mexican Health Foundation 1999; Moser 1999; Villoro and Teruel 2000). This methodology involves summing the monetary and nonmonetary losses that are attributable to the various categories of costs suffered by individuals and/or countries as a whole.[2] The resulting figure is then presented either as an absolute amount or is compared to aggregate indicators, such as GDP or governmental social expenditure. This methodology provides insight on the relative magnitude of the costs that arise from the different crime categories. An additional advantage of this methodology is that it requires only partial information: if data are missing on some category of costs, a partial estimate can be provided using data for those categories for which information is available (Buvinic and Morrison 1999).

Emerging evidence suggests that such costs to Latin America's economies are substantial. A series of six country studies commissioned by the Inter-American Development Bank estimated that national expenditures on security (including spending by governments, individuals, and private firms) ranged from 1.4 to 6.6 percent of gross domestic product (GDP). Health losses, including both expenditures on health systems as a result of violence and the estimated value of healthy life years lost to violence, range from 0.3 to 5 percent of GDP (Londoño et al. 2000); see Table 5.1 for the list of security and health costs by country.

The accounting method, however, has some important disadvantages. It is invariably open to the criticism that some important category of cost has been omitted; furthermore, any categorization of costs is essentially arbitrary, and alternative classifications can always be suggested. Moreover, as the vast majority of the information that is used in this approach comes from official records of institutions such as the police, judiciary, and medical institutions, weak statistical systems are reflected in inaccurate estimates of costs (Mexican Health Foundation and World Bank 1999). Perhaps the greatest weakness of the accounting methodology is that the estimates it

Table 5.1. Economic costs of violence using an accounting framework (percent of GDP)

Cost category	El Salvador	Colombia	Venezuela	Brazil	Peru	Mexico
Security costs	4.9	6.4	6.6	1.4	1.4	3.6
Health costs	4.3	5.0	0.3	1.9	1.5	1.3

Source: Londoño et al. (2000).

generates are not a particularly useful tool to help allocate government resources for crime prevention and control. The reason is obvious: although the methodology captures current spending—both governmental and private—on crime control and restorative measures, these amounts may be an imperfect measure of the value to citizens of reductions in crime. Put more succinctly: the current allocation of crime prevention, control, and restorative resources may be far from optimal.

Disability-Adjusted Life Year Calculations

Burden-of-disease studies, which estimate the healthy life years lost to different types of injuries and disease, have become a standard tool for measuring the socioeconomic cost of different afflictions. Perhaps the most widely accepted metric is the disability-adjusted life year (DALY). The DALY is a measure of time lived with a disability and time lost due to premature mortality. In order to operationalize DALY calculations, researchers must choose a standard life expectancy for men and for women; decide whether to value time lived at different ages equally, or whether to assign higher weights to the more productive, middle-aged years; decide whether and, if so, how much to discount future loss of life or disability; and determine the severity of various disabilities and the amount of time that one is afflicted with these disabilities. Time lived in different classes of disability is multiplied by a weight representing the severity of the disability, in order to obtain a measure comparable to years lost due to premature mortality (Murray and Lopez 1994).

In their DALY calculations, Murray and Lopez (1994) opted for assigning a higher weight to individuals in peak earning years; they used a discount rate of 3 percent against future disability or loss of life. In addition, they developed a categorization that contains six classes of disability, ranging in severity from limited ability to perform at least one activity in one of the areas of recreation, education, procreation, or occupation to needing assistance with daily living activities, such as eating or using the toilet. Higher weights are assigned to more severe classes of disability.

Recent estimates by the World Health Organization (2000) using this methodology document that homicide and violence worldwide account for more loss of healthy life than lung cancer, breast cancer, leukemia, or asthma. Violence against women—including domestic violence and rape—accounts for more than 5 percent of the healthy life years lost by women of reproductive age in developing countries (Heise et al. 1994).

Both DALYs and healthy life years (YHLs) lost are excellent shorthand measures of the health impacts of violence. They both include health losses not only to mortality, but also to injury and disability. Use of these measures makes a strong case that violence is a public health problem, and allows specialists to compare the health impacts of violence with those of other public health concerns. Thus, they are a very valuable aid in setting public health priorities based on hard data rather than on subjective perceptions. Perhaps the only drawback to these two measures is that they do not provide guidance as to the optimal level of interventions to be undertaken; while diseases and social ills that produce the highest loss of DALYs or YHLs presumably should receive priority attention, the cost of reducing loss of healthy life for each ill is not taken into account. If, for example, the ill that produces the largest loss of healthy life is particularly intractable, then policymakers may be ill-advised, at least in the short run, to devote scarce resources to attempts to prevent it.

Willingness-to-Pay Methodologies

Cost-benefit analysis (CBA) is the standard technique that economists use to decide whether to undertake a public policy or public investment. In CBA, the costs should be measured as opportunity costs and the benefits should be measured as the maximum willingness to pay (WTP) for the project or the maximum willingness to accept for enduring a particular loss or damage.

The appropriateness of using a methodology that measures benefits in terms of the WTP has been widely discussed. The main criticism arises from the fact that results might be biased by and correlated with the ability to pay of individuals, thus leading to equity problems in the design of public policies (Donaldson 1990; Williams 1990). However, most authors agree that the dependence of WTP on income level is not a major problem, because one can always either hold constant variables like income or use "equity" weights assigned to the benefits of persons with different incomes (Johannesson and Jonsson 1990; Pearce and Nash 1981).[3]

The most commonly used methods to measure willingness to pay are hedonic models and contingent valuation analysis, both of which attempt to measure the WTP of individuals for a given benefit.

Hedonic Models

The hedonic approach is the most frequently used revealed preference approach to gauge WTP for nonmarket goods. It allows direct identification of WTP through its estimation from market data. Therefore, one must identify a market in which implicit valuations of crime reductions may be found in order to infer the implicit value of those characteristics that are similar to a reduction in the rate of crime of a commodity that is actually sold in a market (Sheppard 1999). Housing and land markets are two such markets frequently analyzed (Cheshire and Sheppard 1995, 1998; Palmquist 1984; Rocha-Macedo 1998; Sheppard 1999; Witte et al. 1979). The hedonic approach looks at a house or a parcel of land as a bundle of characteristics (number of square feet or meters, number of bedrooms, type of materials used in construction, distance to city center, neighborhood characteristics, etc.), and it is the "hedonic value" of each one of those characteristics that is estimated. The hedonic value of a particular attribute or characteristic represents the marginal WTP for an extra unit of the attribute or characteristic. It is important to point out that the hedonic approach assumes that any negative externality present in the neighborhood (e.g., air pollution, traffic congestion, high crime rate) will affect property prices adversely, and any positive externality (e.g., good schools) will affect them positively.

In environmental economics, hedonic models have been used to estimate the value that society places on particular environmental issues or programs, such as pollution reduction or the preservation of a particular animal or plant species. Hedonic models have also proved useful in health economics, where the value of life can be inferred from hedonic functions of the wage in the labor market, using wages as the dependent variable and the risk of death as one of the characteristics on which wage depends (Jones-Lee et al. 1985). In this case an increase in the negative externality (risk of death) is expected to have a positive impact on the wage level, and the increase in wages resulting from an increase in the risk of death is interpreted as the "willingness to accept" increased risk of death in exchange for higher wages.

Apart from several technical issues,[4] the main disadvantage of the hedonic method is that it is often difficult to find an appropriate surrogate market. Yet, in the case of crime, the housing market seems appropriate enough, since it is reasonable to believe that neighborhood crime rates will be reflected in housing prices. By estimating the impact of crime and violence on housing prices, this methodology allows us to assess the willingness to pay of individuals to live in less dangerous neighborhoods. In a hedonic study of land prices in metropolitan areas of the United States, for example, Clark and Cosgrove (1990) found that a doubling of the homicide rate was associated with a reduction of 12.5 percent in the per-acre price of land. Although hedonic housing studies have been done for several Latin American cities (Aryeetey-Attoh 1992; Figueroa and Lever 1992; Rocha-Macedo 1998; Stumpf Gonzalez and Torres Formoso 1997), these studies do not include crime and violence among the neighborhood characteristics analyzed.

Contingent Valuation Methodology

Contingent valuation (CV) is the most popular type of "stated preference" method used to elicit values or preferences. CV relies on asking survey respondents what choices they would make in a hypothetical setting and interpreting their answers under the assumption that the choices they report are the ones they prefer most. CV has been used to value changes in health risks associated with environmental pollution, transportation, food, and medical technologies (Hammitt and Graham 1999). It has also been used to value changes in environmental quality that do not affect health directly (such as visibility), as well as many other goods (Mitchell and Carson 1989).

CV is extremely flexible, as individuals can be questioned about how they would choose in a great variety of hypothetical situations. The hypothetical nature of the choice is also the greatest weakness of the method. Since survey respondents may be unfamiliar and inexperienced with the hypothetical choices they are offered, may have limited incentive to carefully consider the choices, or may respond to other aspects of the survey setting unrelated to their preference for the hypothetical choices, such as a desire to provide an answer that will please the interviewer, CV results are often viewed as less persuasive than revealed preference estimates.

Under CV, survey respondents are presented with a clearly defined choice between two alternatives differing in the attribute to be valued (such as risk of homicide), the method by which the change in the attribute is to be produced (such as a police retraining program), the monetary cost to the individual, and the form in which the cost would be paid (such as higher taxes). Although the choice is hypothetical, it is recommended that it be described as realistically as possible both because WTP may depend on details of the good and in order to encourage respondents to take the choice seriously (Mitchell and Carson 1989). A concern about CV is that results can be sensitive to apparently inessential aspects of the choice (e.g., question ordering and the format in which numerical risks are presented) but insensitive to essential aspects, such as the quantity of the good to be valued (Baron 1997; Carson and Mitchell 1995; Covey et al. 1998; Diamond and Hausman 1994; Frederick and Fischhoff 1998; Hanemann 1994).

Several forms of CV questions have been employed, including open-ended and dichotomous choice. In an open-ended question, the respondent is asked, "What is the most that you would be willing to pay?" (to obtain the good). This question has the virtue of providing a single-valued answer for each respondent, but one that may be biased downward because the question suggests a bargaining process in which people are conditioned not to state their maximum willingness to pay.[5]

In a dichotomous-choice question, the monetary cost of the good to the respondent is specified and he is asked whether he would or would not purchase the good (or vote in favor of a referendum to have the government provide it). This question should yield an unbiased response, but it provides only a single bound on the value of the good to the individual. To improve the efficiency of this method, it is conventional to ask a second, follow-up question where the stated cost is higher than the original cost if the respondent indicates that he would purchase the good, and lower if the respondent indicates he would not (Hanemann et al. 1991).[6]

Hedonic Housing Estimates of the Value of Crime Prevention in Mexico City

Crime Trends in Mexico City

The Mexico City Metropolitan Area (MCMA) includes the Federal District (D.F.), which is formed by sixteen political counties (*delegaciones*), and eighteen municipalities pertaining to the Estado de México. In 2000, the population in the metropolitan area reached almost seventeen million inhabitants (INEGI 2000). Counties in the MCMA can be classified in three large groups according to their crime frequency. High crime incidence counties, with a maximum of 4,500 crimes per 100,000 inhabitants, are located in the downtown area, with high population density and economic activity. Medium crime incidence counties, with between 1,200 and 2,000 crimes per 100,000 inhabitants, tend to have slow population growth and middle-class populations. Low crime incidence counties, with less than 1,200 crimes per 100,000 inhabitants, are located in semirural areas, with a low population growth and low levels of economic activity.

Crime began to become an issue of serious concern in the MCMA in the 1990s. From 1990 to 1994, criminal activities rose 40 percent. In 1995 alone, the crime increased another 45 percent; reported crimes rose from 180,000 in 1994 to 252,000 in 1995 (Mexican Health Foundation and World Bank 1999). According to official statistics (INEGI 1997), homicide rates increased 75 percent for men (predominantly concentrated among the young) and 67 percent for women in Mexico City between the early 1980s and the mid-1990s.

The advantage of using homicide rates as a proxy of general crime is that homicides tend to be reported to the authorities, unlike other types of crime. Underreporting is especially severe in the case of nonviolent crime; according to a study conducted by the municipal government in 1995, only 44 percent of nonviolent crimes were reported (PGJDF 1995). Some studies put the percentage even lower: a recent study by the Mexican Heath Foundation and the World Bank (1999) estimates that only 17 percent of victims of nonviolent crimes reported them to the authorities.

The Hedonic Methodology

The extent to which crime and violence rates experienced by a population can be treated as one of the characteristics that determine the price of housing is an empirical question. We will estimate a hedonic pricing model that includes standard characteristics in addition to a variable that approximates crime and violence in Mexico's metropolitan area. The technical details of the hedonic estimation are presented in the Appendix. Here we note only that we use a semilogarithmic functional form for the regression equation because this is the form that best fits the data.

Data Sources

We use information from the third quarter of the 1996 Encuesta Nacional de Ingreso–Gasto de los Hogares (ENIGH), a consumer expenditure survey collected from August to November by the Mexican National Institute of Statistics, Geography, and Informatics (INEGI).[7] The sample size is 14,265 households; the survey is nationally representative when properly weighted with inflation factors. This survey has information on personal characteristics of household members, total household and individual labor and nonlabor income, household monetary expenditures (commodities that were actually purchased), household nonmonetary expenditures (commodities received or paid as in-kind, gifts, and consumption of home-produced goods), and dwelling characteristics. For the present study we restrict the sample to all households in the MCMA,[8] which contains 1,686 households.

The ENIGH survey contains information on the amount spent on rent for those households who are renting, or on mortgage payments for those households that are paying a home mortgage. In addition, it contains an imputed rental amount for all households that either already own the house or received the house as a payment or benefit, and for those households that are borrowing the house payment from a relative or friend. Dwelling characteristics, such as number of rooms, number of bedrooms, materials used in floors, walls and ceilings, availability and type of sewerage and water connection, availability of electricity and telephone service, and treatment of garbage, are the most important characteristics included in the survey.

Unfortunately, ENIGH does not contain information about the individual's or household's perception of crime. We therefore employ aggregate statistics from official databases on homicides collected by INEGI (1997) to impute a homicide rate for the county (*delegación*) in which a dwelling is located. This homicide rate is used as a proxy variable for the level of crime, violence, and insecurity at the household level. The county level is the smallest level of disaggregation available.

From additional official data published by INEGI, we obtained general characteristics about the infrastructure of the counties, such as population density, schooling supply, green areas, number of kilometers of road, and employment rates, which are among the most important locational amenities. Unfortunately, these are only available for the Federal District and not for all of the MCMA. The number of observations for this subsample is 834 households, in sixteen counties. The definitions of the variables can be found in Table 5.2; descriptive statistics appear in Table 5.3.

Estimation Results

Column 1 of Table 5.4 presents the results of the simplest hedonic specification of the price-attribute relationship, with only dwelling characteristics included. For the MCMA, the number of rooms, the number of bathrooms,

Table 5.2. Variable definitions

Variable	Definition
Rent	Actual or imputed rent
Number of rooms	Number of rooms inside the dwelling
Wall material	Whether the wall material is cement block (as opposed to a more rustic material)
Ceiling material	Whether the ceiling material is concrete
Floor material	Whether the floor material is cement or mosaic
Indoor plumbing	Whether municipal water supply/treatment system supplies water
Bathrooms	Number of bathrooms
Sewage connection	Whether the household has a connected sewage system
Garbage service	Availability of garbage collection system
Electricity	Whether the household has electricity
Telephone	Whether there is a telephone line inside the dwelling
Homicide rate	Number of homicides per 100,000 residents in county
Literacy rate	Percentage of residents that are literate in county
Unemployment rate	Percentage of residents unemployed in county
Green area	Square meters of green space per capita in county
Population density	Population density per square kilometer in county

availability of refuse removal (garbage service), and connections to electrical and telephone service all increase the rent associated with a dwelling.

The second column adds the county homicide rate for all counties in the MCMA (the sixteen counties of the Federal District plus nine surrounding counties). Although the homicide rate has the anticipated negative sign, the coefficient is not statistically significant.[9]

Finally, the third column adds variables that refer to the infrastructure and amenities available in the counties, in an attempt to control for other county-level factors that might influence housing rents. In this regression, the sample is restricted only to the Federal District due to data availability problems.[10] In order to correct for the biased standard errors on the variables measured at the county level, we ran a cluster analysis at the county level. The results of the impact of crime on the rental price of housing stand out in this specification. Again, the sign of the coefficient observed is as expected, and this time it is significantly different from zero.

In general, the estimates of the standard model (in column 1) are robust to the changes in specification. The number of rooms in the house, the number of bathrooms, availability of electricity, and access to telephone services are statistically significant determinants of housing rents in all formulations, and their coefficients retain the same approximate magnitudes.

Table 5.3. Descriptive statistics

	Mean	Standard Deviation
Rent (1996 pesos)*	120,666.80	2,777,856.40
Imputed rent value (1996 pesos)*	375.38	2,776.53
Number of rooms	3.22	1.55
Wall material	0.98	0.16
Ceiling material	0.82	0.38
Floor material	0.98	0.14
Piped-in/running water	0.95	0.21
Bathrooms	0.91	0.29
Sewerage connection	0.92	0.28
Garbage service	0.99	0.10
Electricity	0.996	0.06
Telephone	0.47	0.50
Homicide rate	21.39	10.87
Literacy rate	96.87	0.76
Primary school enrollment	0.26	0.21
Secondary school enrollment (7th to 9th grade)	0.13	0.11
High school enrollment (10th to 12th grade)	0.09	0.1
Primary school teachers (working in schools in neighborhood)	0.006	0.009
Secondary school teachers (working in schools in neighborhood)	0.006	0.004
High school teachers	0.006	0.005
Unemployment rate	7.65	6.07
Green area	6.6	4.54
Population density	108.78	52.76
Number of observations	1,686	

Sources: Authors' calculations using ENIGH (1996); official county-level statistics from INEGI.
* The average peso/dollar exchange rate in 1996 was 8 pesos/dollar.

The coefficient on sewerage connection is consistently of the wrong sign in all specifications.

The coefficients reported in Table 5.4 are not particularly helpful in terms of gauging the importance of the different explanatory variables. In order to gauge the relative importance of the different determinants of housing rents, we calculate the elasticities of housing rents with respect to all the explanatory variables that have statistically significant coefficients. Elasticity is the percentage increase or decrease in housing rents that will arise from a 1-percent change in a given explanatory variable. Thus, the higher the elasticity with respect to an explanatory variable, the more responsive are housing rents to a 1-percent change in this variable. Positive elasticities

Table 5.4. Hedonic estimates of price-attribute relationship

	Basic Specification	+Crime	+Infrastructure
Number of rooms	0.46	0.46	0.46
	(0.041)	(0.040)	(0.072)
Wall material	0.26	0.26	−0.77
	(0.320)	(0.330)	(0.430)
Ceiling material	−0.14	−0.14	0.12
	(0.150)	(0.160)	(0.190)
Floor material	−0.02	−0.02	−0.61
	(0.340)	(0.340)	(0.720)
Indoor plumbing	−0.44	−0.44	−0.69
	(0.290)	(0.300)	(0.370)
Bathrooms	0.60	0.60	1.14
	(0.250)	(0.250)	(0.380)
Sewer connection	−0.80	−0.81	−0.74
	(0.260)	(0.260)	(0.430)
Garbage service	0.15	0.15	1.31
	(0.570)	(0.570)	(0.340)
Electricity	3.16	3.17	2.82
	(0.580)	(0.580)	(0.390)
Telephone	0.67	0.68	0.73
	(0.130)	(0.120)	(0.170)
Homicide rate		−0.0003	−0.02
		(0.0020)	(0.003)
Literacy rate			−0.02
			0.003
Primary school enrollment			0.0
			(0.0)
Primary school teachers			−0.0001
			(0.0)
Secondary school enrollment			0.0010
			(0.0003)
Secondary school teachers			—0.0
			(0.00003)
High school enrollment			0.0020
			(0.0010)
High school teachers			−0.0001
			(0.00002)
Unemployment rate			0.0005
			(0.0001)
Green areas			−0.11
			(0.0200)
Population density			−0.0700
			(0.0200)
			−0.0230
			(0.0030)
Number of observations	1,681	1,681	834
Clusters			13

Table 5.5. Computed elasticities of housing rents vis-à-vis explanatory variables

Variable*	Computed Elasticity
Number of rooms	1.48
Bathrooms	1.04
Garbage	1.30
Electricity	2.81
Telephone	0.34
Homicide rate	–0.42
Literacy rate	0
Primary school enrollment	0
High school enrollment	0
High school teachers	0
Unemployment rate	–0.84
Green areas	–0.46
Population density	–2.50

*Elasticities are presented only if the coefficient on the variable in question is statistically significant (at the 0.05 level). The computations are based on the coefficients from column 3 of Table 5.4.

mean that housing rents increase, while negative elasticities mean that rents decrease.

Elasticities are reported in Table 5.5. A doubling of the homicide rate in a county is associated, on average, with a 42 percent decline in housing rents. A doubling of the county unemployment rate produces an even larger drop in housing rents (84 percent), while a doubling of population density produces a huge 250 percent reduction in housing rents.[11] Note that the county unemployment rate refers to the rate of residents living in that county; these residents may well work in other counties. The bottom line is that people seem willing to pay a significant amount of money to live in safer neighborhoods, but safety is not the only concern. People would also like to live in neighborhoods characterized by low unemployment rates and low population density.[12]

Conclusions

The introduction outlined the rationale for studies that can identify willingness to pay for crime and violence reduction. The primary justification for such studies is that they provide policymakers a convenient metric with which to gauge the importance to the citizenry of crime reduction. In the case of the Federal District of Mexico City, a doubling of homicide rates is associated with a 42 percent decline in housing rents. Put another way, residents would be willing to pay more than 20 percent higher rents in order to live in neighborhoods in which homicide rates were lowered by 50 percent. Personal safety is not a market good, but it is a public good for which citizens of the Federal District are willing to pay.

Further research on the willingness to pay for crime reduction should advance in two directions. First, it is important to distinguish between the willingness to pay for reductions in different types of crime. Homicide is clearly one of the most serious—if not the most serious—crime, and the willingness to pay to reduce homicide rates presumably exceeds the WTP to reduce other crimes. This hypothesis should be confirmed by including county-level data for other types of crimes. This is an important policy question, because policies and interventions should be targeted at reducing those forms of crime that citizens deem most important, as measured by their WTP. Important crimes for which WTP should be calculated include rape, armed robbery, burglary, and auto theft. Neighborhood-level data on these other crimes are increasingly available in Mexico and other countries as police forces begin to use geographic information systems to produce hot-spot maps of crime; these new data systems have the capability of providing rich new data sets to researchers—assuming that police forces are willing to make these data available.

A second direction in which WTP work should proceed is in identifying the mechanisms that the citizenry believes capable of delivering violence prevention or control services. Here, contingent valuation analysis should be the analytical tool employed. A quick example will illustrate this point. In a CV analysis, citizens can be queried about their WTP for a program that delivers a 50-percent reduction in homicide rates. But their WTP will presumably depend on how likely they think the program is to succeed, and their views about probable success are very likely to be influenced by the capabilities and reputations of the institutions undertaking the program. Indeed, in a pilot test of a CV instrument to measure willingness to pay for crime reduction in Mexico City, respondents expressed great skepticism about any measures that relied on the police as an implementing agency. Thus, CV analysis can be used to identify the service delivery mechanisms (for a given outcome) to which the citizenry is most willing to devote scarce resources.

The hedonic methodology used in this paper is not universally applicable. Its use for any given country depends on the existence of high-quality data on housing prices or rents and housing characteristics, as well as data on neighborhood-level amenities and disamenities. Such rich data sets, obviously, are not available in all countries. In particular, many Central American countries do not have regular systems of street addresses—which makes the use of application of hedonic models extremely difficult, since it is difficult to spatially locate houses and associate houses' locations with neighborhood characteristics. For countries with the rich data required for this analysis, however, the hedonic approach permits analysts to estimate the willingness to pay for crime reduction and—if neighborhood-level data on various types of crime exist—establish which types of crime should be public policy priorities.

Appendix: Details of Hedonic Price Estimation

Hedonic studies have used linear, semilog, or double-log functional forms. The choice of functional form is essentially an empirical issue, since any one of these specifications allows for straightforward interpretation of the coefficients (Cheshire and Sheppard 1995, 1998; Cropper et al. 1995). Here we use the Box-Cox transformation to explore different functional forms. The Box-Cox transformation provides the most flexible form and has been widely used in hedonic studies since a linear functional form may be faced with errors not distributed normally. We then select the best fit to estimate the price-attribute relationship.

The results from the Box-Cox estimation are presented in Tables 5.A1 to 5.A3. Figures 5.A1 to 5.A3 present the results graphically. Table 5.A1 (Figure 5.A1) exhibits the results from a hedonic model that includes standard variables such as dwelling characteristics. The variables that were used in this estimation are the following: number of rooms, whether there is a separate kitchen in the house, controls for different materials used in the walls, ceilings and floors of the house, controls for the different types of sewage system, whether the house has access to telephone service, types of water availability, number of bathrooms and/or types, disposition of garbage, and whether the household has access to electricity. Results from this regression suggest a semilog functional form. In addition, we tried two more estimations, the first of which (Table 5.A2 and Figure 5.A2) includes, in addition to the previous dwelling characteristics, the crime variable. The third regression (Table 5.A3 and Figure 5.A3) includes variables that measure the infrastructure of the county. Examples of the latter are number of green areas in the county; degree of schooling in the county; degree of literacy; number of students in primary, secondary, and high school; teacher/pupil ratios; kilometers of road constructed; and employment rates. The semilog functional form is suggested in all cases and is very robust.

Following Rocha-Macedo (1998), the hedonic model we estimate is

$$\frac{P^\lambda - 1}{\lambda} = \alpha + \sum_{i=1}^{m} \beta_i \left(\frac{Z_i^\theta}{\theta} \right) + u \tag{1}$$

where:
P = rental price or imputed value of housing
Z = vector of housing characteristics
u = vector of error terms
α, β_i = parameters to be estimated
λ, θ = parameters to be estimated used in the Box-Cox transformation

The Box-Cox transformation represents a family of transformations and embeds the three most used in hedonic analysis:

$$y^{(\lambda)} = \begin{cases} y - 1 & if\ \lambda = 1 \\ \ln(y) & if\ \lambda = 0 \\ 1 - \frac{1}{y} & if\ \lambda = -1 \end{cases}$$

Once the parameters of the Box-Cox transform are estimated, the unobserved marginal price of the ith characteristic can be estimated as:

$$P_i = \delta P / \delta Z_i$$

$$\frac{\delta P}{\delta Z_i} = \beta_i Z_i^{(\theta - 1)} \left[(1 + \lambda \alpha) + \lambda \sum_i \beta_i \frac{(Z_i^\theta) - 1}{\theta} \right] \frac{1}{\lambda}$$

$$\frac{\delta P}{\delta Z_i} = \beta_i Z_i^{(\theta - 1)} P^{(1-\lambda)}$$

λ and θ may take different values. If $\lambda = 1$ and $\theta = 1$, the result is the linear hedonic equation, which shows coefficients with implicit marginal characteristic price. For other values of these parameters, the estimated marginal price of the attributes can be calculated either using the mean, median, or any other value of the distribution of the P_is.

We use maximum likelihood estimation in the Box-Cox transformation and ordinary least squares with correction for clustering and heteroscedasticity in the estimation of the price-characteristics relationship.

Table 5.A1. "Specification results," Box-Cox transformation

Rent (all)
Number of rooms
Kitchen
Wall material
Ceiling material
Floor material
Sewage connection
Telephone
Indoor plumbing
Bathrooms
Disposition of garbage
Electricity
L = −1   Pr>chi2=0.0000
L = 0   Pr>chi2=0.3427
L = 1   Pr>chi2=0.0000

Source: Authors' calculations using ENIGH (1996).

Figure 5.A1. Box-Cox transformation

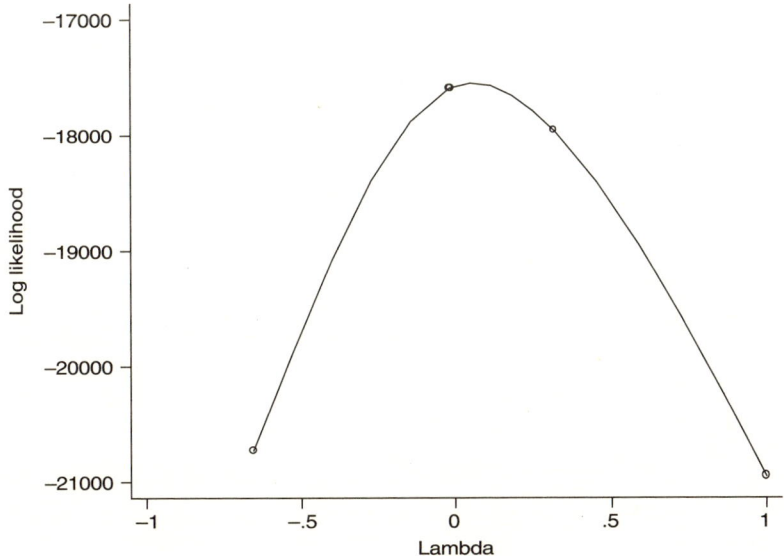

Table 5.A2. "Specification results"

Rent (all)		
Number of rooms		
Kitchen		
Wall material		
Ceiling material		
Floor material		
Sewage connection		
Telephone		
Indoor plumbing		
Bathrooms		
Disposition of garbage		
Electricity		
Homicide rate		
	L = −1	Pr>chi2=0.0000
	L = 0	Pr>chi2=0.3431
	L = 1	Pr>chi2=0.0000

Source: Authors' calculations using ENIGH (1996).

Figure 5.A2. Box-Cox transformation

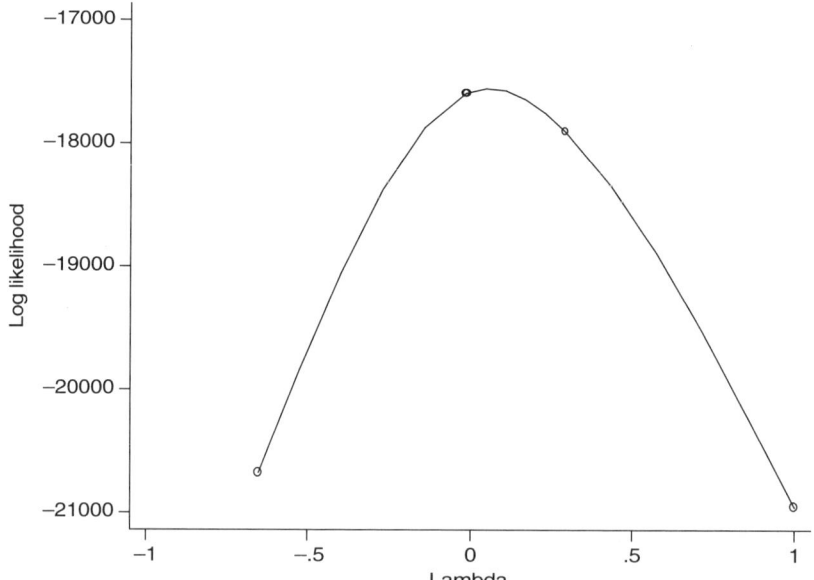

Table 5.A3. "Specification results"

Rent (all)		
Number of rooms		
Kitchen		
Wall material		
Ceiling material		
Floor material		
Sewage connection		
Telephone		
Indoor plumbing		
Bathrooms		
Disposition of garbage		
Electricity		
Homicide rate		
Green areas		
Number of students in primary school		
Number of students in secondary school		
Number of students in high school		
Employment		
	L = −1	Pr>chi2=0.0000
	L = 0	Pr>chi2=0.6414
	L = 1	Pr>chi2=0.0000

Figure 5.A3. Box-Cox transformation

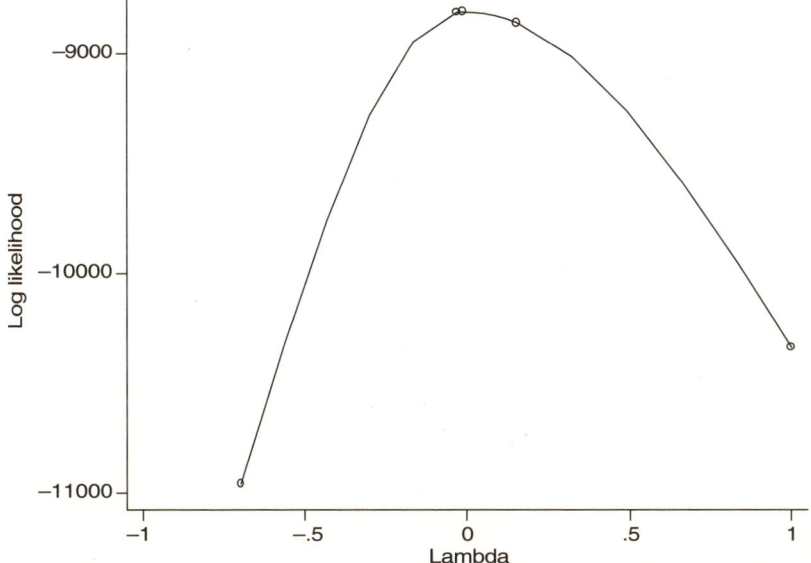

Notes

1. It should be noted, however, that markets for the right to emit pollutants do exist in the United States and a few other countries.

2. Monetary costs usually include governmental expenditure on crime control, national security and justice, and health services provided to victims of violence, as well as individuals' expenditures on self-protection, expenditures on the process for recovering the losses, opportunity costs of time, lost productivity, and medical expenses. Nonmonetary costs generally include reduced quality of life, including the value of pain, suffering, fear, and changed behavior as result of fear of crime and/or victimization by crime. Some authors classify loss of life as a nonmonetary cost due to the difficulty of estimating the value of a human life, while others include loss of life in the category of monetary costs.

3. As a monetary measure of benefits, WTP is the only acceptable measure in accordance with economic theory. According to Pauly (1995), all other methods of valuing benefits in monetary terms are to be judged in terms of their closeness to the definition of WTP. Indeed, other concepts like the addition to measured gross national product associated with a program, the additional wages to beneficiaries or providers, or the additional returns from investment now or in the future are valid only to the extent that they proxy WTP.

4. First, for the hedonic technique to be tenable on theoretical grounds, consumers must be utility maximizers, and the housing market (or any other surrogate market that is used) must contain no imperfections such that individuals are constrained by anything other than their income. This assumption is unlikely to hold in the housing market, where many factors other than income determine the choice of location. Second, the price of any attribute or characteristic is assumed to be independent of any other factor affecting the house price (or the surrogate commodity price). This also seems an assumption that is unlikely to be met, for the utility obtained from the combinations of the attributes is generally unlikely to be the same as the sum of utilities from individual attributes. Despite these technical issues, hedonic models continue to be the most popular revealed preference technique for measuring WTP. For a critique of the meaningfulness of hedonic prices in practice, see Pearce and Nash (1981) and Edwards and Pierce (1979); for a defense, see Freeman (1979).

5. An effort is currently underway, led by the authors of this paper, to undertake a CV survey in Mexico on willingness to pay for crime prevention.

6. Data obtained using the dichotomous-choice format are interval censored. The analyst typically interprets respondents' value as being larger than any stated cost at which they said they would purchase the good, and smaller than any stated cost at which they stated they would not. These models can be estimated using maximum likelihood methods and assuming a parametric form for the distribution of values, or using nonparametric methods (Hanemann and Kanninen 1999). The possibility that some people would not be willing to pay anything for the good can be incorporated using a mixture model, in which there is a probability that WTP is zero, and a probability distribution for WTP conditional on it being positive (Werner 1999).

7. For comparability, only the data pertaining to the third quarter of each year is used in this study.

8. Housing prices will vary among cities for a host of reasons, including levels of economic activity and cost of living differences. Since we cannot control for all these

sources of housing price variation, we must restrict the geographic scope of the sample in order to avoid potentially serious problems of omitted explanatory variables and in order to focus on the importance of crime as a determinant of housing prices.

9. It is important to note that the standard error of this coefficient will be biased downward because this variable does not have the same degree of variation at the household level that the other regressors have. Economists refer to this as a problem of heteroscedasticity.

10. Column 3 of Table 5.4 is estimated using a subsample of the original Mexico City Metropolitan Area sample. This is due to the fact that variables related to infrastructure at the county level are only available for the Federal District. Although the results are not presented here, ordinary least squares robust regressions of columns 1 and 2 of Table 5.4 are very similar to those obtained in column 3 when estimated using the smaller sample.

11. The coefficient of green area per capita is the wrong sign, so the elasticity makes little sense. It is difficult to imagine why an increase in green area per capita should be associated with a decline in housing rents.

12. The fact that high unemployment rates and high population densities have been shown to be associated with increases in crime may suggest that the willingness to pay for crime reduction is at least partially captured by these variables and that, consequently, the WTP for crime reduction—as measured by the homicide rate—is underestimated.

References

Aryeetey-Attoh, S. 1992. "An Analysis of Household Demand Valuations and Preference Structures in Rio de Janeiro, Brazil." *Growth and Change,* 183–98.

Baron, J. 1997. "Biases in the Quantitative Measurement of Values for Public Decisions." *Psychological Bulletin* 122, 72–88.

Bourguignon, F. 1998. *Crime as a Social Cost of Poverty and Inequality: A Review Focusing on Developing Countries.* Washington, DC: World Bank.

Buvinic, M., and A. Morrison. 1999. *Violence Prevention: Technical Notes.* Washington, DC: Inter-American Development Bank.

Buvinic, M., A. Morrison, and M. Shifter. 1999. *Violence in Latin America and the Caribbean: A Framework for Action.* Sustainable Development Department Working Paper. Washington, DC: Inter-American Development Bank.

Carson, R., and R. Mitchell. 1995. "Sequencing and Nesting in Contingent Valuation Surveys." *Journal of Environmental Economics and Management* 28, 155–73.

Cheshire P., and S. Sheppard. 1998. "Estimating the Demand for Housing, Land, and Neighborhood Characteristics." *Oxford Bulletin of Economics and Statistics* 60, no. 3: 357–82.

Clark D., and J. Cosgrove. 1990. "Hedonic Prices, Identification, and the Demand for Public Safety." *Journal of Regional Science* 30, no. 1: 105–21.

Cohen, M., T. Miller, and B. Wiersema. 1996. *Victim Costs and Consequences: A New Look.* Washington, DC: National Institute of Justice, January.

Covey, J., M.W. Jones-Lee, G. Loomes, and A. Robinson. 1998. "Valuing the Prevention of Food-borne Illness: Some Limitations of Consumers' 'Willingness to Pay.'" *Risk Decision and Policy* 3: 245–59.

Cropper, M.L., B.D. Leland, and K.E. McConnell. 1988. "On the Choice of Functional

Form for Hedonic Price Functions." *The Review of Economics and Statistics,* November.

Diamond, P., and J. Hausman. 1994. "Contingent Valuation: Is Some Number Better than No Number?" *Journal of Economic Perspectives* 8: 45–64.

Donaldson, C. 1990. "Willingness to Pay for Publicly Provided Goods: A Possible Measure of Benefit?" *Journal of Health Economics* 9: 103–18.

Edwards, R., and D.W. Pierce. 1979. "The Monetary Evaluation of Noise Nuisance: Implications for Noise Abatement Policy." In *Progress in Resource Management and Environmental Planning,* vol. 1, edited by T. O'Riordan and R. D'Arge. Chichester and New York: Wiley.

Figueroa, E., and G. Lever. 1992. "Determinantes del precio de la vivienda en Santiago: Una estimación hedónica." *Estudios de Economía* 19, no. 1: 69–84.

Frederick, S., and B. Fischhoff. 1998. "Scope (In)Sensitivity in Elicited Valuations." *Risk, Decision, and Policy* 3, 109–24.

Freeman, A.M. 1979. *The Benefits of Environmental Quality.* Baltimore: Johns Hopkins University Press.

Hammitt, J., and J. Graham. 1999. "Willingness to Pay for Health Protection: Inadequate Sensitivity to Probability?" *Journal of Risk and Uncertainty* 18, 33–62.

Hanemann, W. 1994. "Valuing the Environment through Contingent Valuation." *Journal of Economic Perspectives* 8, 19–43.

Hanemann, W., and B. Kanninen. 1999. "Statistical Considerations in CVM." In *Valuing Environmental Preferences: Theory and Practice of the Contingent Valuation Method in the US, EU, and Developing Countries,* edited by I.J. Bateman and K.G. Willis. Oxford: Oxford University Press.

Hanemann, W., J. Loomis, and B. Kanninen. 1991. "Statistical Efficiency of Double-Bounded Dichotomous Choice Contingent Valuation." *American Journal of Agricultural Economics* 73: 1255–61.

Heise, L., et al. 1994. *Violence against Women: The Hidden Health Burden.* World Bank Discussion Paper Number 255. Washington, DC: World Bank.

Instituto Nacional de Estadística, Geografía e Informática (INEGI). 2000. *XII Censo general de población y vivienda.* Vol. I. Mexico City: INEGI.

Johannesson, M., and B. Jonsson. 1990. "Economic Evaluation in Health Care: Is There a Role for Cost-Benefit Analysis?" *Health Policy* 17, no. 1: 1–23.

Jones-Lee, M.W., et al. 1985. "The Value of Safety: Results of a National Sample Survey." *Economic Journal* 95, 49–72.

Londoño, J.L., and R. Guerrero. 1999. *Violencia en América Latina: Epidemiología y costos.* Working Paper No. R-375. Washington, DC: Inter-American Development Bank, August.

Londoño, J.L., R.A. Gaviria, and R. Guerrero. 2000. *Asalto al desarrollo: Violencia en América Latina.* Washington, DC: Inter-American Development Bank.

Mexican Health Foundation (MHF) and World Bank. 1999. *Trends and Empirical Causes of Crime in Mexico.* Mexico City: MHF; Washington, DC: World Bank.

Mitchell, R., and R. Carson. 1989. *Using Surveys to Value Public Goods: The Contingent Valuation Method.* Washington, DC: Resources for the Future.

Moser, C. 1999. "La violencia en Colombia: cómo construir una paz sostenible y fortalecer el capital social." In *Ensayos sobre paz y desarrollo: El caso de Colombia y la experiencia internacional,* edited by A. Solimano, F. Sáez, C. Moser, and C. López. Washington, DC: World Bank.

Murray, C., and A. Lopez. 1994. "The Global Burden of Disease in 1990." In *World Development Report 1993: Investing in Health.* Background Paper Number 12. Washington, DC: World Bank.

Palmquist, R.B. 1984. "Estimating Demand for the Characteristics of Housing." *The Review of Economics and Statistics* 66 (August): 394–404.

Pauly, M. 1995. "Valuing Health Care Benefits in Money Terms." In *Valuing Health Care,* edited by F.A. Sloan. Cambridge: Cambridge University Press.

Pearce D., and C. Nash. 1981. *The Social Appraisal of Projects: A Text in Cost-Benefit Analysis.* London: Macmillan.

Rocha-Macedo, P.B. 1998. "Hedonic Price Models with Spatial Effects. An Application to the Housing Market of Belo Horizonte, Brazil." *Revista Brasileira de Economia* 52, no. 1 (January–March): 63–81.

Sheppard, S. 1999. "Hedonic Analysis of Housing Markets." In *Handbook of Regional and Urban Economics,* edited by P. Cheshire and E.S. Mills. Vol. 3, *Applied Urban Economics.* Amsterdam: North Holland.

Stumpf Gonzalez, M.A., and C. Torres Formoso. 1997. "Estimaciones de modelos de precios hedónicos para alquileres residenciales." *Cuadernos de Economía* 34, no. 101: 71–86.

Villoro, R., and G. Teruel. 2000. *The Social Costs of Crime in Mexico: Is There an Impact on the Distribution of Income?* Washington, DC: Inter-American Development Bank.

Werner, M. 1999. "Allowing for Zeros in Dichotomous-Choice Contingent-Valuation Models." *Journal of Business and Economic Statistics* 17: 479–86.

Williams, A. 1990. "Ethics, Clinical Freedom, and the Doctors' Role." In *Competition in Health Care,* edited by A.J. Culyer, A.K. Maynard, and J.W. Posnett. London: Macmillan.

Witte, A.D., H.J. Sumka, and O.H. Erekson. 1979. "An Estimate of Structural Hedonic Price Model of the Housing Market: An Application of Rosen's Theory of Implicit Markets." *Econometrica* 47 (September): 1151–73.

World Health Organization (WHO). 2000. *The World Health Report, 2000. Health Systems: Improving Performance.* Geneva: WHO.

Part II

Case Studies

Chapter 6

Paths toward Police and Judicial Reform in Latin America

Paulo de Mesquita Neto

Democratic regimes are now established in most countries in Latin America. In democratic regimes, police and judicial institutions are expected to be (1) independent from the government, the military, political parties, and interest groups and accountable to the law and the community; (2) effective and efficient in performing their mission, defined as providing security and justice to the citizens; and (3) equally accessible and responsive to all citizens and groups. Reforms have developed in response to the growing perception that police and judicial institutions in most of these countries are none of the above.

Some countries have advanced more than others in the process of reforming police and judicial institutions inherited from authoritarian regimes and in developing institutions committed to the protection and promotion of democratic values and capable of fulfilling the difficult task of providing security and justice in extremely unequal societies with a high incidence of crime, including organized crime, and a growing concern with the problem of insecurity and injustice.

However, democratic police and judicial institutions are far from established in the region (Mendez et al. 1999; Yamin 1999; Agüero and Stark 1998), where the demand has grown faster than the democratic governments' ability to provide security and justice services to their citizens. In many cases, police and judicial institutions are perceived as part of the problem, captured by organized crime and permeated by corruption and violence. Democratic governments are frequently criticized and attacked by groups on both sides of the political spectrum: from the right, they are criticized for being weak, "soft" on crime, and therefore not capable of controlling crime, particularly organized crime; from the left, they are also criticized as weak, "soft" on police and judicial misconduct, and therefore not capable of containing state violence, including executions, torture, and arbitrary detention, or reducing the corruption involving police officers, prosecutors, and judges.

The objective of this chapter is to characterize different paths toward police and judicial reform in Latin America, examine their possibilities and limitations, and explore the implications of each path for the nature of the new, democratic police and judicial institutions in the region. It focuses on three paths, emphasizing differences in the nature and outcome of the reform depending on the extent to which the process is initiated and driven by (1) international actors, (2) the government, or (3) civil society.

A series of historic, economic, social, cultural, and political factors condition the development and the outcome of police reform in Latin America. Yet, in the same way that the paths toward democracy may have an impact on the consolidation and the quality of the democratic regime (Linz and Stepan 1996; Stepan 1986), the paths toward police reform may have an impact on the consolidation and quality of democratic police and judicial institutions. More specifically, I argue that the nature of leadership in the reform process has implications for the balance between three basic characteristics mentioned above in the new, democratic police and judicial institutions: (1) independence and accountability; (2) effectiveness and efficiency; and (3) accessibility and responsiveness.

In countries where judicial and police reforms are monitored by international actors, the independence of the police and the judicial institutions in relation to the government, the military, political parties, and interest groups, and accountability to the law and the community tend to be the key objectives of the reform process.

In countries where such reforms are led by the government, the effectiveness and efficiency of police and judicial institutions and the establishment of internal and/or governmental control of the police and the judiciary tend to be the key objectives of the reform process.

There are no examples of police and judicial reforms led by civil society in the region. However, in countries where civil society's pressures are strong, and police and judicial reforms result from political agreements between the government and civil society, the accessibility of police and judicial institutions and their responsiveness to citizens tend to gain importance. The strengthening of societal control of police and judicial institutions tends to be emphasized as an important objective of the reform process.

The three paths toward police and judicial reform presented here are not the only possible ones, but appear to be the more important reform paths followed in Latin America during the wave of democratization that happened in the region from the 1970s to the 1990s. Furthermore, there are significant differences in the nature and outcome of reform processes following similar paths depending on the relationships among international actors, the government, and civil society, which are not the focus of this study. The process of reform in particular countries may also change course and follow or combine more than one of the three paths described here. This chapter is intended to open and not conclude debate on these different paths.

Reform Monitored by International Actors

On this path, police and judicial reforms follow an intervention by international actors (foreign governments and/or international organizations) or a peace process supported or facilitated by international actors. International support for reform increases the chances that national actors committed to the reforms will prevail over those that oppose them, thus opening the possibility of significant changes in police and judicial institutions. However, the extensive participation of international actors in the reform process may undermine the legitimacy of the new institutions and render them highly dependent on international assistance for their survival and development.

In the case of reforms following peace accords between the government and an armed opposition, international actors have less influence over the process than when reform follows an international intervention. However, the greater the intensity of the conflict between the government and the armed opposition, the greater the chances of international influence in the reform process.

In both cases, the alignment of police and judicial institutions with the previous authoritarian regime or military government—and their participation in or at least tolerance of human rights violations—makes the independence of these institutions from the government, the political parties, and the military a central component of the reform process. These reforms include the professionalization of the police, judges, and prosecutors, with investments in education and training and the development and strengthening of police and judicial careers. There may be efforts to create new police and judicial institutions. Haiti is an example of police and judicial reform following an international intervention; Guatemala is an example of reform following a peace process.

Haiti

In Haiti, an international intervention led by the United States reestablished the government of Father Jean-Bertrand Aristide in October 1994 and unseated the military government that had deposed him in 1991. Aristide's government dismantled the Haitian armed forces and created the Interim Public Security Force four months after the U.S. intervention, and the Haitian National Police in 1995, with strong support from the U.S. Army, the U.S. International Criminal Investigations Training Assistance Program, and the United Nations Mission in Haiti (Maingot 1996; Washington Office on Latin America 1997a, 1995a).

The creation of the new police force was relatively rapid and recruited many members from the very armed forces that had been abolished by the government. Despite professional training by international experts, members of the new police force engaged in serious human rights violations and demonstrated little experience and insufficient resources and skills in crime control and maintaining order.

The U.S. Agency for International Development, France, Canada, the United Nations Development Program, and the European Union supported a process of judicial reform that included emergency training for four hundred judges and prosecutors, the creation of a national academy for training judges and prosecutors, the improvement of law schools, the creation of a special secretary within the Ministry of Justice to support the work of judges and prosecutors, the rebuilding and rehabilitation of the courts, and the development of judicial assistance services with the participation of nongovernmental organizations (NGOs) (Brody 1999).

Despite the technical and financial support for police and judicial reforms, international actors, particularly the United States, were strongly criticized by NGOs because the reforms were planned and implemented with little consultation with relevant social groups. In particular, international actors did not support the prosecution and judgment of state officials responsible for human rights violations, defined as a crucial step in the process of police and judicial reform not only by human rights organizations but also by the government of Haiti (Brody 1999).

Guatemala

In Guatemala, the peace accord between the government and the Unidad Revolucionaria Nacional Guatemalteca in 1996 ended a thirty-six year period of armed conflict during which two hundred thousand people died or disappeared as a result of political violence. The limitation of the role of the armed forces in the area of public security and the creation of the new Civilian National Police were central components of the peace accord.

Until 1996, initiatives toward police reform had failed. In 1997, as a result of the peace accord, the government dismantled the National Police, Treasury Guard, and Mobile Military Police, which were deeply involved in political repression during the period of civil war. The government created the Civilian National Police and the Academy of the Civilian National Police, subordinate to the Ministry of Government, with the support of Spain through the Civilian Guard, the United States, through the International Criminal Investigations Training Assistance Program, and the United Nations Mission in Guatemala (Byrne et al. 2000). The government also constructed new police stations and offices for receiving complaints about crimes, and established Juntas Locales de Seguridad as a permanent forum for dialogue between the police and the community (Byrne et al. 2000; IEPADES 2000a, 2000b).

Guatemala faced many problems recruiting and training members for the new police: of the 17,339 members of the Civilian National Police in 1999, 64 percent were members of the former police forces. Furthermore, the new police did not include members from indigenous groups, as established in the peace accord (Byrne et al. 2000).

The armed forces also continued to play an important role in the area of public security. The National Congress authorized the participation of the armed forces in joint patrols with the police; 33 to 45 percent of army personnel were employed in public security in the year 2000. An agreement was also established through which the Ministry of Government pays the Ministry of Defense for the participation of the military in patrols and their collaboration in prison security (IEPADES 2000a, 2000b).

In a referendum for changing the constitution in 1999, the majority of the population supported the employment of the armed forces in the area of public security. Civil society and human rights organizations had limited ability to influence the process of police reform after the peace accord, but are now increasingly involved and support the separation between the military and the police (Byrne et al. 2000).

Regarding judicial reform, the United Nations Mission for the Verification of Human Rights in Guatemala supported legal reforms, including laws limiting the scope of military justice and the treatment of prisoners; strengthening the national governmental and nongovernmental organizations responsible for the protection of human rights, particularly the judiciary, the Public Prosecutor's Office (separated and differentiated from the attorney general), and the Public Defender's Office; and the creation of integrated justice centers in rural areas and legal aid programs (Franco 1999). A school for judges was established in 1992 (Sutil 1999).

There are significant differences among national organizations regarding the capacity and willingness to promote judicial reforms. International actors have focused attention on new and smaller organizations, such as the Public Prosecutor's Office and the Public Defender's Office. The problem is that the improvement of the judicial system requires reforms at many levels, including the police, the courts, and the prisons (Franco 1999). In practice, both the police and the judges struggle to maintain control over criminal investigations and judicial processes and therefore resist and oppose the development of the Public Prosecutor's and Public Defender's Offices (Palmieri 2000).

Reform Led by the Government

On this path, as in the one to be described below, the influence of international actors is more limited. Police and judicial reforms follow a significant increase in crime, violence, and corruption. Political actors within the government and/or the police and the judicial system, perceiving that these conditions undermine the stability of the government and/or the legitimacy of the police and the judicial system, initiate a process of reform to a significant extent independent of pressures from international actors or demands from civil society.

The main objective of reform in this case is to improve the effectiveness and efficiency of the police and judicial systems—that is, their ability to respond to the increase in crime and violence, including organized crime, as well as to the growth of judicial conflicts over economic and social issues. However, there are variations, depending on the extent to which the reform process is controlled by government authorities or by police and judicial authorities. If government authorities control the reform, the strengthening of external—governmental—control of the police and the judiciary is likely to be a central component of the process; if police or judicial authorities are in control, the strengthening of internal control of the police and the judiciary is likely to be a central component.

Government authorities would hardly be able to assume control of the reform process or even initiate it without support from either civil society or the military. The reform process, if it happens, would probably be highly influenced or controlled by the police and the judicial authorities. In the absence of civil society support, given a situation of armed conflict and/or severe crisis in the area of public security, the government may be able to gain the support of the military to promote police and judicial reform. The nature of the reform process, however, will be completely different depending on whether government support comes from civil society or the military.

Colombia and Peru are cases of a severe public security crisis, in which reform processes were led by the government and supported by the military, with the objective of increasing the effectiveness and efficiency of the police and the judicial systems (Stokes 1996; Kline 1996). Chile, which is another case of reform led by the government, does not have the problems of drug traffic and armed conflict as do Colombia and Peru, but common crime is a growing problem (Frühling 1998a). In Chile, the government does not have the same capacity—including military support—to impose reform projects upon the police and the judiciary. The reforms are to a significant extent driven by the police and the judiciary. In the three cases, but particularly in Peru and Colombia, the pressures from civil society for police and judicial reform were not as strong as in Argentina or Brazil.

Colombia

In Colombia, the 1991 constitution maintained the subordination of the National Police to the Ministry of National Defense (Guizado 1999; Riedmann 1996). In 1993, Minister of Defense Rafael Pardo Rueda established two commissions to propose reforms in the National Police: an "internal" commission composed of police professionals, and an "external" commission of representatives from the National Congress, regional and local governments, civil society, and retired police professionals. Within forty days, the two commissions proposed a law that kept the police subordinated to the Ministry of National Defense but created the National Council of Police and Citizen Security; the National Police Commissioner; specialized police units for urban areas, rural areas, criminal investigation, and special operations; and the National System of Police and Citizen Participation.

The National Congress approved the law in the same year (Law 62/1993) but the process of police reform largely ignored the content of the law. In 1994, General Rosso José Serrano, head of the "internal commission," became general director of the National Police. With the support of the

University of Los Andes and the United States he initiated a process of police reform centered on the expansion of the police force, the reduction of police corruption, the creation of an intelligence unit independent of the judicial police, the inclusion of women, and changes in police management, attitudes, and behaviors. Nine thousand police officers were dismissed. In 1998, the National Police's Institutional Strategic Plan established six priorities: community participation, new work culture, strengthening of operational capacity, management development, education and training, and administrative improvement.

The 1991 constitution had created the Judicial Council, the Public Prosecutor's Office, the Human Rights Ombudsman, and the Public Defender's Office. The Judicial Council has the power to appoint judges; the Public Prosecutor's Office is in charge of criminal investigations and the coordination of military and civilian agencies investigating crimes; the Human Rights Ombudsman is in charge of investigations focusing on human rights violations; and the Public Defender's Office is subordinated to the Human Rights Ombudsman (Sutil 1999; Frühling 1998b; Hammergren 1998).

The government of Colombia supported the development of the Public Prosecutor's Office over that of the Human Rights Ombudsman and the Public Defender's Office. The Public Prosecutor's Office grew rapidly to 23,000 members, many drawn from preexisting organizations, with 3,600 prosecutors and another 2,000 investigators who are supposed to coordinate the activities of 6,000 investigators from police and military organizations. The United States also supported the Public Prosecutor's Office through large-scale training of prosecutors and police investigators. The Public Defender's Office, by contrast, is poorly financed, staffed, and managed (Hammergren 1998); it has approximately 470 members, almost all of whom are poorly paid contract workers without job security, who are also allowed to work outside the institution.

Peru

In Peru, the government of Alan García created the National Police of Peru by integrating the Civilian Guard, the Investigative Police of Peru, and the Republican Guard in 1988. Alberto Fujimori assumed the presidency in 1990 and appointed active duty military officers to the Ministry of Interior and the General Direction of the National Police, in practice subordinating the police to the military. Police activities were also subjected to the control of the military-led National Intelligence System and to politicomilitary commands in emergency zones (Costa 1998, 1999; Varona 1998; Rospigliosi 1998).

The 1993 constitution, promulgated after Fujimori's coup in 1992, did not produce significant changes in the organization of the National Police. The National Congress approved the Organic Law of the National Police of Peru only in 1999, shaped by the police more than by the government or civil society. The law promotes the professional education and training of police officers and relations between the police and the community through the formation of neighborhood groups, but does not promote significant changes in the organization of the National Police (CED 2000; Costa 1998, 1999).

Regarding the judiciary, Fujimori's government suspended judicial activities for ten days after the coup in April 1992. The government removed judges, intervened in the Judicial Council, and imposed a series of changes allegedly to reduce corruption and politicization and increase the effectiveness and efficiency of the courts (Sutil 1999; Frühling 1998b). In Peru, as in Colombia, the government emphasized the importance of modernizing and professionalizing the judiciary. A national school for judges was established in 1996 (Sutil 1999).

Chile

Chile has two police forces: the Carabineros, the largest police, with 38,000 agents, and the Policía de Investigaciones. The two continue to be formally subordinated to the Ministry of National Defense rather than the Ministry of Interior; the Carabineros particularly maintain a high degree of autonomy in relation to the government since the transition to democracy (Quintana 1998). Democratic governments have tried unsuccessfully to establish a formal subordination of both forces to the Ministry of Interior. In 1992, the Ministry of Interior created a commission to formulate a National Plan for Citizen Security, but the Carabineros opposed the initiative. They proposed their own Modernization Plan in 1994, but it was not fully implemented due to the resignation of General Director Rodolfo Stange in 1995. In 1996, the Carabineros began the implementation of a strategic plan for the modernization of the police (CED 1999, 2000; Frühling 1998a).

In 1998, the government established a commission with representatives from the Carabineros, the Policía de Investigaciones, the Ministry of Defense and the Ministry of Interior for the elaboration of a plan for police reform with the objective of increasing police effectiveness and efficiency.

On the recommendations of the commission, the government initiated a reform process with four objectives: the improvement of the professional education and training of police officers; the introduction of new technologies in the police force; the improvement of relations between the police and the community; and the development of mechanisms for evaluating police performance (CED 1999, 2000).

Patricio Aylwin's government proposed the creation of the National Council of Justice, with representatives from the Supreme Court, courts of appeals, the Senate, the president's office, and law schools. The council would set standards for the appointment and promotion of judges, formulate judicial policies, and be responsible for the administration of the courts. The National Congress approved the establishment of a school for judges in 1995, and a change in the rules for selecting and promoting judges, but not the proposal to create the National Council of Justice (Sutil 1999; Frühling 1998c).

Reform through Political Agreement

On this path, as in the above, police and judicial reforms follow a significant increase in crime, violence, or corruption. However, in this case, civil society plays a more important role through protests and pressure to force government authorities to initiate reforms. Although such protests and pressures are not sufficient to produce reform, and define their objectives and outcomes, they might lead the government to start the reform process and also influence its scope. Police and judicial reform develop by means of an (explicit or implicit) agreement between political actors in the government and in civil society. A reasonably organized civil society and the presence of moderate groups within the government and civil society, capable of jointly supporting police and judicial reform, increase the chances of reform through this path.

On this path, the reduction of state violence and corruption and the accessibility and responsiveness of police and judicial institutions to all citizens and groups are likely to become important objectives. A central component of the reform process will be the strengthening of mechanisms of external—societal—control of police and the judicial institutions.

The government and civil society may have to overcome the resistance of police and judicial institutions. Increases in crime and violence and serious cases of state violence and corruption may weaken institutional resistance, strengthen the government and civil society, and create favorable conditions for the initiation of the reform process. However, without support from police and judicial institutions, the scope of the reform is likely to be limited and the sustainability of the reform process is very difficult. Furthermore, even in the absence of institutional resistance, the conditions that allowed the convergence of political actors in the government and civil society may change and their conflicts may undermine the reform process.

The nature of the reform depends largely on the strength of the government and civil society, the position of police and judicial institutions regarding the reform, and the degree of public concern with crime and violence in society versus human rights violations by the police.

Police Reform

Argentina and Brazil are cases of police reform initiated by political agreement. In both countries, in contrast with the other cases presented here, the government has a federal structure. Argentina has a federal police, federal security forces linked to the armed forces, and provincial police forces. Brazil has a federal police and, in each state, a military police, which is also a reserve of the army, and a civilian police. In both countries, the transition to democracy led to limiting the role of the military in public security and the expansion of civilian and democratic control over the police, but did not lead to the creation of new police forces or to major reforms of the police forces inherited from the authoritarian regime. The police have been criticized by NGOs and distrusted by the population not only for their ineffectiveness in crime control and maintaining order, but also for the persistence of police violence and human rights violations (CELS 2000; CELS and Human Rights Watch 1998; Cardia 1999; Pinheiro 1998; Pinheiro and Mesquita Neto 1999).

Buenos Aires

Buenos Aires Province has the largest police force in Argentina, with 48,500 officers. Police violence and corruption have persisted since the transition to democracy and have been exposed by national and international human rights organizations. Police reform in Buenos Aires followed public protests after confirmation of the participation of police officers in the explosion that caused the death of 87 people in the Asociación de Mutuales Israelitas de Argentina in 1994 and the assassination of journalist José Luis Cabezas in 1997.

In December 1997, responding to public pressure, Governor Eduardo Duhalde dismissed the police high command and appointed a civilian director with extraordinary powers for ninety days to implement the reorganization and decentralization of the provincial police. More than three hundred high-ranking police officials and four thousand police officers were dismissed and regional units and special investigation brigades were dismantled. The police were reorganized into eighteen police districts and eighteen investigation departments related to the eighteen judicial departments of the province.

In 1998, the legislature approved the Organic Law of the Police of the Province of Buenos Aires establishing the division of the provincial police into four forces: judicial police, security police, traffic police, and police in charge of the detention and transportation of prisoners. The government of Buenos Aires created the Ministry of Justice and Security, the Office for Controlling Corruption and Abuse of Power, and the Court of Police Ethics. The government also reformed the systems of recruitment, education, and training; introduced new laws in accordance with international norms regulating the use of force by the police; and encouraged the formation of community groups to improve relations between the police and the community.

Even though the problem of police violence and corruption was at the heart of the civil society's pressures for police reform, the resolution of this problem was not at the center of the reform process. On the contrary, increases in crime and violence strengthened conservative groups, which limited extension of the scope of police reform based on the discourse opposing the defense of law and order and the protection and promotion of human rights. In 1999, Carlos Ruckauf, as a candidate for governor of Buenos Aires Province, proposed that criminals be executed. After the election, as governor, Ruckauf appointed Aldo Rico, a retired military officer who organized a coup against the government of Raúl Alfonsín as minister of justice and security and undermined the process of police reform.

São Paulo

In São Paulo State, Brazil, as in Buenos Aires Province, the problem of police violence and corruption persisted after the transition to democracy. National and international human rights organizations, as well as the Office of the Police Ombudsman created in 1995, systematically documented and published reports on police violence. The legitimacy of the police was further undermined by the growth of crime and violence during the transition to democracy.

In 1997, two events placed the question of police reform on the national agenda. In March, military police officers were videotaped beating and torturing people and killing a person in Diadema, a city in the São Paulo metropolitan region. In June–July, the police initiated strikes and the federal government employed the armed forces to contain the police and maintain law and order in nine states.

In São Paulo in September 1997, Governor Mário Covas changed the general-commander of the military police. The new general-commander immediately announced the adoption of community policing as an organizational strategy for the military police in the state and established a commission for the implementation of community policing with representatives from civil society (Mesquita Neto 1999; Mesquita Neto and Affonso 1998). In 2000, the military police created the Department for Community Policing and Human Rights (Mesquita Neto 2000). Similar initiatives happened, although on a smaller scale, in other states (Muniz et al. 1997).

In 1999 and 2000, respectively, following his reelection in 1998, Governor Mário Covas integrated the operational areas of the military and civilian police and introduced computer technology to record crimes, analyze crime trends, and monitor police performance. In 2000, the federal government announced the National Plan for Public Security and created the National Fund for Public Security, with the objective of supporting processes of police reform in the federal states, particularly improvements in criminal statistics, police training, police integration, and community policing.

Judicial Reform

Regarding the reform of the judicial system, a crucial difference between Argentina and Brazil was the prosecution and punishment of military authorities responsible for human rights violations during the authoritarian regime in Argentina and the absence of that process in Brazil.

Argentina's constitutional reform in 1994 included changes in the judicial system: the creation of the National Judicial Council, the Jurado de Enjuiciamiento de Magistrados, and the establishment of the independence of the Public Ministry (CELS 1996).

The National Judicial Council was established in November 1998, in accordance with Laws 24.937 and 24.939/1998 and Decree 816/1999. The council has twenty members: the president of the Supreme Court, four representatives each from the judiciary, the Senate, and the Chamber of Deputies, one representative from the executive, four representatives from the law profession, and two representatives from academe. The council is responsible for the selection of candidates entering the judicial career track, budget administration, organizational norms, judicial discipline, and decisions regarding the initiation and termination of proceedings for the removal of judges. The same laws defined the structure and functioning of the Jurado de Enjuiciamiento de Magistrados, responsible for the judgment and removal of judges, which was established in March 1999.

The Public Ministry, organized in accordance with the 1994 constitution and Law 24.946/1998 (Organic Law of the Public Ministry), combines the Public Prosecutor's Office and the Public Defender's Office. Since 1999, the Public Ministry has developed a program for establishing closer relations with the population and NGOs, the Programa de Acercamiento a la Comunidad.

Brazil

In Brazil, the 1988 constitution strengthened the Public Ministry and the Public Defense Office. In 1996, the National Congress approved the law transferring from the military courts to the civilian courts the judgment of military police officers accused of intentional homicides. The 1996 National Program for Human Rights, developed by the federal government in consultation with NGOs, included a series of proposals to facilitate the people's access to the judicial system and increase the responsiveness of the judicial system to the people. In accordance with the National Program for Human Rights, the federal government created the National Program for the Protection of Victims and Witnesses of Crimes (Law 9.807/1999).

As had happened in Chile and contrary to what happened in Argentina, however, the National Congress has not yet approved the creation of the National Judicial Council, nor has it approved proposals for reforming the Criminal Code and the Criminal Procedures Code.

Conclusions

All paths toward police reform characterized in this chapter can lead to the development of new, democratic police and judicial institutions, but the nature and the chances of consolidation of these institutions are not the same. Particularly in Latin America, there are many obstacles to be overcome to consolidate democratic police and judicial institutions, including mainly legacies from a long history of authoritarianism and military control over these institutions. Consolidation depends ultimately on overcoming these legacies, increasing the independence of the police and the judiciary in relation to the government, military, political parties, and interest groups, as well as the development of internal and external control mechanisms for ensuring these institutions' accountability, effectiveness, accessibility, and responsiveness (Stone and Ward 2000).

The organization and mobilization of civil society are crucial factors for advancing processes of police and judicial reform, and specifically for strengthening external control mechanisms, a factor that, despite the strengthening of civil society during the transitions to democracy in the region, is often missing or plays a relatively limited role in reform processes in Latin America. Even in Argentina and Brazil, where civil society pressures for reform were stronger, these pressures were sufficient for pushing the government to initiate reforms but were not sufficient for defining the objectives and outcomes of the reform processes. As a result, external, societal control mechanisms of police and judicial institutions have been difficult to establish, reducing the chances of consolidating democratic police and judicial institutions. Democratic governments, even those that have the support of active civil societies, have been unable and sometimes unwilling to support more comprehensive police and judicial reforms, and have instead focused attention on particular dimensions of the reform process. The problem with this strategy is that police and judicial reforms cannot be effectively consolidated and produce significant results if they do not address the questions of accessibility and responsiveness to the public as well as the questions of independence, accountability, effectiveness, and efficiency.

In countries where the independence of police and judicial institutions is more established, and civil society is more organized and mobilized, as in Argentina, Brazil, and Chile, legislators and policymakers frequently engage in long debates and intense conflicts over the relative value of internal, governmental, and societal controls over police and judicial institutions. The debate is extremely important for defining priorities. However, the experience of democratic societies shows that there is no incompatibility between the three types of control, and the consolidation of democratic police and judicial institutions depends on the combination of these three types of control. The experience of Latin American countries shows that a stronger priority should be given, by all political actors but especially civil society leaders, to the development of external, societal controls of police and judicial institutions.

The development and consolidation of democratic police and judicial institutions, with the ability to provide security and justice to all citizens and groups, is a complex and difficult process. The chances of success can be expected to increase if the relevant political actors, particularly legislators, policymakers, and civil society leaders, as well as police and judicial authorities have a comprehensive view of the reform process and focus attention on both the independence, accountability, effectiveness, efficiency, and responsiveness of police and judicial institutions, as well as on the internal, governmental, and societal mechanisms of control over those institutions.

References

Agüero, Felipe, and Jeffrey Stark, eds. 1998. *Fault Lines of Democracy in Post-Transition Latin America.* Coral Gables, FL: North Center Press.

Brody, Reed. 1999. "International Aspects of Current Efforts at Judicial Reform: Undermining Justice in Haiti." In *The (Un)Rule of Law and the Underprivileged in Latin America,* edited by Juan Mendez, Guillermo O'Donnell, and Paulo Sergio Pinheiro. Notre Dame, IN: University of Notre Dame Press.

Byrne, Hugh, William Stanley, and Rachel Garst. 2000. *Rescatar la reforma policial: Un reto para el nuevo gobierno guatemalteco.* Washington, DC: Washington Office on Latin America.

Cardia, Nancy. 1999. *Atitudes, valores e normas culturais em relação à violência.* Brasília: Ministério da Justiça, Secretaria de Estado dos Direitos Humanos.

Centro de Estudios para el Desarrollo (CED). 1999–2000. *Policía y sociedad democratica.* Santiago de Chile: CED.

Centro de Estudios Legales y Sociales (CELS). 1996. *Informe anual sobre la situación de los derechos humanos en Argentina—1995.* Buenos Aires: CELS.

———. 2000. *Derechos humanos en Argentina: Informe anual 2000.* Buenos Aires: Eudeba.

Centro de Estudios Legales y Sociales and Human Rights Watch. 1998. *La inseguridad policial: Violencia en las fuerzas de seguridad en Argentina.* Buenos Aires: Eudeba.

Costa, Gino. 1998. "La propuesta de nueva ley orgánica de la Policía Nacional del Perú: novedades y limitaciones." In *Control democrático en el mantenimiento de la seguridad interior,* edited by Hugo Frühling. Santiago de Chile: Centro de Estudios para el Desarrollo.

———. 1999. *Las Comisarías por dentro: un estudio de caso en Lima Metropolitana.* Santiago de Chile: Centro de Estudios para el Desarrollo.

Franco, Leonardo. 1999. "Comments on Brody and a Discussion of International Reform Efforts." In *The (Un)Rule of Law and the Underprivileged in Latin America,* edited by Juan Mendez, Guillermo O'Donnell, and Paulo Sergio Pinheiro. Notre Dame, IN: University of Notre Dame Press.

Frühling, Hugo. 1998a. "Policía y consolidación democrática en Chile." *Pena y Estado* 3: 81–116.

———. 1998b. "Judicial Reform and Democratization in Latin America." In *Fault Lines of Democracy in Post-Transition Latin America,* edited by Felipe Agüero and Jeffrey Stark. Coral Gables, FL: North Center Press.

Guizado, Álvaro Camacho. 1999. *La policía colombiana: Los recorridos de una reforma.* Bogotá: CESO, Universidad Los Andes.

Hammergren, Linn A. 1998. *Institutional Strengthening and Justice Reform.* Washington, DC: Center for Democracy and Governance, U.S. Agency for International Development.

Instituto de Enseñanza para el Desarrollo Sostenible (IEPADES). 2000a. *Informe de avance sobre la investigación 'Relaciones Policía–Comunidad en Guatemala.'* Guatemala City: IEPADES.

———. 2000b. *Analysis of Police Reform in Guatemala.* Guatemala City: IEPADES.

Kline, Harvey F. 1996. "Colombia: Building Democracy in the Midst of Violence and Drugs." In *Constructing Democratic Governance: Latin America and the Caribbean in the 1990s,* edited by Jorge L. Domínguez and Abraham F. Lowenthal. Baltimore and London: Johns Hopkins University Press.

Linz, Juan J., and Alfred Stepan. 1996. *Problems of Democratic Transition and Consolidation: Southern Europe, South America, and Post-Communist Europe.* Baltimore and London: Johns Hopkins University Press.

Maingot, Anthony. 1996. "Haiti: Four Old and Two New Hypotheses." In *Constructing Democratic Governance: Latin America and the Caribbean in the 1990s,* edited by Jorge L. Domínguez and Abraham F. Lowenthal. Baltimore and London: Johns Hopkins University Press.

Mendez, Juan, Guillermo O'Donnell, and Paulo Sergio Pinheiro, eds. 1999. *The (Un)Rule of Law and the Underprivileged in Latin America.* Notre Dame, IN: University of Notre Dame Press.

Mesquita Neto, Paulo. 1999. "Policiamento comunitário: A experiência em São Paulo." *Revista Brasileira de Ciencias Criminais* 7 (25): 281–92.

———. 2000. "Violência e segurança pública nas grandes cidades: A experiência de polícia comunitária em São Paulo." Paper presented at Seminar on Violência e Segurança nas Grandes Cidades, Experiências Comparadas: São Paulo, Rio de Janeiro, Buenos Aires. Buenos Aires, 20–21 July.

Mesquita Neto, Paulo, and Beatriz Affonso. 1998. *Policiamento comunitário: A experiência em São Paulo.* São Paulo: University of São Paulo, Núcleo de Estudos da Violência.

Muniz, Jacqueline, et al. 1997. "Resistências e dificuldades no programa de policiamento comunitário." *Tempo Social* 9, no. 1: 197–213.

Palmieri, Gustavo. 2000. "Criminal Investigations." In *Themes and Debates in Public Security Reforms: A Manual for Civil Society.* Washington, DC: Washington Office on Latin America.

Pinheiro, Paulo Sergio. 1998. "Polícia e consolidação democrática: O caso brasileiro." In *São Paulo Sem Medo: Um Diagnóstico da Violência Urbana,* edited by Paulo S. Pinheiro, et al. Rio de Janeiro: Garamond.

Pinheiro, Paulo Sergio, and Paulo de Mesquita Neto. 1999. *Primeiro relatório nacional sobre os direitos humanos no Brasil.* Brasília: Ministério da Justiça.

Quintana Benavides, Augusto. 1998. "Informe nacional: Control democrático de los organismos de seguridad interior en Chile." In *Control democrático en el mantenimiento de la seguridad interior,* edited by Hugo Frühling. Santiago de Chile: Centro de Estudios para el Desarrollo.

Riedmann, Arnold. 1996. "La reforma policial en Colombia." In *Justicia en la calle: ensayos sobre la policía en América Latina,* edited by Peter Waldmann. Medellín: Fundación Konraud Adenauer, CIEDLA, ISLA, and Biblioteca Jurídica Diké.

Rospigliosi, Fernando. 1998. "Informe nacional: carencia de control democrático sobre las fuerzas de seguridad en Perú." In *Control democrático en el mantenimiento de la seguridad interior,* edited by Hugo Frühling. Santiago de Chile: Centro de Estudios para el Desarrollo.

Stepan, Alfred. 1986. "Paths toward Redemocratization: Theoretical and Comparative Perspectives." In *Transitions from Authoritarian Rule: Comparative Perspectives,* edited by Guillermo O'Donnell, Philippe C. Schmitter, and Laurence Whitehead. Baltimore and London: Johns Hopkins University Press.

Stokes, Susan. "Peru: The Rupture of Democratic Rule." In *Constructing Democratic Governance: Latin America and the Caribbean in the 1990s,* edited by Jorge L. Domínguez and Abraham F. Lowenthal. Baltimore and London: Johns Hopkins University Press.

Stone, Christopher E., and Heather Ward. 2000. "Democratic Policing: A Framework for Action." *Policing & Society* 10, no. 1: 11–45.

Sutil, Jorge Correa. 1999. "Judicial Reform in Latin America: Good News for the Underprivileged?" In *The (Un)Rule of Law and the Underprivileged in Latin America,* edited by Juan Mendez, Guillermo O'Donnell, and Paulo Sergio Pinheiro. Notre Dame, IN: University of Notre Dame Press.

Varona, Ciro Alegría. 1998. "Policía y sistema de defensa nacional en el Perú." In *Control democrático en el mantenimiento de la seguridad interior,* edited by Hugo Frühling. Santiago de Chile: Centro de Estudios para el Desarrollo.

Washington Office on Latin America (WOLA). 1995a. *Demilitarizing Public Order: The International Community, Police Reform, and Human Rights in Central America and Haiti.* Washington, DC: WOLA.

———. 1995b. *Policing Haiti: Preliminary Assessment of the New Police Force.* Washington, DC: WOLA.

———. 1997a. *Haiti's Police Reform: Can Slow Progress Be Sustained?* Washington, DC: WOLA.

———. 1997b. *The Human Rights Record of the Haitian National Police.* Washington, DC: WOLA.

Yamin, Alicia. 1999. *Em caminho ao século 21: Desafios e estratégias da comunidade de direitos humanos.* Washington, DC and Lima, Peru: Washington Office on Latin America and Instituto de Defesa Legal.

Chapter 7

Police Reform in Latin America: Brazil, Argentina, and Chile

Heather H. Ward

Throughout Latin America, crime has become a top concern of citizens, politicians, international donors, the media, and police. As democracy consolidates throughout most of the hemisphere, public safety replaces concerns about national security, political violence, and economic stability in many countries. Crime and violence have grown steadily: between 1984 and 1994, the homicide rate in the region increased 40.9 percent (Morrison et al. 2003; author's calculations based on Pan American Health Organization data), and fear of crime seems to be outpacing the actual increase. Citizens look to their government to do something about crime, and when the state fails, they lose confidence in government and feel even more insecure.

Citizens concerned about crime often want a powerful state—and powerful law enforcement agencies—to fight crime with a heavy hand. In many developing democracies in Latin America and other regions, citizens are often willing to cede more authority to police today than they wielded during authoritarian regimes (Stone and Ward 2000, 11–12). For example, in 1997—because of rising crime—the Hungarian parliament authorized police to detain and hold suspects incommunicado for longer than they were able to under the communist regime. And in South Africa, police have wider discretion to search and seize property than during apartheid.

There are many approaches to reducing crime and violence. Some tackle the root causes through programs to alleviate poverty, income disparity, unemployment, and gender inequality. Others believe the problems are the product of an outdated criminal justice system and look to improve the way prosecutors, defense attorneys, courts, police, and correctional institutions work together. Although the need to address all these issues is real, the task of crime control falls most immediately to the police. Only police have the explicit mandate of providing public safety, a concept that can be broadly defined. Police are on duty twenty-four hours a day, seven days a week, making them the agents of first response to any disorder problem, however minor or severe.

In the decade or two since most Latin American countries left authoritarianism behind, they have undergone huge transformations to realize democracy. They introduced new constitutions, penal codes, electoral procedures, rules of trade and commerce, and more. Barring only a handful of exceptions, police reform was not part of the initial transformation. There are several possible explanations for this. First, in some countries, including Chile and Brazil, police services have strong legal, cultural, and historical links to the military and were, in fact, auxiliary forces during those countries' military regimes. After weakening the military's control, further "demilitarizing" the police could have meant jeopardizing democracy's tenuous hold. Second, changes to other institutions, such as adopting new constitutions that guaranteed human rights or strengthening the judiciary, seemed more pressing (and received more support from international donors). Third, the law enforcement system—however ineffective or brutal—offered some measure of much needed stability while the rest of government was transformed. Conservatives were likely to support the police, who in turn could help preserve the status quo. Finally, there is the persistent obstacle that police, like any bureaucracy in any country, tend to resist change. This chapter will highlight the conditions under which the police are willing to accept change and demonstrate the types of reforms that may cause the police to resist.

Today, it is apparent that democratic policing is not merely a by-product of a democratic government. Beginning in the late 1990s, there has been a swell of projects and programs to reform the police, representing a second wave in the transition to democracy. State officials and civil society institutions—as well as police leaders—want a police service consonant with the rest of society. The proposals for how to do this are diverse: some aim to turn police into crusaders for human rights, some aim to flatten the hierarchical chain of command, some try to scrap the existing police institution and start over, and some try to make police more effective through new tools and technology.

Ultimately, there is no tried-and-true way to bring about a democratic police service. Unlike judicial reform, there has never been a coherent model of policing for energetic reformers to pursue. Many scholars and practitioners have attempted their own definitions of what democratic policing really means. Policing scholar David Bayley argues that what distinguishes democratic police from any other is that they are responsive and accountable: a democratic police force "responds to the needs of individuals and private groups as well as the needs of government," and is "accountable to multiple audiences through multiple mechanisms" (1997). In Latin America today, the demands placed on police by individuals, private groups, and government are many, but principal among them are two: reduce crime and respect the rule of law.

For lessons in how to effect democratic policing, many look to the examples of Guatemala, Haiti, and El Salvador—or even Bosnia and South Africa. These countries, often with international assistance, created new police services from scratch, following armed conflict and humanitarian crises. When starting a new police service, these examples can illuminate complex questions about structure, mission, staffing, and administration.

But starting over is not an option in most countries. The challenges facing police reformers in Argentina, Brazil, Chile, Colombia, Mexico, and many other countries of Latin America are different, and it would serve them to learn from each others' police reform experiences. Although there is a growing body of police research and evaluation in Latin America, it is still small, making it difficult to access these lessons. Time is one factor: most processes of police reform are recent and unfinished.[1]

Nevertheless, it is possible to compare what we do know about some of the police reform efforts underway today. This chapter reviews recent or ongoing processes of reform within police organizations in three countries: Brazil, Argentina, and Chile. In all three countries democratic governments are trying to cope with the same police organizations that formerly served military regimes.

The impetus for police reform can come from many places—politicians who find themselves in command of rogue police or under pressure from citizens to get tough on crime, human rights organizations that document police abuse, community organizations that want better police service, or police commanders who want to improve the professionalism and self-image of their departments. Drawing on a framework laid out by Stone and Ward (2000), it is possible to place these sources of influence and accountability of police in three groups: civil society, state institutions, and police organizations.

Each of the three case studies presented in this chapter represents profound changes to police organizations initiated by a different one of the set of actors. In Minas Gerais, Brazil, civilian experts at the Centro de Estudos de Criminalidade e Segurança Pública (Center for Studies of Crime and Public Security, or CRISP in Portuguese), which is affiliated with the state-sponsored Federal University, helped police create new information management systems and trained police to analyze crime. In the province of Buenos Aires, the government faced such an acute crisis of public security and police misconduct that it sacked the 243 highest-ranking police officers and called for a complete makeover of the force. And in Chile, the national uniformed police service, the Carabineros, launched their own plan to increase community presence and improve efficiency.

The relationship among the three sets of actors is interdependent and complex. Police, state officials, and civil society all share a stake in public security. Police try to control crime on the front lines, but their effectiveness depends on the other two actors. For example, individual citizens and community groups can offer police important information about crime and suspects and can sometimes work with police to address local maintenance or disorder problems that contribute to crime. State institutions guide public security policy, allocate funding for police, and determine the legal parameters of police work.

The sources for this chapter are first- and second-hand accounts of what led to the reforms in each of the three cases, who was involved in shaping and implementing the reforms, what the reforms aim to accomplish, and what they have achieved so far. The chapter does not attempt to evaluate the reforms, only to compare the approach that police—and the government and civil society actors involved—have taken to improve crime-control effectiveness and responsiveness to the public. The chapter focuses on how the reforms have affected the work of frontline police officers, not special units for drug interdiction or organized crime.

Each case study reviews the circumstances that brought about the police reform initiative, such as rising crime and frustration at police ineffectiveness, how the reforms were implemented, and any initial outcomes.

Minas Gerais: Policing with Results

It is hard to talk about the events in Minas Gerais as significant "reform" efforts, because they are not. The Military Police in Minas Gerais introduced a series of small changes to police management, information systems, deployment, and in-service training over many years that had a profound impact. The changes are the product of a partnership among the Military Police, the

Federal University of Minas Gerais, and the Fundação João Pinheiro begun more than fifteen years ago. At that time, as Brazil was realizing its transition to democracy, the state's Military Police commander and his change-minded colleagues within the police foresaw the new demands that democracy would place on the organization. To improve the professionalism and public service orientation of the police force, they looked to the two educational institutions to provide public policy education for police. Some of the officers who participated in those first courses are now in charge of the police service, and they are further institutionalizing professional, scientific methods of crime detection and enforcement.

Factors Leading Up to Police Reform

In the early 1980s, a partnership emerged among the Federal University of Minas Gerais, the state's Military Police, and the Fundação João Pinheiro, a semiautonomous state-funded research center and graduate school for public policy. As institutions throughout the country became more democratic, some members of the Military Police leadership—particularly the state's commander, Colonel Klinger Sobreira de Almeida—understood that if the police did not keep pace with the changes democracy brought, they might not survive it. Klinger was known as a tough-on-crime leader during the last years of the military regime, when the Military Police functioned as an auxiliary to the army.[2]

Colonel Klinger formed an unlikely friendship with Antonio Luiz Paixão, a leftist critic of the military regime and a research pioneer in the areas of violence, crime, and policing in Brazil, who was affiliated with the Fundação João Pinheiro. Paixão believed that the role of police in the process of democratization was extremely important.[3] Paixão and his like-minded academic colleagues organized graduate level courses in public administration required for police promotion. According to Claudio C. Beato F., director of CRISP and a Paixão disciple, this was a critical step in "civilianizing" the Military Police. The courses, which covered topics such as public relations and sociology, helped the police convert from a quasimilitary organization into a public service, partly because of their day-to-day experience in the classroom with nonpolice professors and students. Today, the youngest of those first students occupy the highest ranks of the state's Military Police.[4]

The relationship between the Federal University and the Military Police, along with the Fundação João Pinheiro, has grown since those early days.

In 1994, Paixão, Beato, and a third researcher from the Federal University of Minas Gerais, Renato Assunção, with the then-colonel of the Military Police, Lúcio Emílio, and the Fundação João Pinheiro embarked on a research collaboration. They wanted to examine the role of police in controlling violent crime, which had been increasing in Brazil's urban centers since the 1980s, but the police had no way of comparing crime across the state. They assembled a computer database of violent crime incidents in Minas Gerais between 1986 and 1997. This is where the expertise of university staff could serve police. According to Beato, it was this project that proved to police that outside researchers could be worthy partners.[5]

In the spring of 1997, two shocking incidents of police brutality were captured on videotape in São Paulo and broadcast nationally. It seemed Brazilians' tolerance for abusive and ineffective police—even for the sake of crime control—had reached its limits. Never before had criticism of the police reached such a tenor, and the need for police reform and increased oversight seemed urgent. Police, for their part, resented being lumped by the media and the public into the same barrel with the bad apples. They felt unappreciated for doing dangerous work, with long hours and low pay. In June and July 1997, police in seventeen states, including Minas Gerais, went on strike (Ward 1998). Reconciliation between the state and its Military Police, and restoration of public confidence in the police, would require changes in police management and culture.

Similar events generated reforms in the states of Rio de Janeiro, São Paulo, and others. The São Paulo Military Police initiated a statewide community policing program to try to rescue its public relations. The new "pilot program," launched in December 1997, started in forty-one locations and was scheduled to expand to two hundred sites by December 1998 (Mesquita Neto and Affonso 1998, 39). In 1999, Rio's governor Anthony Garotinho and his team of public security specialists launched an ambitious plan that would replace the Military and Civil Police with an improved hybrid service, among other changes (Soares 2000).

As violent crime increased steadily in the late 1990s—and fear of crime with it—the Minas Gerais Military Police felt continuous pressure to improve. Since 1997, both the Military and Civil Police have sent captains and colonels to specialized courses offered by the Fundação João Pinheiro. In 1999, the Military Police command of Belo Horizonte, the state capital, introduced a new program for crime reduction, "Policing with Results," with help from CRISP.

Policing with Results

Policing with Results is a department-wide program introduced by Colonel Severo Augusto da Silva Neto, the Military Police commander for the city of Belo Horizonte, to manage police activity. It divided the city into twenty-five administrative regions, each led by a commander and staffed by a company, and made each commander responsible for coming up with his own strategies and operations to produce measurable reductions in crime (Beato F. 2000, 11). The essence of the program is that results matter, and area commanders are evaluated on the basis of their results.

In 1999, Beato proposed a joint project between CRISP and the Military Police that would support Colonel Severo's Policing with Results program. Severo was one of the early students in the police courses offered by the Fundação João Pinheiro in the 1980s, and since then, he had grown into a strong leader with the courage to innovate. The idea was to use new computer technology to create a crime mapping system that would pinpoint crime hot spots and identify patterns, helping police better target specific problems and use resources more efficiently. CRISP's first step was to create a database from the official crime incident reports that could be used for a geoarchive (the information needed to make maps). Then CRISP trained police officers to use the mapping and crime analysis software, effectively creating the first crime analysis unit within the local Military Police command. Every six months the unit sends lengthy reports to the twenty-five area commanders detailing the most frequently reported crimes and areas of concentration. Based on the information contained in the reports, every commander must draw up a six-month operations plan outlining major priorities (Beato F. 2000).

So far, the crime analysis team mainly serves police managers, who use aggregate data for planning, resource allocation, training, identifying crime trends, and developing information for the community. The team at CRISP, however, hopes to expand the users to include all ranks of the police command (Beato F. 2000). Frontline officers, for example, need different kinds of information and analysis. They are likely to want to know about current crime incidents within a small geographic area to help them respond to calls for service, investigate, and apprehend suspects.

The Military Police–CRISP partnership has grown into much more than a crime mapping exercise. Since mapping and other types of crime analysis require specialized skills, training has been an important part of the collaboration. In 1999, the university offered a sixty-hour course in crime analysis for twenty-three police officials, a group of planning unit directors, and battalion commanders. They learned how to use crime mapping software to see the distribution of crime incidents and how to use descriptive statistics to better understand crime.

The information system developed by CRISP and the Military Police has been a critical element of Colonel Severo's Policing with Results program, not only because it helps them analyze crime and target police activity, but because the information it contains can be used for measuring the performance of the twenty-five area captains. However, Beato warns that it is difficult to evaluate police officers on purely quantifiable marks because so much of police work is not directed at things that can be counted, in the way arrests can be. Effective policing also includes a considerable amount of time devoted to crime prevention, order maintenance, and reducing fear of crime, which are much harder to measure. What can be measured, says Beato, is the impact of a particular police strategy or intervention on very specific categories of crime (Beato F. 2000, 6).

The team at CRISP would like the system they developed to help police work together with communities to address neighborhood crime and disorder problems. The Military Police in Belo Horizonte began experimenting with a model of community policing in 1993, but it has not expanded beyond the initial test sites. Early results of the experiment were mixed. One study found that the program has made citizens feel safer, boosted police morale, and, combined with new resources and equipment, prepared them to be more effective crime-fighters. However, the study points out that soliciting funds from community members in order to buy new equipment was a major motivation for the program, and it concludes that no crime reduction could be attributed to the program. Although community policing is grounded in collaboration between community members and police to resolve problems that lead to crime, the study found that genuine collaboration and prevention activities were largely absent from the Belo Horizonte program. The study concludes that, although the program did not generate sufficient public, political, and police support to expand, it opened up unprecedented dialogue between police and civilians and dispelled much of the mythology, suspicion, and fear that surround policing (De Souza 1999). The information and maps now available to the Military Police could be a platform for working with community members on specific, local problems and to plan crime prevention efforts together.

Higher education for police is still at the heart of the arrangement among the Military Police, Federal University, and Fundação João Pinheiro. They are now working together to start a two-year master's program in public administration with a specialization in public security. Eventually, they hope the foundation—where Professor Paixão first held courses for the police—will become a center of police research and policy and a repository of technical expertise in public security topics in service to police administrators (CED 1999a, 3–4).

Conclusions from Minas Gerais

In 1985, Military Police leaders saw that, unless police were involved in the reform of their own organization, change would be forced on them. Police initiated the process of change, with help from two academic institutions. The partnership that formed has helped the Military Police periodically reflect and reorient to keep pace with social and political changes. Today, their willingness to innovate, often with the use of new technology and management practices, is a great source of pride.

It is important to note, however, that even when reform is initiated by police leadership, there may still be an "old guard" that resists. Some officers, particularly those who have served longest, view the new technology and partnerships as unnecessary. These officers believe security is achieved with weapons,[6] not prevention and strategy.

The role of the Federal University and the Fundação João Pinheiro as genuine partners with police has been critical to police reform in Minas Gerais. With the expertise of sociologists and specialists in public administration from both institutions, the Military Police have tried to build a more professional, technical, and soundly administered public service.[7] The partnership evolved because police could depend on the neutrality of the scholarship, teaching, and assistance that it received from members of both institutions. According to one researcher at the Fundação João Pinheiro and his police officer coauthor, the partnership has evoked a more open popular image of the police and is to credit for an approval rating (43 percent) that is slightly higher than that of the Civil Police (Sapori and de Souza 2001).

The incremental, long-term approach taken in Minas Gerais is unusual in the world of police reform, particularly in Brazil, where it sometimes seems as though only drastic measures can arrest severe crime and police misconduct problems. For example, other police reformers in Brazil have attempted to eliminate the Military Police, to strip it of its "military" character and hierarchical structure, to combine the Military and Civil Police services, or to decentralize police command to create local police services. Claudio Beato at the Federal University in Minas Gerais says he has found that "the best way to not change anything is to change everything" (2001). Police resist efforts to modify their structure and attempts to do so will put them on the defensive. Instead, Beato finds that modest changes in police management, planning, technology, and some strategies can cause profound changes in the police organization's relationship to the public and, sometimes, in its ability to control crime.[8]

Where Policing with Results has been most successful, according to Beato, is in identifying specific patterns or trends in crime and taking action to disrupt them. For example, with the new crime analysis techniques that CRISP helped introduce, the Belo Horizonte Military Police were able to detect a troubling pattern of taxi robberies. The police then adopted a series of measures to prevent them—such as safety inspections for taxis on well-traveled routes—and measured the change. Taxi robberies plummeted. Beato notes that overall crime figures for the city have not changed much since Policing with Results was introduced, although the rate of increase of crime has slowed.[9]

Policing with Results in Minas Gerais aims to improve police effectiveness at controlling crime by giving police reliable information on which to base their activities, limiting discretion and arbitrary enforcement activities. Although reducing police misconduct was not a primary goal of the program, it may indeed have that effect by offering more systematic, structured and accountable work routines for police. (Unfortunately, there is not yet conclusive evidence to make that claim more strongly.) As Beato notes, police with real skills do not have to resort to brutality in their work.[10] The information system he has helped create also gives police the tools for objectively evaluating individual and department-wide performance with quantitative indices (Beato F. 2000, 15).

The long-standing relationships between the Military Police and the two academic institutions have not produced the overnight turnaround that many police reformers seek. However, with time, the police have institutionalized the changes, making them more difficult to reverse. Beato says that the Minas Gerais Military Police are still at the beginning of a long process and that there is much left to do. So far, the most important thing he and his colleagues have learned is that they have discovered an effective way of introducing change in a police organization through cooperation with universities (Beato F. 2000, 15). What exists now is a better functioning apparatus for taking on strategic or operational changes in the future.

Buenos Aires Province: The Intervention

In December 1997, then-governor of Buenos Aires Province, Eduardo Duhalde, took drastic measures to reinvent the province's public security system. Crime was on the rise, public fear of crime was outpacing the real increase, and illegal activity permeated the police ranks. The situation was so bad, that, to Duhalde and many others, drastic measures seemed the only option. In a span of ninety days, Duhalde dismissed more than three hundred of the highest ranking officers of the Bonaerense (as the province's police force is known), divided the Bonaerense into eighteen administrative police departments, created four separate police forces to perform different tasks, and named the province's first minister of justice and security, a civilian, to whom the police would report. Duhalde declared the police, as well as the rest of the criminal justice system, out of date and incapable of responding to the demands of modern life (Saín 1998).

Duhalde's measures tackled the problems of police corruption and abuse; they did not deal head-on with the crime problem, which the citizenry was much more concerned about. Just a few months after setting the reforms in motion, the Duhalde administration's efforts were discredited when they produced no reduction in crime. Still trying to score a political victory, Duhalde replaced his minister of justice and security and began emphasizing crime reduction over cleaning up the police.

Two years after launching the "intervention," Duhalde failed to win the presidency and was succeeded by Carlos Ruckauf, who ran on an anticrime, "zero tolerance" platform. Upon taking office, Ruckauf named Aldo Rico, a former military officer with a well-established record of human rights abuse, as minister of justice and security. More recently, Ruckauf separated the Ministry of Justice from the Ministry of Security and appointed a retired police official to lead the latter—a move that weakened civilian control of the police. He has created the new role of "operations chief" to oversee the province's eighteen regional departments, thereby reasserting centralized authority over local police.

The problems of crime and insecurity persist in Buenos Aires, and increasing the ability of the provincial police to address those problems is important to Governor Ruckauf. But whether he will commit his administration to realizing a new ethos for respectful and effective police work is not clear.

Factors Leading Up to Police Reform

Many factors contributed to the urgency of police reform in Buenos Aires in 1998. All types of crime had increased from 81 incidents per 100,000 persons in 1980 to 204 per 100,000 in 1995 (IDB 1999). In the late 1990s, crime levels continued to rise; jumping from 16,000 incidents per month in 1994 to 25,700 in June of 1999.[11] Along with the actual rise in crime grew the public's preoccupation with crime and feelings of insecurity. In 1997, one study found that the growth of crime had become citizens' second largest concern after unemployment.[12]

The police were increasingly unable to control crime. According to Ciro Annicchiarico, former advisor to the government on its reform plan, the Bonaerense was falling apart by the late 1990s. Management systems were weak: there was a lack of information about basic things like human and material resources as well as ineffective oversight of police activity. Many police officers were doing janitorial and administrative work, detaining and transporting prisoners (1,700 prisoners were being held in police stations, although detention is the responsibility of the corrections administration), and many vehicles were out of service (Annicchiarico 1999, 68, 86–87).

Some say the Bonaerense did more to contribute to the crime problem than resolve it (Estévez 2000, 5). Argentina's largest law enforcement agency was also the country's most corrupt and abusive. The involvement of Bonaerense members in two brutal events revealed the extent of the problem: the 1997 murder of photojournalist José Luis Cabezas—who was working on a story about corruption within the police—and the bombing of the Mutual Association of Argentine Israelites community center in 1994. In the late 1990s, Bonaerense members responsible for drug enforcement got involved in drug trafficking, there were numerous unjustified shootings of suspects, and they were unnecessarily tough on student protesters (Human Rights Watch 1998).

Public confidence in the police was steadily eroding. A public opinion survey in August 1996 showed that 37 percent of citizens feared the police, and another found that 83 percent mistrusted the police (CISALP 1996). Citizens perceived police misconduct and the increase in crime as evidence that the provincial government was failing (Saín 1998). Those with the resources turned to private security for added protection. The private security industry reached thirty thousand strong in Buenos Aires alone, constituting a "parallel armed force" (Annicchiarico 1999, 8).

Despite the organization's weaknesses, the public depended increasingly on police to solve all varieties of public order problems (Saín 1998). In fact, when the Bonaerense created a hotline for complaints against police in 1997, 32 percent of the first 1,400 calls were from citizens complaining that they needed more police presence in their neighborhoods (CISALP 1997). The public reliance on the police, combined with the lack of oversight by external authorities, produced a largely autonomous and unaccountable organization.

Duhalde, with his eye on the 1999 presidential campaign, attempted to prove that his government could indeed do something about police ineffectiveness and abuse.

"The Intervention" and Reforms That Followed

On 19 December 1997, Governor Eduardo Duhalde presented the Plan de reorganización general del Sistema Integral de Seguridad e Investigación de los Delitos de la Provincia de Buenos Aires (Plan for General Reorganization of the Integral System for Security and Investigation of Crime of Buenos Aires Province).[13] Duhalde declared that the problems of public security bore structural roots, that the situation had reached crisis proportions, and that the entire public security system had broken down.

The plan cast reform of the province's public security system in two phases: the ninety-day intervention that would dismantle the Bonaerense, and longer-term administrative and structural changes to the overall public security system (Secretaría de Seguridad [1997], 11). In the first phase, Duhalde declared the Bonaerense defunct and proposed a new public security system for the province. The intervention dissolved the Bonaerense's regional police units and investigative brigades. Worried that the Bonaerense's leadership would try to sabotage the reforms, the Duhalde administration dismissed all personnel occupying the ranks of general commanders, major commanders, and inspector commanders—243 in all (Abregú 1998, 10; see also Annicchiarico 1999, 62).

The goal of the intervention was to eliminate the Bonaerense's command structure, authority, networks, internal culture, and corruption rings, which many believed emanated from the top of the organization. The changes also attempted to decentralize the force, mainly by creating geographic divisions and by giving more authority to regional commanders. This, the reformers hoped, would bring police into closer contact with the public, increase transparency, and give more control to civilian government officials (Beraldi 1998). Duhalde named the province's first minister of justice and security, a civilian, and established the Instituto de Política Criminal y Seguridad (Institute for Crime and Security Policy), a semi-independent organization that would lend technical support and expertise to the ministry on a range of public security issues.

The plan divided the provincial police force, the Bonaerense, into eighteen police "departments," whose jurisdictions corresponded to that of the province's courts. Each department was made responsible for local police administration, crime prevention, and patrol. The plan also created three additional police forces to perform other tasks that previously fell to the Bonaerense—such as traffic enforcement and investigations—making it possible for the eighteen new police departments to focus more attention on crime reduction.

The Buenos Aires parliament outlined a detailed plan for how the reforms would be implemented. In Argentina, Brazil, and many other countries, both in Latin America and elsewhere, the internal organization of the police is prescribed by law, and changes such as those initiated by Governor Duhalde require changes in law. According to one observer, Duhalde tried to create a multiparty parliamentary commission to cosponsor the reforms, but members of other political parties did not want to be so closely aligned with his policies. They did agree, however, to form a bicameral parliamentary committee to monitor and oversee the reform process. The committee would be included in policy formation, it would be responsible for allocating funding for the reforms, and it would produce public reports from time to time (Saín 1998).

Although there was wide political consensus that reform of the province's public security system was necessary, there were many proposals for how to achieve it. Proposals were submitted by the Institute for Crime and Security Policy, the Alianza (an alliance between the Unión Cívica Radical and Frepaso parties), the Partido Justicialista, and the government itself (Saín 1998). They addressed a range of topics, from recruitment and training plans, to effective investigations, to mechanisms of external oversight of police (Abregú 1998, 11).

In August 1998, the Partido Justicialista proposal became the Ley Provincial de Seguridad Pública (Provincial Public Security Law). Incorporating many elements of Duhalde's reform plan, it provided for:

1. An integrated public security system based on the creation of three distinct police organizations: Departmental Security Police, Investigative Police, and Traffic Safety Police. The existing uniformed police would be divided into eighteen regional departments (corresponding with court districts), and would have general responsibility for preventing crime and maintaining order. A General Directorate for Communication and Information would collect and track crime incident data for the entire province and assist the eighteen regional police departments (Human Rights Watch 1998).
2. Creation of a provincial council for public security that would develop proposals for coordination, cooperation, and training in the public security system, whose members would include several provincial ministers, heads of the three provincial police services, the chief prosecutor, and representatives of citizen safety forums.
3. Community participation, through the creation of neighborhood and municipal safety forums and departmental safety councils, which would provide feedback to the police about their activities and participate in crime prevention planning and activities.
4. Municipal Defenders of Security, who would meet with and facilitate communication among the neighborhood and municipal safety forums, local and provincial government authorities, and police forces; evaluate police activities and produce triannual and annual reports about the three police services; make recommendations for institutional improvements; help plan crime prevention activities; and receive complaints from citizens about any of the province's public security agencies.
5. A bicameral commission for monitoring police performance in the province's parliament.
6. An independent Institute for Crime and Security Policy that would give technical and strategic support to the Ministry of Justice and Security for the implementation of the new public security law. The institute's initial staff members represented diverse political parties and focused on the areas of police reform, judicial reform, drug control, violence prevention, and police training.
7. The province's first Ministry of Justice and Security.
8. The Office for the Control of Corruption and Official Abuse, made up of an auditor for internal affairs and an ethics court. The auditor's job would be to investigate complaints of ethics violations or official abuse committed by police and to present the cases to the ethics court. The court would be responsible for finding fault and issuing punishment.

9. Ethics and behavior guidelines based on the principles of rationality and proportionality, which called for police to try to avoid abusive, arbitrary, or discriminatory actions that result in physical or moral violence and to reserve force as a last resort (Estévez 2000, 7–10).

The New Departmental Police

In February 1998, the eighteen regional police departments officially began operations. Each department was to have functional, administrative, and financial autonomy and focus exclusively on crime prevention and control (Annicchiarico 1999, 93). If all went as planned, the eighteen chiefs of police—each in command of twenty to thirty *comisarías,* or precincts—would be more attuned to local problems and would improve their abilities to respond rapidly and effectively (Beraldi 1998). The chiefs would conduct their own recruiting, training, and personnel management, which were previously handled by a central authority. Eventually, the eighteen departments would conduct their own basic crime analysis and planning.

The reason for the breakup into eighteen departments, according to a publication by the Secretary of Security, was to better coordinate the work of police and the courts by placing them in the same jurisdictions, and strengthen the relationship between police and municipal governments (Secretaría de Seguridad [1997], 17–18). Previously, police personnel rotated throughout the province, which prevented them from establishing ties in the communities where they worked.

Meanwhile, the Delegados Departamentales de Investigaciones, or departmental investigative police, which replaced the Bonaerense's Investigative Brigades, would be responsible for conducting investigations under the supervision of the judiciary, but also for producing studies about crime and police tactics, maintaining a public security information system, and operating a system for suspect identification. The reforms restricted the involvement of regular uniformed (sometimes called "preventive") police in investigations, which previously occupied a large portion of the work at the *comisaría* level.

Although the guiding principle behind both the governor's plan and the new public security law was decentralization of authority in order to better control the province's police forces, decentralization was not complete. Marcelo Saín notes this contradiction in the creation of a special directorate—a central provincial official—for all police intelligence (Saín 1998). In addition, the eighteen department chiefs were placed under the supervision of a general director of operations for the province.

Outcome

Although Governor Ruckauf represented the same political party as former Governor Duhalde, his approach to public security proved contradictory (Estévez 2000). Duhalde had focused on cleaning up the Bonaerense's dirty reputation, but his changes did not succeed in reducing crime. Ruckauf, by contrast, called for crime control at any price, including sometimes "shooting thieves."[14] Upon taking office, Ruckauf launched a "counterreform" to Duhalde's intervention. Although by this time many of the points of the reform plan were secured by law, others were not yet institutionalized or were only functioning in a few jurisdictions.

The restructuring of the police, based on decentralization of command through the division into eighteen regional departments, was completed. However, little changed on the front lines. A report by the Centro de Estudios Legales y Sociales (Center for Legal and Social Studies) (CELS) in Buenos Aires notes that, at the precinct (*comisaría*) level, the day-to-day work was unaffected by the government's large reform package. Basic management systems remained in place, and police violence and corruption persisted (CELS 1999, 118). The only perceptible change to many police officers was that they were free to spend more time on patrol, having passed their investigative duties to the new departmental investigative police (Abregú 1998, 10).

By the time Ruckauf took office, many neighborhood and municipal security councils had been formed, with varying levels of police and community participation. And early in 1999, the Office for Control of Official Corruption and Abuse and the Police Ethics Tribunal began operations. The first cases presented, however, pertained to disputes between lower- and higher-ranking officers, not the severe abuse for which the Bonaerense had become notorious (CELS 1999, 117, 120).

Other aspects of the Duhalde reforms, such as the creation of "defenders of security," had not yet been realized, and the Ruckauf administration did not pursue them further. Budget cuts by the Ruckauf administration forced the Institute for Crime and Security Policy to close at the end of 1999.

Ruckauf further undermined the spirit of the Duhalde reforms through his appointments and the creation of some new positions. As his first Minister of Security, Ruckauf named Aldo Rico, a former military colonel known for his participation in human rights abuses in the years Argentina was ruled by military junta (1976–1983) (CED 2000a, 6). Then, in early 2000, the governor divided the ministry into two separate offices, one for justice and one for security, and installed a retired police officer as security minister.

Although the reforms had eliminated any uniformed police chief for the province, Ruckauf created a new position, the "superintendent of coordination," that would function much as a provincial chief, and named a uniformed officer to the post. These moves revoked civilian leadership of the police that the Duhalde reforms had tried to establish.

The most alarming aspect of the counterreform has been the increase in deaths of civilians caused by police officers and deaths of police officers in armed confrontations. Ruckauf's rigid anticrime attitude has given police license to get tough on criminals, and officers who put themselves in danger receive "bravery rewards." The governor has even recommended that police "use maximum fire power to stop criminals." The daily newspaper *Clarín* reports that a study by the San Isidro courts showed that in the first eight months of Ruckauf's administration, the number of complaints of police mistreatment of youths doubled.[15] Research by CELS found that 273 civilians were killed by police and 76 police officers died in armed confrontations during 1999, compared with 172 civilians killed by police and 51 police deaths in 1998 (CELS 1999, 98–99).

Some observers note problems inherent in the reform plan attempted under Duhalde that facilitated its reversal. For one, the intervention created eighteen provincial departments but did not allow them to function autonomously, probably because of the deep mistrust of higher-ranking officers held by provincial officials. Commanders still depended on central administration for their budgets and for hiring, firing, and transferring personnel. The disciplinary system continued to be run by the central command, through the province's internal auditor and ethics tribunal. And the Bonaerense's training system remained more or less intact. To an innovative commander interested in using this new authority—in trying out new police strategies to deal with particular problems at the local level, in building a new culture of discipline within his or her ranks, or in retraining existing staff to improve their performance—these were serious constraints.

Conclusions from Buenos Aires

The approach taken by Duhalde and his team fell apart for at least three reasons: First, it alienated police and made them defensive of old ways. As noted by Sofía Tiscornia (1998), an Argentine anthropologist who specializes in institutional violence, the exclusion of police in the reform process was a fatal error in Buenos Aires. Any private sector business, she notes, before conducting such a drastic reform, would undertake extensive consultation with its employees. Tiscornia advises that successful reform requires consensus with the very people who will be called upon to comply with the changes. In the Buenos Aires case, because the government believed that police were contributing to the crime problem, it did not want them to be part of the solution.

After Duhalde's call for the reforms, the Buenos Aires parliament became a forum for the debate around how to structure the province's public security institutions, and a new law prescribed in detail just how the police would change. But the parliamentary process was more symbolic than real (CED 1999c, 32). Although legislators no doubt represent the will of their constituents, they are not experienced in policing—nor did they seek contributions from police in drafting the new law. Ultimately, realizing any reforms spelled out in the law would depend on police to go along with them.

Second, the reforms did not give police options for doing better police work. Although the reforms redistributed authority, both geographically and within the police hierarchy, the administration did not present a new model of police work for the commanders to follow. Some observers say the intervention was Duhalde's personal project, aimed at removing an obstacle to the presidency, not at consolidating a competent new public safety apparatus. By subordinating his ideas for reforms to his political agenda, Duhalde weakened his own power to actually cause long-lasting changes in the police force.

Third, the reforms produced no immediate results in crime reduction. Police misconduct seemed like a more urgent (and potentially more embarrassing) problem to the administration when it declared the intervention. Indeed, civil society organizations and the general public were exasperated with their rogue police. What the governor and his team underestimated, however, was the growing public will to do something about crime and make the police more effective. Tiscornia (1998) notes that the reforms instigated by Duhalde marked the first time that the "political class" in Argentina had concerned itself with the problems of bad policing. To Duhalde's and others' surprise, crime mattered more than corruption.

Chile: The Plan Cuadrante

Chile's 36,500 uniformed, preventive police, known as the Carabineros, have a reputation for integrity and discipline. However, their historical link to the defense forces has produced a militaristic culture that is widely regarded as closed, autonomous, and distant from the public. From 1973 to 1990, the Carabineros' general director was a member of the country's military junta, and the police force was used by the regime to suppress political subversion. Today the Carabineros' fundamental mission is crime control, not political control, but accompanying shifts in police strategies and orientation have not followed suit. The Carabineros remain accountable to their superior officers, but critics note that they are unresponsive to civilian officials and to local communities. Traditionally, Carabineros have granted outsiders little access to information about their mission, policies, and practices (Ward 1997, 1).

Although Chile still enjoys a low per-capita crime rate relative to other countries in Latin America, increasing crime and fear of crime have put pressure on the Carabineros—as well as other criminal justice institutions—to look for new strategies for preventing and controlling crime. In Minas Gerais, the police have looked to university experts to help them address similar pressures; in Buenos Aires, the provincial government stepped in; in Chile, it is the police themselves who have recently proposed institutional changes to improve their ability to fight crime and meet the demand for police services.

In the fall of 2000, the Carabineros began implementing the Plan Cuadrante, which has three elements: (1) increased presence of Carabineros on the street, (2) revised personal and human resource management systems, and (3) a new way of measuring performance based on a set of objective, quantifiable indicators. Although the plan does not call for a more community-oriented policing style, some observers say it is the first step in bringing Carabineros and communities closer together. Others warn that the plan only increases the Carabineros' capacity to carry out traditional—even repressive—law enforcement strategies.

Because the Plan Cuadrante is so new, we do not yet know how far the Carabineros will go in carrying out the plan or what its outcome will be. However, the mere fact that the Carabineros have engaged in a process to improve and modernize their institution is a step that seemed far less possible only a few years ago. For those interested in bringing about more open, accountable, and democratic policing in Chile, the Carabineros' plan—even if it fails—gives them hope that the institution is becoming more receptive to new ideas.

Factors Leading Up to Reform

It is difficult to know whether the Plan Cuadrante is the product of long-term planning by the organization's leadership, a reaction to increasing crime and public concern about crime, or the initiative of energetic leaders. One thing is sure: public security has become a more prominent political issue than ever before in Chile.[16]

Although Chile has the second lowest rate of victimization in South America behind Uruguay (Gaviria and Pagés 1999, 32), crime and fear of crime have grown in the late 1990s. In 1997, two surveys revealed that 68.6 percent of Chileans thought that crime had increased over the previous year, and that 84.2 percent thought that crime had become more violent than in 1996 (Frühling 1999, 69).[17] In 1989, 21.5 percent of Chileans placed crime first on their list of concerns, and in 1995, 35 percent put crime first.[18] The increase of armed robbery and robbery with intimidation, in particular, has made citizens feel more threatened.[19] Between 1999 and 2000, these and other crimes against persons increased 23.5 percent (Ministry of the Interior 2001).

The rise in crime has led Chileans to demand more police service. Public security has traditionally been dealt with by the national government—the Carabineros and the Policía de Investigaciones (Investigative Police) are both national institutions. In the last several years, however, this change in public opinion has led communities to begin pursuing their own solutions to local crime problems. Municipal governments are now more involved than ever before in policing and public safety issues. Some municipalities have begun supporting, or increased their support for, local police units. Throughout Chile, city governments typically donate equipment and material resources to local police stations, assist in the construction of station houses, and form local police support committees. In some cases, city agencies have taken over responsibilities that traditionally belonged to the Carabineros—such as delivering court papers to residences—in order to free up police for other duties (CED 1998, 5–6).

The Chilean Association of Municipalities reported that local support for Carabineros totaled US$10.8 million over twenty months in 1998 and 1999 (CED 1998, 5–6). Because crime continued to rise in the late 1990s, the association asked the Carabineros to account for how the money was spent. The public embarrassment this caused the Carabineros may be one factor motivating the Plan Cuadrante's new resource management system.

As local communities and municipal governments get more involved in public security policy, questions arise about equality. Rich communities are more likely to sponsor their own auxiliary police forces, to purchase private security services, or to increase the local capacity of the Carabineros. One researcher used "units of service equivalents" to compare the level of police service among communities in Santiago and found that the richest communities indeed received the most policing.[20]

Some observers say the Plan Cuadrante is less a response to external factors than the Carabineros' own recognition that society has changed in recent years and that the organization must keep up with the changes, the same conclusion reached by the leadership of the Military Police in Minas Gerais. The gradual but persistent increases in crime in the late 1990s have caused the Carabineros to rethink the effectiveness of their traditional approach to policing, grounded in law enforcement and absent public cooperation. In 1996, then–General Director of Carabineros Rodolfo Stange began drafting a strategic plan for the organization that would reflect Chile's recent social, demographic, and economic changes. In September 1998, a special commission with representatives from the Carabineros, the Interior Ministry, and the Defense Ministry began drafting a comprehensive plan to improve citizen security. Among the changes the commission recommended were the gradual shift of twelve thousand officers from administrative to operational functions; the creation of a system of *cuadrantes,* or patrol sectors; the introduction of better management techniques; and improvements to information management (CED 1999d).

It is difficult to say why the Carabineros embarked on the Plan Cuadrante when they did. At least one observer attributes the timing to the director general of Carabineros, Manuel Ugarte, who was appointed in 1998. Unlike previous directors general, Ugarte's career inside the Carabineros includes extensive experience in police operations, not just management and policy. He has often traveled outside Chile to learn about policing models in other countries, particularly England.[21]

The Plan Cuadrante

The Plan de Seguridad Vecinal Integral y Plan Nacional de Difusión de Acciones Policiales Preventivas (Plan for Integrated Neighborhood Security and the National Plan for Dissemination of Preventive Police Activities), or Plan Cuadrante, proposes to reverse the trend of increasing crime by putting more police on the streets (CED 1999e). The plan has three main parts: first, it carves out new patrol sectors and estimates the amount of policing needed to control crime in each; second, it puts in place rigorous systems for control of human and material resource; and third, it establishes objective, quantitative measures for individual and departmental performance.

The Carabineros first tested the Plan Cuadrante in the Santiago Sur precinct. Early results from the pilot showed that relations between police and citizens improved and citizens' fear of crime decreased, but reported crime actually increased. A possible explanation for the increase is that citizens felt more confident in the police and were more inclined to report crime. Evaluations of the pilot site and further implementation of the Plan Cuadrante will be conducted by Carabineros personnel based on official statistics and citizen surveys,[22] but such evaluations are typically for internal use only. At the time of this writing, the plan has been extended to the entire metropolitan region, as well as to certain neighborhoods in the 5th and 8th regions (Frühling 2003, 12).[23]

Deployment by Cuadrantes

The cuadrante system attempts to address two problems the Carabineros face: the increase in demand for police services and the emerging imbalance of police service among rich and poor communities.

According to official publications of the Carabineros, the Plan Cuadrante creates patrol sectors based on diversity of the sector, urban layout, composition of the population, activities that occur in the sector, and its crime profile.[24] Based on the level of crime, the Carabineros assign each *cuadrante* a rating of one, two, or three corresponding to the number of times per day that a pair of officers is needed to patrol every street in the area by car, foot, or motorcycle in order to control crime. The resources for adequate service in each *cuadrante* are distributed on the basis of "units of vigilance equivalents" (see below).

Carabineros expect that more street presence will result in better community relations, and they concede that community input is needed to improve safety (Bobadilla Rojas 1999). With adoption of the Plan Cuadrante, patrol assignments will increase from two to four years to allow stronger bonds to develop between police and local residents.[25] Some officers will be assigned to attend neighborhood association meetings, where they will hear residents' complaints about crime, and they will set up networks for neighbors to share information about crime and pass information to Carabineros. Carabineros also plan to improve coordination of crime reduction activities with mayors, neighborhood groups, and community organizations (Bobadilla Rojas 1999).

Resource Management

The Plan Cuadrante attempts to systematize the distribution and control of human and material resources so that Carabineros are able to ensure public safety and a minimum level of police service for every community. Under the plan, resources will be distributed on the basis of objective criteria—namely the crime level of each *cuadrante*—not political or economic importance.

Ideally, every *cuadrante* of the same rating (one, two, or three) will have the same or equivalent resources. A *cuadrante* with a rating of one would have one "unit of vigilance equivalent" at all times, a ranking of two would require two units, and so forth. The composition of each unit varies among *cuadrantes*. The value assigned to persons, equipment, or vehicles is based on how well they enable police to cover territory and the quality of coverage they provide. For example, one patrol car with three officers equals one unit, one motorcycle with one officer equals 0.45 units, one mounted officer equals 0.3 units, and one foot patrol officer equals 0.2 units.[26]

At the core of the Carabineros' new resource distribution plan are the basic economic principles of supply and demand. The unit-of-vigilance equivalence concept is an attempt to quantify police service in order to fit it into a supply and demand equation. The Plan Cuadrante provides that Carabineros will assess local conditions and measure the need for police service in each *cuadrante;* that they will quantify and price the resources necessary to deliver that level of service; that they will determine other factors that influence service delivery, such as size of the territory to be covered and population density; and that they will judge whether existing resources are enough (Marabolí B. 1999, 4).

When the Carabineros assessed their ability to provide basic police coverage according to the *cuadrante* system, they found that demand far outstripped supply. They would need more resources. First, they looked for ways of reallocating what they had. Over a period of three years, they have proposed to shift twelve thousand personnel from administrative to operational duties. This would require reorganizing four daily work shifts into three, hiring civilians to perform administrative tasks, and freeing Carabineros from tasks that are not purely police related (CED 1999e). They are also closing down some station houses and reassigning personnel to others. Next, Carabineros obtained extra funds from the Interior Ministry to cover, among other things, the addition of two thousand personnel.[27]

Information Management and Performance Measurement

The third element of the Carabineros' Plan Cuadrante involves the creation of new information management systems. The Carabineros intend for the new systems to provide objective criteria for evaluating individual personnel as well as overall crime prevention and control strategies. The Carabineros' existing information system tracks data recorded in crime complaints at each station house, making it difficult to examine crime conditions and patterns for an entire city or region. Eventually, Carabineros plan to install a network that will link stations to central command. They also hope to use the system to improve community relations by sharing local crime information—possibly even digitized maps—with residents (CED 2000b, 8).

The Carabineros are also preparing staff to make better use of the information they track. In 2000, four Carabineros attended a crime analysis course in the United States, where they learned how to perform crime mapping, and traveled to England for two weeks to work inside a crime analysis unit. As a result, the Carabineros established an office of Community Relations and Crime Analysis that is responsible for crime analysis for the director general's use.

A complex challenge facing the Carabineros (and any other police force) is measuring police performance to include the many different things that police do. Carabineros' existing performance measurement system is based only on tangible or quantifiable factors, such as the conditions of physical installations and equipment, response time to calls for service, and crime incidents. But because police are available twenty-four hours a day, because they have local community presence, because they are equipped to respond rapidly, and often because of a lack of basic social services, much of their time is spent interacting with citizens to address all sorts of problems. The productivity of this activity is not easily measured. Carabineros say they are trying to develop performance measures that include public opinion surveys, reports by other agencies and private organizations, as well as internal evaluations (Carabineros de Chile 1998, 5–7). A newly created Department of Control and Management will periodically evaluate the performance of local units (Barrientos Ramírez 2000, 20).

The Carabineros' current system for measuring individual performance is largely subjective and includes factors such as commitment to the organization and patriotism. The Carabineros plan to replace this system with one that measures progress toward goals. Officers will set goals for each region related to resource management and crime reduction and will be evaluated according to their progress toward meeting them.[28] In addition, Carabineros are working now to select a set of six or eight key indicators against which area commanders can compare their performance over time, or which central command can use to compare *cuadrantes* against each other.[29]

Outcome

So far, the Carabineros' Plan Cuadrante consists of a written plan, an initial pilot experiment, and implementation in a few sites. How the plan will affect crime and community relations is still unknown. It seems unlikely, however, that the Carabineros will abandon their commitment to implement the plan, after having obtained special funds for it and eliciting support from neighborhood organizations and the media.[30]

While solid conclusions are distant, early expectations for the Plan Cuadrante are numerous. Some observers are skeptical that the Carabineros may follow the letter of the plan but not permit deeper strategic or cultural changes. Carabineros are adept at public relations, and in the newly democratic Chile, they suffer from their militaristic image. The cynical view is that improving the Carabineros' public image will satisfy their interest in reform, unlike the case of Minas Gerais, where a culture of reform is deeply rooted in the police force.

There is wide agreement on what the Plan Cuadrante is not: it is not an attempt to introduce community policing to Chile. Although some aspects of the plan are aimed at improving police-community relations, they do not alter the Carabineros' basic crime control approach, which relies on arrest and detention rather than working with citizens to solve the root causes of crime. It should be noted here, however, that in spring 2001, the government announced a new plan to support community-led public safety initiatives. The Plan Comuna Segura—Compromiso 100 (Community Safety Plan—Promise 100) calls for community councils for citizen security and the role of technical secretaries to assist them. The Interior Ministry will sponsor citizen-led projects in twelve of the councils.

Although no one expects that the Plan Cuadrante will revolutionize policing in Chile, some observers are optimistic that the Carabineros have engaged in reform at all. The willingness of police leadership to try something new opens a space for dialogue on the topic of public security reform—and for introducing new ideas—that did not exist just a few years ago. At a minimum, they say, the Plan Cuadrante provides a more rational, objective basis for management and resource allocation.

Conclusions from Chile

As in the example of Buenos Aires, when problems with rising crime and police ineffectiveness are severe, it is tempting for police reformers to try to change everything at once. In Chile, the Carabineros do not face such acute problems, although they are under pressure to be more effective and open. The Plan Cuadrante is designed to address specific deficiencies identified by the Carabineros and no more. It is not an attempt to change police culture or style, only to install more rigorous management systems. If they succeed, the Carabineros will have produced a better managed organization.

Historically, the Carabineros have retained tight control over their operations, crime control tactics, and even crime statistics. They are also in the driver's seat of the Plan Cuadrante, even though government, NGOs, and academics are making some important contributions. In addition to authorizing funding to pay for the Plan Cuadrante, for example, the government has organized a special commission to measure demand for police service among communities, and resources will be distributed among *cuadrantes* based on the commission's findings. In addition, Carabineros have consulted a handful of academics and representatives of NGOs on different aspects of the plan.

Although concentrating the reform process within the police organization helps police take ownership of the changes and makes internal resistance less probable, the lack of involvement by civil society institutions—particularly community organizations—may prove detrimental. Improved police-community relations is one of the Plan Cuadrante's major goals, and yet there seems to have been no consultation with community organizations to learn citizens' or community leaders' views on how to best accomplish this.

Measuring the Plan Cuadrante's success will be no easy task, especially on such vague scores as police-community relations or citizen satisfaction with police service. Yet here Chile stands to learn from the example of Buenos Aires province. In Buenos Aires, the provincial government seized a political opportunity to shake up its police but had to abandon the entire reform package when it did not produce the changes that people desired most. The Plan Cuadrante has received a lot of media attention and citizens are forming expectations. If they do not perceive real changes, the moment for Carabineros to bring about the changes both they and the public hope for could be lost. Public opinion does matter in the process of reform.

Conclusions

Who Is Involved in Police Reform?

A central theme of this chapter is that police reform efforts can be strengthened by the involvement of multiple actors. Those actors are identified as the police organizations themselves, government or state authorities, and civil society (including NGOs, research organizations, community groups, the media, and individual citizens). Police-led reforms can better address citizens' insecurity, for example, when they consult citizens (directly or through associations that represent them) to find out what they want. State-sponsored reforms, even when there is great political will behind the changes, can be stalled without the involvement of multiple ranks of the police organization. Of course, every situation is different; there is no specific combination of actors or minimum level of involvement that will guarantee the success of police reforms. And for historical and political reasons, it is not always possible for all three or even a combination of these actors to work together in Latin America. But, as discussed below, each stands to gain from the contribution and support of the other in striving to make their societies more safe and, ultimately, more democratic.

Police

The locus for police reform is, of course, the police organization itself. Even in a deficient police organization, some members will have technical expertise about crime control, extensive knowledge of the communities where they work, and experience in running their own organizations—and many will simply be motivated to improve their self-image and professionalism. Ultimately, police determine whether reforms succeed and endure, since they must carry out and live with the changes.

Changes within the police organization require strong leadership and the courage to innovate. Yet even when changes are led by police commanders, other parts of the organization may try to block them (Stone and Ward 2000, 19). Police reform must offer something positive for police, and that is best assured when police of multiple ranks participate in the reforms.

At the other extreme, particularly in Chile, police sometimes attempt reforms without the participation of other government institutions and civil society. Such efforts can produce skepticism about the depth of commitment and the extent of real change. This is especially true in societies where police are mistrusted, either for their commitment to crime control or their conduct.

Government or State

Although it is difficult to sustain state-sponsored initiatives without support from the police, the state confers political legitimacy on new initiatives and, when necessary, allocates funding for them.

When a crime problem or police misconduct is severe, and when the initiative within the department to address these problems is weak, the role of the state may have to be larger (Stone and Ward 2000, 30). However, in such cases the tendency is often to propose radical solutions to sometimes intractable problems. The changes proposed in Buenos Aires, for example, were too extensive to produce any measurable results within a short time frame—a serious problem for politicians under pressure to show quick results.

What happened in Buenos Aires also illustrates the potential problem of politician-led police reform. A change in political administration may result in funding cuts and programmatic shifts that cancel out or even reverse the reforms. This can serve as a warning for other Latin American states that embark on state-led police reforms.

Civil Society

In Latin America, there is little history of collaboration between the state or its police and civil society. Public security is traditionally the responsibility of the state, which—through its police—is charged with protecting citizens from crime. However, police in Chile and elsewhere are learning that they can control crime better when they share more of this responsibility with citizens.

Public perception of the police and of crime—whether real or exaggerated—is often the impetus for police reform. Yet there are few mechanisms for police or state entities to consult average citizens about what they want from their police, other than the occasional public survey or election. Consultation with local citizens committees and neighborhood watch groups helps police target their activities and helps state officials shape public security policy to meet citizens' expectations.

Although there may be few ways for average citizens to contribute to processes of police reform, there are many NGOs and community organizations that can articulate public concerns about crime and police abuse. The obstacle for these groups is that police are unaccustomed to working with outsiders toward their shared goal of public safety. Instead, so-called civilians are often invited to give lectures at the police academy or to attend public meetings with police. Police overlook these groups' potential to organize residents and merchants around crime prevention activities.

Police also stand to gain from partnerships with researchers, who can lend expertise and skills. In Minas Gerais, for example, the Center for Studies of Crime and Public Safety at the Federal University has helped the Military

Police collect and interpret crime data. Based on this information, the police have changed their deployment patterns and enforcement strategies to better target crime.

Different Paths and Results

There is no set model or prescription for police reform. To be sure, there is a limited menu of things that one can try to change: recruitment practices, training programs, deployment patterns, the nature and tone of interaction with members of the public, information systems, and tools and equipment, to name just a few. But changing any of these things may produce different effects in different places. For example, in Minas Gerais, the introduction of new skills and work habits aimed at improving police effectiveness have, according to some observers there, begun to improve the self-image and professionalism of the police organization. In Buenos Aires, on the other hand, Governor Ruckauf's tough-on-crime message to police produced an increase in civilian deaths and a perception that police are out of control. The difference here may be due to the individual leadership of the persons in charge, and that is part of the problem. Although goals and reform plans may seem similar at face value, the tone of the persons leading the changes and the attitudes of those who accept or reject them dictates their outcome.

Should there be a model of police reform? Should some international group of persons committed to better policing sit down and write out a series of guidelines or objectives? If the goal is to bring about a method of policing that is more consistent with democratic values, then each society deserves its own policing system. Choosing an approach to policing and setting priorities for crime reduction can be opened up to a more democratic process and determined locally—ideally through a process of consultation among police, government, and citizens.

The Need for Evaluation

Lessons from different police reform experiments would be useful to police reformers, but they are hard to come by in Latin America. Although the body of literature on policing in the region is growing rapidly, there is still a dearth of evaluations measuring the impact of police reforms. That is understandable for many reasons. First, policing became a subject worthy of serious study in Latin America only in the early 1990s. Second, researchers and police have not traditionally worked together in Latin America, with the notable exception of the twenty-year partnership between the Center for Studies of Crime and Public Security in Minas Gerais and the state's Military Police. Forging such a partnership is not easy. Police must believe that they will gain something from the partnership. They may be reluctant to turn over sensitive crime and personnel data to outsiders for study and, possibly, criticism. Researchers have their work cut out for them in earning police trust.

A third impediment to the development of police research in Latin America and elsewhere has been the challenge of measuring the success of police reforms. One problem is knowing what to attribute to good or bad police work. If crime drops, is it because police did something different? It is impossible to know. Researchers must use more specific factors that are more easily attributable to policing. For example, instead of measuring the fluctuation of overall crime, researchers could compare specific categories of crime—such as burglary—before and after police adopt new tactics for reducing burglary in a particular geographic area. Researchers could employ similar methods for measuring the impact of other changes in policing, including new training programs. In order for researchers to carry out these sorts of before-and-after impact evaluations, however, they need to gather reliable baseline data, and this requires them to have a good working relationship with police in advance of the reforms.

Another challenge is identifying factors that are useful for comparing before and after reform is initiated. Many systems for measuring police effectiveness are based on easily quantifiable factors, such as the number of citations given out, the number of arrests made, or the number of investigations closed by detectives. However, much of police work is spent walking or driving a beat, talking to residents and merchants, observing neighborhood conditions, attending community meetings, visiting schools, and many other things that cannot be easily counted.

More scientific evaluation of police reform could help police learn from the mistakes and achievements of their counterparts across Latin America. And if the evaluations include a broad range of variables—the effect on crime, the incidence of police abuse, the success of investigations, possibly even job satisfaction among police and public opinion of police—it would help the other police leaders identify aspects of the reforms that they might adapt best to their own precincts.

There are many brands of police reform in Latin America. Some police organizations in the region have adopted elements of policing models developed in other countries, such as community policing, and through trial and error they have tailored them to local circumstances. Police commanders in Minas Gerais and in Chile have offered their own innovations, and still others continue to draw from the same old menu of police strategies without knowing for sure how well they are working. Lessons from all these experiences, when shared among reform-minded police leaders, government officials, and citizens would go a long way toward advancing better policing in the democracies of Latin America.

Notes

1. This is particularly the case in Chile, where reforms were first implemented in fall 2000.
2. Claudio C. Beato F., electronic personal correspondence with the author, 6 November 2000.
3. Ibid.
4. Ibid.
5. Ibid.
6. Ibid.
7. Ibid.
8. Ibid.
9. Beato, personal electronic correspondence with author, 14 May 2001.
10. Ibid.
11. CED (1999b), based on reports in *Clarín* in September 1999.
12. Centro de Estudios Unión para la Nueva Mayoría, cited in Saín (1998).
13. Cited in Estévez (2000).
14. CED (2000a, 6), based on reports in *Clarín*, 9 February, 31 March, and 2 April.
15. "Ruckauf y su vice polemizan sobre la Policía Bonaerense," *Clarín*, 28 September 2000.
16. See Frühling (2003).
17. Survey by Fundación Paz Ciudadana and Adimark, *La Segunda*, 26 May 1996, p. 16; cited by Frühling (1999, 70).
18. Encuestas CEP-Adimark, 1989–1993 and CEP, 1995, cited by Frühling (1999, 71).
19. Fundación Paz Ciudadana, *Anuario de estadísticas criminales, 1996 y 1997*, cited by Frühling (1999, 69).
20. Iván Silva, unpublished research; cited by Frühling (1999, 85).
21. Carlos Valdivieso, General Manager of Fundación Paz Ciudadana, phone interview with author, 15 November 2000.
22. Guillermo Holzmann, professor of political science, Universidad de Chile, telephone interview with author, 8 November 2000.
23. In March 2006, President Michelle Bachelet promised to continue implementing the plan in even more areas, bringing coverage by the Plan Cuadrante to 66 percent of the country's districts.
24. "Plan Cuadrante," http://www.carabineros.cl/base.htm.
25. Valdivieso interview.

26. "Plan Cuadrante: Qué es?" http://www.carabineros.cl/objetivo.htm.
27. Valdivieso interview.
28. Ibid.
29. Ibid.
30. Holzmann interview.

References

Abregú, Martín. 1998. "La reforma policial en la Provincia de Buenos Aires." *Policía y Sociedad Democrática* (Centro de Estudios para el Desarrollo, Santiago, Chile), no. 1.

Annicchiarico, Ciro. 1998. "El desafío de reformular la política de seguridad y de intervenir la Policía Bonaerense." In *El final de la maldita policía? El Frepaso ante la reforma del sistema de seguridad de la provincia de Buenos Aires*. Edited by Eduardo Sigal, Alberto Binder, and Ciro Annicchiarico. Buenos Aires: Ediciones FAC.

Barrientos Ramírez, Franklin. 2000. *La gestión policial y sus métodos de evaluación*. Santiago: Centro de Estudios para el Desarrollo, April.

Bayley, David H. 1997. "The Contemporary Practices of Policing: A Comparative View." Paper presented to the Center for Strategic and International Studies and the Police Executive Research Forum, Washington, DC, 6 October.

Beato F., C. Claudio. 2000. "Informação e desempenho policial." Paper presented at the Fourth Brazilian Seminar for the project Police and Democratic Society, São Paulo, 1 February.

———. 2001. "Ação e estratégia das organizações policiais." In *Policía, sociedad y estado: Modernización y reforma policial en América del Sur,* edited by Hugo Frühling and Azun Candina. Santiago: Centro de Estudios para el Desarrollo.

Beraldi, Carlos. 1998. "Response to Marcel Saín." Seminar on Police Reform in Argentina, Centro de Estudios Legales y Sociales, Buenos Aires, 1–2 December.

Bobadilla Rojas, Alfons. 1999. "Carabineros y su relación con la comunidad: Planes y programas desarrollados e implementados." Third International Course on Policy Design and Evaluation of Citizen Security Projects, Santiago, 19 August.

Carabineros de Chile, Dirección General. 1998. *Foro panel: Los medios de comunicación y su responsabilidad en la seguridad ciudadana, Municipalidad de San Joaquín*. Santiago: Política Comunicacional de Carabineros de Chile, 1 July.

Centro de Estudios para el Desarrollo (CED). 1998. "Chile: La nueva trascendencia del municipio para el desarrollo de la policía." *Policía y Sociedad Democrática*, no. 2, December.

———. 1999a. "Programa de investigación y capacitación conjuntos en Minas Gerais: Las policías y la universidad trabajando juntos." *Policía y Sociedad Democrática*, no. 5, October.

———. 1999b. "Argentina: Renuncia del Ministro de Seguridad y Justicia de Buenos Aires: cambio de rumbo en la reforma policial." *Policía y Sociedad Democrática*, no. 5, October.

———. 1999c. "Las reformas policiales en Argentina." *Proyecto Policía y Sociedad Democática: Resumen de actividades y informes de reuniones realizadas*. Summary of seminar organized by the Centro de Estudios Legales y Sociales, Buenos Aires, 1–2 December 1998. Santiago: CED, July.

———. 1999d. "Chile: Balance de la reforma policial en Chile." *Policía y Sociedad Democrática*, no. 5, October.

———. 1999e. "Chile: Nuevo plan de seguridad ciudadana." *Policía y Sociedad Democrática*, no. 3, March.

———. 2000a. "Argentina: Renuncia del Ministro de Seguridad de la Provincia de Buenos Aires." *Policía y Sociedad Democrática*, no. 7, June.

———. 2000b. "Chile: Anuncios sobre la nueva gestión en Carabineros de Chile." *Policía y Sociedad Democrática*, no. 7, June.

Centro de Estudios Legales y Sociales (CELS). 1999. *Derechos humanos en Argentina: Informe anual 2000*. Buenos Aires: CELS.

Centro de Investigaciones Sociales y Asesorías Legales Populares (CISALP). 1996. *Boletín Informativo*, no. 4. Buenos Aires: CISALP, September.

———. 1997. *Boletín Informativo*, no. 131. Buenos Aires: CISALP, 27 September.

De Souza, Elenice. 1999. "Policiamento comunitário em Belo Horizonte." Master's thesis, Federal University of Minas Gerais.

Estévez, Eduardo E. 2000. "Reforma de sistemas de seguridad pública e investigaciones judiciales: Tres experiencias en la Argentina." Paper presented at the conference Crimen y Violencia: Causas y Políticas de Prevención, World Bank and Universidad de los Andes, Bogotá, Colombia, 4–5 May.

Frühling, Hugo. 1999. "La policía en Chile: Los nuevos desafíos de un coyuntura compleja." *Perspectivas en política, economía y gestión* (Universidad de Chile, Santiago) 3, no. 1.

———. 2003. "Police Reform and the Process of Democratization." In *Crime and Violence in Latin America*, edited by Hugo Frühling and Joseph Tulchin with Heather A. Golding. Washington, DC: Woodrow Wilson Center Press.

Gaviria, Alejandro, and Carmen Pagés. 1999. *Patterns of Crime Victimization in Latin America*. Working Paper 402. Washington, DC: Inter-American Development Bank, 29 October.

Human Rights Watch. 1998. *Exacerbating Insecurity: Police Brutality in Argentina*. Translated by Jill Hedges. Washington, DC: Human Rights Watch and CELS.

Inter-American Development Bank (IDB). 1999. *Perfil I, Argentina: Programa de prevención de la violencia y el crimen*. Profile: Project No. AR-0247. Washington, DC: IDB, August. http://www.iadb.org/exr/doc98/pro/par0247.pdf.

Mesquita Neto, Paulo, with Beatriz Stella Affonso. 1998. *Policiamento comunitário: A experiência em São Paulo*. São Paulo: Núcleo de Estudos da Violência da Universidade de São Paulo, September.

Ministry of the Interior (Chile). 2001. *Informe anual de estadísticas nacionales y regionales 2000: Denuncia por delitos de mayor connotación social y violencia intrafamiliar, situación nacional de narcotráfico, período 1999–2000*. Santiago, February. http://www.interior.gov.cl.

Marabolí B., Marcos. 1999. *Administración de recursos de vigilancia policial: Concepto de nivel mínimo de vigilancia efectiva*. Versión preliminar. Santiago: Carabineros de Chile, Consejo Asesor Superior, Departamento Planificación y Desarrollo, August.

Morrison, Andrew, Mayra Buvinic, and Michael Shifter. 2003. "The Violent Americas? Risk Factors, Consequences, and Policy Implications of Social and Domestic Violence." In *Crime and Violence in Latin America: Citizen Security, Democracy, and the State*, edited by Hugo Frühling and Joseph Tulchin with Heather A. Golding. Washington, DC: Woodrow Wilson Center Press/Johns Hopkins University Press.

Saín, Marcelo. 1998. "Democracia, seguridad pública y policía. La reforma del sistema de seguridad y policial en la Provincia de Buenos Aires." Working paper presented at the seminar on Police Reform in Argentina, Centro de Estudios Legales y Sociales, Buenos Aires, 1–2 December.

Sapori, Luis Flávio, and Silas Barnabé de Souza. 2001. "Violência policial e cultura militar: Aspectos teóricos e empíricos." *Teoria e Sociedade,* no. 7, 173–214.

Secretaría de Seguridad, Gobierno de la Provincia de Buenos Aires. [1997]. *La transformación del sistema de seguridad.* Buenos Aires: [Secretaría de Seguridad].

Soares, Luiz Eduardo. 2000. *Meu casaco de general: 500 dias no front da segurança pública do Rio de Janeiro.* São Paulo: Companhia das Letras.

Stone, Christopher E., and Heather H. Ward. 2000. "Democratic Policing: A Framework for Action." *Policing & Society* 10, no. 1, 11–45.

Tiscornia, Sofía. 1998. "Response to Marcel Saín." Seminar on Police Reform in Argentina, Centro de Estudios Legales y Sociales, Buenos Aires, 1–2 December.

Ward, Heather. 1997. *Country Overview: Chile.* Internal Report. New York: Vera Institute of Justice, March.

———. 1998. *Brazil: Focus on Rio de Janeiro and São Paulo.* Internal Report. New York: Vera Institute of Justice, March.

Chapter 8

Citizen Participation and Public Security in Argentina, Brazil, and Chile: Lessons from an Initial Experience

Catalina Smulovitz

Introduction

Most Latin American societies have recently experienced an increase in crime rates and in citizens' perception of insecurity. Because of the central importance the issue of security has assumed, it has made its way onto governments' agendas and onto the broader public agenda. However, despite consensus regarding the seriousness of the problem, the numerous policies aimed at dealing with the issue have sometimes been contradictory. On the one hand, there have been policies designed to correct deficiencies in the state's punitive systems and increase the repressive capacities of the security forces. Policies of this type include measures such as increasing the severity of sentences, lowering the age of legal accountability, bringing greater police presence to bear, and expanding police powers. On the other hand, with the marked decline in the reputation of the police during the 1990s, there was a flurry of proposals aimed at bringing about police reform, many of which included community policing programs inspired by measures tried in the 1980s in the United States, Canada, and Europe (see Goldstein 1990; National Institute of Justice 1988–1990; Trojanowicz and Bucqueroux 1993; Chinchilla and Rico 1997; Neild 1998).

In the following pages, selected community policing programs implemented in Argentina, Brazil, and Chile will be considered. An exploratory map of current experiences will be drawn, and an attempt will be made to extract lessons from some of the experiments. The experiences under consideration differ in terms of their stage of development and availability of relevant information. Thus, in some cases it is possible to make preliminary impact assessments, while others provide little more than a rough list of the efforts currently underway. Moreover, although a number of the programs are characterized as examples of community policing, many are limited to promoting some degree of citizen participation in security issues, rather than being community policing programs *per se*.

Community Policing: Initial Definitions

The ineffectiveness and failure of the policing model based on increased use of repressive mechanisms were instrumental factors in prompting the emergence of alternative policing projects (Chinchilla 1999). In these alternate models, the policing function is not limited to enforcement, but includes a preventive dimension of promoting public peace and security. In order to achieve these expanded goals, the community policing model proposes that the police work in close contact with other state agencies and the community. By consulting with members of the local community, problems affecting it can be identified and policing measures can be adapted to address its needs. Moreover, the model proposes participation by the community and by local state agencies in designing ways to reduce crime rates, reduce the sense of citizen insecurity, and increase public acceptance of the police, while also improving social monitoring of police actions. Implementation of community policing entails a number of changes, namely (1) expanding the traditional police mandate; (2) greater emphasis on preventive vs. reactive policing functions; (3) incorporation of strategies for local action; and (4) inclusion of mechanisms for cooperation among the police, political authorities, public service providers, and members of the community.

From this brief description, it can be seen that certain conditions are needed in order to implement community policing programs. However, the superimposition of, and conflict between, two policy approaches are hindering the chances of bringing about those conditions: measures are currently being designed to control and limit police discretion, while at the same time police powers are being enhanced to give them greater punitive authority. Measures of the former type seek to increase citizen participation, and are based on the premise that security can only be achieved through cooperation between the protector and the protected. Measures of the latter type, on the other hand, are based on the view that providing security, rather than being a shared responsibility, is solely the job of the police—a system that tends to reinforce the adversarial relationship and lack of trust between the police and the citizenry. Although there has been no detailed evaluation of community policing programs in Latin America, the few existing assessments tend to show that, in addition to this superimposition of contradictory policies, another factor affecting their implementation is that one of the primary objectives of these programs is to change the public image of the police. Thus, rather than being an alternative model for achieving citizen security, community policing appears to be merely a tool for ameliorating the increasingly poor reputation of the police.

Experiences with Community Policing

In recent years, community policing projects—or projects presented as such—have been implemented in Peru, El Salvador, Colombia, Venezuela, Haiti, Brazil, Chile, Argentina, and Guatemala (Chinchilla and Rico 1997; Chinchilla 1999). The scope and definition of these efforts have varied widely, as have the reasons for their emergence and the identity of those promoting them. Beyond these differences, an evaluation of the results of these experiences must consider at least the following[1]: (1) the impact of community policing on the reduction of crime and violence, (2) the perception of citizen insecurity, (3) the levels of police violence and corruption, (4) on the levels of trust/distrust between the community and police, and the organizational structure of the police (changes in professionalization, education, etc.), (5) on the expansion and continuity of community participation in community policing programs; and (6) on the extent and level of collaboration on community policing programs by other bureaucratic agencies. It should be pointed out, however, that available data are not sufficient to allow for a detailed evaluation of each of these variables, given the wide disparities in information available on the selected cases. The primary objective here is to provide a map of some of the existing experiences, so consideration will be given to certain programs currently in development in Argentina, Brazil, and Chile.

Argentina

In the 1980–1999 period, statistics from the National Crime Policy Bureau of Argentina (Dirección Nacional de Política Criminal de la Argentina) show an increase in crime rates for the entire country. A recent work by Lucía

Dammert (2000) indicates a threefold increase in crime.[2] In 1980, on a national level, there were 80 crimes reported for each 10,000 inhabitants, compared to 174.2 in 1990, and 319.7 in 1999 (Dammert 2000). Data on the perception of citizen insecurity mirrors this situation: 86.2 percent of the population indicated that they believe they live in an insecure environment (Dammert 2000). In this context of insecurity and increasing crime rates, efforts were undertaken to implement reforms in public security policies and, particularly, in the policing apparatus.

The subject of police structure reform received the highest visibility and attracted great public interest, since it arose primarily in response to an ongoing decline in the reputation of the police.[3] The issue of insecurity and the problem of the police became topics of discussion on the political agenda and a subject of public debate, encompassing a wide range of actors. In addition to political officials and the police agencies themselves, the discussion included technical experts from the political parties, members of various nongovernmental organizations (NGOs), and citizens who, having been victims of police violence, organized themselves for the purpose of influencing the debate. Because the debate encompassed such a broad array of actors, police policy will no longer continue to be made "in camera," as was true in the past, and such policy is now beginning to be debated in a fairly public way.

Currently, a number of districts are in the process of implementing or designing police reforms. Despite the recent nature of these efforts, it should be noted that one of their common characteristics has been citizen involvement in formulating security policies. The national government has enlisted the assistance of specific institutions in an effort to ensure that the community plays a role in public security (Smulovitz 2003); examples of this are police programs in Buenos Aires Province,[4] the reform carried out by Santa Fe Province (Rosúa 1998), and the reform of the city government of Buenos Aires.[5] Buenos Aires Province secured the participation of national government agencies in security programs involving neighborhood, municipal, and departmental councils, while also calling on the participation of Municipal Defenders of Security.[6] In Santa Fe Province, Neighborhood Community Security Councils were formed to promote discussion between police and local residents (Rosúa 1998). Beginning in July 1997, the Buenos Aires city government promoted the formation of neighborhood Crime and Violence Prevention Councils to provide residents a channel for their security demands and give them a role in implementing and monitoring security measures.

In addition to these institutional efforts, numerous civil associations and neighborhood movements have emerged, made up of those actually affected by safety concerns. In the vast majority of cases, these groups arise as a consequence of dissatisfaction with the results obtained through police action. In some cases these associations attempt to control local criminal activity, while in others they seek to monitor police performance. In all cases, however, they are managed by the local residents themselves.

Thus, Argentina provides two scenarios: in one, state agencies and citizen representatives interact in institutional venues; in the other, programs are managed by the neighborhood residents themselves, with no regulation of interactions between the police and the community. While more or less institutionalized experiences can be found in most of the provinces (Buenos Aires, Chaco, Córdoba, Chubut, Entre Ríos, La Pampa, La Rioja, Santa Fe, and Río Negro), this chapter concentrates on only a few of them. Moreover, the section that follows is organized according to whether the existing programs include some degree of participation by state agencies or are focused on the activity of locally formed neighborhood associations.

Citizen Security Programs with Participation of State Agencies

Experiences with community participation in Buenos Aires Province highlight police efforts to address societal needs and give local councils an active role. Police chiefs from other provinces have also indicated that actions have been undertaken to advance community policing programs in their respective jurisdictions. The police chief of La Rioja province maintains that meetings with different neighborhood centers in different areas are taking place, that the community supported the use of private vehicles for patrolling, and that street patrols have doubled in urban areas.[7] Likewise, the area chief of the Police Institute of Chubut Province stated that an education and training program in community policing was initiated in September 1996, inspired by the Catalan policing model emphasizing the "local" element, and that pilot experiments have been carried out in the neighborhoods of the cities of Trelew, Puerto Madryn, and Rawson.[8] Reports from the police departments of Río Negro, Santa Fe, Chaco, Córdoba, and La Pampa also indicate that local, regional, and provincial security councils have been established in those provinces in order to voice the concerns and needs of residents regarding security issues and bring these to the attention of relevant state entities. However, reports from the different provincial police organizations reveal that the definition of citizen participation in community policing programs is a limited one. The main actor in citizen security continues to be the police, while the community appears to be merely the beneficiary of renovated service, rather than a partner in providing security as a public good.

In 1997, in certain neighborhoods of the nation's capital (Saavedra, Mataderos, Liniers, Villa Devoto, Flores, Floresta, Nuñez, Palermo, Barracas, and La Boca), crime and violence prevention councils were formed (Martínez et al. 1998). The launching of these councils had no formal institutional origin, as there was no law or resolution establishing their creation. Rather, they appeared as part of the Crime and Violence Prevention Program, under the Secretariat of the Interior of the City of Buenos Aires government, and were initially proposed as a venue for neighborhood-level discussion, intended to function within the Management and Participation Centers.[9] These councils appeared on the political scene as a mechanism to channel the strained social atmosphere of those years, characterized by growing public alarm regarding security, demands by citizens and civic organizations, and major public debate on the issue of citizen insecurity.

Evaluations of the experience of the various councils showed marked differences in the degree and form of local participation. In some locations, the rapprochement was immediate and the participation ongoing, while in others there were problems in securing the participation of residents (Martínez et al. 1998): in the Palermo neighborhood, council meetings were organized rapidly, with considerable participation on the part of local residents; and in the Flores neighborhood, meetings were sporadic and there was never extensive participation by residents. The difference in participation levels is probably attributable to whether there were previously existing local organizations: Palermo had a network of organizations, such as the Neighborhood Security Monitoring Committee, Sensitive Citizens of Palermo, Los Vecinos de Campaña del Desierto, Citizen Initiative, and Club Palermo, with experience in putting forward claims and demands and in mobilizing; while in Flores, preexisting organizations did not become involved in the initiative, and organizing councils depended primarily on the efforts of local city government officials (Martínez et al. 1998).

Surveys conducted by the National Crime Policy Bureau indicate that between 1997 and 2000, citizen perception of police activity in the city improved slightly: in 1997, 52 percent of those surveyed believed that the police had not done a good job in their neighborhoods, while 31.4 percent had the opposite opinion; in 2000, 44.9 percent indicated disapproval of police activity, while 34.2 percent had a positive opinion (Ministerio de Justicia de la Nación 1997–2000). This improvement was perceived both by those who had been victims of a crime and those who had not. The surveys also showed that the passage of time had not produced any increase in the number of persons informed about police activities in their neighborhoods: in 1997, 16.6 percent of those interviewed stated that they had no knowledge of such operations, while in 2000 this proportion rose to 20.9 percent. Surveys conducted in 1999 and 2000 by the city government and by the national government (Ministerio de Justicia de la Nación 2000), regarding measures needed to solve the security problem, indicate that while the population preferred increased police presence, an increase in the severity of sentences, adoption of repressive measures, and policies to alleviate unemployment; in 1999, only a minority of those interviewed proposed preventive measures (6.1 percent), reforms within the police system (7.6 percent), or training of police personnel (6.3 percent) (Ministerio de Justicia de la Nación 1999, 2000).

There has also been a variety of experiences in the provinces involving citizen participation within state agencies responsible for security. In 1998, Buenos Aires Province promulgated a new public security law (No. 12.154) that states:

> [I]t is a right of the inhabitants of the province, and an obligation of the government, to promote effective community participation in developing, implementing, and monitoring public security policies and—in order to achieve that objective—to create Neighborhood Security Councils, Municipal Security Councils, Departmental Security Councils, and Municipal Defenders of Security [Article 12].[10]

In order for Neighborhood Security Councils to achieve their objectives,[11] they should be made up of local citizens, neighborhood organizations, and any NGOs concerned with public security. Their main functions are (1) to intervene in issues related to neighborhood public security, (2) to evaluate the functioning and activities of the police of the province and of private security service providers, (3) to formulate suggestions and request reports from precinct officials, and (4) to participate in crime prevention plans.

In Castelar Sur (a residential area and marketing center in Morón municipality), a neighborhood security council was formed, with support from the Foundation for Democratic Change.[12] Although such a council is not actually part of the municipal councils established by provincial law 12.154, it emerged as the result of residents' request that their local legislators implement the provisions of the law. This experience was the product of cooperation between residents and local police precincts, in light of the need to create a new precinct in the southern part of the locality. Given the lack of resources, it was agreed that, until construction of the new police station was completed, local residents and police would hold meetings at the development association, and that the police would allocate certain resources to the construction of the new police station. The council has continued to function, although without participation of the local government. This demonstrates a trend that shows up repeatedly: where citizen participation in security issues increases, public authorities tend to withdraw from the scene.

Another experience with programs involving participation of state agencies occurred in Presidente Perón, where a municipal security council was formed comprised of thirty institutions from the region. Council participants (sixty persons) decided to create committees concerned with monitoring police management and crime prevention. The former, in collaboration with the local police, implemented a situational prevention project developed to address the neediest areas of the neighborhood, focusing on the particular locations most vulnerable to potential crime. The residents supported the police's request for additional resources (vehicles and patrol cars) needed to carry out the plan. The second committee selected a "highly vulnerable" neighborhood—where there were high rates of vandalism and/or violence, an absence of community organization, and the presence of "addictive behaviors" (Ministerio de Justicia y Seguridad 1999, 1–2)—and designed a social prevention plan. Within the selected neighborhood, the committee identified three social groups with specific needs. The first group included children between ages seven and eleven with high dropout and school-violence rates; the second group included adolescents between the ages of eleven and fifteen who were addicted to narcotics, had no plans for their future, and were experiencing conflict within their families; and a third group consisted of young people between age sixteen and twenty who lacked jobs, had an excess of free time, displayed aggressive attitudes, and had problems with alcoholism or drug addiction. Once the groups had been identified, the council and the Undersecretariat of Security, through the Multiple Response Program, began to establish activities aimed at these sectors (Ministerio de Justicia y Seguridad 1999, 1–2).

Statistics from the National Crime Policy Bureau show that, as of 1998, the perceptions of the citizens of the Province of Buenos Aires regarding the crime prevention activities implemented by the police and the provincial government improved: in 1997, 26.6 percent of those interviewed expressed the opinion that the police were doing a good job, while 58.2 percent expressed an opposite view; one year later, the percentage that believed the police were doing a satisfactory job increased nearly 10 percent, to a total of 35.3 percent, while those who believed the opposite represented 51.3 percent (almost 7 percent less than the previous year) (Ministerio de Justicia de la Nación 1997, 1998). These figures remained nearly constant until 2000 (Ministerio de Justicia de la Nación 1999, 2000). As in the case of the residents of the city of Buenos Aires, persons who had been victimized by crime had a more negative assessment of police activity than those who had not: in 1997, 64.3 percent of those victimized and 53.3 percent of those who had not been victimized said the police had not done a good job, while 21.8 and 30.8 percent, respectively, believed the opposite. In 1998, the positive image of the work of the police had increased to 29.6 percent among those who had been victimized, and to 39.1 percent among those who had not, while a negative opinion prevailed among 58.4 and 46.5 percent, respectively. Likewise, inhabitants of the province indicated that in order to solve security problems, various measures needed to be taken, including solving the problem of unemployment (22 percent), increasing police presence, and providing for more severe sentences (Ministerio de Justicia de la Nación 1999, 2000).

In Entre Ríos Province, and specifically in the city of Gualeguaychú, crime prevention plans were also instituted.[13] Given the increase in the crime rate resulting from the growing popularity of Mardi Gras festivities, as well as the city's strategic location,[14] the provincial government expressed interest in implementing a process for citizen participation in crime prevention in Gualeguaychú. To this end, a cooperation and technical assistance agreement was signed among the National Crime Policy Bureau, Foundation for Democratic Change, University of La Plata, and the town council of Gualeguaychú for the mapping of the area. A cooperative planning methodology was used, since the central objective was to bring together the various social actors in assessing, planning, and executing the program.[15] The results of this joint effort were (1) involvement of the different sectors of society (citizens, businesspeople, merchants, government agencies, and NGOs) in formulating social policies regarding crime prevention and citizen security; (2) application of community management processes in one of the neighborhoods of Gualeguaychú, with the intention of extending the methodology to the entire city; and (3) strengthening of mediation structures in civil society.

The Foundation for Democratic Change worked with young people from low-income neighborhoods of the city. The purpose of this effort was to provide young people the space to engage in sports, recreational activities, social events, and other activities, as well as giving them the freedom and opportunity to establish social bonds. The absence of evaluations prior to the implementation of this program makes it difficult to assess the results. Nevertheless, the town council of Gualeguaychú expressed interest in continuing the activities associated with the crime prevention program.[16]

Citizen Security Programs Managed by Local Residents

There have also been efforts by residents affected by neighborhood insecurity to control local criminal activity, as well as police activity, independent of the actions of state agencies. The perception of citizens regarding the inaction of local and national government authorities led neighborhood residents to form groups to enhance security in their neighborhoods. These have flourished in various localities. Unfortunately, due to the chaotic and noncontinuous nature of such efforts, there are virtually no evaluations of their impact and results.

The first neighborhood crime and violence prevention associations were formed in Saavedra.[17] In later years, associations such as Neighbor Alert, JUVESA (the Saavedra Neighborhood Council), and the Neighbors United Group became models for groups in other neighborhoods. One of their major achievements was the creation of Plan Alert in 1997.[18] The most immediate result of the plan was that authorities gave prompt attention to complaints, after years of inaction and bureaucratic red tape. These complaints related to lack of public lighting and tree pruning and hazards posed by abandoned lots, houses, and cars, among other things. Section 49 of the Argentine Federal Police established a direct line for emergencies and, with support from the residents, requested an increase in the number of police officers in the neighborhood.[19] Contacts were also initiated with a public school to study potential educational campaigns to combat violence in the region's schools. Due to the fact that Saavedra was considered a pilot case, the national Attorney General's Office decided to create a Circuit Prosecutors' Office. This office, in collaboration with the Public Prosecutor's Office and with the community, was designed to increase the efficiency of criminal investigations and, hence, benefit both victims and witnesses.

Beyond the good intentions and the support that Plan Alert received, several outcomes can be noted. First, due to the limited geographic scale of this experiment, there were no problems in terms of police coverage. However,

Table 8.1. Selected general crime statistics for Saavedra area, October 1999–May 2000

Offense	October 99	November 99	December 99	January 2000	February 2000	March 2000	April 2000	May 2000
Auto theft	90	101	81	59	101	54	49	112
Auto theft and assault	10	20	14		4	7	3	15
Armed robbery	109	80	139	82	109	113	109	135
Attempted armed robbery	1	2	4	4	2	3	5	2
Purse snatchings	38	21	47		37	30	42	52
Burglary (theft in absence of victim)	10	12	12		11	8	10	17

Source: District Prosecutor's Office, based on reports by victims. See http://members.tripod.com/~Daniel_E_Cantoni/Mapas/MapaDelito.htm.

if the plan had been extended to the entire Saavedra neighborhood, new personnel—such as bicycle police—would have been necessary. Second, the plan was implemented due to the efforts of a small group of citizens who used door-to-door (personal contact) methods to get residents to participate in the meetings, thus making the neighborhood a central and indispensable actor. Third, according to the data cited above, and taking into account that the period under consideration was very short, it would appear that the plan did not produce any significant changes in crime rates in the neighborhood. Nevertheless, the residents who participated in this experiment state that there was a reduction in the perception of insecurity, and that they succeeded in maintaining an open dialogue with the police.

Such self-managed activities had little effect on Buenos Aires city residents: in 1997, 85.6 percent of respondents believed they had a high probability of becoming crime victims, while in 2000 this figure was 85.9 percent. There were slight changes in the perception of insecurity: in 1998, the percentage of persons who felt very or fairly secure was 29.6 percent, while in 2000 this figure was 33.8 percent; in 1998, 69.6 percent felt somewhat or very insecure, while in 2000 this figure was 64.5 percent (Ministerio de Justicia de la Nación 1997–2000).

As in the nation's capital, in some provinces self-formed neighborhood groups were created to deal with the issue of insecurity. In Buenos Aires Province, the Cabildo Abierto del Pueblo en Ciudadela (Open Meeting of the People of Ciudadela)[20] was created, along with Vecinos Unidos por la Seguridad ¡Asaltados! en La Plata.[21] Likewise, in Villa Alonso, in Santa Rosa (La Pampa Province), a neighborhood committee was established to implement a crime prevention plan.[22]

In this set of experiences, the case of Vecinos Unidos por la Seguridad ¡Asaltados! en La Plata is worth considering. This group was formed when a kiosk owner, after being repeatedly robbed, and "tired of sending notes, along with other people, to the police and to the Ministry of Security requesting a greater uniformed police presence in the area" (*Diario El Día,* 10 September 2000), decided to join with a number of merchants and residents—also victims of violent crime—to formulate a plan. They put together a website for people to relate their experiences and describe the crimes of which they had been victims. The site provided a forum for people to post detailed accounts of robberies and thorough descriptions of the assailants. According to the members of this association, the site serves to differentiate the "criminals" from the "good people," and ensure that complaints do not get relegated to files buried in government offices. However, these accounts do, in effect, constitute computer "lynchings" that skirt due process guarantees. This phenomenon reveals the degree of neglect suffered by the victims and demonstrates one of the risks posed when the provision of the public good of security rests on the decentralized actions of citizens lacking government authority to regulate, monitor, or support them.

As in the national capital between 1997 and 2000, perceptions of the inhabitants of Buenos Aires Province regarding the probability of being crime victims remained constant: in 1997, 85 percent of those interviewed perceived themselves as having a high probability of being a victim, while in 2000, the same figure was 87.7 percent. Unlike the results of the statistics from the national capital, however, the residents of the province showed a slight increase in the perception of insecurity: in 1998, 69.6 percent felt somewhat or very insecure—a figure that increased to 72.8 percent in 2000 (Ministerio de Justicia de la Nación 1997–2000).

Brazil

In Brazil in recent years, NGOs, the media, and various social organizations have reported an increase in social and police violence and have demanded that the government come up with a solution (Mesquita Neto 1999a). Moreover, in the same period there has been a major change in the concept of public security. While in the past there tended to be a preference for options that relied on strengthening repressive and punitive measures (Mesquita Neto 1999b), the government has recently promoted the use of strategies to control violence that rely on citizen participation, including community councils, human rights councils, and community policing.

In this section, consideration will be given to the manner in which these informal policies for controlling violence have occurred in São Paulo and Rio de Janeiro.[23] Although similar principles served as the starting point in both cases, with emphasis on the need to foster community participation and give local agencies a role, sociocultural and governmental differences between the two cities led to a continuation of the policy in São Paulo and a decision to abandon it in Rio de Janeiro.

São Paulo

Prior to the implementation of community policing programs, the media indicated that the increase in crime and police violence was reaching critical levels. The homicide rate in São Paulo, which in 1980 was 13.8 persons per 100,000 inhabitants per month, had increased in 1985 to 25.35, and to 34.20 in 1995 (Mesquita Neto 2000). According to sources at Fundação SEADE (State Data Analysis System, www.seade.gov.br), in 1996 the homicide rate in the city and in the metropolitan region reached levels of 55 per 100,000 persons. Jardim Ângela and Diadema were the most violent areas, with figures of 94.42 and 129.49 homicides per 100,000 inhabitants, respectively. In turn, data from the Secretariat of Public Security indicated that the number of civilians killed by police continued to be very high, although it had fallen between 1995 and 1997: an average of 51.5 civilians per month died in 1995; the figure for 1997 was 36.6.

This was the context in which reform of the public security system occurred when, in December 1997, a community policing program was initiated in São Paulo. The project began in 41 areas within the region with both high and low rates of violence; by the beginning of 1999, there were already 204 programs in operation. For its part, the Community Police Department of São Paulo's Military Police established a series of programs and, in 1997, brought together thirty-eight organizations to provide advice on the implementation of community policing.[24] In tandem with this, the government implemented actions to foster citizen participation in monitoring police activities, including the establishment of an ombudsman, strengthening of community security councils, regular publication of statistics on crime and police violence, and regulation of actions by the Public Prosecutor's Office in their external monitoring of police activity. It should be pointed out, however, that there are conflicting opinions and conflicting evidence regarding the degree of civilian involvement in these programs, as well as the composition of groups participating in the community policing activities.

The São Paulo Community Police Department is of the opinion that these programs moderately reduced the crime rates in localities where they were implemented, and considers the experiment to have been "successful" in the case of the Jardim Ângela neighborhood. According to police sources, prior to instituting the community policing security system, there were 132 crimes per month, a figure that fell to 14 per month after the community policing system was in place.[25] In contrast, data from the Secretariat of Public Security show different results: the homicide rate for the 1996–1999 period increased by 23 percent: in 1996, 94.42 crimes were reported per 100,000 inhabitants, while in 1999, there were 116.23 per 100,000 inhabitants. Regarding police violence, the Secretariat's data show no reduction in this figure in the last four years: the number of civilians killed by police was 446 in 1997, 546 in 1998, 647 in 1999, and reached 260 killed in the first three months of 2000 (Mesquita Neto 2000).

One of the most important challenges these programs face is restructuring of the police organization. The first structural change in the São Paulo State Police was the creation of a Department of Community Police and Human Rights. However, as acknowledged by the São Paulo Community Police Department, these changes are resisted by the police because they are viewed as a reduction of police powers and they involve a different concept of policing.[26] Another source of resistance to organizational change is that many police view the program as merely the mandate of the current government; inasmuch as the police see the program as temporary with little chance of continuing into the future, they have little commitment to its success.

It is difficult to evaluate these programs because of the lack of research before their implementation. Although the absence of previous statistics hinders evaluation of the changes in perceptions of insecurity and confidence in police institutions, recent research by ILANUD (United Nations Latin American Institute for the Prevention of Crime and Treatment of Offenders) shows that, following the installation of these programs, 55 percent of those surveyed stated that they felt more secure, while 25 percent indicated that they did not feel more secure and 17 percent maintained that the programs did not change their perceptions. Another interesting datum emerging from the ILANUD survey is that 60 percent of those surveyed believed that community policing had been responsible for the reduction in crime in their neighborhood, while 30 percent believed that it had no impact. According to ILANUD, in São Paulo, community policing programs have not increased the community's trust in the police: in 1995, 51 percent of the population feared and distrusted the police, compared to 74 percent in 1997 and 66 percent in 1999 (Mesquita Neto 2000). The ILANUD research also shows that 35 percent of survey respondents had contact with the community police, and research conducted by the Community Police Department maintains that 60 percent of respondents stated that they were familiar with the program. Finally, in regard to citizens' perception of community policing, the ILANUD research determined that 13 percent of those surveyed were very satisfied with the program, 52 percent described it as good, 11 percent as bad, and 22 percent said they did not know or had no opinion. The survey also reported that 88 percent of those surveyed believed that this policing should continue, and 94 percent stated that they would like to have this type of community policing in their neighborhoods. Paradoxically, although the majority (56 percent) of those surveyed believed that the community police were more courteous and helpful than traditional police, only 14 percent believed that the system was more efficient in combating crime. In the words of Tulio Kahn, "[P]art of the population still associates effectiveness with repression."[27]

Rio de Janeiro

Rio de Janeiro has a population of 5.5 million, 18 percent of whom live in shantytowns. During the first administration of Governor Leonel Brizola, an attempt was made to bring the community and the police closer together. The program, known as Neighborhood Policing, included meetings of community leaders and neighborhood residents through the Pastoral de la Favela (Shantytown Church) to gather suggestions and complaints from the community. In June–July 1991, a pilot project of policing by sectors was implemented in the Grajaú and Andaraí neighborhoods.[28] The results were inconclusive, given the failure to mobilize the participation of many neighborhood associations and the inability to cover all inhabitants. By contrast, in Urca, Laranjeiras, and Alto da Boa Vista, where the initiative remained within the communities themselves, the results were positive. However, these experiences never became more than pilot projects.

In 1994, members of the VIVA RIO movement, which had been formed in December 1993 in the wake of a series of traumatic events, demanded the installation of community policing in the city.[29] It was officially launched with the support of the then–Rio de Janeiro State Military Police commander. Designing the program was not an easy task, and from the start, there were problems with and obstacles to carrying out the plan, which ultimately undermined its implementation. Problems of cooperation between the state government and the prefecture of Rio de Janeiro frustrated this initial attempt to implement the proposal in various city neighborhoods. At that time, the prefecture of Rio de Janeiro was launching the Favela-Barrio project, to which it shifted its priorities and efforts (Conde 1998). As a result, after a series of advances and setbacks, a decision was made to implement the community policing program with the collaboration of VIVA RIO in the Copacabana area only.

The police patrolled the neighborhood on foot in order to become familiar with the behaviors, routines, and habits of the population, so as to be able to relate better to the community and address its needs. Meetings of the community councils were held in public establishments to identify the neighborhood's security problems, propose solutions, discuss and evaluate police activities, and establish a work agenda. A special police program was also established for the protection of tourists, along with a competitive sports program. Given that the program functioned during daytime hours, it secured only limited participation, mostly from building doormen, merchants, street vendors, *franelinhas* (people who wash automobile windshields), beggars, and street children; participation of area residents was limited.[30]

The collaboration of VIVA RIO was aimed at mobilizing the local community. It was assumed that the organization's heterogeneous base would help to reach diverse sectors of the population.[31] However, because it was only recently established, the number of people it could attract to participate in the program was variable and unreliable. Leonarda Musumeci,[32] coordinator of Instituto de Estudos da Religião (ISER) research on monitoring community policing programs, suggests that the discontinuous nature of grassroots participation reflects the dynamic that typically characterizes voluntary groups: initial euphoria and high expectations, followed by disappointment and disbanding (Musumeci 1995). This cycle, attributable to the impossibility of solving the problems in the short term and to the obstacles imposed by other state agencies, ultimately undermined the initiative's continuity.

Another element to be considered in evaluating this experience is the role that VIVA RIO assumed. The inclusion of figures such as Rubem César Fernandes and Elizabeth Sussekind (respectively, director and coordinator of VIVA RIO), whose contribution initially spurred participation in the meetings, in the end proved counterproductive, inasmuch as the residents and council members came to feel "abandoned" when members of VIVA RIO later failed to attend the meetings (Musumeci 1995). National visibility and access to the media, politicians, businesspeople, and civil organizations made VIVA RIO into a vital component of the community policing program; however, this advantage ultimately made the sustainability of the program dependent on the presence of its leaders.

Sectors with fewer resources had another view of the role of the association and of the program: they perceived the councils and VIVA RIO as an elitist, opportunistic movement of conservative forces. They believed that the new security system was benefiting the most privileged classes and that repression continued to exclude and marginalize the poorest sectors of society (Musumeci 1995). This judgment had some foundation: the community policing program was not put into practice in shantytowns, since there was a widespread belief that the problems in these areas were different from those in higher-income urban areas, and that they therefore required a special program based on different police training.[33] Paradoxically, six years after the Copacabana community policing program had been dismantled, the Special Areas Policing Group (GPAE) was carrying out community policing tasks in the Pavão/Pavãozinho and Cantagalo shantytowns, based on the same parameters as the old community policing program.[34]

The community policing programs began in September 1994 and ended in June 1995. In the summer of 1994–1995, an evaluation was conducted: according to data from the Registro de Ocorrência and bulletins of the Rio de Janeiro Military Police, the homicide rate increased 144 percent between summer 1993–1994 and summer 1994–1995 (Fernandes 1995). The number of robberies fell 15 percent from one summer to the next, with drops in auto theft (–11 percent) and auto theft with force (–14 percent).

In terms of organizational changes, unlike what had occurred in São Paulo, the implementation of community policing did not involve the creation of an autonomous structure. The battalion that worked on the implementation constituted a part of the police structure already in place, and their training was rather minimal.[35] Another problem, mentioned by the police themselves, was the lack of a coordinator, which made them feel that they were on the streets with no supervision or advice.[36] An additional source of difficulty was the lack of support from or coordination with other state entities, particularly those of the prefecture. Moreover, there were obstacles within the police itself, due to the persistence of structures from the military period and confrontations with the traditional police, who had little regard for the community police. According to statements by the community police, the greatest external problem they faced was the lack of support from government entities, and the greatest internal obstacle was the lack of equipment and insufficient autonomy (Piquet Carneigo and Musumeci 1996).

It was also difficult to establish direct relationships between the police and community because of the program's failure to operate when residents and police could participate effectively: Copacabana residents worked during the day, and so could not attend meetings; the police, who lived far away, could not attend the meetings at night.

Chile

As with Argentina and Brazil, issues linked to citizen security and crime prevention have been a priority concern of the Chilean population in recent years. However, unlike these other cases, the promotion of citizen participation has not been driven by distrust for public institutions responsible for the judicial and penal system, but primarily by rising crime rates and the public's security concerns. It must be remembered that in Chile the question of increases in police abuse and violence does not have the same importance on the public agenda as it does in Brazil or Argentina (Fuentes 2001).

There are disparities in statistics from Chilean sources regarding the number of complaints received for muggings and theft in 1999. Official sources registered 142,383 cases, while the Citizen Peace Foundation indicated 395,508 reports during the same period.[37] Despite this difference, Chile's Ministry of the Interior did state that during the 1998–1999 period, there was an increase in the number of crimes committed.[38] A 1999 report by the Citizen Peace Foundation indicated that the number of reports received by the police represents only a small percentage of total crimes committed, due to the fact that many victims do not resort to the police or court system. The percentage of victims making criminal complaints to the justice system varies according to city, but in broad terms, more than half of the victims do not go to the police. In the metropolitan region of La Granja in 1999, a total of 8,245 crimes were committed; only 2,921 (35.4 percent) of them were reported to the police.[39] In the municipality of Pedro Aguirre Cerda, more victims resorted to the justice system in 1999: 45.1 percent of those affected (10,729) made reports to the police.[40] Of the reports made to the police and the justice system, only a small number of cases were ultimately resolved; according to the Citizen Peace Foundation, barely 3 percent were resolved through judicial means, while 97 percent of the cases remained unsolved.[41]

Given that the citizenry does not perceive itself as threatened by police actions, its forms of intervention—unlike those in the other cases—involve institutional channels and official support, rather than self-structured organizations that take an adversarial approach to monitoring public authorities. Some of the elements that characterize the Chilean situation and differentiate it from the other cases considered here are (1) the relationship with the Carabineros, (2) the continuity of security policy from one national administration to another, (3) more developed interbureaucratic functional relationships, and (4) low level of spontaneous participation in security programs by the citizenry.

Chile's Carabineros are, along with Chile's Investigative Police, one of the few Latin American police forces that a considerable proportion of citizens "trust to a large degree" (23 percent) or to a "moderate degree" (35 percent) (Cox 2000).[42] Since the restoration of democracy, the three government administrations (Aylwin/Frei/Lagos) have maintained an ongoing and consistent policy regarding crime prevention and public security. This has led to the implementation of plans and programs sustained over time, despite changes in the government and despite the influence of the "zero tolerance" rhetoric by right-wing parties and the media. Unlike the other cases considered here, political continuity has allowed Chile to establish a high level of cooperation and articulation between government and nongovernmental actors involved in preventing crime and violence. This cooperation translates into better relationships and an absence of competition among government agencies.

The case of Chile also presents few experiences involving self-management of citizen participation efforts to prevent crime and violence. Citizens who become involved tend to have experience with existing government programs and participate as program collaborators or partners at the urging of official agencies, whether through the Division of Social Organizations (under the General Secretariat of Government Ministry), Carabineros, or Division of Public Security and Citizen Participation (under the Interior

Ministry). At the same time, civil society organizations, such as the Citizen Peace Foundation and FORJA (Formación Jurídica para la Acción), provide technical assistance within the governmental context. NGOs such as the Center for Development Studies (CED) or the Liberty and Development Foundation, which is dedicated to studying the issue, are not involved in implementing participatory experiences in the area of crime prevention.

Following is an examination of four experiences in which some form of citizen participation in preventing crime and violence can be seen. In all cases, the policies and/or programs have functioned in an articulated manner, independent of their governmental or NGO origin. This factor is significant in light of the experiences in citizen participation on public security matters seen in the other cases considered here.

Citizen Security and Protection Committees

As in other Latin American countries, crime is one of the greatest concerns of the public at large (Sandoval 2001, 2), and, since the beginning of the 1990s, the national government, municipalities, and police have put forth a series of measures to address this. Jorge Araya Moya, head of the General Secretariat of Government Ministry's Citizen Security Program, stated that "at the beginning of the 1990s, when there was an increase in insecurity, Citizen Security Committees, Citizen Protection Committees, and Civil Protection Committees began to emerge in many neighborhoods. These were spontaneous organizations aimed at providing defense against a rash of muggings. Residents met and considered measures such as the installation of alarms and organizing community alerts."[43] Starting in 1993, during the first democratic government of President Patricio Aylwin, this citizen movement was welcomed by the national government through the Division of Social Organizations, which, in conjunction with the Santiago city council and the National Office of Emergencies, promoted citizen participation on natural disaster issues.

Although the government encouraged the creation of these committees throughout the country, they had the greatest impact in Santiago, where approximately seventy such neighborhood committees now function along with another twenty in schools where problems of drugs or crime were identified. Participation is open to residents and community organizations.[44] Training programs developed with committee participants highlight the important role of state authorities in the life of the community. This training, which emphasizes preventive activities and is implemented through agreements with various universities, includes the participation of municipal officials, police, and local residents. According to Araya Moya, "this was a means of putting into practice the objective of bringing together these actors, which in theory is highly positive but in practice is very difficult to achieve. The results were positive, since after two months, bonds of trust and increased communication had been established." Public authorities have had a central role in organizing and institutionalizing citizen participation in the committees: although the committees "start up spontaneously, they later become a government-promoted policy."[45]

Araya Moya maintains that it is difficult to evaluate the impact of Citizen Protection Committees because no ex-ante or ex-post measurements of the programs have been implemented. Officials interviewed also indicated that the committees functioned better in some *comunas* (municipalities) than in others. Residents' failure to consistently follow through in attending meetings, once the committees were formed, was the main reason given for these varying results.[46] Another factor that affected their functioning was the political orientation of municipal authorities. According to Hernán Ortega, of the Interior Ministry's Public Security and Citizen Participation Division, in municipalities governed by the right, local authorities tended to show little support for citizen participation in the committees or for their activities.[47]

In line with what has been confirmed in the other countries considered here, those analyzing the Chilean case have underscored the point that the benefits of this form of policing are primarily seen in the reduced perception of insecurity among the citizenry. Araya Moya suggested that "the mere fact that the people are organizing dispels the 'ghosts' of perceived insecurity."[48]

Communal Citizen Security Councils

In August 2000, the government presented a new proposal to address problems of citizen insecurity. Communal (Municipal) Citizen Security Councils were put forth as a continuation of the experience of the Citizen Security and Citizen Protection Committees. The relevant public officials explained their creation as being the product of the need to "provide a strong push toward articulation, because there is merit in the spontaneity with which these have emerged, but they also have the disadvantage of being highly disorganized, with no common institutional unity."[49] In order to implement this new mechanism, agreements were signed with the Chilean Association of Municipalities and the Citizen Peace Foundation.[50] The first type of organization sets the role of the municipality in the field of citizen security, while the second provides technical assistance in implementing the government's crime prevention strategy.

Apparently, the need to ensure the political feasibility of these programs was the driving factor in bringing about these agreements. The reticence of some municipalities in participating in the plan, and the government's interest in ensuring the support of all municipalities, led to the first agreement. The need to build a bridge with the municipalities governed by right-wing parties that are not in tune with the government led to the establishment of a strategic alliance with an institution like the Citizen Peace Foundation. Carlos Valdivieso, general manager of the foundation, explained that the objective was to institutionalize a community-based citizen security policy, since this is "one of the most successful features of the countries in which the crime rate is being reduced."[51]

The fact that it was necessary to forge such agreements highlights the fact that implementation of the plan, which relies on the committees, faced various problems.[52] According to Valdivieso, several studies have shown that voluntary initiatives have not functioned well when coordination between the mayor and the police is weak or nonexistent, whether because the mayor wishes to control the police or because the police do not trust the mayor, who is a political figure.

The Quadrant Plan

The third experience, in which some form of citizen participation is included, is the so-called Quadrant Plan supported by the Carabineros. The police force formulated a strategic plan in 1995 that included a series of programs aimed at strengthening the police's operational functions, as well as a number of actions designed to increase mutual familiarity and good relations with the community. The objective of the system of patrolling by sectors (quadrants)[53] is to improve the efficiency of police actions and create a more personal and direct relationship between the Carabineros and residents of each quadrant. The aim is to make the residents "feel" more comfortable with the Carabineros, while increasing police efficiency by giving officers a greater sense of responsibility for what occurs in their individual quadrants, thus leading to their taking a stronger leadership role in preventing crime and establishing security.[54] The plan began as a pilot experiment in certain municipalities; in early 1999 it was extended to the entire Santiago metropolitan region, based on the fact that it had produced positive results in its experimental phase, even though there have been no formal evaluations of its achievements or failures.

The statements of a member of the Carabineros indicate the way in which the institution views the scope and nature of community participation: "The corporal's work consists of getting to know the community, within his specific grid, in order to gain information on various problems facing the community, such as drugs, alcohol, youth gangs, abandoned houses, et cetera, and to subsequently provide a report to the Operations Office." Directives from community organizations, as well as direct contact with residents and children—through crime prevention talks in the schools within the officer's area—serve as links in this relationship. The officer participates in meetings called by the Citizen Security Committees or by the Residents' Councils, and organizes meetings at the police precinct with residents and organizations. The purpose of these meetings is to "give an account of the actions taken based on information provided by the residents—for example, the fact that patrols were increased in a given area, or that in another area, a certain number of persons were arrested in connection with a crime."[55]

The Carabineros have established efficiency criteria for implementing the plan[56]; however, evaluations of its effectiveness do not yet exist. Specialized researchers on this issue anticipate that there will be difficulties in carrying out such evaluations, due to the closed nature of the Carabineros institution and the fact that external control is still a new and undeveloped concept.[57] Moreover, according to those responsible for implementing the security and protection committees, the relationship between the committees and the Carabineros has been varied, generally attributable to the degree of goodwill and conviction of the police officer in charge. In some municipalities, the officers have been receptive to implementing the committees, while in others they have shown reticence, believing "that the people should not interfere in security issues."[58]

Communal Citizen Security Committees

In collaboration with FORJA, the O'Higgins regional government (administrative region VI) implemented the fourth security program, which has gained some degree of citizen participation. As the result of a public competition, FORJA was selected as the executing agency for the government program, Applying Preventive Citizen Security (Aplicación Seguridad Ciudadana Preventiva). The program began in September 1999 for a ten-month period, and covered seven municipalities selected from the three provinces that comprise the region.[59]

The program's primary objective was to apply, to the greatest extent possible, the principle that "solidarity is the foundation of citizen security." In order to achieve this objective, the program implemented preventive social intervention strategies designed to reduce risks to persons and property, strategies to achieve community participation in establishing security, and a program of assistance and guidance for victims of any attack on security.[60] In practice, the program involved four types of action: (1) a survey of social actors who were to participate in the program in each of the selected communities; (2) a diagnostic assessment of citizen security issues, based on surveys conducted among directors, leaders, and residents selected in the previous stage; (3) training these leaders in priority issues identified in each commune; and (4) formation of Communal Citizen Security Committees in each of the selected municipalities.

In order to solve the problem these programs face in gaining citizen participation, FORJA developed a methodology designed to select leaders or local directors, who were called upon to participate actively in the program. The search for people who were genuinely representative of their communities delayed the start of the program, since the organizers wanted to avoid having the group "limited to the municipality's list of persons, who are usually persons close to or known by the municipality, with common residents excluded."[61]

Based on the surveys completed by the selected leaders and residents, the program prepared a diagnostic assessment of citizen security issues. The survey included questions such as: "How is security in your municipality?" and "What areas in your municipality are dangerous?" In addition, there were questions asking for a list of citizen security problems affecting each *comuna,* questions regarding community initiatives to be promoted in the area of crime prevention and control, and questions concerning the importance of social organizations in achieving citizen security. Of those surveyed, 30 to 60 percent were willing to participate in citizen security programs in their municipalities, and similar percentages believed that civic organizations were important to citizen security in their *comunas.*

The training was conducted on the basis of the teaching guides prepared by FORJA. These included statistical data, suggestions for legal actions to deal with contingencies identified in each municipality, and recommendations for promoting citizen participation. The directors and leaders who were trained (a total of eighty-two persons) belonged primarily to grassroots community organizations. In at least one of the training sessions, a representative of the Carabineros was present, and the participants expressed fear that their participation in the program could lead to reprisals, since they might be regarded as informers. Moreover, inasmuch as most participants already occupied positions in community organizations, many indicated that they did not have sufficient time to take on new tasks.

As already mentioned, the primary objective of the program was the formation of Communal Citizen Security Committees and Provincial Security Councils, which were to formulate proposals and solutions for dealing with security problems and advising the municipalities. The intention was that the committees should secure legal status, so as to guarantee autonomy and be able to access competitively awarded funds. The most successful experience was that of Rancagua Comuna. According to FORJA, in this case a fluid connection was established with the municipality, which assigned one person to deal specifically with the issue, and the effort was successful in gaining the participation of a diverse group of people. In Colchagua, FORJA has continued to act as a collaborator, and the government expressed its interest in expanding the experience to other municipalities. As of this writing, of the seven committees created, four are in operation, meeting on a monthly basis, carrying on contacts with the municipal government and seeking other persons to expand the committees. Its tasks include meeting with other institutions and channeling the opinions of the community to institutions such as the Carabineros.

The relationship with the Carabineros has been variable. At the start of the program, the Carabineros feared that the committees were intent on "arming" the residents, or looking to protect themselves unaided. Later, they officially signed onto the program. Despite this, they have not participated actively in all of the municipalities. Meanwhile, in Region VI, the existence of the Quadrant Plan compelled the Carabineros to take the program seriously, since it allowed them to become familiar and establish closer relations with the community.

Similar to other past and present initiatives in Chile, the fact that the municipal committees are so recent makes it difficult to evaluate their impact on crime rates and on feelings of insecurity. However, officials and others whom I interviewed agree that these programs are changing the perception of insecurity, inasmuch as they show that something can be done and that solutions can be found. Members of the FORJA team point to the following results of the experience: (1) collaboration among the residents was achieved; (2) the need to train communities to acquire the skills that will put them on an equal footing with the police or with government agencies was confirmed; and (3) there was confirmation of the fact that unless these communities access competitively awarded funds, it will be impossible to gain sufficient autonomy to generate and implement their own proposals.

Final Observations

Argentina, Brazil, and Chile exemplify three diverse situations in terms of the degree of development of community policing programs. There is growing public and private concern for security/insecurity issues in the three countries. However, while in the case of Argentina the persistent presence of the problem has led to chaotic, contradictory, and voluble policies, the case of Chile highlights a policy that is more constant through time, with greater control over the content of the agenda on the part of government authorities. In the case of Brazil, by contrast, there is significant intervention on the part of public authorities in defining the agenda, while citizen organizations would appear to have the capacity to mold that agenda and make demands on government and police.

The greater presence of government authorities in Chile also highlights a difference with the other cases, in terms of the type of citizen participation. Thus, while in Argentina and Brazil there are major signs of spontaneous, although not continuous, citizen participation; in Chile, participation tends to be mobilized by state agencies themselves. The public and police authorities make explicit efforts to frame and institutionalize the types of spontaneous citizen participation that might emerge. This institutionalization is perceived as necessary, not only by the public authorities but also by some civil society organizations.[62]

In all three cases, there are few evaluations of results, and the ones that do exist are not highly specific. However, Brazilian experts have made greater progress than their counterparts in Argentina and Chile in evaluating results. Despite the scarcity of research on the impact of the programs, interviews in the three countries indicate that they reduce the perception of insecurity by citizens, although they do not appear to affect the level of criminal activity. This fact, however, is not insignificant, given the discrepancy between the perception of insecurity and crime rates.

Finally, it should be noted that although these programs are being characterized as community policing, they do not fit the conceptual definition of the phenomenon. In Argentina, Chile, and Brazil, initiatives aimed at bringing the police and the community closer together, or efforts to create channels to express society's demands to the police agencies, are characterized as community policing. However, these experiments include few changes in the police organization overall, scant commitment by other state agencies to design crime prevention policies, and an unsophisticated and underdeveloped attempt to establish ongoing, institutional mechanisms for citizen participation in security policies. Moreover, in some cases, such as Argentina, the community-based nature of these initiatives consists primarily of the emergence of a spontaneous and autonomous organization of affected citizens, rather than the establishment of formal mechanisms for collaboration with public and police authorities.

The following, therefore, is a summary of the problems that have been faced in implementing these programs in the countries under study.

Trust

The introduction of these programs involves expanding the base of actors participating in security issues. The purpose of altering the types of interaction between residents and police is to change the forms of local social interaction, thus changing the perception of insecurity. One of the requirements for designing community policing programs, therefore, is that the community and the police collaborate to resolve security problems. This collaboration presupposes the existence of trust between the police and citizenry—indeed, this is essential to the success of the programs. However, as reported by numerous surveys conducted in the countries of the region, the relationship between the police and the community is typified by mutual distrust.[63] Beyond the historical reasons for this, the fact is that such distrust can hardly be expected to be easily reversed based solely on a showing of goodwill on the part of those involved in introducing these types of alternative policing. Therefore, in order to successfully implement these programs, efforts must be undertaken to expand over time and consolidate the mutual trust between police and community.

Building trust is a long-term process. Rebuilding broken trust or creating it anew requires time. However, given the urgency of the insecurity problem, this is not an option available for the police, who must show results, neither for the community, which needs to resolve more immediate problems. The urgency of obtaining clear and immediate results conspires against the possibility of establishing a link that will change mutual judgments and prejudices. However, inasmuch as the justification for, and permanence of, public policies tend to depend on immediate results, it can be anticipated that attempts to institute community policing programs will be sporadic. Both the urgency of obtaining results and the mutual distrust and reticence of those involved argue against their continued existence. Thus, it is likely that the sporadic nature of this process will not only jeopardize the trust-building process required by community policing programs, but will also result in bringing into question the overall validity of the community policing approach.

Restructuring Police Agencies

Community policing theorists have suggested that implementation of these programs requires changes in the organizational structure of the police force (Waddington 1999). First, there needs to be a change in the internal organization of the police itself, inasmuch as there is a need for greater autonomy on the part of line officers. Second, in order to promote collaboration and interaction with the community, the strict division of tasks between citizens and police, on which traditional policing is based, needs to be changed. Both of these changes tend to be perceived by the police as threatening, since they appear to be reductions in their functions. Consequently, another difficulty in implementing this type of program is resistance among line officers and commanders, who tend to view these programs as a threat to their powers and resources.

Any policy designed to promote the implementation of community policing, therefore, needs to give special attention to needed changes in the organizational structure of the police force. The few analyses that have been done in Brazil and Argentina are in agreement on the problems that programs of this type face within the police structure. In São Paulo and Rio de Janeiro, as well as in Buenos Aires and Santiago, the police have tended to interpret required changes as being restrictive. Rather than being viewed as changes in the internal organization designed to facilitate community collaboration and participation, the police have interpreted the meaning of the change as an *aggiornamiento* aimed at improving their public relations with the community (Eilbaum 2000). Unless these changes in the internal organization of the police institution occur, community policing in the region will be, for the police, merely a campaign to improve public relations and, for residents, merely a self-managed and uncoordinated exercise of security functions.

Relations with Nonpolice Bureaucratic Agencies

Another typical source of problems in implementing community policing programs is the lack of coordination and collaboration among different state agencies, police forces, and community organizations. The community policing perspective regards citizen security as being the product not only of reactive and repressive police activities, but essentially as the result of practicable preventive measures. Consequently, the success of these programs requires that the various nonpolice state agencies act in concert with and contribute to solving in each community problems that have been identified as sources of insecurity. Thus, while the community understands that in order to improve prevention, public lighting needs to be installed, urban conditions need to be improved, and opportunities for residents to socialize must be provided, state agencies responsible for providing these services must perceive themselves as playing a part in security policy, so as to be able to be more responsive to residents' demands. However, inasmuch as these state agencies have not been jurisdictionally involved in community policing programs, they tend to believe that they are not obligated to respond, or that their response can be delayed. In the eyes of a community mobilized to deal with the problem of insecurity, this lack of response is seen as disinterest and translates into an increased perception that these programs are ineffective. Consequently, offices need to be created to provide coordination and serve as liaisons, in order to ensure that community demands are addressed.

Citizen Participation

Finally, there is one problem highlighted and agreed on by members of the various community associations participating in programs of this type: sustaining, over time, the extended participation of community members. Given that community policing programs rely in part on the participation of residents, if this participation cannot be sustained over time, success of the programs will remain in question. Moreover, if the participation remains limited to a small group within the community, the programs face the risk of being coopted by individual interests. Consequently, given that the continuity and expansion of participation is a major factor when evaluating the fate of these programs, measures need to be considered to promote and maintain community participation.

The literature on participation has identified various reasons for problems of citizen participation in contemporary societies (Verba and Nie 1978). These same factors affect the expansion and continuity of participation in community policing programs. Empirical research has shown that participation is positively correlated with socioeconomic strata, perceived efficacy of the actions being undertaken, and perception that involved parties are affected in a clear and immediate way. At the same time, rational choice theories have emphasized that when the object of the participation is a public good, incentives to participate decrease, since the individuals believe that their participation will have miniscule effects on the ultimate results, or that they can obtain the good by free-riding. Consequently, given the difficulties with participation in general, and with participation aimed at obtaining a public good such as security in particular, measures need to be considered that can counteract these foreseeable problems.

In the three cases analyzed here, the extent and continuity of the participation were presented as a problem affecting the implementation and success of the programs. Despite this fact, in all three cases there were indications that the main benefit of implementing these programs was that citizen participation in community policing seemed to reduce the perception of insecurity among those involved. Therefore, although these programs do not necessarily reduce crime rates, in order to measure their success one must evaluate their effects on the perception of insecurity. Participation in the programs by those who are victims of fear allows community members to move from being defenseless victims of an intolerable problem to being actors in a solution. If this is the case, it can be anticipated that those who decided to participate because of the urgency of the problem will opt to remain involved over time because they perceive that the act of participating provides them an unexpected benefit—namely, a reduction in their perception of insecurity.

Notes

This report was made possible by the field research of Andrea Castagnola, María Poli, and Carolina Varsky in Brazil, Chile, and Argentina, respectively.

1. Some of these evaluation criteria have been used by Mesquita Neto (2000).

2. During the 1990–1999 period, the city of Buenos Aires has had a greater increase in crime (206 percent) than any other city in the country (Dammert 2000).

3. Those analyzing the issue agree that reports of police corruption and violence, and the high public exposure gained by cases such as the attack on the Jewish Community Center (AMIA), the murder of journalist José Luis Cabezas and that of the teenager María Soledad Morales in Catamarca, in which police involvement was confirmed, have

made the issue of the police one that political authorities perceive as a potential problem in elections.

4. See Articles 11 and 12 of the Provincial Public Security Law.

5. An analysis of the functioning of these institutions can be found in Martínez et al. (1998).

6. See Articles 11 and 12 of the Provincial Public Security Law.

7. See Dirección Nacional de Política Criminal, *Resumen ejecutivo de experiencias de policía comunitaria en la Argentina. Informe policial de la Provincia de La Rioja* (Buenos Aires: Dirección Nacional de Política Criminal, May 1999).

8. Comisario Mayor Sergio A. Díaz, *Resumen ejecutivo de experiencias de policía comunitaria en la Argentina. Informe policial de la Provincia de Chubut* (Buenos Aires: Dirección Nacional de Política Criminal, May 1999).

9. The Management and Participation Centers are agencies of the city government, located in various neighborhoods with the responsibility of mediating the resolution of conflicts, among other functions. The councils are made up of the director-general of the Management and Participation Center, a representative of the Crime and Violence Prevention Program, and representatives of various civil society organizations (NGOs; educational, religious, and trade associations; independent neighborhood committees, etc.). The meetings are held every fifteen days and deal with a list of previously determined issues. The explicit objectives of these councils include (1) increasing social awareness of crime prevention through the preparation, dissemination, and discussion of security measures, and by bringing together citizens and police; (2) compiling neighborhood crime maps; (3) collaborating on control and execution of security measures; and (4) contributing to the design of databases to optimize the security services provided by each police station.

10. Municipal Councils, which are to operate in each municipality of the province, will be promoted by the mayors, and will be made up of the mayor or his representative, representatives of the Deliberative Council, representatives of community and sectorial organizations, and a representative of religious institutions. For their part, the Departmental Councils, corresponding to the territory of each Judicial Department of the Province, will be made up of Defenders of Security, the Court of Appeals Prosecutor, four provincial legislators, municipal mayors, and one representative of each of the following: Bar Association, Chamber of Commerce, agricultural sector, professional schools, trade organizations, and religious institutions.

11. The law provides for the creation of a neighborhood security council within the territorial purview of each police station that is part of the Departmental Security Police (Article 13).

12. The Foundation for Democratic Change, a nonprofit NGO, was established in Argentina in early 1998; it was the first organization in Latin America to become part of the Partners for Democratic Change network (www.cambiodemocratico.org).

13. Information was provided by the Foundation for Democratic Change.

14. Gualeguaychú is one of the main routes of communication with MERCOSUR member countries.

15. Cooperative planning is a process used to deal with complex issues and build consensus in a given community. It involves citizens' participation in peacefully resolving social problems, in cooperation with the government and other institutions with jurisdiction over the matter in question.

16. Unfortunately, we did not have access to surveys assessing this program.

17. See http://www.bigfoot.com/~vecinos. See also "Orígenes y desarrollo del Plan Alerta," presentation given by Neighbors United Group (Grupo Vecinos Solidarios) on 11 September 1998, Academia Federal de Policía, Centro de Orientación de la Víctima, IV Jornada sobre Violencia. This presentation summarizes the activities, experiences, and conclusions of the Grupo Vecinos Solidarios, Saavedra neighborhood, in the first ten months of the Plan Alert pilot experiment.

18. The objectives of Plan Alert were to (1) develop individual behavior patterns aimed at reducing opportunities for crime, (2) develop solidarity in the community in order to protect residents, and (3) coordinate community activities with area police.

19. In meetings, the commander of section 49 spoke of the need to have a motorcycle and four officers to carry out street patrols over the 24-hour period in the designated area. In response to this concern, the Ministry of Justice arranged the necessary additional resources through the Argentine Federal Police headquarters (Subsecretaría de Relaciones con la Comunidad [n.d.]).

20. See http://orbita.starmedia.com/~cabildociudadela. Ciudadela is a critical area, located on the outskirts of the city of Buenos Aires. Among the main problems reported by residents are isolation, floods, and security issues. The construction of the Autopista del Oeste highway gave rise to the creation of the Cabildo Abierto del Pueblo de Ciudadela in February 1998. Residents met with the police commander and formulated recommendations for their protection: Internet guides to "block organizing," increased contact between residents and police, establishment of a telephone network, and improvements in public lighting. Members of the Cabildo Abierto make special mention of the Saavedra neighborhood Plan Alert, whose experience and information have been used on the website. After a while, it became evident not only that the police were providing little help, but also that they lacked the human and economic resources to address neighborhood needs.

21. See http://habitantes.elsitio.com/ciudad21/asaltados.htm.

22. See http://members.xoom.com/Villa_Alonso/. In April 1999, the residents of Villa Alonso conducted an investigation to determine the true situation in the neighborhood. This investigation revealed that (1) one in five residents interviewed had been the victim of a crime in the last 12 months; (2) areas with a higher level of socioeconomic development had been victimized more than those with lower levels of development; (3) the feeling of insecurity was not high; and (4) this feeling was attributable to the fact that most of the crimes were robberies that occurred when residents were not present. Following this investigation, the Villa Alonso Steering Committee put into practice a Neighborhood Crime Prevention Plan, designed to rectify individual and family habits and customs, identify infrastructure deficiencies, and increase voluntary collaboration and solidarity among residents of each block. The position of the Villa Alonso residents was similar to that of the residents of Saavedra, with whom they were in contact. Their information bulletin indicates that "among ourselves, on a voluntary basis, we agreed on simple, cost-free measures, based on the experience of the residents and the police, a plan under which the Neighborhood Council disseminates, supervises, and provides advice on the plan; includes the residents; and provides contact with the police."

23. There are also community policing efforts in other cities and regions of the country, such as Espiritu Santo, Minas Gerais, Rio Grande do Sul, and Pará.

24. Participating in this commission were business organizations, such as FIESP, the Korean Chamber of Commerce and Industry, and the Trade Association of Brazil; religious organizations, such as the Council of Priests of the State of São Paulo and Youth

Pastoral; public entities, such as the Secretariat of Justice and Defense of the Citizenry, Secretariat of Justice, Civil Police of São Paulo, and Violence Research Center of the Universidade de São Paulo; NGOs, such as ILANUD (United Nations Latin American Institute for the Prevention of Crime and Treatment of Offenders), Peace and Justice Movement, Center for Citizenship Integration, Citizen Security Association (ASSEC), football (soccer) clubs, the Afro-Brazilian community, and Friends of Belém Society; and several security councils, such as those of Butana and Santa Cecilia; and council coordinators.

25. Interview with Major Miguel Libório Cavalcante Neto, São Paulo Community Police Department, São Paulo, 23 October 2000.

26. Interviews with Major Miguel Libório Cavalcante Neto and Captain Marco Antonio, São Paulo Community Police Department, São Paulo, 23 October 2000.

27. Interview with Tulio Kahn, ILANUD, São Paulo, 24 October 2000.

28. The policing of quadrants tends to decentralize activities, such that each police officer obtains a sector in which to operate; however, this does not mean more direct contact with the community in which the officer functions, nor does it entail the creation of a special battalion.

29. In July 1993, eight street children were murdered next to the Candelaria Church, in the downtown area. One month later, twenty-two residents of the Vigário Geral shantytown, in the northern section, were murdered.

30. According to a survey conducted by the Instituto de Estudos da Religião, the primary participants in these programs were doormen, accounting for 38 percent; residents represented only 17 percent.

31. The movement arose as a practical response to immediate problems. Its objective was to promote interaction among the private sector, state enterprise sector, unions, NGOs, charitable institutions, universities, other citizen movements, religious institutions, advertising agencies, the media, and state, municipal, and federal agencies. Participation was of a personal and voluntary nature, and the organization was nongovernmental and nonpartisan. See Gaspar Pereira (1996).

32. Interview with Leonarda Musumeci, Rio de Janeiro, 27 October 2000.

33. Interview with Major Antonio Carlos Carballo Blanco, Commander of the Special Areas Policing Group (GPAE) of Rio de Janeiro, Rio de Janeiro, 26 October 2000.

34. In September 2000, a new program was launched in the Pavão/Pavãozinho and Cantagalo communities in Copacabana. This program, under the direction of GPAE, has one hundred police officers dedicated to "integrated policing." The police patrol these communities on foot, enter into contact with residents and merchants, attend meetings of the security councils, establish relationships with area neighborhood associations, and participate in events carried out in the communities (celebrations, competitions, and dances). The objective of the police is to establish ongoing contact with residents, merchants, and people who frequent the neighborhood, in order to discuss actions that would ensure the security of the community. Interview with Major Carballo Blanco.

35. Interview with Leonarda Musumeci, Rio de Janeiro, 20 October 2000.

36. Ibid.

37. *La Tercera,* 28 April 2000.

38. The report published by the Ministry of the Interior gives the percentage increase in complaints. Some of the indices that increased most for the 1998–1999 period were robbery involving violence against the victim, 32.2 percent; robbery involving damage to victim's property, 16.3 percent; theft, 15 percent; domestic violence, 19.3 percent; and rape, 10 percent. See www.inec.gov.cl.

39. *La Tercera,* 28 April 2000.
40. *La Tercera,* 12 June 2000.
41. The cities reporting the highest number of muggings of residents include Santiago, with 7,349 cases; Rancagua, with 5,750; and Iquique, 4,874 cases. In those cities, only 4 percent of the cases were cleared—that is, 294, 230, and 195, respectively; see *La Tercera,* 28 April 2000.
42. According to a Centro de Estudios para el Desarrollo report (CED 2000), Houston is the only place where fewer people (7 percent) have a negative opinion of the police than in Chile.
43. Interview with Jorge Araya Moya, Santiago de Chile, October 2000.
44. The authorities established the need for a minimum of fifteen persons to make up a committee. These could be in a building, on a block, or in a territory (that is or is not within a territory of the Neighborhood Council). Depending on the characteristics of the neighborhood, merchants, businesspeople, or only residents might participate. Interview with Hernán Ortega, Division of Public Security and Citizen Participation, Ministry of the Interior, Santiago de Chile, October 2000.
45. Interview with Araya Moya, Santiago de Chile, October 2000.
46. Interview with Ortega.
47. "There is undoubtedly a political segment—on the political right—that is not promoting participation, and that therefore is attempting to establish citizen security plans that rely on local authority, for example, the experience of Lavín in Las Condes, which is restricted to organizing 'red beetle' patrols with retired officers and locating guards in the parks, et cetera, without contemplating improving relations with the community, much less organizing committees. . . . I think that in Las Condes there probably isn't a single one." Interview with Ortega, Santiago de Chile, October 2000.
48. Interview with Araya Moya.
49. "La Seguridad Pide Ayuda. Hay que Involucrar a los Vecinos," interview with Chilean Undersecretary of the Interior Jorge Burgos, *El Mercurio,* 4 September 2000.
50. Ibid.
51. Interview with Carlos Valdivieso, general manager, Citizen Peace Foundation, Santiago de Chile, October 2000.
52. The plan involves formation of Communal Citizen Security Councils "with the power and authority to set local citizen security policy." These councils are established by a Law of Communal Councils. The former are to be chaired by the mayor and comprised of representatives of the Carabineros, Investigative Police, community organizations, and members of health, education, and other service organizations, as well as representatives of the private sector. Organizing these councils would provide information about people's concerns regarding citizen security and offer a means of channeling and coordinating local initiatives. On this basis, those interested would be able to access competitively awarded funds to finance community initiatives that might emerge. The functions of the Councils in terms of crime prevention would be to foster the participation and training of commune residents in the area of crime prevention and control, conduct a diagnostic assessment of the local situation and publicize it, design an action plan to address needs, and call for a competition for the community to develop projects. They would also have the responsibility of evaluating and selecting the best projects for the community, proposing them as possible recipients of competitively awarded funds, and supervising the fulfillment of goals and objectives of projects being implemented. See Ministerio del Interior, División de Seguridad Ciudadana, http://www.seguridadciudadana.gob.cl/.

53. The *communes* were divided into quadrants (251) on the basis of patterns related to the distance that can be covered, or the number of persons, on average, that can use a radio patrol car in an eight-hour shift. In terms of the allocation of human and logistical resources for each quadrant, the criteria employed involved equivalencies among different types of police patrols (cars, vans, foot patrols, mounted patrols, etc.), which are expressed in equivalent patrol units and take into account variables of the coverage and quality of each patrol system, as well as factors such as crime rates, demographic density, number of households, locations where alcohol is sold, areas of uncultivated land, and so on, in each *commune*. The Carabineros established patrol levels from one to four, with these levels indicating the number of times that a given block should be patrolled, according to whether the risk associated with the particular area is higher or lower. Information from internal Carabineros' report.

54. Ibid.

55. Interview with Corporal First Class Carlos Bastidas Martínez, Station 14, Commune of San Bernardo, October 2000.

56. The officers of each sector must meet quantitative targets—such as reducing the number of robberies in the area by 10 percent—in relation to the crime index and the management of resources allocated to each officer. These targets will make it possible to periodically evaluate each sector officer. Included in the evaluation will be indicators that take account of the opinions and priorities of the residents. Finally, it is assumed that this system of performance control will influence the careers of the officers in charge of the sectors. In April of each year, the police will be required to give a public accounting of the use of their resources and the extent to which targets were met.

57. Interview with Azún Candina, researcher at the Center for Development Studies, Santiago, October 2000.

58. Interview with Araya Moya.

59. In this region there were no previous initiatives in citizen security, except for assessments carried out by the Citizen Peace Foundation and one early initiative in Rancagua, which, being very much in line with this program, decided to join up with the present one. In Pichilemu, there was a specific program for the summer period; information sharing was carried out with its crisis committee. For more detailed information on the objectives and aims of the program, see FORJA (2000).

60. FORJA (2000).

61. Interview with Claudio Valdivia Rivas, official of the FORJA Aplicación Seguridad Ciudadana Preventiva program, Santiago de Chile, October 2000.

62. These organizations are demanding mechanisms to access state funds without considering the fact that the process of distributing and accessing such funds could limit their actions.

63. Even in the case of Chile, where the population has higher levels of trust in the police, the statements of Carabineros and of high-level public authorities indicate a considerable lack of confidence in terms of what the citizenry is able to accomplish on security issues.

References

Centro de Estudios para el Desarrollo (CED). 2000. "Policía y sociedad democrática." *Boletín,* 2, no. 8 (September).

Chinchilla, Laura. 1999. "Policía de orientación comunitaria. Una adecuada alianza entre policía y comunidad para revertir la inseguridad." Paper presented at the Inter-American Development Bank Seminar "Dialogos sobre Convivencia Ciudadana," Washington, DC, October.

Chinchilla, Laura, and José María Rico. 1997. *La prevención comunitaria del delito: Perspectivas para América Latina.* Miami: Florida International University, Center for the Administration of Justice.

Conde, Luis Paulo. 1998. "O Projeto Favela-Barrio." In *O Brazil e o mundo no limiar do novo século,* vol. 2, edited by João Paulo dos Reis Velloso. Rio de Janeiro: José Olympio Editora.

Cox, Sebastián. 2000. *Ciudadanía y protagonismo comunitario para la gobernabilidad democrática. Algunas experiencias de Chile.* Santiago: Formación Jurídica para la Acción, May. (Citing United Nations Development Programme. 2000. *Desarrollo humano en Chile—2000. Más sociedad para gobernar el futuro.* Santiago: United Nations Development Programme, March.)

Dammert, Lucía. 2000. *Violencia criminal y seguridad pública en América Latina: La situación en Argentina.* Political Science Series. Santiago, Chile: Economic Commission on Latin America and the Caribbean.

Eilbaum, Lucía. 2000. "La policía 'al servicio de la comunidad': Viejas prácticas policiales y nuevas políticas." Undergraduate thesis, Universidad de Buenos Aires.

Fernandes, Rubem César, ed. 1995. *Monitoramento quantitativo da violencia em Copacabana.* Rio de Janeiro: Instituto de Estudos da Religião/Núcleo de Pesquisas, June.

Formación Jurídica para la Acción (FORJA). 2000. *Aplicación seguridad ciudadana preventiva.* Resumen de Programa. Santiago: FORJA, June.

Fuentes, Claudio. 2001. *Denuncias por actos de violencia policial.* Chile: Facultad Latinoamericana de Ciencias Sociales.

Gaspar Pereira, Hilda Maria. 1996. *The Viva Rio Movement: The Struggle for Peace.* London: Institute of Latin American Studies.

Goldstein, H. 1990. *Problem-Oriented Policing.* New York: McGraw-Hill.

Martínez, Josefina, Mariana Croccia, Lucia Eilbaum, and Vanina Lekerman. 1998. *Consejos de seguridad barriales y participación ciudadana: Los miedos y las libertades.* Buenos Aires: Centro de Estudios Legales y Sociales.

Mesquita Neto, Paulo. 1999a. "Violência policial no Brazil: Abordagens teóricas e prácticas de controle." In *Cidadania, justicia e violência,* edited by Dulce Chaves Pandolfi, et al. Rio de Janiero: Editora Fundação Getulio Vargas.

———. 1999b. "Crime and the Threat to Democratic Governance in Latin America." Paper presented at the Conference on Crime and the Threat to Democratic Governance, Woodrow Wilson International Center for Scholars, Washington, DC, 29 September.

———. 2000. "Violência e segurança pública nas grandes cidades: A experiencia de polícia comunitária em São Paulo." Preliminary version presented at the seminar Violência e Segurança nas Grandes Cidades, Experiencia Comparadas: São Paulo, Rio de Janeiro e Buenos Aires. Buenos Aires, 20–21 June.

Ministerio de Justicia de la Nación. 1997–2000. *Encuesta de victimización de la Ciudad de Buenos Aires.* Buenos Aires: Dirección Nacional de Politica Criminal.

Ministerio de Justicia y Seguridad, Gobierno de la Provincia de Buenos Aires. 1999. *Revista Foros de Seguridad* 2, no. 5 (September).

Musumeci, Leonarda. 1995. *Policiamento comunitário em Copacabana: Monitoriamento qualitativo. Primeiro relatório parcial.* Rio de Janeiro: Instituto de Estudos da Religião/Núcleo de Pesquisas, February.

National Institute of Justice. 1988–1990. *Perspectives on Policing.* Washington, DC: U.S. Department of Justice.

Neild, R. 1998. *Temas y debates en la reforma de la seguridad pública: Una guía para la sociedad civil, policía comunitaria.* Washington, DC: Washington Office on Latin America, January.

Piquet Carneiro, Leandro, and Leonarda Musumeci, eds. 1996. *Um ano de policiamento comunitário: A experiencia de Copacabana.* Rio de Janeiro: Instituto de Estudos da Religião/Núcleo de Pesquisas, January.

Rosúa, Fernando. 1998. "La reforma policial en la Provincia de Santa Fe." In *Las reformas policiales en Argentina.* Buenos Aires: CELS, December.

Sandoval, Luis. 2001. "Prevención local de la delincuencia en Santiago de Chile." In *Policía, sociedad y estado: Modernización y reforma policial en América del Sur,* edited by Azun Candina and Hugo Frühling. Santiago: Centro de Estudios para el Desarrollo.

Smulovitz, Catalina. 2003. "Citizen Insecurity and Fear: Public and Private Responses in the Case of Argentina." In *Crime and Violence in Latin America: Citizen Security, Democracy, and the State,* edited by Hugo Frühling and Joseph Tulchin with Heather A. Golding. Washington, DC: Woodrow Wilson Center Press/Johns Hopkins University Press.

Subsecretaría de Relaciones con la Comunidad. [N.d.] *Experiencias de participación en temas de seguridad. En nuestro país y en el mundo.* Buenos Aires: Gobierno de la Provincia de Buenos Aires, Secretaría de Relaciones con la Comunidad y Formación.

Trojanowicz, R., and B. Bucqueroux. 1993. *Community Policing: How to Get Started.* Cincinnati, OH: Anderson.

Verba, Sidney, and Naomi Nie. 1978. *Participation and Political Equality: A Seven Nation Comparison.* Cambridge; New York: Cambridge University Press.

Waddington, P.A.J. 1999. *Policing Citizens: Authority and Rights.* London, Philadelphia: UCL Press.

Chapter 9

Citizen Security Policy in Argentina: The National Crime Prevention Plan

Alberto Föhrig, Julia S. Pomares, and Cecilia Gortari

This chapter is an analysis of an initiative implemented by the government of Argentina in August 2000—the National Crime Prevention Plan (Plan Nacional de Prevención del Delito [PNPD])—designed to establish urban security. The plan is of particular interest in that it is the first national initiative on this topic, and it brings together various state agencies and departments that, until now, have worked on the issue separately, without linking their efforts.[1]

A year after launching the initiative, two of the country's twenty-four districts—the Province of Neuquén and the City of Buenos Aires—began implementing the plan. Given that the process is in a more advanced stage in the latter, an evaluation will be made of its functioning in that district. First, an analysis is made of the context in which the PNPD emerged; then, consideration will be given to its main characteristics, as conceived in the design and development of the implementation process in the City of Buenos Aires; and last, some conclusions will be set forth regarding its functioning.

The Emergence of Security as a Priority on the Public Agenda

Security has become a major concern on Argentina's public agenda. Although to a lesser extent than in other Latin American countries, there has been an increase in certain types of crimes, particularly those involving physical violence. According to official statistics, from 1990 to 1999, the rate of alleged criminal acts reported in the country grew from 1,722 to 2,904 per 100,000 inhabitants—that is, an increase of 68 percent. The majority of these were crimes against persons and property.[2] Added to this are crimes not reported in the police statistics (constituting the so-called *cifra negra* of crime): in the last five years, in the main urban centers, approximately seven out of ten crimes were not reported to the police.

In tandem with this growth in crime, in the last decade there has been an increase in the feeling of insecurity. Public opinion surveys indicate that insecurity due to crime is the second-ranking social concern of Argentines, after unemployment. This is reflected in the high percentage of citizens who believe they have a good probability of being the victim of a crime in the future. In the last five years, victimization surveys conducted in the country's main urban centers show that this figure has remained above 80 percent.

Against this background, the political context in which the debate on security occurs can be characterized as one in which the state's ability to produce public goods is extremely poor. The issue of security is being discussed amid decreasing public acceptance of political parties and state institutions, as well as a marked decline in the public's assessment of the national government's management abilities.

Security, unlike most public policy issues, has generated intense controversy, not only in academic circles, but in politics. One of the sources of impetus for the debate has been the government of the Province of Buenos Aires—the most important district in the country, where one-third of the total population is concentrated. Here, a policy to deal with crime, known as Iron Fist, was implemented in 1999, granting the police greater discretionary powers in suppressing crime,[3] and allowing them to be less concerned with the individual rights of those who have been arrested or prosecuted.[4]

The national government, for its part, took an ambivalent stance, combining inconsistent initiatives that, on the one hand, were a response to the social demand for greater security through more severe sentences and increased police powers and, on the other, applied preventive and participatory concepts to combating crime. In the first instance, greater autonomy was given to the Argentine Federal Police (Policía Federal Argentina [PFA]) to search individuals,[5] more severe penalties were provided for crimes involving firearms,[6] and sentences were stiffened.[7] The National Crime Prevention Plan analyzed here is an example of the second of these trends, since it uses preventive actions, beyond the scope of the penal system, to complement repressive measures.

As never before since the restoration of democracy in 1983, a debate confined to legal issues—such as the question of giving more or less weight to safeguarding individual guarantees for citizens in seeking to solve security problems—became a competition between two alternative approaches to solving the public policy problem.

It should also be noted that within the state structure, security creates major challenges, in terms of patterns of state response to an increasingly complex issue. No individual state agency is capable of dealing with this issue alone. Thus, new interagency institutional arrangements have begun to be developed within the Argentine government. At the same time, the planning of specific actions has been hindered by a lack of reliable figures—crime rates and victimization surveys—that could provide sufficiently disaggregated geographic information on the different crime-related issues. Consequently, the analytical framework for security policy places the increase in crime within a context of institutional weakness and political competition regarding the type of policies to be implemented.

The social situation that frames this issue has also changed markedly throughout the 1990s. Its qualitative change is directly related to the increase in crimes committed by minors and to changes in the types of crime. The reasoning involved in criminal behavior takes on a new perspective once the actions of minors are taken into account. In a significant proportion of cases, there is no cost-benefit calculation, nor any consistency between means and ends at the time the crime is committed. This spike in youth crime rates is positively correlated with changes in cultural patterns among young people. Statistically, the proportion of young people from large urban centers who neither study nor work has grown throughout the 1990s.[8] Qualitative studies on violence indicate that these youth are the main sources of the breakdown in traditional codes in the very heart of the low-income sectors—codes such as the dictate that one not "work" in one's own neighborhood.

The middle and upper classes have responded to this situation in two ways. The first has been to withdraw into their private worlds. During much of the 1990s, there was a proliferation of gated and country club–type communities on the outskirts of the major urban centers. As a by-product of this new form of urban structure, there has been an increase in the demand for private security in these neighborhoods. The second response, by society as a whole, has been the significant increase in the possession of weapons by civilians.[9]

This set of factors had a decisive influence on the origin of the PNPD and on its subsequent implementation. The plan arose out of the consensus of the country's twenty-four jurisdictions, brought together in the Domestic Security Council[10] (February 2000), which signed the "Foundation for

Consensus for a Federal Security Plan"; one of its points was to implement a crime prevention plan that fostered citizen participation. As a result, a number of provincial governments subsequently demanded its implementation in their respective jurisdictions.

Implementation of the National Crime Prevention Plan in the City of Buenos Aires

In the City of Buenos Aires over the course of the 1990s, criminal acts reported in official statistics increased by 207 percent, equivalent to an increase of 4,255 crimes per 100,000 inhabitants. This is far above the increase registered in the same period for the country overall (68 percent). In 2000, the total number of crimes rose to 199,587, equivalent to 545 crimes per day, approximately 23 per hour. According to data from the victimization survey for the same year, one out of three inhabitants of the City of Buenos Aires had been the victim of some kind of property crime in the past twelve months.[11]

Although Buenos Aires acquired the status of an autonomous city in 1994 (with the last reform of the national constitution), security services in the city are still provided by the Argentine Federal Police (through the Superintendency of Metropolitan Security).[12] The law guaranteeing the interests of the national state in the City of Buenos Aires (Law 24588 of November 1995) establishes that "the Argentine Federal Police shall continue carrying out police security functions and acting as an auxiliary arm of the justice system of the City of Buenos Aires, while being organizationally and functionally answerable to the national executive branch."

In 2000, some changes were made in the organizational structure of the Federal Police, but their impact on the distribution of personnel is difficult to assess; 49 percent of the total force of approximately 17,250 officers carries out policing functions in the City of Buenos Aires. These serve a population of 3 million, plus an additional 1.5 million people who work in the city and come primarily from the Province of Buenos Aires.[13]

A number of different crime prevention and citizen participation initiatives have been tried in recent years, at both the governmental and nongovernmental levels. In terms of official initiatives, two immediate predecessors of the PNPD can be identified, both of which began in 1998. The first was the creation of Community Prevention Councils by the Argentine Federal Police. These were to be made up of approximately ten residents, who would be representative of the neighborhoods to which they belonged. The councils were coordinated by the police precinct of the jurisdiction concerned and, in general, addressed issues related to police patrolling. The other was the creation by the government of the City of Buenos Aires of Neighborhood Crime and Violence Prevention Councils. These would be made up of neighbors, residents, merchants, nongovernmental organizations, recognized local or neighborhood entities, representatives of all types of official institutions (schools, social welfare centers, and so on) located in the area in which the council has authority, a representative of the respective Management and Participation Center (Centro de Gestión y Participación [CGP]), officials and technical staff of the Ministry of Interior's Citizen Security Program, and officials from other areas of government.

Beyond the specific characteristics of each of these initiatives, their short duration was related primarily to the lack of political coordination and the threat of competition between the two politically distinct types of agencies (the Ministry of the Interior—responsible for the Argentine Federal Police—and the city government). The 1999 change in national government and the resulting political similarity between the two levels of government were conducive to implementation of the PNPD in the City of Buenos Aires.

The primary objectives of the PNPD are to reduce predatory or street crimes, particularly crimes against property and persons, involving physical violence; diminish the feeling of insecurity in the face of such crimes; and foster the active participation of nongovernmental actors (citizens, civil society organizations, and so on) and establish a network of commitment, cooperation, and articulation with government actors to deal with crime prevention and the feeling of insecurity.

Complementary objectives of the plan are to encourage active participation by citizens and their organizations in each of the communities, ensuring their involvement in defining specific problems and viable solutions; promote the transformation of police institutions and security forces, in order to assist them in adapting to new strategies and actors concerned with crime prevention; build new relationships of mutual trust between police institutions and security forces on the one hand, and NGOs on the other; execute interventions designed to prevent crime through social policy, developing coordination and complementarity for the purpose of improving the quality of life of the citizens; and collaborate in producing a new urban security culture, through the production and dissemination of new language to propose and publicly debate related needs and demands, in ways consistent with the democratic system.

In order to achieve these objectives, the PNPD outlines a series of strategies and approaches that share three central characteristics: (1) an organizational structure based on a multiagency and interagency approach, (2) a key role given to citizen participation, and (3) an integrated crime prevention approach.

Organizational Structure

The organizational structure of the PNPD attempts to emulate certain experiences of the developed countries and is innovative in terms of Argentina's public administration, given that:

> the plan will have, as a central feature, an interagency approach, since it brings together a range of governmental actors that traditionally carry out their activities in an isolated fashion—belonging, as they do, to different levels of government (national, provincial, municipal)—and will produce a "collective entity" with its own structure and management model. This interagency approach seeks to optimize the use of public resources, avoiding the superimposition of actions generated from different agencies and seeking to extend their scope, while increasing their effectiveness and efficiency in establishing urban security (Ministry of the Interior and Ministry of Justice and Human Rights 2000).

Organizational engineering based on the partnership approach begins with the assumption that crime prevention and community security lie beyond the competence of any individual entity alone. Crime is, by its nature, multifaceted, both in its causes and its effects. However, the social response to crime is segmented and shared. Thus, different agencies must interact in different ways in relation to the specific problems of crime, and contribute different types of knowledge.

This multiagency approach can have various levels of cooperation. If cooperation is measured by the effect it has on redefining the objectives and functions of the agencies, there is, on one extreme of the continuum, multiorganizational partnerships, which involve bringing together different agencies to deal with a given topic, without this affecting or transforming their tasks significantly. The PNPD, for its part, promotes partnerships of this type with programs or agencies that oversee social development programs (Ministries of Health, Social Development, Labor, and so on) but lie outside the plan's structure. At the other extreme are interorganizational partnerships that affect and permeate normal internal relationships. They involve collaboration and interdependence and generate new structures, in terms of teams, identifiable units, and forms of work.

The implementation and functioning of the PNPD is the result of an interagency partnership between the Ministry of Interior—responsible for security forces, and the Ministry of Justice and Human Rights—in charge of crime statistics and the prison system. According to the regulations created by the plan, this consists of a General Coordination Team composed of six coordinators (three for each ministry) and a technical team, known as the General Technical Unit, made up of twenty professionals from both ministries.

Implementation in each jurisdiction is carried out through interagency partnerships between the different levels of government involved (national, provincial, and municipal). This cooperation translates into the formation of teams with representatives from the three levels (known as regional, when related to the provincial level, and local, when related to the municipal level).

Beyond the advantages that it provides to these partnerships at the international level, this complex framework takes on vital importance in the case of Argentina, since it makes it possible to take account of Argentina's political structure and security system. Given its federal character, police powers fall within the provincial sphere. Hence, in order to be effective, any intervention concerning citizen security at the municipal level requires the backing of the government of the province of which the municipality is a part. Argentina's federal structure has historically meant that certain powers were reserved for the provinces and were not constitutionally delegated to the federal branch. Added to these "nondelegated" areas have been, over the course of the 1990s, other functions that, to date, have been overseen at the federal level, such as health and education. This profound process of decentralization produced new opportunities for solving interjurisdictional problems. Thus, new interagency and multiagency structures were established. These new practices demonstrate the growing complexity of public policies, such as the appearance of new mechanisms to institutionalize these practices. There are numerous federal councils that bring together the nation and the provinces to deal with various public matters in multijurisdictional councils that include national and provincial ministers with various areas of responsibility.[14]

In the city of Buenos Aires, a Regional Coordination Team was formed, composed of the coordinator of the PNPD in the city (director-general of security and crime prevention policy), two members of the General

Coordination Team, and a representative of the Argentine Federal Police. This management structure, although it made it possible to reach consensus, often highlighted the lack of defined leadership, which poses several problems, given that this is generally a critical factor in implementing such policies.

In regard to the multiagency partnerships, it is worth mentioning the problems in achieving coordination and efficiency between the different agencies of the government of the City of Buenos Aires. The effort and management time required even for simple matters, such as pruning trees or installing lighting, raises questions as to whether the PNPD will be capable of implementing effective strategies. The results from coordination with the Argentine Federal Police have been much more encouraging. The support that was not forthcoming from the high levels of the police hierarchy was indeed received from many of the precincts, perhaps due to the greater accountability they have to the residents in their jurisdictions.

Role of Citizen Participation

The second characteristic of the PNPD is citizen participation and its role in crime prevention. A series of basic guidelines was defined, in terms of the nature of the participatory process and the points at which participation should have an effect. Citizen participation in the framework of the plan should:

1. Provide appropriate information to citizens regarding the scope of citizen participation anticipated at the various points in the plan.
2. Create ongoing mechanisms for citizen participation—individually or through civil society organizations—and for governmental actors in each of the local communities.
3. Provide an open invitation, so that all citizens have a chance to be involved in the participatory mechanisms.
4. Create spaces for effective exchanges and deliberation concerning ongoing mechanisms for participation among citizens and government actors.

Citizen participation in implementing the plan will occur at various "moments" or points, and will have four facets: (1) consultative, inasmuch as it will act as a provider of information for developing the diagnostic assessment of the urban security situation in the local community; (2) decision making, since it will participate in the decision-making process by developing options and alternatives, in conjunction with government actors, on the type of interventions to be carried out in the local community; (3) executive, inasmuch as it will be able to participate in carrying out interventions in collaboration with government and oversight actors; and (4) oversight, since it will carry out ongoing monitoring of the progress of interventions determined through public deliberation within the framework of the plan and based on the consensus reached during the citizen participation process (Ministry of the Interior and Ministry of Justice and Human Rights 2000).

In terms of the basic guidelines for citizen participation and the general and specific objectives of the plan, citizen participation is first a means of political socialization that involves creating new spaces and mechanisms for articulation between the state and members of society and, second in importance, a way of strengthening civil society, by seeking to recover public spaces and creating bonds of social solidarity.

This sets an ambitious goal for the early participatory processes that have been set in motion in the country: it means moving beyond consultative participation (the first stage) and foresees participation of a decision-making, executive, and oversight nature. This involves greater commitment on the part of the citizenry and the state, not only in terms of operational requirements, but also in terms of accountability, in light of greater pressure on state authorities to provide an accounting to the citizenry.

Mention should also be made of the role that citizen participation must play (pursuant to the first basic guideline) in facilitating access to information—an issue no less important to the institutional practices of the Argentine state (and of other Latin American states). In the City of Buenos Aires, the CGPs—territorial divisions of the municipal administration—represented the unit responsible for implementing the participatory mechanism. As a result of the decentralization set in motion in 1996, the city is divided into sixteen regions, each of which has a CGP, to which certain municipal functions have been delegated (bureaucratic procedures relating to vital records, revenues, and violations, as well as regional social service, and so on). It is anticipated that in a second (political) stage of decentralization, some of the district legislators will be elected to these divisions.

In an initial stage, the PNPD was implemented in five CGPs, covering approximately 650,000 inhabitants and seventeen neighborhoods.[15] Each CGP was, in turn, divided into subregions (on average, four per CGP) according to various criteria, such as police jurisdiction, geographic boundaries of the neighborhoods, common problems, and so on. In each of these subregions, a neighborhood meeting is convened on a monthly basis. The plan promotes the direct participation of both citizens and civil society organizations, but under different scenarios: the direct participation of citizens in neighborhood meetings of each subregion, and the participation of civil society organizations in another space, through the CGP, based on geographic criteria. Due to the fact that this second type of participation—in this first stage—has received little promotion, the analysis here will focus on the development of participatory mechanisms in the neighborhood meetings.

The implementation of the plan, at this stage, involved holding twenty neighborhood meetings per month. About forty residents participated in each of these meetings; their average age, in most cases, was approximately sixty. The mechanism for convening people has been face-to-face dissemination of information, overseen by the coordinators. To date, no massive campaign to disseminate the PNPD—through television, radio, or newspapers—has been carried out at either the local or national level.

Due to the method of bringing people together, access to information may have been limited and of limited breadth. Added to this is the lack of experience in the country with citizen participation, the distrust of government initiatives due to the failure of previous experiences, and certain material constraints. There may be limitations on participation due to economic hardship, long work hours, or working multiple jobs. Given these difficulties, the people who are able to participate in such meetings are often not economically constrained. Therefore, there is a selection bias in favor of middle class or older, retired participants; this bias directly influences the outcomes of the debates. All of these factors affect the possibility of or willingness to participate in meetings, which casts their representativeness in doubt; this confirms a criticism of citizen participation strategies—that they make the erroneous assumption that everyone will be able to participate.

There is a low level of attendance of young people (who are often pointed to as the culprits in various social problems) at neighborhood meetings. This reflects a serious flaw in the process, which is that the meetings represent the only opportunity for participation, and this participatory mechanism is the only source of information for designing crime prevention strategies. This can be traced to the design of the plan itself: although citizen participation is not limited to holding meetings, neither are other forms of participation specified (e.g., multisectoral boards or the forming of focus groups with young people).[16]

Nonparticipant observation at numerous meetings and analysis of records of these meetings shows that the initial discourse of the residents reflects a number of discriminatory and repressive features, replete with prejudices toward and stigmatization of the youth and immigrants from neighboring countries (mostly with poor socioeconomic conditions). This rhetoric is associated, in general, with demands for greater police presence (this, as will be seen further on, is the main demand) and, to a lesser extent, with proposals such as the prohibition of alcohol consumption on public streets, use of assault tanks at the exits of local dancehalls, the closing off of squares through the use of fences and padlocks, and so on. This brings up another frequent criticism of the community strategy: a given practice can have different meanings depending on whether the community has a reputation for being intolerant or punitive. This can have positive consequences in that it promotes creativity, but it can also obscure certain features; in the extreme case, as Nuria Cunill mentions (1991), the same guideline can be adopted in support of values as contradictory as those of democracy or dictatorship.

The citizen participation process, as put into practice by the PNPD, is most susceptible to these risks—even more so if one considers that the positive value associated with the practices makes them fertile terrain for artificially built consensus and the legitimization of inequalities. Added to this is the lack of a response or clear definition on the part of the PNPD, in terms of what position to take regarding this type of rhetoric. On numerous occasions, meeting coordinators have shown "fear" of the residents and a consequent silence and compliance regarding their rhetoric. Thus, a type of relationship is created between the plan and the residents in which the coordinators attempt, to the extent possible, to avoid conflict. This can be attributed in part to a certain deficit in the education of the community coordinators regarding group dynamics, as well as a lack of support from the neighborhoods in which they carry out their role as plan officials.

Another characteristic of the participatory process evidenced in this first stage is the reticence of residents to assume active, committed roles beyond the simple presentation of complaints and demands. There have been few cases in which residents prepared proposals and collaborated in their development, despite the fact that both the coordinators and the technical teams have tried various mechanisms to encourage them.[17] In other words, participation has assumed a primarily consultative character, without taking on a decision-making or executive function. This is closely linked to the fact that, in many cases, participation in meetings is sporadic and fragmentary. Residents who voice a given demand do not always attend the following meeting, which makes it difficult to evaluate the impact of the actions taken on the demand. In terms of the design of the plan, this means that citizen participation in many cases fails to exercise its oversight role.

Finally, a central question that permeates the entire participatory process is that, in the City of Buenos Aires, as with the rest of the country, political practices associated with clientelist approaches are highly entrenched and are marked by the different politico-territorial jurisdictions. This reality has had a significant effect on the National Crime Prevention Plan, from the setting of criteria for the selection of local implementation teams to the methods of convening meetings. Coordinators for the local implementation teams were selected by giving priority to balancing the political parties: for each CGP, two coordinators were named (one for each party of the coalition). In addition, the coordinators carry out their political activities in the same geographic space as that which they use in their capacity as plan representatives, thus creating a major conflict of interest.

In CGPs in which the clientelist approach predominates, the meetings have been more numerous (with an average of forty attendees per meeting, there are subregions in which one hundred residents attended), since attempts to convene the residents were carried out with partisan militancy; for obvious reasons, the representativeness of these meetings is seriously compromised.

Integrated Crime Prevention Strategy

The plan emphasizes "integrated prevention," meaning converging a set of diverse crime prevention strategies on a single object, in order to enhance potential and obtain better results. Integrated crime prevention represents the most appropriate means of responding to the needs and demands of security at present, since it acts before the crime is committed, preventing it from occurring, and creating a feeling of security. Moreover, by bringing into play mechanisms beyond the penal system, it not only reduces the human and social costs brought about by crime, but also those generated by the penal system.

Integrated prevention, as understood in this plan, brings together the strategy of social prevention (designed to affect the social causes of crime) with the strategy of situational-environmental prevention (designed to reduce the opportunities for carrying out crimes). Both contribute significantly to the objective of reducing crime and the feeling of insecurity, but the situational-environmental strategy, which provides greater effectiveness over the short term, does not produce lasting effects over the medium and long term. Thus, this strategy should be linked to the social strategy, given that its scope, as a stand-alone measure, is extremely limited. The plan favors medium- and long-term interventions and makes social strategy primary, with the situational environmental strategy having a secondary role (Ministry of the Interior and Ministry of Justice and Human Rights 2000).

The PNPD defines situational environmental prevention as "a collection of measures directed at highly specific forms of crime which involve the management, design or manipulation of the immediate environment in which these crimes occur in as systematic and permanent way as possible so as to reduce the opportunities for these crimes as perceived by a broad range of potential offenders" (Hough et al. 1980, cited in Crawford 1998, 66). There is a great range of situational intervention techniques available, from the use of closed-circuit television and the recomposition of police patrols to redefining the public space (lighting, bus stops, etc.).

In regard to social prevention, the PNPD provides that interventions will be directed primarily at the secondary level of potential offenders (primary prevention relates to social policies in general; tertiary prevention, linked to social reintegration of the prison population, is beyond the area of competence of the PNPD). Among the main risk factors dealt with by this strategy are poverty, particularly among children and young people; unemployment, especially among youth; overcrowding and the absence of public housing; peer pressure; school attrition; and family violence.

The implementation of crime prevention strategies by the PNPD is intimately linked to the participatory dynamic because it is confined to responding to the priority demands arising out of meetings, which, as already pointed out, have limited representativeness. One of the arguments to justify this dynamic is the need to regain citizens' trust in government, to demonstrate that participation makes sense and that it can produce results (relating political results to the demands of the citizens). However, although this argument has validity, other preventive strategies need to be developed that go beyond and complement the demands of the residents. Practically speaking, statistical assessments of the status of security for the City of Buenos Aires have not to date played a role as inputs, which demonstrates the lack of experience in the country, in terms of using this type of tool in decision making—an issue that is particularly relevant to security policy.

In terms of the demands put forth by residents at the meetings,[18] these relate—in approximately 98 percent of cases—to situational environmental prevention strategies, primarily in the form of greater police presence (68 percent). Demands related to social prevention alone represent the remaining

2 percent; this datum, in view of the foregoing, poses certain contradictions in terms of the priority importance that the plan's design assigns to social strategies for crime prevention. The demands are categorized and analyzed at bimonthly meetings by the Regional Coordination Team. They are prioritized according to previous occurrences of the crimes—as reported by the residents.[19] At these meetings, responsibilities are also established for carrying out the actions that have been defined.

Given the results of this processing of demands, the crime prevention strategies outlined in the plan's design can be characterized as follows: the situational environmental strategy plays the greatest role in interventions, primarily related to restructuring police patrols. The cooperation of the police forces becomes vitally important to the success of the interventions. These, being for the most part responses to specific demands of residents, ultimately are isolated strategies, without any comprehensively planned interventions. As already mentioned, in the period under consideration few interventions were carried out in the framework of the social prevention strategy. However, these have a common feature: not having specific resources of its own for social prevention, the PNPD relies on coordination with other social programs for its implementation. The problems in establishing effective cooperation mechanisms have hampered interventions in this area.

Conclusions

In regard to the structuring of state space for implementing security policy, certain conclusions can be drawn based on the development and implementation of the PNPD at several levels: intergovernmental relations, the political leadership required to move it forward; citizens' access to information; and use of this information by the state as input for designing public policy.

In regard to inter- and intra-governmental relations, it is safe to say that despite the limitations and problems in the design and implementation process, the PNPD is an important step in defining a state policy on security that takes account of the complexity of the issue and the multiplicity of actors involved in dealing with it. Until now, there had been no attempt in Argentina to achieve effective coordination among different levels of government and among various public agencies in regard to public security.

Moreover, beyond the strong political resolve demonstrated in creating the plan, a major flaw can be seen in the implementation stage in terms of the conviction and will to make substantial changes in the method by which those at the highest decision-making levels oversee public security. Changes in the ministerial cabinet and internal political splits, as well as the implementation of different security-related measures in a disjointed (and, in some cases, even contradictory) manner, has had highly negative consequences for the legitimacy of the initiative and for its effective functioning. In public ventures of this scale, the absence of definitive political leadership makes its implementation highly problematic.

Statistical and qualitative information on the matter of security is scarce—in both quality and quantity. The lack of theoretical work and empirical research in the country on the subject of citizen security is an obstacle to designing and evaluating public policy. Because of this gap, there is little experience in using this information as a tool for public management. In the specific case of the PNPD, the existing material—for example, statistical assessments of the City of Buenos Aires—were not used as inputs in the implementation process.

In terms of the relation between state and civil society concerning the design and implementation of public policy, the participatory component has constituted a significant step in more closely linking the two elements. The creation of venues for consultative participation, as well as the prospect of expanding participation to the decision-making, executive, and oversight phases, are positive features in an area historically linked to the job of security "professionals." The prerequisite to the proper functioning of participatory mechanisms, such as those described, is a qualitative leap in management to generate solid work teams and smooth coordination of action at the governmental level. Setting in motion participatory processes at the state level involves the complicated task of creating legitimate spaces for citizens. This is made difficult by the fact that the plan's meetings are presented as the only ongoing participatory space promoted by the state to deal with public problems. Because of this, the level of enthusiasm of the discussion by those attending the meetings is not confined to the issue of crime prevention, making it more difficult to achieve positive results from the participatory exercise. This is even more true, given that the topic is so socially sensitive. The state's invitation to the citizenry to participate should not be confused with removing the state from its primary responsibility of promoting public security, nor with promoting direct action by citizens to oversee security.

Finally, a number of considerations need to be highlighted regarding the relation between executing programs, as described here, and the security forces and Federal Police. It is essential to coordinate crime prevention initiatives with reforms of the security forces and of the prison system. Improving citizens' trust in police institutions must go hand in hand with a process of reform of the security forces. Restructuring crime prevention policies is inconceivable without providing effective coordination with crime suppression policies. In both instances, policy plays a key role. Crime prevention strategies can only be carried out, in practice, to the extent that this link is established.

Attempts to incorporate the Argentine Federal Police in the management of the plan have had uneven results—at least, to date. One positive aspect, as mentioned earlier, was having a representative of the force be part of the team in charge of coordinating the PNPD in the City of Buenos Aires. Another positive element is that networks of trust and cooperation are starting to be established at this level. However, there are numerous indications that this process needs both a chance to develop over time, in order to establish itself successfully, and—far more profoundly—an integrated reform of the security forces. Such reform must cover aspects such as educating police commanders on matters related to interdisciplinary crime prevention policies, the demilitarization of crime prevention analysis, and the decorporatization of the police institution. Finally, mechanisms must be set in place within the force to provide external controls of police actions and provide an accounting to citizens.

Notes

1. The authors participated directly in the plan—both in its coordination and as part of its technical team—from the design stage in April 2000 to April 2001.

2. National Criminal Information System, Ministry of Justice and Human Rights of the Republic of Argentina.

3. For example, an internal circular of the Buenos Aires Provincial Police (2001) gave the order to all departmental headquarters that "children and homeless youth be detained" in operations to be implemented "on an ongoing basis," and that they would conclude by placing minors "at the disposal of the Justice system as many times as necessary."

4. According to a finding by the Supreme Court of Justice of the Province of Buenos Aires (Ruling No. 3012 of 24 October 2001), the "list of children and youth in State custody killed in alleged confrontations with police during 1999 and 2000, verified from relevant information provided by magistrates of specialized jurisdiction, included at least 60 cases." The Court also expressed "its great concern about acts of institutional violence that, as a result of acts or omissions, violate recognized international norms of human rights to the detriment of minors who are wards of the State."

5. A national law passed in June 2001 (No. 25434) establishes that PFA officers may "require a suspect, at the location where the crime occurred, to provide information or a brief description of the circumstances, in order to guide the ongoing investigation," and that they shall have five days (extendable by five additional days) to complete investigation of the case and submit it to the judge. In terms of searches, they may "in case of obvious risk" enter alone while witnesses wait outside until the danger has passed. They are also authorized to seize evidence different from that which they were seeking and may, without a warrant, search any person, their belongings, and their vehicles for items "deriving from or connected with a crime or that could be used to commit a crime."

6. Based on the sanction provided in Law 25297 (2000), "When one of the crimes is committed with violence or intimidation against persons using a firearm, the length of the sentence provided for the crime involved shall be increased by at least one-third and by no more than the legal maximum for the corresponding type of sentence."

7. By means of the sanction provided in Law No. 25430 (2001), the "two for one" law—which governed as of 1994 and was a response to Argentina's signature of the Pact of San José, Costa Rica—was repealed. In accordance to the Pact, no one may be detained beyond a "reasonable period" without receiving a final sentence. The "two for one" law established that "reasonable period" may not be more than two years (extendable by one additional year). After this time period, the detained person must be released. At the same time, the law established that, as of the second year in prison with no final sentence, each day shall be calculated as two days of imprisonment.

8. In Argentina, 14 percent of young people between 15 and 24 years of age are neither studying nor working, nor do they manage households (known as NET youth); in 1991, this figure was 11 percent. Today, the percentage of NET youth in the low-income quintile is 22.4, and was 20.5 percent in 1991 (Household Survey, Encuesta permanente de hogares, Instituto Nacional de Estadísticas y Censos, 1991–2001). In terms of Argentina's population aged under 14 years, half (10.5 million persons or 29 percent of the total population) live in households below the poverty line. Methodologically, the poverty line is defined as for nuclear families of four persons with income under US$495 per month. For this social sector, families on average have five members and their real median income is US$355 per month, or US$2.20 per day. In 1997, young people living in poor households represented 45 percent of the total (Social Development Survey, Sistema de Información, Monitoreo y Evaluación de Programas Sociales-Instituto Nacional de Estadísticas y Censos, 16 June 1999).

9. As of March 2001 (according to the National Arms Register) there were 740,416 users of firearms in the entire country. More than 75 percent of the nation's users reside in the Province of Buenos Aires, the nation's capital, Santa Fe, and Córdoba (42.5 percent, 13.1 percent, 11.4 percent, and 8.8 percent, respectively). In total, 2.25 million arms are registered, although police authorities indicate that there are an additional 1.5 million that are not registered.

10. The Domestic Security Council is a consultative body that brings together all of the country's provinces for the purpose of providing advice on domestic security to the national executive branch.

11. National Office of Criminal Policies, Ministry of Justice and Human Rights.

12. In its own constitution approved in 1996, the City of Buenos Aires establishes that "public security is an unrenounceable obligation of the State and is offered equally to all inhabitants. The service shall be the responsibility of the security police, under the executive branch. . . ."

13. In terms of perceptions regarding the actions of the police in the city, 45 percent of Buenos Aires residents believe that they are not doing a good job, while 34 percent believe that they are. At the same time, 49 percent of those interviewed state that the police pass by their house (on foot or by car) every day; 14.5 percent indicate that the police never do so; and 13.7 percent state that they pass by three times per week. In evaluating this frequency, more than 60 percent believe that the police should pass by their house more often, while 27 percent believe that it is sufficiently frequent. As stated earlier, the city also has a high rate of unreported crime: 70 percent do not report crimes. However, the perception of treatment received at the police stations by those who report crimes or transact other formalities is very satisfactory: 69.5 percent believe the experience was good or very good (Victimization Survey, Ministry of Justice and Human Rights, 2000).

14. The most important councils, besides the Domestic Security Council referred to earlier, are the federal public policy councils, and those of education, infrastructure, and investment.

15. The neighborhoods covered by these CGPs (7, 10, 11, 12, and 14 East) are Saavedra, Villa Urquiza, Coghlan, Villa del Parque, Villa Devoto, Monte Castro, Villa Real, Paternal, Parque Chas, Chacarita, Agronomía, Villa Pueyrredon, Villa Santa Rita, Flores, Floresta, Colegiales, and Belgrano.

16. Multisectoral boards refer to the meeting of different representative neighborhood entities and state officials; focus groups refer to qualitative studies based on empirical research.

17. These initiatives were linked to the construction of telephone communication networks between residents who live on contiguous blocks, designed to alert each other to potential dangers.

18. Directorate General of Security and Crime Prevention Policy of the Government of the City of Buenos Aires, based on demands presented at meetings held up to 31 March 2001.

19. The requirement that demands should have, as a foundation, the occurrence of some concrete act, is questionable, in that one of the objectives of the PNPD is to reduce the feeling of insecurity.

References

Crawford, Adam. 1998. *Crime Prevention and Community Safety: Politics, Policies, and Practices*. London, New York: Longman. Citing J.M. Hough, R.V.G. Clarke, and P. Mayhew, "Introduction," in *Designing Out Crime,* edited by R.V.G. Clarke and P. Mayhew. London: HMSO, 1980.

Cunill, Nuria. 1991. *Participación ciudadana. Dilemas y perspectivas para la democratización de los Estados latinoamericanos*. Venezuela: Centro Latinoamericano de Administración para el Desarrollo.

Ministry of the Interior and Ministry of Justice and Human Rights. 2000. *National Crime Prevention Plan*. Buenos Aires: Ministry of the Interior and Ministry of Justice and Human Rights.

Chapter 10

Civilian Oversight of Security in Peru: The Testimony of a Participant

Carlos Basombrío Iglesias

Several years ago, as part of the first phase of its project on citizen security and democratic governance in Latin America, the Woodrow Wilson Center's Latin American Program commissioned me to write a paper dealing with the way in which the issue of citizen security was being dealt with by authoritarian regimes like the one that existed then in Peru. My approach to the question at that time was shaped by two factors. One was my concern, as an academic, to understand the processes connected with citizen security and their impact on political life; the other was my commitment, as a democratic activist, to call attention to politically motivated decisions on the subject, and to stress their impact on the rights of individuals.

The present chapter, commissioned four years later, is being written against a very different background. First, the Peruvian situation changed abruptly with the collapse of the authoritarian regime, which ushered in a peaceful transition to democracy and the election of a democratic government that finds itself, however, in difficulty halfway through its term. On the personal side, I am emerging from an intense experience in which I was directly responsible for managing the country's domestic security. During my tenure, major changes occurred in the police and in the country's approach to security.

This chapter attempts to describe the changes, principal challenges, and achievements of this recent period, as well as some important lessons learned and the enormous task remaining. It is important that the reader understand that this testimony is that of one party to the situation, given just months after the conclusion of what was, for me, an intensely personal experience. It should not be read as an academic paper by a distant observer, but as an expression of the thinking of one of the leading players in the process.

Background

Throughout the 1990s, Peru was governed by Alberto Fujimori and Vladimiro Montesinos. They took advantage of the collapse of democracy that resulted from Peru's inability to deal with the great national problems of the moment, and created an authoritarian regime that hid one of the most corrupt governments in recent Latin American history behind a façade of technocratic efficiency and feigned departure from traditional politics.

Most state institutions lost their autonomy and were used as tools to support the regime. This was true of institutions such as the judiciary, Congress, and the national Office of the Comptroller General. Particularly notable, however, is the fact that this also encompassed the armed forces and the National Police. During the decade in question, the armed forces were transformed into a political support system for the authoritarian regime. Their prerogatives and authority grew in areas and in ways no democratic government would have permitted.

Such is the background against which the situation of the National Police in the 1990s and the management of public security must be understood. The areas falling within the Ministry of the Interior's purview, which included the National Police, were under the direct control of the armed forces. In a budgetary sense, it was one of the greatest sources from which Vladimiro Montesinos, through the National Intelligence Service, extracted funds destined for corrupt political purposes.

The decade was a difficult one for the National Police. There was a tendency toward a greater degree of militarization, as a result of the years spent combating terrorism—a struggle that consumed a major proportion of the overall energies of the police. Fearing indiscriminate attacks by the Shining Path, the police reduced its presence in the country's cities and towns and in its streets, and became, from the public's perspective, a distant force. Citizen security was not a central priority for them, and the country saw the emergence of the *serenazgo*—a community policing arm of the municipal police—whose functions competed with those of the National Police. Meanwhile, the institutional structure of the police was strongly affected. Promotions, personnel assignments, and incentives were politicized and became a force for corruption. The National Police lost prestige in the public eye, a situation that has proven difficult to reverse.

In the late 1990s, the Fujimori regime attempted to use citizens' legitimate fear of crime and insecurity as a means of legitimizing the government.

It created a legal and institutional framework for this purpose that attempted to equate common crime with terrorism. The legal category of "aggravated terrorism" was created, encompassing common criminal behavior. As is well known, the Fujimori-Montesinos regime collapsed unexpectedly in November 2000 with the flight of its leaders. In their wake, a network of corruption unequalled in Peru's history, and probably in the history of Latin America, came to light. A highly legitimate transition government took the reins and oversaw an impeccable election from which the democratic government in power today emerged. In the process of restoring democracy, major institutional changes were initiated.

As a reaction to the fact that the previous government's power was heavily invested in the security apparatus, the citizenry and politicians had a highly favorable attitude toward changing institutions that, at other times in Peru's history, had been untouchable by civilian authority. In the case of the armed forces, an intense purge took place, with the departure of many senior officers. For the first time in the country's history, there was a civilian minister of defense, and legislation redefining the role of the ministry was passed. It strengthened the minister's authority over the budget, administration, and functions of the armed forces. A similar phenomenon occurred with the National Intelligence Service, which was dismantled after Montesino's exit. It was replaced by the National Intelligence Center, created by Congress and granted limited authority, as is appropriate for an intelligence agency in a democratic system.

An ambitious reform of the National Police was also launched, taking advantage of the fact that the president's inaugural address announced a restructuring of the National Police as one the objectives of his government. Many observers agree that the president was really thinking of the armed forces rather than the National Police, but Minister of the Interior Fernando Rospigliosi took him at his word, immediately creating a commission in charge of restructuring the police. After four months of work (the last months in 2001), the commission issued a report with a set of recommendations that began to be implemented over the course of 2002.

This chapter deals with major change, but it is a process of change that is still in its early stages. It describes the dynamics of the process as it has unfolded to date, the changes contemplated for the National Police, progress made in modernization, and the new guiding concept of citizen security. Finally, the limitations of the process and the factors that could prevent its consolidation and permanence are indicated.

Special Commission for Restructuring the National Police

The Special Commission for Restructuring the National Police was created by executive decree in October 2001. One initial decision of importance concerned the composition of the commission: whether the members would be civilian opinion makers in various fields, police, or ministry staff. The final decision was to create a pluralistic and broad-based commission.

It was agreed, in principle, that the National Police must be represented, given their knowledge of the field, the need for them to feel identified with the process, and the importance of their future support for the process. Thus, the decision represented an approach that was neither reform "for" nor "against" the police, but rather reform "with" the police. The highest level of the force was represented on the commission: three generals, including the director-general of the force, were included, as well as a number of colonels and—a bold step in such a hierarchical body—a representative of the noncommissioned officers, that is, the street officers who are usually excluded from institutional decision making.

Political representation of the highest level was also deemed important. Then-Minister of the Interior Rospigliosi and Vice Minister Gino Costa were incorporated into the process and took an active part in the commission's deliberations and activities. Moreover, a decision was made to include "user representatives," that is, individuals with varied experience, who represent community life and who could voice to the commission the views of those benefited or harmed by police action. Among the most distinguished civilians on the commission were Susana Villarán, who is now a member of the Inter-American Commission on Human Rights; constitutional expert and former congressman Jorge Avendaño; journalist Zenaída Solís; and businessman Arturo Woodman.

The commission was given four months in which to work, and it agreed, at its first session, to adopt measures to ensure that its work would not be merely an academic assessment. It decided that the internal and external political process surrounding its work was every bit as important as its final report.

The commission set forth four principles that were to define its activities. It was to be transparent, seeking continuous openness in order to ensure that all of its activity and the measures it adopted would be public knowledge and would be subject to public evaluation; it was to be participatory, activating multiple channels of communication within and outside the police force, in order to garner contributions and suggestions; it was to be pluralistic, soliciting the views of different sectors of the community, public and private organizations, and all levels of the police force; and it was to be a technical body, drawing on the specialized knowledge accumulated within and outside the institution.

The commission's work itself represented a process of change within the National Police, in that it facilitated (indeed, mandated) institutional openness to civilians in the course of the assessment, allowing the realities within the organization to be seen, and inviting debate on its problems and achievements.

One of the basic elements of the commission's work was broad consultation with the police institution and with the public. Various mechanisms were employed, including public hearings in many of the country's departments, with participation by both police and citizens. A national survey of members of the National Police was also carried out with the support of the University of Lima, in order to solicit their opinions on a variety of subjects. The survey which was wide-ranging, with questions regarding all aspects of the professional life of police officers, corroborated many of the commission's concerns. The survey, conducted with the help of a prestigious university, was a useful tool to know the perceptions of police officers of all ranks. Unfortunately, due to the dynamics of the process, it was not analyzed as much as we originally wanted. The results were partially published in the report of the Reform Commission.

Another factor given strong emphasis was consultation with national experts, many of whom were retired members of the police force who, over the years, had conceived intelligent alternative solutions to the institution's problems. With a similar objective in mind, technical support from police in various countries was obtained (Spain, Chile, Colombia, France, and the United States, in particular). Representatives of these countries' police forces were invited to Peru to advise the commission, in order to ensure that it would have access to a variety of experiences in formulating its conclusions.

Also of note was the academic support provided by the Woodrow Wilson International Center for Scholars, with whose collaboration an international seminar was held to share and compare experiences of police reform. The seminar was attended by many Peruvian National Police officers. Although the participation of retired police officers who were critical of the reform process constituted a major and unforeseen problem at the seminar, it alerted the commission to issues that would cause the most difficulty for the process of change once it got underway.

The commission's work concluded in February 2002, and was quickly followed by the creation of a Modernization Commission, which was slightly smaller but more action oriented in nature. Its function was to monitor the implementation of the recommendations of the Restructuring Commission. This monitoring was made possible by the fact that the commission's final report emphasized concrete recommendations, with deadlines and mechanisms to verify implementation.

The Restructuring Commission laid out three stages for the reform. First, there were recommendations for immediate implementation; these were implemented within two months of the release of the report. Second, there were short-term recommendations requiring six months for implementation. Finally, the commission provided medium-term recommendations that required two and a half years to be implemented. The entire set of recommendations was to be in force by the end of 2004.

Guiding Principles for Change

The Restructuring Commission made a detailed assessment of the reality of police work in all of its major aspects, and suggested policies and specific measures in regard to each issue. It is impossible here to cover all of the issues addressed by the commission, but it is important to describe their eight guiding principles for change:

1. The police must contribute to consolidating democracy in the country, promoting a culture of rights and obligations within the organization, demonstrating respect for the constitution and for human rights, giving increased importance to ethical issues, and demilitarizing the organizational culture.
2. The police must assume the challenge of improving relations with the community, developing public security policies, encouraging active community participation, and supporting the work of local authorities.
3. The quality of life of police officers must be improved, salaries increased, working conditions improved, and health and welfare systems strengthened.
4. Corruption must be squarely confronted, with policies to ensure transparency and accountability. Citizen participation must be encouraged, financial oversight facilitated, complaints addressed, coordination with state oversight entities developed, and internal controls strengthened.
5. A modern system of police education must be developed, identifying new institutional needs and specific skills required, improving recruitment

and selection procedures, opening channels of communication with the country's educational community, promoting international exchange, and establishing follow-up and evaluation mechanisms for training.
6. A new administrative system must be created. Competitiveness and productivity must be encouraged, and units serving the public must receive funding priority; new administrative procedures must make organizational structures simpler and more flexible; and police research and development must be encouraged.
7. Up-to-date technology must be incorporated in all police procedures. Technological innovations must be adopted on a priority basis, and communications systems modernized. Technology must be used to free up personnel and support police services, while reducing the time citizens must wait for the completion of bureaucratic procedures and increasing personnel training in the area of technology.
8. New forms of organized crime must be confronted, taking into account current trends and new types of criminal activity, strengthening relationships with international organizations, participating in systems designed to combat crime, and training police personnel to deal with transnational crime.

Purging the Police

In the 1990s, promotions in the National Police force reflected two types of distortion. Objective professional criteria were set aside in favor of political considerations, personal favoritism, and even corruption. At the same time, there was an attempt to compensate for poor pay through promotions, in hopes of deflecting pressure for better salaries. This led to promotions that were not based on the institution's functional needs. This dual distortion was highly detrimental to the institution's functioning. It was top heavy, lacking in rank-and-file personnel, and had lost the pyramidal shape of an efficient hierarchy.

Although purging the organization began under Antonio Ketín Vidal during the transition government, Minister Rospigliosi found fifty-eight generals and over eight hundred colonels in the force when he assumed his post. By comparison, the Colombian National Police, with equivalent total numbers, had fewer than ten generals and just over eighty colonels. The hypertrophy of the Peruvian National Police led to irrational action. Since there was no work for many of these senior officers, positions had to be invented for them, with concomitant additional bureaucratic costs.

Many senior officers who attained their rank as part of this distorted process that was not based on merit, did not have the professional capabilities needed for the positions they occupied. Moreover, in many cases they owed their position to political favors under the Fujimori-Montesinos regime, and their presence in the organization was an impediment to any possible renovation of the institution. A purge of the command ranks was therefore indispensable if the new government was to make the changes proposed for the National Police.

Peruvian law gives the president broad powers in the area of police personnel, enabling him to retire majors, command-level colonels, generals, and lieutenant generals, in order to renew the ranks. This system unquestionably lends itself to potential abuses of political power, and the commission's view was that it should be changed in favor of clear rules governing career development. In the period under discussion, however, after a decade of the Fujimori regime, presidential power was the only tool available to reform the institution.

The process took place in two steps: in late 2001, under Minister Rospigliosi, and in late 2002, under Minister Costa. In the first phase, over six hundred officers were retired. Despite this enormous figure, there was neither political nor institutional resistance to the measure. The second phase was significantly more difficult, for a number of reasons. First, the process of selecting officers to whom retirement was to be offered was problematic, since the obvious candidates for retirement had already departed. Second, there was far more resistance inside the institution, beginning with the director-general himself. Nevertheless, approximately four hundred officers were retired in this second phase.

Regardless of the political repercussions, there is no doubt that the decisions of Ministers Rospigliosi and Costa produced major change in the police command structure. The number of generals and colonels as of 2003, for example, is half what it was in 2001 and is much more closely aligned with the institution's real needs. In the case of the generals, all but two of those currently on active duty were promoted to their positions by democratic governments. Hence, one can accurately speak of new leadership.

Internal Controls and Efforts to Combat Corruption

The Restructuring Commission's assessment concluded that one of the most serious problems affecting the National Police and other national institutions was top-down corruption, which it viewed as widespread, affecting all members of these institutions. Corruption was, and continues to be, the primary obstacle to change. It has impeded proper use of scarce resources, while severely affecting the efficiency and image of the police.

This situation clearly needs to be reversed. A series of reform and modernization measures has been proposed, and initial implementation has begun. First, state secrecy, which was used to justify enormous arms acquisitions and other internal security measures beyond normal state oversight, has been eliminated. All procurement and bidding are now part of a standard contracting process under the supervision of the Comptroller General of the Republic. Second, an attempt was made to find mechanisms to involve citizens in oversight functions and in combating corruption. Thus, respected civil society organizations, such as ProÉtica, have been involved as supplementary oversight agencies to monitor bidding for police procurement. One emblematic case concerned bids for National Police uniforms, a contract worth approximately US$18 million.

Third, an effort was made to strengthen the Office of the Inspector General of the Police, providing for more systematic functioning and preventing immediate superiors from interfering with the application of sanctions. Attention was given to creating better working conditions, so that the inspector general's office would attract members of the police when they were up for reassignment, rather than being a place where—as had become the practice—officers were assigned as a means of punishment. Efforts were also made to modernize the organizational structure of the Office of the Inspector General, and to equip it properly. Another important measure in combating internal corruption was the creation of the Internal Affairs Office, reporting directly to the Minister of the Interior, with responsibility for selectively investigating probable cases of corruption and producing expeditious results, in order to set an example. In its first months of operation, the office's achievements were promising. The Office of Internal Affairs was as expected deeply resisted by high-ranking police officers. In spite of that it was extremely efficient while the reform team remained in office. The fact that a civilian—strongly supported by the minister himself—and not a police officer led the office was a key factor for its initial success.

Finally, an intense media campaign was undertaken, along with counterintelligence actions, to detect everyday, minor bribery on the part of street officers. This occurs primarily in connection with traffic enforcement, and seriously affects the image of the police. The campaign's motto was, "Respect for the Police." It attempted to create public awareness that bribing members of the National Police is not only a crime punishable by up to five years in prison but also that it weakens their authority and capacity to enforce the law.[1]

New Citizen Security Policies

Shortly after the Restructuring Commission proposed a comprehensive reform of the Peruvian National Police in 2002, the Modernization Commission began to gradually implement the reform, following the schedule set forth in the Restructuring Commission's assessment and policy recommendations. Although it is impossible to consider here all of the areas in which reform was initiated, a few thoughts in regard to the purge and the attempts to combat corruption—prerequisites for any change—will be offered. The approach to a new democratic citizen security policy, in the context of police reform, must take into account the primary concerns given below.

Proper Assessment

Concrete experience in managing security suggests that it is essential to recognize that citizen security issues are among the most difficult to address. With all of its complexities, the experience in the ministry showed that it is much easier to define the measures required to effectively combat organized crime (drugs, terrorism, kidnapping, etc.) than to design actions to deal with the theft of wallets and watches, the breaking of automobile windows at traffic lights, neighborhood gang activity, and local drug dealing. In the case of organized crime, well-designed plans, properly trained professionals, good intelligence, and the appropriate use of modern technology can produce major results. The relevant variables can be controlled, or at least identified. In the case of common crime, however, its very simplicity, its massive scale and multiple causes, and the fact that it is reproduced continually make success far more difficult to achieve.

As a starting point, the public can be provided with a serious and honest assessment of the problem, along with an evaluation of what can or cannot be done to address it. First, a difficult fact must be acknowledged: this is an evil found in large and medium-sized modern cities, and no city in the world—much less Third World cities—can eliminate it completely. Any assessment should acknowledge the futility of militarizing the crime-fighting effort, given the complex and diverse nature of both the causes and the necessary solutions.

Allocating More Police Resources

Faced with widespread demands for greater effectiveness, the institutional response of the police has been to insist that they require more funds and greater powers. Based on our experience, it is erroneous to believe that funding alone can produce good results without proper strategy and institutional change. There is, however, a serious lack of resources for citizen security, and attacking the problem on a priority basis requires reasonable spending increases.

The greatest deficit in Peru is in human resources. The number of police, rather than increasing, has dropped, falling from 120,000 in the late 1980s to slightly over 90,000 in 2003. Meanwhile, both the population and the complexity of the problem have grown. Thus, the gap between the resources available and the demand for resources is even greater than the absolute numbers suggest. Moreover, like all of Peru's state institutions, the police are lacking in material resources and suffer from innumerable technological deficiencies.

This does not mean that the police should compete for funding priority with education or health care. However, security issues should be given sufficient priority to provide for more and better-paid police, and provide for investment in modern technology and transportation, as well as in communications equipment. The most difficult of these requirements to satisfy is the first: given the number of police, a rise in pay would be difficult for the national budget to absorb.

The second factor can more feasibly be addressed in the short term. During our time at the ministry, we made significant progress in identifying and beginning to negotiate international loans that could efficiently, albeit with austerity, provide the communications and technology tools needed to improve security in Peru's largest cities.

Strengthening Police Stations as a Central Pillar of Police Functioning

The police station is the basic unit for responding to the population's immediate, everyday problems. However, it has been neglected over the last two decades. It is an unattractive workplace for police personnel, its funding and infrastructure are deficient, and its relations with the community are poor.

Current reform seeks to make the station into the basic cell of police functioning, empowering it with human and economic resources. This must take place within a new community policing model that stresses openness to society and readiness to work with local authorities to ensure public security and respect for citizens' freedom and rights. The reform proposes that stations be given priority in the allocation of material and logistical resources, in order to provide an improved environment in which to function. The proposal emphasizes communications, information, and infrastructure.

Even more important than material resources is providing stations with higher-quality human resources. A current reform aims to assign personnel to stations according to location, population density, socioeconomic conditions, and availability of resources. In determining allocation of resources in Lima for 2002—as well as in other major cities for 2003—a rigorous selection process was undertaken to identify and select the most competent and professional commissaries. They were given a three-week training course in 2002, in which new guidelines for conduct were presented, and the new commissaries were closely monitored throughout the year.

Finally, it is important to establish professional and economic incentives for police who work at the stations, in order to promote competitiveness and productivity. Evaluation by the community should be taken into account in determining promotions. We conducted an initial experiment along those lines in Lima, in 2002, with a competition to reward the best stations for their performance. The evaluation used a set of indicators, with community opinion—expressed by various means—given considerable weight. Points toward promotion were offered as an incentive for performance, and economic resources were provided to improve infrastructure and equipment. This experience is to be replicated in 2003, not only in Lima but in Arequipa, Moquegua, Tacna, and Trujillo.

Legitimizing the Police in the Eyes of the Public

Attempts to combat crime—much less joint action with the police—cannot be effective if the community lacks confidence in the institution or considers it corrupt or abusive. Initiating (or continuing) police reform is essential if this confidence is to be gained. Changes that are underway, which include redefining the police's mission, education, career structure, organizational structure, financial management, disciplinary regimes, community relations, welfare, crime-fighting efforts, and so on, can be expected to enhance the new image of the police among the public. The most effective and striking tool for this change in image, to date, has been the "Respect for the Police" campaign, which was referred to above. The campaign included efforts to uncover flagrant abuses, punish those who corrupt the police, and publicize these occurrences in the media.

Encouraging Citizen Participation

Despite the problems that the National Police faced during the Fujimori period, it is important to recognize that in the mid-1990s, it did create effective programs to promote public participation on citizen security issues. This work was, and continues to be, the responsibility of the Office of Citizen Participation (Dirección de Participación Ciudadana, or DIRPACI), which has many programs to encourage civil participation. The most important of these are the Neighborhood Councils, of which there are roughly forty thousand in the nation, involving hundreds of thousands of individuals, particularly in the poorest neighborhoods. The success of these councils demonstrates the value of preventive strategies and shows that it is possible to involve organized civil society in crime prevention. Based on the proposals of the Restructuring Commission, these citizen participation programs should be closely associated with proposed new institutional structures, in order to coordinate local efforts.

Creating Local Institutional Spaces

Following the recommendations of the Restructuring Commission, legislation in late 2002 created the National Citizen Security Council. This is a technical regulatory agency focusing on public security policy at the national level. It is an institutional response that represents the new approach to crime, and is a practical tool for involving other governmental entities and civil society in efforts to combat crime and insecurity. The functions of the National Citizen Security Council are to develop a medium- and long-term plan for the nation's public security, with specific objectives and goals, to conduct studies on public security problems, to formulate national policy to address public security problems, and to evaluate and monitor the impact of such policy.

Even more important than the council are the district, provincial, and regional public security committees referred to in the legislation. These involve local government officials and civil society organizations working toward the following main objectives: to produce an assessment of local citizen security, to create and implement local public security plans, to channel communal resources to support police work, and to evaluate and oversee police activity in each locality.

The local and provincial Citizen Security Committees should also function as the place for police authorities to coordinate with local governments in order to rationalize services, increase the efficiency of both the police and the *serenazgos,* put aside conflicts, and prevent duplication of effort.

Ensuring That Minor Offenses Do Not Go Unpunished

It is indispensable, when creating realistic crime policy, not to resort to absurd extremes. A dichotomy between widespread impunity and converting the country to one vast prison is not a sensible approach. There is a broad sense that minor crime generally goes unpunished and that drastic measures are needed to deal with this situation. Such an approach is based on the idea that stricter measures need to be put in place, including unrestricted arrest authority on the part of the police. Such a tactic, in addition to affecting individual rights, is entirely impractical in a country with a lack of penal facilities to house arrestees.

In the opinion of the Restructuring Commission, the best solution to this dilemma would be to implement an aggressive program of alternative sentencing options for minor violators, with priority given to community service. Although a legal structure for this type of program already exists, it is not being used. Community service sentences are provided for in Articles 31 and 34 of the Penal Code, and their application is regulated by Law 27030. To eliminate the bottlenecks that have made these provisions impractical, Congress passed supplementary legislation in late 2002, at the request of the Ministry of the Interior. The additional provisions simplify procedures so that trials for minor violations can be conducted in a single hearing at police stations, where justices of the peace will now be in place. The police will also have greater authority to enforce community service and arrest those who evade it: violators will serve the alternative sentence determined at trial.

Some Major Mistakes

Although we believe that the reform has been largely successful, some important mistakes were made, and these should be underscored to allow for a proper evaluation of this experience with police reform. The first mistake was our profound distrust of intervention on the part of political actors who were not part of the Ministry of the Interior's reform team. We kept a relatively low profile precisely to avoid being "contaminated" by the types of problems we saw in the general institutional political process occurring in the country.

In particular, we attempted to keep the reform separated from Congress. Thus, we tried to make decisions that did not require congressional legislation, since we thought that, given the lack of control over the Congress and the limited knowledge on the part of its members regarding police reform, the reform could be distorted to the point of caricature if the Congress became involved. In fact, we succeeded in making important changes, simply by modifying regulations that were under the control of the executive branch. This was a double-edged sword, however, since the reform would have become state policy much more quickly if the Congress had participated in a productive way, and this would have made backsliding much less likely.

Second, we did not invest sufficient time in explaining, within the police institution, the reform being undertaken. Although internal discussions did occur, they should have been far more systematic and should have been given the highest political priority. The majority of police do not have an overall sense of the reform. They are familiar with changes in different areas, but not all members of the police—indeed, perhaps very few—have a broad grasp of the extent of the changes.

Third, we did not invest sufficient time and energy in explaining the content and orientation of the reform to the public. In an environment dominated by political theater and news of crises, it was difficult to attract the public's attention concerning changes occurring far beneath the surface, which lack drama and luster. Toward the end, we understood the need to engage the public's interest, and launched the Respect for the Police campaign. The campaign was very well received, generating expectation and enthusiasm on the part of citizens concerning our efforts. Unfortunately, the political effects of the campaign in furthering the reform were essentially invisible, since the campaign coincided closely with the exit of the ministry's team.

Fourth, we took too long to produce concrete benefits for members of the police force. Had we been quicker, we could have gained their support for the reform process. Toward the end, real benefits, associated with eliminating arbitrary salary deductions of various types and providing access to quality housing, were put in place. In the area of health care, where we had a clear roadmap for what needed to be done and knew what specific measures were needed, we hesitated for political reasons that, in retrospect, did not justify the delay.

The Halfway Point

At the end of January 2003, the entire civilian team overseeing reform of the Peruvian National Police left the Ministry of the Interior, as a result of the resignation of Minister Gino Costa. This occurred in the wake of a crisis involving the director-general of the police over differences on measures regarding promotions and retirements, which were designed to renew the force. The president, who could—and should—have immediately resolved the crisis in favor of his minister, did not choose to do so, compelling the minister to resign. In light of later changes in key areas, it is clear that the replacement of the minister had no relation to police resistance to reforms, although the government attempted to convey that impression. Rather, the replacement of the minister was related to a desire to pack the executive branch with people who were closer to the president's circle.

As is often the case, there are reasons for optimism regarding the results achieved and their permanence, as well as reasons for concern about possible backsliding. First, let us consider the reasons to believe that the changes will remain in place and continue to unfold over time.

Police reform, and its importance in improving citizen security, has already gained a place in the public mind. Unlike military issues, police reform had never been on the public agenda in Peru. The presidential candidates did not make it a subject of discussion or political proposals during the electoral campaign, and the president's mention of it in his inaugural address was, as explained above, incidental, and only occurred because of the habit of including the police in references to the armed forces.

Subsequent civilian intervention at the ministry created an issue where none had been present. Thus, only recently has police reform become part of the political agenda. The progress achieved to date is valued, and any backsliding would be strongly challenged by the public.

It was also demonstrated that a different role was possible for the Ministry of the Interior. It had always been assumed that the Peruvian Ministry of the Interior was a shadowy place in which military wealth, crises, and police performance (good or bad, but in any case far from the public eye) were managed. During a period of almost two years, however, the Ministry of the Interior was one of the focal points of political change in Peru, and one of the most transparent. The police reform proposal, in particular, was perceived by the majority of the population as exemplary, given the type of action involved. The public's negative reaction to the president's dismissal of the minister related, in large part, to the fact that the continuity of the reform would be affected. A second element is that to many groups within the National Police, the proposed reforms had come to be seen as advantageous to the institution. More important still, they generated an expectation that, for the first time in many years, the job would acquire greater public prestige, with the possibility of truly professional careers on the horizon.

This is not to suggest that there was not (and is not) resistance to change, as in any institution. Indeed, resistance of three types occurred, and was far from insignificant. First, there was resistance based on the desire to protect vested interests, mostly in connection with corrupt management of institutional resources. Second, there was resistance by what might be called institutional traditionalists. These were primarily senior officers, mostly retired, who feared that demilitarizing the police would lead to a lack of discipline and a loss of the traditions with which they identified. Third, there was an understandable fear of change on the part of rank-and-file officers, given the difficulty of adapting to new rules of the game. However, it was also true that many officers of rank were great allies of change, and contributed substantive proposals to the process.

A third element is that many of the measures were implemented and have begun to produce concrete results within and outside the institution. For example, new institutions emerged from the reform process, and these now have important areas of authority. Specifically, the Office of the Police Ombudsman, and the Office of Internal Affairs of which the former is part, have an important presence in their respective areas. In addition, there are substantial changes in how the National Police is structured institutionally. The creation of the three executive offices (operations, administration, and human development) marks a radical change in organizational structure, decentralizing power and creating a management approach to a process that goes far beyond any previous system. None of these institutional or organizational changes can easily be reversed.

At the same time, new institutions have been created to deal with citizen security, for example, the Local Citizen Security Committees. Their very creation marks a qualitative change in the notion of citizen security work, generating potential demand from other sectors of government and from citizens interested in participating in this field. Beyond these examples, concrete changes have occurred in every area of police life and institutional spaces have been created, all constituting initial reform and providing a foundation for further change.

Fourth, there are many individuals today outside of public administration or police work who are familiar with citizen security and police issues. Because their successful management experience gives them legitimacy in the public eye, they are in a position to oversee police work and the political management of the ministry.

Perhaps the most important finding from these two years of civilian management of security reform is that it indeed proved possible to effect the desired changes. It is therefore reasonable to believe that reform will continue. These hopes, rather than being an illusion of academic idealists, turned out to be eminently achievable. Moreover, if current political circumstances change, either those who were involved in the experience or other people driven by similar visions, will be able to reshape the process and take it further without major problems, benefiting from the progress made and the experience acquired in this first stage.

It is also worth examining what weighs on the other side of the scales, that is, the problems that hinder the democratic reform of security in Peru, and its continuation. The first problem is the profound weakness of the government of Alejandro Toledo and the constant crises that threaten its continued rule. Despite the importance of economic advances and progress in gaining efficient sectoral policy in many areas, the government is facing severe public criticism. The government's approval rating is very low, and fears that it may have difficulty completing its term are on the rise. In this context, it is difficult to make structural changes that require strong political will and commitment at the highest level.

Second, the political authorities in charge of the sector are in a precarious position. The new administration, which came under question from the start and had little expectation of remaining in power for a sufficient period of time, lacks the staff, ideas, and political will to carry on the process.

Third, there are very few high-ranking officers in the National Police who have a clear overall vision and support the more political dimensions of the reform project—that is, who wish to adapt police functioning to the features and needs of a democracy. This is entirely understandable; political vision and sense of direction are associated with leadership in the context of an overall government program, while immediate issues of institutional life are the natural concern of police officials. Many officers understand and identify with specific aspects of the internal modernization of the institution, which is an important—but not the sole—component of the reform process. All signs, to date, indicate that the National Police, as an institution, is creating mechanisms to permit the modernization process to advance.

Fourth, there is pressure for concrete results, given the problems with citizen security and police efficiency. As in all countries in the region, citizen insecurity is one of the most acute problems for the population. There are no easy or immediate solutions, especially when the police have a chronic lack of human and economic resources. There is a risk that the country's political sectors will again argue for militarization as a response, and will blame the current type of police reform for security problems. There are already public calls from some officials, for example, to have the armed forces participate in crime-fighting efforts.

Symbolic solutions to the problem of police reform can be tempting to the public, which can be easily drawn into supporting demands for such solutions. It is even conceivable that the government, for pragmatic reasons, could decide to support this type of policy, abandoning reform entirely.

None of this, however, has taken place. We are still facing an open process of police reform in which the profound changes that have occurred, although they are not immune to the possibility of being reversed, have the political possibilities for survival and even for potential growth.[2]

Notes

1. More information about the campaign and its effects and shortcomings can be found in the book, Carlos Basombrío and Gino Costa, *Liderazgo civil en el Ministerio del Interior. Testimonio de una experiencia de reforma policial y gestión democrática de la seguridad* (Lima: Instituto de Estudios Peruanos, 2004).

2. Further discussion of the issues and proposals analyzed in this chapter can be found in the essay "The Militarization of Public Security in Peru," in the previous volume of this series, Hugo Frühling and Joseph Tulchin with Heather A. Golding, eds., *Crime and Violence in Latin America: Citizen Security, Democracy, and the State* (Washington, DC: Woodrow Wilson Center Press/Johns Hopkins University Press, 2003).

Chapter 11

Elements for a Study of Crime in Mexico City

Arturo Alvarado Mendoza

Introduction

For the past decade, crime and the inability of government to reduce crime have been the main sources of concern about public safety in Mexico. While crime is not a recent problem, it has become a matter of everyday preoccupation in Mexico City and throughout the country. Guaranteeing the safety of people, protecting property rights and the patrimony of Mexican citizens, and upholding the rule of law traditionally have been the most persistent challenges facing the national and local governments.

The concept of public safety has both objective and subjective components, that is, crime and perceived crime, respectively. The perception of insecurity in Mexico has increased because government anticrime efforts have produced meager or substandard results. In recent years, particularly between 1995 and 1998, the crime wave seemed unstoppable, and the government was apparently incapable of dealing with it. The increase in all types of criminal activity—from assaults in the streets to organized crime, political assassinations, terrorist acts, and combat between narcotraffic gangs—has created both exaggerated perceptions and genuine conditions of growing insecurity among residents of the Mexico City metropolitan area (hereafter, metropolitan area), dominating public debate and constraining residents' everyday activities.[1]

This chapter focuses on crime trends in the metropolitan area. Trends in official statistics as well as how residents of the metropolitan area (specifically the Federal District) perceive the crime problem will be examined. I will also attempt to estimate the proportion of specific crimes not reported to authorities. In order to explain the crime situation in Mexico, this chapter addresses two central issues. The first has to do with defining and describing crime, and the second concerns the challenge of building a data set that allows us to understand the phenomenon. Thus, the main objectives of this chapter are to estimate the dimensions of the phenomenon and to develop a set of hypotheses to explain it. These objectives are based on the premise that crime can be explained in the context of a criminal justice system that is inefficient, inequitable, and unfair, and understood as a product of the actions of the principal actors and institutional and legal regimes in the metropolitan area.

Government in the Mexico City Metropolitan Area

Mexico City's unique crime and law enforcement situation stems from a vast, heterogeneous array of measures, laws, and codes. Because Mexico City is located at the intersection of three federal entities—Federal District, México State, and part of Hidalgo State—no fewer than fourteen laws and codes apply to criminal activity, such as the General Constitution of the Republic, the Constitution of the State of Mexico, the Statute of Government and the Organic Law of the Federal District, civil, criminal, and procedural codes of the aforementioned states, and the federal criminal code (e.g., for drug-related offenses or those committed by civil servants). In addition, there are other anticrime decrees, laws, regulations, and programs at the national and state level, such as the National Public Security Program.[2] The criminal and procedural codes of Hidalgo State, which govern suburban municipalities of the capital city, must also be taken into account. The various jurisdictions report different types of offenses in their official crime statistics, some of which may not be defined as offenses or may not be codified in the same way elsewhere. Similarly, some criminal behaviors are penalized but are not classified or specified as offenses in the criminal codes. This is true of the *secuestro express,* or the "kidnapping express," the popular term for this phenomenon that has spread throughout the metropolitan area, but which the Federal District defines as aggravated robbery. Consequently, the body of statistics I will use includes a huge quantity of "other" offenses, and focuses on those occurring at higher rates and of greatest concern to the public and government: robbery, aggravated assault and battery, homicide, rape, fraud, breach of trust, and plunder.

Codes and Penalties

In order to organize crime data, I use the government catalog of crimes that includes approximately 200 offenses from the federal to the local level. The definition of an offense is not based only on, or limited to, how the phenomenon is defined in the legal codes. On the contrary, the true understanding of an offense is found in its application, that is, in the actions taken by law enforcement entities, particularly the Ministerio Público, whose agents decide whether to prosecute a given charge ("claim"). In this regard, the Ministerio Público, together with the police forces and the attorney general of every state, are the first links in the chain of the justice system.

There is also a vast array of police, justice, and other public security institutions in the metropolitan area. This institutional framework includes approximately ten police forces (in addition to officers in over forty-two municipal police forces) consisting of some 130,000 public and private police agents. Further, there are several local and federal prosecutors and various judicial and penal systems. While all of these officially form part of the national public security system, there is no coordination at the government administrative or law enforcement level to combat crime in the metropolitan area. Each force operates within its own territorial boundaries and enforces the law pursuant to its own criminal code. The criminal justice system in Mexico City includes the Office of the Attorney General of the Federal District (Procuraduría General de Justicia del Distrito Federal) (PGJDF), which prosecutes "ordinary" crimes, as well as the Offices of the Attorney General (PGJ) of México and Hidalgo States. The Office of the Attorney General of the Republic (PGR) prosecutes federal offenses.[3]

The relationship between police and the Ministerio Público constitutes the first problem of the criminal justice system. The Ministerio Público's agent or prosecutor for the case (although without the same legal status as in the United States) is the authority in charge of the prosecution. The prosecutor is responsible for receiving claims and arresting suspects, but police officers perform the prosecution's investigations. Police officers then are the most important actors for the prosecution by detaining suspects and gathering evidence. The effectiveness of the police related to detentions and arrests is low. Arrests "on site" (*en flagrancia*) account for nearly 60 percent of all arrests (Alvarado 2004). Even though police have internal mechanism of control, there is no transparency in the process, nor is there accountability to the citizenry. Analysts of the prosecutor's office have used the following terms: inefficient, lacks legitimacy, arbitrary, and capricious (Carbonell 2004; Castillo 1992; Castro 2002; Concha 2005; Fix Zamudio 2002; Sarre 1997; Zepeda Lecuona 2004).

By 2000, the Mexico City government had imposed arrest quotas (unprecedented in the metropolitan area) for particular types of crimes, such as auto theft (www.df.gob.mx), and police officers receive compensation upon meeting quotas. Recruiting and training police continue to be problems. Salaries and compensation for street police are low, considering tasks performed and level of risk (although their median income is higher than the national average) (Alvarado 2004; Arzt and Arroyo 2006).

One way to develop a sociological taxonomy of crime is to categorize offenses in terms of victim, that is, crimes against the state, against society, and against individuals. Another classification method is based on the split between crimes against persons and crimes against property. It should be noted that offenses by state and government officials must also be taken into account; these offenses include arbitrary detention, torture, extrajudicial execution, and other human rights violations.

Description of Crime and Violence in the Metropolitan Area

This section traces the evolution of crime statistics in the Mexico City metropolitan area. I draw upon official statistics as well as a series of victimization surveys. I also present a taxonomy of offenses aimed at exposing the social and political framework within which these offenses must be studied. In 1999, Mexico City and outlying metropolitan areas in the State of Mexico accounted for 10 percent and 8 percent of reported crime in the country, respectively. Figure 11.1 illustrates trends in crime rates in the country as a whole and in the metropolitan area from 1988 to 2001.

Based on Figure 11.1, between 1988 and 1994, the crime rate declined in the metropolitan area, but did not return to pre-1985 levels. During the administration of Mayor Oscar Espinosa Villarreal, crime increased over a three-year period and did not start to decline again until Cuauhtémoc Cárdenas assumed the office in December 1997. Yet the rate never dropped to 1994 levels. Figure 11.2 illustrates the rates of four types of crime for the Mexico City metropolitan area from 1995 to 1999.

There are indications that crime rates in the capital will remain constant or increase gradually in the long term. Nonetheless, during the 1995–1997 period, there was a notable increase in crime that contrasts with average rates for the past decade. During that three-year period, the daily average number

Figure 11.1. Crime trends throughout Mexico and the capital metropolitan area, 1988–2001

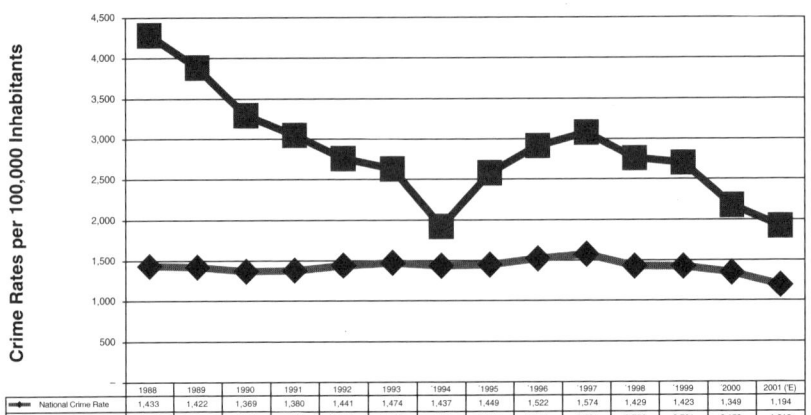

Sources: Instituto Nacional de Estadística, Geografía e Informatica [INEGI], *I Censo general de población y vivienda*, 2000, http://www.inegi.gob.mx/difusion/espanol/poblacion/definitivos/iter/INITER09.PDF; INEGI, *Indicadores sociodemográficos de México, 1930–2000*, http://www.inegi.gob/mx/di; PGJDF, Presidencia de la República, *Informes Presidenciales, 1988–2201*; INEGI, *Cuaderno de estadísticas judiciales, México, 1998–2003*.

of crimes reported to the PGJDF rose from 550 to 720, and there was an average of 1,061 crimes per day in the metropolitan area. It is important to note that all categories of crime did not increase at the same rate. Robbery increased the most, eventually accounting for 57 percent of all crimes reported, followed by assault and battery (14 percent), property damage (6.8 percent), and sex offenses (4.7 percent). In contrast, homicide figures declined to 5.5 a day.

Since the three-year upsurge in crime in the mid-1990s, crime rates in the capital have generally decreased in absolute terms as well as in relative terms vis-à-vis population. In fact, population growth has outpaced the crime rate. In 1994, the crime rate in the capital city was 1,918 crimes per 100,000 inhabitants; it peaked in 1997 at 3,081.

A similar trend is observed in the Mexico City metropolitan area, but the increase in crime from 1995 to 1997 was even more pronounced. In 1996, the crime rate was 2,239 per 100,000 inhabitants. Crime rates declined overall from 1997 to 1999, with the exception of the most densely populated municipalities where rates increased from 1,407 to 1,565 crimes per 100,000 inhabitants.[4]

Figure 11.2. Crime rates in Mexico City metropolitan area, 1995–1999

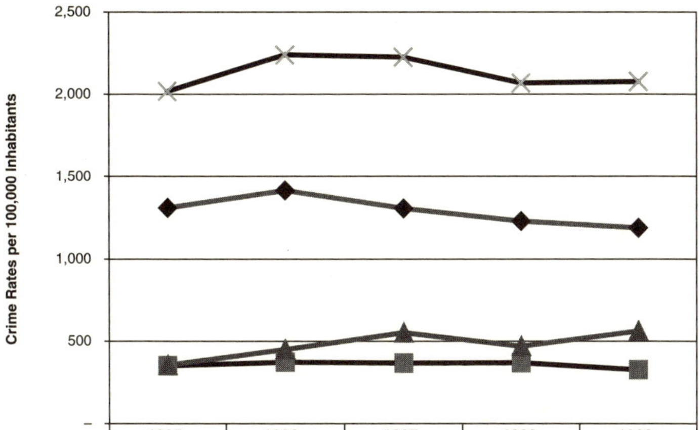

	1995	1996	1997	1998	1999
Property Crime	1,310	1,416	1,306	1,229	1,189
Assault and Battery	352	374	367	370	327
Other Crimes	355	450	552	470	562
Total Crime Record, Metropolitan Area	2,017	2,239	2,225	2,068	2,078

Sources: INEGI, *Anuario estadístico del Distrito Federal, México,* 1988 to 1998; PGJDF, *Total de delitos,* 1999, and *Principales delitos,* 1999; INEGI, *Anuario estadístico del Estado de México,* 1996 to 2000.

The contribution of each municipality and *delegación* (roughly, borough) to the overall crime rate must be ascertained in order to understand the prevalence of crime in the greater metropolitan area. In 1997, 68 percent of all crimes were committed in the Federal District. In contrast, 88 percent of homicides and 94 percent of kidnappings, took place in the metropolitan municipalities of México State. In 1999, 61.32 percent of all crimes occurred in the Federal District. This represents a nearly 7-percent decrease in its contribution to overall crime figures.[5]

Table 11.1 summarizes rates for various offenses in the Federal District and metropolitan municipalities. In 1999, the capital accounted for most robberies (69.49 percent) and cases of assault and battery (56.01 percent). At the same time, the rate for rape was equal to that of the metropolitan municipalities (49.54 percent), and the capital accounted for far fewer homicides (29.83 percent), which are concentrated in México State (70.17 percent). The Federal District accounted for 41 percent of breach of trust, fraud, and plunder offenses, and its contribution to other types of crime is comparable.

Table 11.1. Percentage of crimes reported in the Federal District and metropolitan municipalities of México State, 1999

	Robbery	Assault and Battery	Homicide	Rape	Fraud, Swindling, Breach of Trust, Plunder	Other	% of Total Crime
Federal District	69.49	56.01	29.83	49.54	41.73	50.12	61.32
Metropolitan municipalities of México State	30.51	43.99	70.17	50.46	58.27	49.88	38.68

Sources: INEGI and PGJDF (1999).

While the Mexico City metropolitan area clearly has a serious crime problem, comparing crime rates with other large cities places these phenomena in context. In 1996, the Federal District ranked seventh among the ten most dangerous cities in the world. It was preceded by six cities in the United States, with Washington, D.C. ranking as the most dangerous city followed by Chicago, Houston, Philadelphia, Los Angeles, and New York (Asamblea Legislativa del Distrito Federal 1996). Also, the Federal District ranked sixth in sex crimes and tenth for homicides in the same year (Dueñas et al. 1998).

Comparing Federal District homicide rates with those of other Latin American cities, such as São Paulo, Rio de Janeiro (with an estimated 21 to 24 murders per 100,000 inhabitants annually), Medellín, Bogotá, and Cali (with averages well above 26 per 100,000), the Federal District ranks in fifteenth place.

Classifying Crime in the Metropolitan Area
Description of Offenses

Homicide[6]

In 2000, the official intentional homicide rate in the Federal District was 9.03 per 100,000 inhabitants, and was the eleventh leading cause of death in the city. Mortality rates due to traffic accidents surpassed homicide rates and accounted for most negligent homicides. In contrast, the mortality rate associated with intentional homicide in México State reached 16.34 per 100,000 inhabitants, and was the seventh leading cause of death in the state.

The mortality rate due to traffic accidents was equally high—14 per 100,000 inhabitants—and was the ninth leading cause of death.

To get an idea of the magnitude of the phenomenon, these rates can be compared with those of other jurisdictions. Homicide rates in the Federal District and México State were surpassed by the states of Guerrero, with a rate of 25.02 per 100,000 inhabitants, making homicide the fourth leading cause of death in that state; Oaxaca, with a rate of 19.41, making homicide the fifth leading cause of death; Chihuahua, with a rate of 19.1; Sinaloa, with a rate of 18.91; and Baja California, with 17.21. Traffic fatality rates were higher in other jurisdictions such as Baja California (25 deaths per 100,000 inhabitants), Zacatecas (21.9), and Querétaro (20.74).

While homicide is not the most prevalent offense in the country, accounting for only 3.6 percent of all crimes in 1995, its persistence along with the impunity with which homicides are committed have a devastating effect on perceived public safety. In 1996, most homicides were committed in México State municipalities (77.6 percent of the total). In 1997, the Federal District accounted for 32.7 percent of homicides and the metropolitan municipalities accounted for 67.2 percent. By 1999, homicides represented 1.71 percent of all crimes, and the Federal District accounted for just 29.8 percent of the total, compared to 70.2 percent in the metropolitan municipalities.

In 1997, the municipalities in the Mexico City metropolitan area with the highest homicide incidents were Naucalpan (11.75 percent of total occurrences), Ecatepec (11.14 percent), Nezahualcóyotl (8.8 percent), and Tlalnepantla (5.96 percent), followed by the Delegaciones of Gustavo A. Madero (5.78 percent) and Miguel Hidalgo (4.7 percent). These six jurisdictions accounted for 52 percent of homicide cases. The figures were similar in 1999: Naucalpan (11.8 percent), Ecatepec (11.5 percent), and Nezahualcóyotl (7.96 percent), with the difference that Iztapalapa took fourth place with 5.61 percent, followed by Tlalnepantla (4.99 percent), Gustavo A. Madero (4.42 percent), Atizapan de Zaragoza (3.79 percent), and Texcoco (3.32 percent).

In Mexico City, deaths due to accidental causes and violence occur most frequently in the streets (54 percent), followed by at home (24 percent). Most of the victims are men (78 percent). The vast majority of victims of violent deaths are men (77 percent). In contrast, women account for 34 percent of deaths at home, which are mostly caused by accidents and domestic violence.[7]

Unfortunately, there is no way to consolidate into a single database the types of homicide that occur in the capital and the metropolitan municipalities of México State. Nonetheless, Table 11.1 illustrates the types of criminal behavior in each of these jurisdictions, particularly taking into account that four-fifths of these crimes occur in the suburban municipalities of México State. The adjusted rate for México State rises to 20.3 homicides per 100,000 inhabitants. Homicides are usually committed with firearms in the Federal District, while poisoning is used more frequently in México State. One of the most troubling aspects of intentional homicide is the high degree of impunity associated with it. In the past ten years, only 50 percent of these crimes were prosecuted and solved.

Property Crimes

Property theft is the most profitable crime and various types of criminals engage in it. In 1997, robberies accounted for 59 percent of all crimes reported in the Mexico City metropolitan area. In 1999, robbery was the most frequent type of offense and accounted for 57.22 percent of all reported crimes. The Cuauhtémoc delegación had the highest rate, accounting for 11 percent of all robberies in the metropolitan area. Next in the ranking were Venustiano Carranza (8.7 percent), Iztapalapa (8.73 percent), Benito Juárez (7.58 percent), Nezahualcóyotl (6.28 percent), and Ecatepec (6.08 percent). Taken together, these six delegaciones accounted for 48.4 percent of all robberies.

Statistics from the Federal District classify robbery into two categories:

1. Theft involving violence, the most prevalent being assaults on individuals in the streets, accounted for an average of 18 percent of all robberies in 1997. Next in the ranking is arson to commercial establishments (10 percent), vehicle theft (10 percent), theft from commercial establishments (5 percent), and residential theft (nearly 1 percent).
2. In the robbery without violence category, most incidents involved auto theft (22 percent), followed by theft from commercial establishments (9 percent), and residential theft (over 6 percent). There were 485 cases of bank robbery in 1996, 550 in 1997, and 692 in 1998. In contrast, the amount stolen decreased from 146 million pesos in 1996 to 129 million pesos in 1998 (Coordinación de Seguridad Pública 1999).

Assault and Battery

Assault and battery accounted for 14 percent of all reported crimes in 1997, and 16.4 percent in 1999. The areas reporting the highest assault and battery rates in 1997 were the boroughs of Gustavo A. Madero (9.95 percent), Cuauhtémoc (9.26 percent), and Iztapalapa (7.97 percent); the municipalities of Ecatepec (6.53 percent) and Naucalpan (6.15 percent); the borough of Venustiano Carranza (5.53 percent); and the municipality of Nezahualcóyotl (5.47 percent). These seven jurisdictions together accounted for 50 percent of the total for this type of crime. These crimes probably can be attributable to a tendency toward violent conduct among city dwellers (in contrast to rural locales), and negligent or aggressive driving in the city.

Little had changed in 1999, except that Nezahualcóyotl had replaced Venustiano Carranza in the ranking. It is worth noting, however, that the rates had declined to 8.72 percent in Gustavo A. Madero and 8.07 percent in Cuauhtémoc, while the rate in Iztapalapa rose to 8.07 percent.

Rape

Official records of this offense show relatively constant rates, yet it is said to be one of the most underreported crimes and one that causes the most harm to victims and society. The vast majority of victims are women and minors. In 1997, the Federal District accounted for 51 percent of reported rapes. In terms of geographical distribution, Ecatepec ranked first with 9.51 percent, followed by Gustavo A. Madero (8.94 percent), Iztapalapa (7.24 percent), Nezahualcóyotl (6.71 percent), Naucalpan (5.97 percent), Venustiano Carranza (5.09 percent), Coyoacán (4.84 percent), and Cuauhtémoc (4.77 percent). Taken together, these jurisdictions account for 53 percent of all rapes in the metropolitan area.

The distribution between the Federal District and metropolitan municipalities had changed little in 1999, when the Federal District accounted for 49.5 percent of all rapes. Federal District statistics for that year do not provide information broken down by borough. There was also a significant change in crime patterns in México State. At any rate, the municipality with the highest incidence of rape was Ecatepec (8.99 percent), followed by Nezahualcóyotl (5.85 percent), and Naucalpan (4.24 percent).

Fraud, Swindling, Breach of Trust, and Plunder[8]

In 1996, fraud, swindling, breach of trust, and plunder accounted for 6.16 percent of all crimes reported to the authorities. These types of offenses are most frequently reported in urban areas with concentrated financial, commercial, and service activity. They reflect, in my opinion, a tendency toward disputes over property rights. In 1999, the Federal District accounted for 41.7 percent of all charges involving these offenses, while the metropolitan municipalities accounted for 58.2 percent. In 1997, the Cuauhtémoc borough alone accounted for 55 percent of such crimes, perhaps because the city's financial and commercial center is located there, as are the main courts. Cuauhtémoc is also where statistics are compiled from the central sector of the PGJDF. This may explain the high concentration of these crimes in Cuauhtémoc, which may not reflect their actual prevalence. Ecatepec ranks second (5.5 percent), followed by the boroughs of Benito Juárez (3.6 percent) and Gustavo A. Madero (3.13 percent).

Trends in these types of offenses changed in 1999 due to changes in the law. Statistics varied among the municipalities and more property damage was reported. In addition, the crime of driving under the influence of alcohol was added in México State, which contributed to the altered trends.

Other Offenses

A series of offenses are reported by the PGJ of both jurisdictions based on the way that each Ministerio Público classifies certain activities in respective criminal codes. These offenses represent an enormous miscellany of criminal acts reported in INEGI statistics.[9] This category accounted for 26.4 percent of all offenses in 1997 and 18 percent in 1999. In 1997, the Federal District accounted for 60.1 percent of such crimes and the metropolitan area jurisdictions 39.8 percent. Once again, the Cuauhtémoc borough ranked first, accounting for 19.2 percent of crimes in the miscellaneous category, followed by Naucalpan (6.75 percent), Ecatepec (6.52 percent), Gustavo A. Madero (6.1 percent), Iztapalapa (6 percent), and Tlalnepantla (5.53 percent). Charges filed specifying these offenses are systematically concentrated in these boroughs, which suggests that a wide range of criminal activities occurs in them. On the other hand, the relatively high rates may be the result of fewer difficulties associated with reporting such acts to the authorities. In 1999, the borough of Gustavo A. Madero ranked first (6.83 percent), followed by Ecatepec (6.7 percent), Tlanepantla (6.7 percent), Cuauhtémoc (6.5 percent), Nezahuacóyotl (6.23 percent), Iztapalapa (6.17 percent), Naucalpan (5.74 percent), and Coyoacán (5.3 percent).

There is another group of federal offenses that includes drug trafficking, drug use, piracy, contraband, tax evasion, copyright infringement, electoral offenses, trafficking in archaeological artifacts, environmental offenses, misconduct by public officials, and fencing of stolen goods. Unfortunately, the PGR reports do not break down data of these offenses by jurisdiction. Other crimes include Internet fraud, identity theft, credit card theft, and incitement to commit fraud. Such offenses are grossly underreported and public data are not available. Moreover, there is no organization that is able to maintain accurate information on crimes by government officials or the link between human rights violations and crime.

Unsafe Areas: Spatial Distribution of Crime

The most "unsafe" boroughs and municipalities in terms of crime prevalence consistently have been Cuauhtémoc (with high crime rates per 100,000 inhabitants, usually above the overall average for the Mexico City metropolitan area), Gustavo A. Madero, Iztapalapa, and Benito Juárez. These jurisdictions are followed, in order of crime prevalence, by the municipalities of Nezahualcóyotl and Ecatepec, the borough of Venustiano Carranza, and sometimes the borough of Miguel Hidalgo. These eight jurisdictions consistently account for half of all crimes in the metropolitan area. (See Figures 11.3 and 11.4.)

In 1997, criminal activity was distributed among the boroughs and municipalities as follows: Cuauhtémoc had the highest crime rate, accounting for 14.7 percent of all crimes committed in the Mexico City metropolitan area. It was followed by the boroughs of Gustavo A. Madero, Iztapalapa, and Benito Juárez, which together accounted for 37 percent of the total. The municipality of Nezahualcóyotl ranked fifth with 5.4 percent. Twenty-one municipalities and sixteen boroughs accounted for 85 percent of all reported illegal activity in the Mexico City metropolitan area.

Figures 11.3 and 11.4 compare the evolution of crime from 1997 to 2002. (The data for these maps were grouped based on crime volume to highlight areas with higher crime rates.) Both clearly show that Cuauhtémoc is the most dangerous borough in the greater metropolitan area, followed by Gustavo A. Madero and Iztapalapa, and then a swath of boroughs and municipalities in the central-northern part of the metropolitan area. In 2002, despite an overall decrease in crime, very few changes were noted in terms of crime volume (and rates). This section of the metropolitan area apparently has well-entrenched patterns of criminal behavior. Crime appears to "spread" throughout the central-eastern portion of the metropolitan area, but with lower volumes than those found in the central area.

Figure 11.3. Crime incidence by borough and municipality, 1997

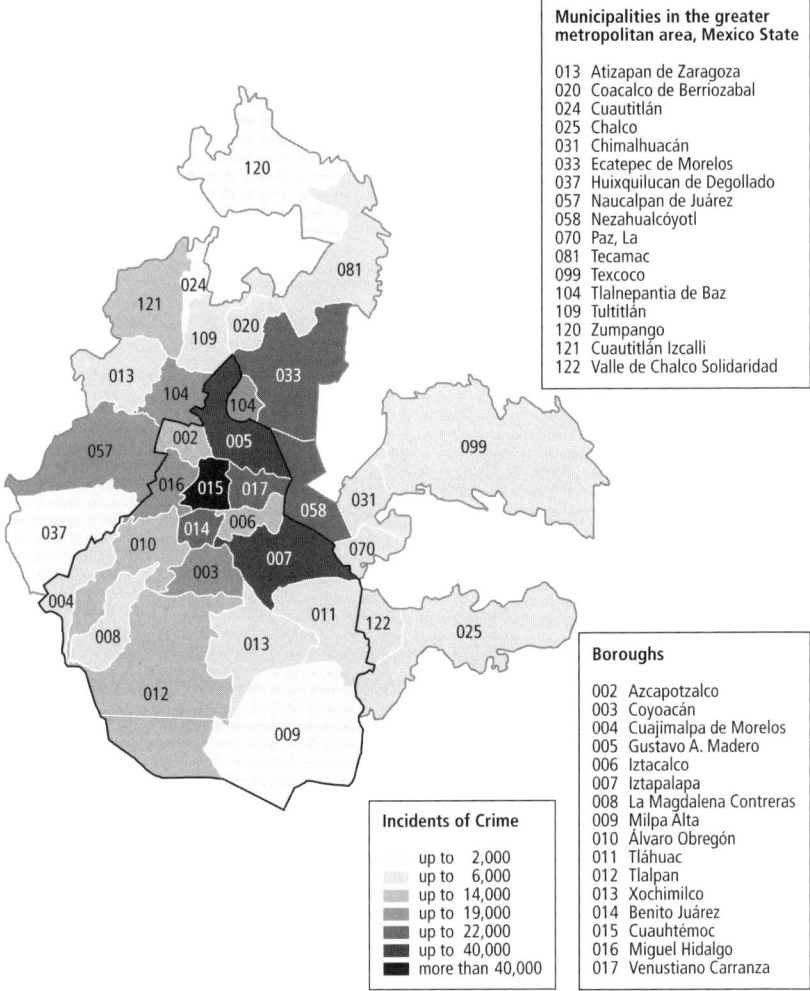

Source: INEGI, *Estadísticas criminales, Distrito Federal y Estado de México* (Mexico City: INEGI, 1998).

The Spatial Logic of Crime

Figures 11.3 and 11.4 reveal a commonality in terms of the metropolitan area where crime occurs. The question that arises from these maps is whether an urban or metropolitan criminal system exists or merely a series of un-

Figure 11.4. Crime incidence by borough in the Federal District, 2002

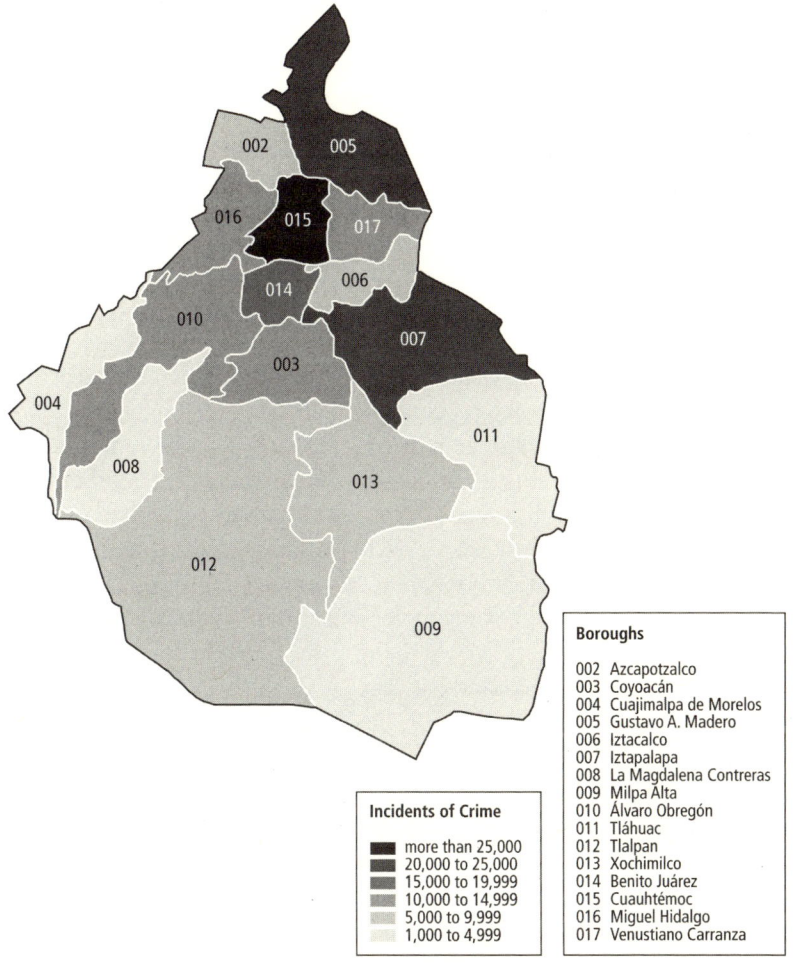

Sources: Agencias del Ministerio Público, Dirección General de Estadística y Política Criminal, 2002.

coordinated events linked in space and time. What we can say is that, first, criminal activity is concentrated in the "old city," from whence it is spread unevenly around the city's metropolitan municipalities.

Second, it is worth asking whether any single activity such as robbery (or homicide as I mentioned earlier) can be considered a marker for criminal activity in general. Looking at the maps, however, there does not seem to be a predominance or correlation among the different types of crimes.

Instead, criminal activities are very diverse. Therefore, a dual logic might be at work: first, criminal activity is competitive (between categories of crime), and second, criminals tend to specialize. This means that certain criminals (individuals or groups) will tend to specialize in a particular type of crime and avoid other kinds of activities. (For example, some robbers specialize in street activity or auto thefts, while a rapist has a certain criminal profile, as does a criminal who commits fraud.) It may also be the case that different criminal individuals and groups in the metropolitan area operate within a defined area and tend not to invade or explore other areas.

Moreover, criminal activity is a system or economy that has important dimensions and links within the informal economy (and certain ties to the formal economy such as in fencing stolen goods and contraband, for example). It acquires its own dynamic vis-à-vis the urban economy and evolves according to its own internal processes and challenges.

Criminal activity tends to be inflexible. It is rigid in the sense that it is not affected by even dramatic changes or developments in the urban economy, by legal reforms (criminal codes), or by public and police efforts to combat it. More particularly, Mexico City's crime rates have been growing during periods of economic boom and bust, major transformations of the local economy, high rates of unemployment, and increasing poverty. The only variable that is closely related to the crime rate seems to be inequality, a historical pattern of social division in Mexican society (Fajzylber et al. 2001).

Criminal behavior is innovative in that it responds to its own inherent challenges and creates new types of offenses. Examples are the kidnapping express, and bank robbers who move toward gang-related and organized crime.

Lastly, patterns of criminal activity are systematic and stable, and have proven durable in time and space in the metropolitan area.

Crime, Impunity, and Arbitrary Police Action

Government failure to prosecute crime severely erodes the rule of law. According to the National Action Party (PAN), only 6.02 percent of investigations led to indictment in 1996, compared to 14.3 percent in 1990 (PAN 1997). In 1999 an estimated 10 percent of crimes were prosecuted (and resolved). It is estimated that between 50 and 60 percent of homicide cases are resolved. Contemporary studies of the issue include Zepeda Lecuona

(2005) and Arroyo (2004); both state that for every 100 "real" crimes committed in the country, only 2 percent are solved. They call this an "impunity rate" of 98 percent.[10]

Figures on alleged criminals (convicted and under prosecution) in Mexico City have risen consistently in recent years to almost 50 percent (Alvarado 2005), although they do not account for even 10 percent of official crime figures. With respect to robberies, the most salient figures are for auto and property theft—cases in which reporting the crime might result in at least partial recovery of losses—battery in general, fraud, and so on. Other variables that affect whether a crime is reported include the need to report the incident for the victim's protection, possibility of recovering losses (e.g., via insurance), "accessibility" of the authorities, intervention of the victim's friends, and hiring an attorney.

Police capacity for law enforcement can be considered a key factor in understanding crime. Little is known about the "operating capacity" of the police forces under the Ministry of Public Security of the Federal District and of the local PGJ offices to prevent and prosecute crime. There is no basic public document that describes personnel levels in each of these entities. Therefore, my assessment is based on the probable crime-fighting capacity of the police forces, according to some official figures. These numbers are very enlightening.

The police forces under the Ministry of Public Security comprise an estimated 35,000 active-duty police agents (Alvarado and Davis 1999; Alvarado 2003). In 1999, they represented approximately one-third of the ministry's 100,000-plus employees. However, a glance at the numbers of police officers assigned to each borough—in other words, those engaged in day-to-day police work as opposed to the grenadiers, special action, or task force agents—shows the official figures for 1997 dropped to 16,667 police officers, about one-half of the total. If these agents were working at full operational capacity, the following situation would prevail: 1.9 police officers per 1,000 inhabitants in the Federal District, and one officer for every eleven reported crimes (2000 crime count).

Further, there is an average of 10.4 charges per suspect (or indicted person). This means that for each police agent, there are 1.07 alleged criminals involved in legal proceedings (apprehended, indicted, prosecuted, etc.). In other words, only 9.59 percent of all alleged criminals become involved in the justice system process.

Regarding the judicial police in the capital, let us assume that 1,500 agents are on duty every day. In this case, there are 0.17 judicial police agents for every 1,000 inhabitants; they are engaged in responding to crime (rather than crime prevention) and they serve as adjuncts to the Ministerio Público in resolving cases. Therefore, there are 124 crime reports, or complaints, per judicial police agent, and 11.9 alleged criminals per agent—an overwhelming caseload. The situation is no better when we add the crimes and police agents in México State to this equation. If we also take into account figures from victimization surveys, we obtain a more complete picture of crime trends and police action in the Federal District.

Crimes committed by police agents against citizens severely exacerbate the climate of insecurity and foster impunity. According to the Mexican Commission for the Defense and Promotion of Human Rights (CMDPHHAC), 55 percent of complaints of human rights violations nationwide implicate the army, the municipal police, and the state judicial police (CMDPDHAC and *Reforma,* June 1998). Statistics from the Human Rights Commission of the Federal District (CDHDF) are very instructive as well. Of the charges submitted to the commission from 1993 to 1997 (around 15,000 cases), 48 percent were against the attorney general of Mexico City, 22 percent against the Ministry of Public Security of Mexico City (SSP), and 4.7 percent against the local judiciary (CDHDF 1999).[11]

From 1995 to 1998, 52 percent of charges against the PGJDF (1,847 cases) involved the Judicial Police, and 59 percent of charges against the Mexico City government involved the Ministry of Public Security. In other words, one out of every two complaints concerned the actions of the capital's police forces. Nonetheless, only 17 percent of accused PGJ employees have been sanctioned, while only 20 percent of Public Security Ministry employees have been sanctioned.

The situation has not improved significantly. By 2000, the Human Rights Commission of the Federal District reported that of the total number of charges filed, 18.6 percent were against local prosecutors' offices and 390 implicated the Judicial Police.[12] In addition, 16.42 percent were made against the Mexico City Ministry of Public Security. Moreover, 36 percent of accused personnel from the PGJDF were sanctioned compared to only 4 percent of accused personnel from the Ministry of Public Security of the Federal District.

In México State, the State Human Rights Commission received a total of 14,600 complaints from 1993 to 1997. Of these, 25.7 percent implicated the judicial authorities, 9.5 percent the public security and traffic directorate, and 12.5 percent the Superior Court of Justice (Tribunal Superior de Justicia)

(CEDHEM 1998).[13] Moreover, 4.5 percent of charges concerned arbitrary detention by the state judicial police.

Crimes by Police

Human rights groups and society in general are particularly concerned about human rights abuses committed by the police against citizens. As mentioned earlier, most complaints of police abuse involve arbitrary detention and abuse of authority, but there are also reports of torture, kidnapping, and even arbitrary execution.

Academics and human rights organizations such as the Lawyer's Committee for Human Rights and Human Rights Watch cite a recurring pattern of abuses, which emerges with particular clarity in cases involving torture.[14] According to Human Rights Watch (1999),

> Almost without fail, in cases in which Federal Judicial Police were involved, the detainees were illegally held and tortured prior to being turned over to prosecutors. Common to almost every case is prosecutors' lack of initiative to follow up on torture allegations or medical exams that describe torture. In some cases, prosecutors simply fail to investigate torture, or they charge police with lesser crimes, such as "abuse of authority." In other instances, even if the human rights violator is indicted, authorities do not follow up on arrest warrants.

This organization has identified numerous cases of torture, although none of them involve the authorities or police of the Federal District.[15] However, two Mexico City newspapers (*Reforma* and *La Jornada*) have documented tragic cases of arbitrary detention, delays in turning detainees over to prosecutors, torture, and deaths of detainees in police custody.

The Human Rights Commission of the Federal District has made a number of recommendations regarding torture in Mexico City. One of the main causes of torture is what Silva (2003, 11) calls "the logic of punishment":

> In June 2000, according to recommendation 7/00, the judicial police repeatedly tortured two detained men who had participated in a robbery in which a judicial agent was killed by a shot fired by one of the assailants. A few years ago, as described in recommendation 11/97, a man was beaten, tortured, and falsely accused of robbery after kicking the

door of a judicial police vehicle that was blocking the entrance to his business. As we will see in other cases . . . involving the [Federal] Preventive Police [PFP], any aggression or contradiction, albeit minor, of the one "in charge" seems to provoke a symbolic and physically excessive response!

According to Silva, police abuse can also be attributed to lack of professional conduct, to police seeking financial enrichment in the course of duty, and to the tendency to punish people who resist their demands. The type of abuse most frequently attributed to the Preventive Police is arbitrary detention, as well as physical injury and mistreatment; there have also been some cases of torture. But this force also tends to commit abuses associated with the types of operations conducted by its officers, such as controlling demonstrations, or stops and searches in public roadways, ostensibly to "catch people en flagrancia" or "suspects" in areas considered problematic. Silva documents at least four cases of CDHDF recommendations involving extortion (10/95, 2/97, 5/02, and 1/99); one in particular involves the use of police officers for personal ends when a person who owed money to a relative of a deputy director of the PGJDF was detained, robbed, and extorted (Silva 2003, 10–11).

To date, government efforts to remedy and prevent this situation have been insufficient. To make matters worse, crimes often are not reported, because doing so does not necessarily mean that the injustice will be rectified. Even when the authorities have demonstrated a positive attitude toward human rights, this alone does not eliminate or even reduce police abuse and torture.

Organized Crime

An important aspect of the crime pattern involves federal, rather than "ordinary" offenses. These offenses include organized crime activities, money laundering, drug trafficking, trafficking of persons, trafficking of human organs, and certain other illegal activities at the U.S. border. In Mexico City, the magnitude and scope of these activities seem relatively minor compared to other problems. However, there is significant discussion as to whether this type of crime undermines the political institutions of the state. Specifically, Bailey and Chabat (2002) discuss the challenges that organized crime poses to government institutions, such as (1) the volume of funds and resources managed by organized cartels may overwhelm the government,

Table 11.2. Organized criminal activity by type of offense, 1994–1998

Year	Drug-Related Crimes	Robbery	Firearms	Contraband	Sum	Annual Average
1994*	1,234	2,581	6,950	302	11,067	2,767
1995	12,773	2,989	8,592	266	24,620	6,155
1996	23,992	10,030	12,827	905	47,754	11,939
1997	21,071	6,235	13,852		41,158	13,719
1998	19,629	9,491	14,761		43,881	14,627
Average	15,740	6,265	11,396	491		

*First year of constitutional and legal reforms to combat these activities.
Source: Arzt (2002, 149).

(2) their ability to generate violence and the magnitude and scope of their activities may undermine government capacity, (3) the police are ill-equipped to tackle activities conducted on a such a large scale, and (4) they pose special challenges for crime fighting institutions, such as specialized international agencies.

Preliminary data on activities involving organized crime show a steady increase in all areas of activity. Table 11.2 shows federal offenses at the national level (or rather, it reveals a steady increase in crime statistics from the federal authorities). The activities reported during this period are concentrated in eight states of the Federation (the metropolitan areas of the Federal District and the states of México, Jalisco, Baja California, Sinaloa, Sonora, Tamaulipas, and Oaxaca [Arzt 2002, 150]). It should be noted that no data are available on trafficking in persons and organs and other related offenses. Such activities seem to be relatively rare in Mexico City. However, it is probably safe to say that federal authorities concentrate their efforts to combat such offenses at the northern border states rather than the capital.

The authorities are keeping records of what they call "suspicious" or unusual banking transactions. As of March 2000, 2,866 cases had been opened by the PGJ offices. An additional 1,422,783 bank transactions involving over US$20,000 each were reported, as well as 107 cases of "unusual" activities (Arzt 2002, 148).

An enormous amount of effort is devoted to combating these crimes. In 2002, Arzt calculated that the Federal Attorney General's Office, known by the Spanish acronym of PGR (*Procuraduría General de la República*), in México State devoted must of its resources to combating such crimes.

Police conduct in this area is also a major concern. SECODAM (Ministry of the Comptroller and Administrative Development of Mexico) reports that the Attorney General's Office ranks among the top five government offices in terms of the number of complaints and accusations of corruption and illegal activities over a two-year period. According to SECODAM, 10 percent of the staff of the PGR had been sanctioned (Arzt 2003, 18).[16]

According to the National Human Rights Commission (CNDH), PGR is also the government agency most frequently implicated in complaints of human rights violations. The CNDH reports that, from 1990 to 2001, the PGR received 179 "recommendations" to resolve human rights complaints (CNDH 2002, 741). The main human rights violations reported in 2002 were failure to administer justice (42 cases), forced disappearance (22 cases), torture (19 cases), and arbitrary use of public security forces (13) (CNDH 2002, 579).

Citizens' Perceptions of Crime

This section offers an alternative to official statistics in measuring the crime phenomenon in Mexico City. What some refer to as the total or under-reported crime rate is actually much higher than reported crime rates. The problem lies in finding a systematic, objective, consistent way to reflect it. An estimate of this "hidden figure" for the Federal District is presented below. I should add that no data are available for the same figure in the metropolitan municipalities.

Official statistics on crime rates and criminal activity do not accurately reflect the magnitude and complexity of the phenomenon. An enormous number of victims and witnesses do not report crimes. Victimization surveys represent one method of estimating crime and weighing the official figures. The Mexican newspaper *Reforma* has published the findings of its victimization surveys since October 1996. The surveys conducted by *Reforma* in the 1996–2002 period are compiled in a database.[17] I will compare several years in order to arrive at a systematic estimate of reported and unreported crimes (victimization). A consistent trend has been established by comparing and adjusting each sample based on population factors. I will also show the discrepancies between this estimate and official figures, and demonstrate that the surveys show realistic trends over time. Significantly, they offer statistically reliable evidence of victimization in specific populations. Based on this, I suggest that government crime data reflect only what the government is able and willing to process.

Elements for a Study of Crime in Mexico City 301

The next section examines the various definitions of criminal trends from the victim's standpoint, which do not necessarily coincide with the definitions of offenses found in the criminal codes. These definitions may be at odds with some legal statutes (e.g., the so-called "kidnapping express," which does not appear in any criminal code).[18]

Comparative Analysis of Crime Rates and Victimization Surveys

In the survey, victims are adults (age eighteen and above) who answered yes to the question, "Have you been the victim of a crime in the past three months?" The following figures compare a series of surveys conducted from 1997 to 2002. The average victimization rate in the surveys was 20.8 percent from 1996 to 2002, with a significant departure in 1996, when 32 percent of Mexico City adult residents reported having been the victim of some type of crime, and in 2000, when the average dropped to 14 percent (Figure 11.5).

Figure 11.5. Proportion of adults reporting being the victim of a crime in the past three months in annual surveys, 1996 to January–May 2002

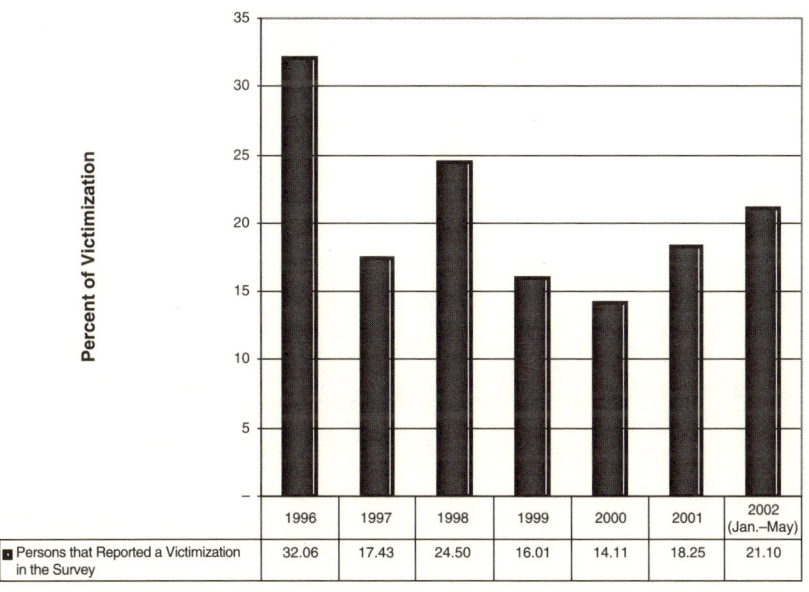

	1996	1997	1998	1999	2000	2001	2002 (Jan.–May)
Persons that Reported a Victimization in the Survey	32.06	17.43	24.50	16.01	14.11	18.25	21.10

Source: Surveys by *Reforma*, 1996 to 2002.

Figure 11.6. Proportion of adults victimized by crime: incidence of crimes reported versus not reported to authorities, 1996 to January–May 2002

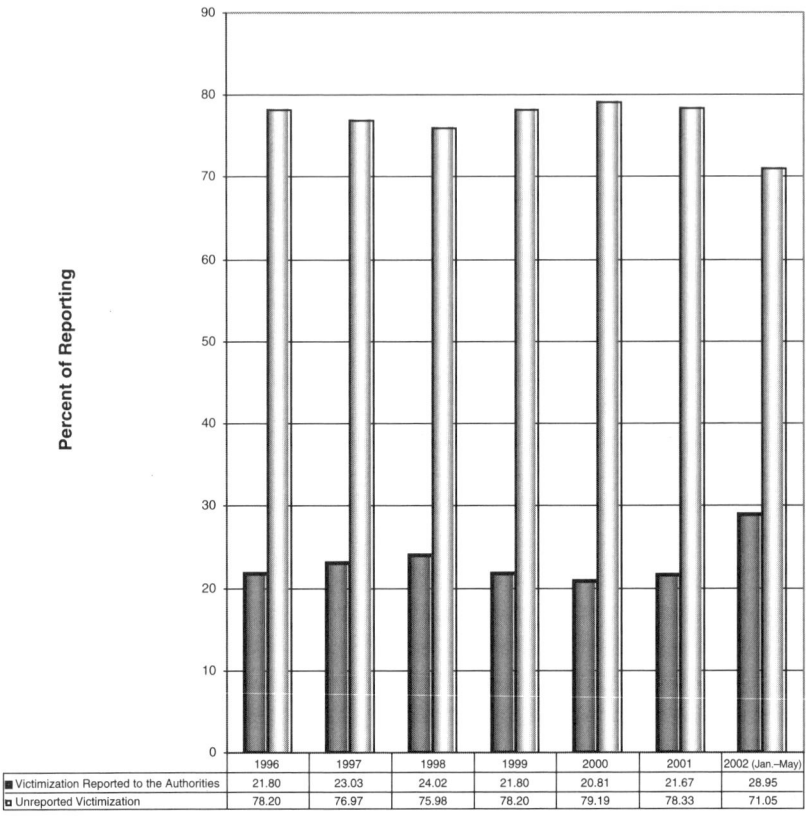

Source: Surveys by *Reforma,* 1996 to 2002.

Interestingly, trends in crime reporting (and not reporting) are consistent. Crimes are reported at an average rate of 22.29 percent, which increased to 24.02 percent in 1998. Thus, an average of 77.7 percent, or three out of four victims, do not report crimes.[19]

A consistent pattern can be observed beginning in 1997. On average, one in four people who stated that they had been victimized also stated that they had reported the incident to the authorities. Most offenses reported are against personal property. The main reason for reporting the crime, according to those surveyed, was to recover stolen property or to file a complaint with the Ministerio Público in order to seek insurance reimbursement.

Figure 11.7. Victimization and crime rates (per 100,000 inhabitants), Federal District, 1996–2002

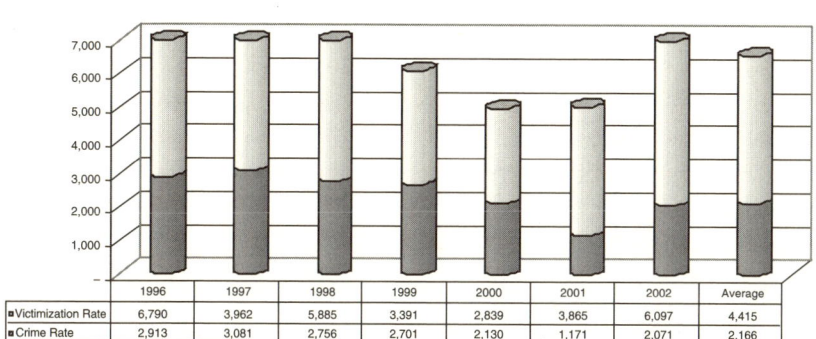

Sources: Reforma surveys; INEGI, Anuario estadístico del Distrito Federal, 1997–2003, and Procuraduría General de Justicia del Distrito Federal.

Figure 11.7 shows the estimated number of adults who would have been crime victims if the trends shown in the surveys were correct. The rates per 100,000 inhabitants were extrapolated from the data on victimization in the surveys and on officially reported crimes.

There is a huge discrepancy between incidents reported to the authorities and the estimates drawn from the surveys, representing an average ratio of more than two nonreported crimes to every reported crime. However, there are exceptions that merit closer attention, such as in 2001 when the ratio was closer to four to one.

The crime-reporting trends in the surveys are consistent, which could lead us to infer that crimes reported in the surveys parallel official trends. Based on this assumption, we can offer an estimate of unreported crime.

Figures 11.8 and 11.9 and Table 11.3 show trends in reported crime in official statistics and victimization surveys. Each of these variables evolves according to its own pattern. While the official statistics tend to decrease systematically, victimization estimates suggest a different trend. Trends in reported and nonreported crimes were similar from 1996 to 1999, but subsequently began to increase dramatically.

Once again, the surveys are consistent. The ratio of nonreported crimes and official figures is four to one.

Based on the above, I created another graph (Figure 11.10) that offers an estimate of the total number of crimes committed in Mexico City from 1996 to 2002. It represents an estimate of crimes committed in the capital and

Figure 11.8. Comparison of crimes reported to authorities and crime incidence reported in victimization surveys, 1996–2002

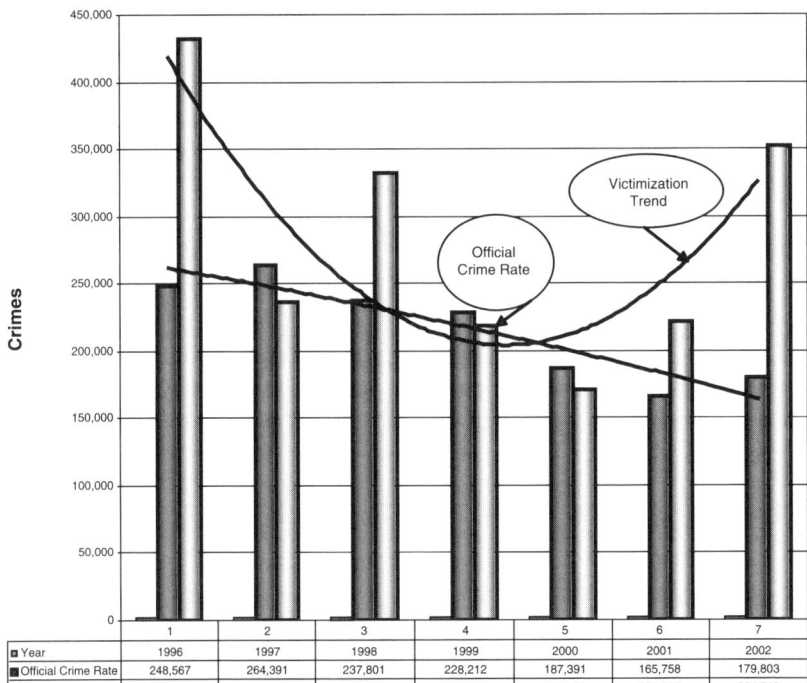

compares its evolution to officially reported crime rates. It is interesting to note that in this diagram, as in the others, the line reflecting crime shows an upward trend beginning in 2000. Therefore, the ratio between estimated and reported crimes also increases even more dramatically.

Of course, the above calculations are preliminary estimates. The surveys are internally consistent over time, except for 1996, when striking differences in victimization patterns are observed. While all surveys offer a more dismal view of the crime situation and strongly substantiate the public's perceptions of public security/safety, there is a certain degree of similarity between crime trends as reported in official statistics and those reported in the surveys.

If we compare victimization rates with the number of alleged criminals, and with the number of police agents, we arrive at an estimated 806,717 victims (adults who reported having been the victim of a crime in the preced-

Figure 11.9. Estimates of unreported crimes

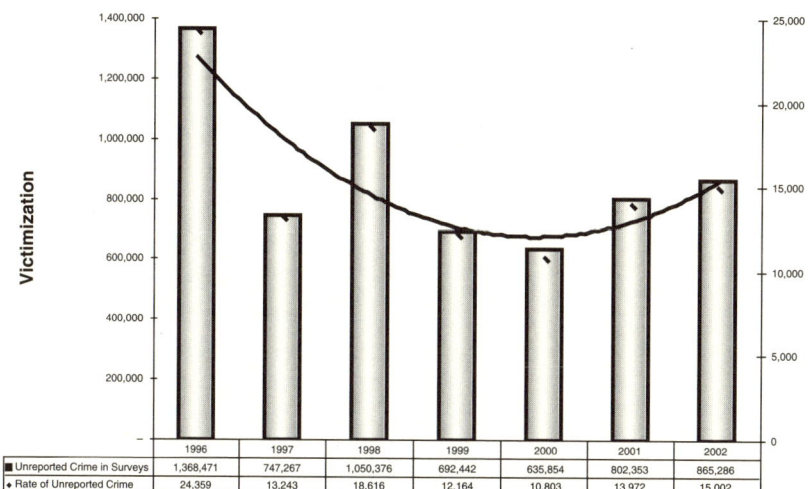

	1996	1997	1998	1999	2000	2001	2002
Unreported Crime in Surveys	1,368,471	747,267	1,050,376	692,442	635,854	802,353	865,286
Rate of Unreported Crime	24,359	13,243	18,616	12,164	10,803	13,972	15,002

Sources: INEGI, *Anuario estadístico del Distrito Federal*. Data for 2000 are preliminary (see http://www.pgjdf.gob.mx/estadisticas/resumen_ng.asp, May 14, 2001).

ing three months) for 2001. This represents a 4:1 ratio compared to alleged crimes registered by the Public Ministry for that year (187,391). At least one in ten people was a victim of a crime in 2001, resulting in a rate of 9,325 crimes per 100,000 inhabitants, compared to the 2,130 alleged crimes reported in the Public Ministry. There is an immense disparity between estimated crimes and police agents, representing forty-eight crimes per Preventive Police agent, and 537 crime victims for each Judicial Police officer.

Table 11.3. Estimates of unreported crimes, 1996–2002

Year	Official Figure on Reported Crimes	Crimes Not Reported by Victims	Ratio
1996	248,567	1,368,471	5.5
1997	264,391	747,267	2.8
1998	237,801	1,050,376	4.4
1999	228,212	692,442	3.0
2000	187,391	635,854	3.4
2001	165,758	802,353	4.8
2002	179,803	865,286	4.8
Average	215,989	880,293	4.1

Source: *Reforma* surveys and PGJDF reports, various years.

Figure 11.10. Ratio of reported crimes and estimated crime incidence from surveys, 1996–2002

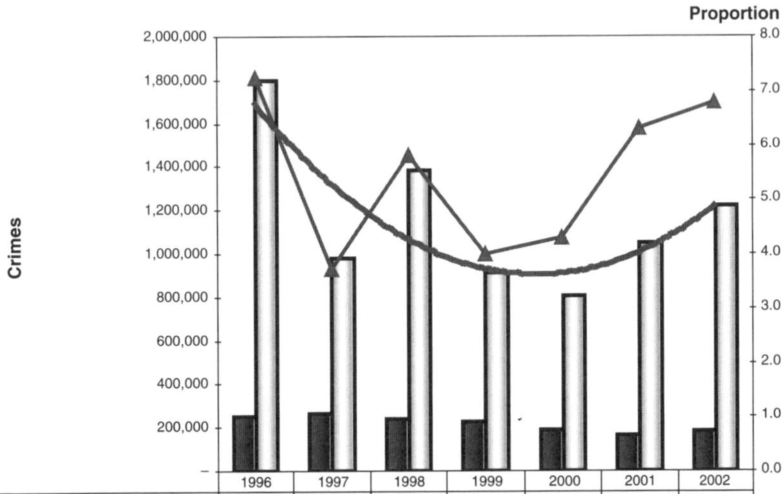

	1996	1997	1998	1999	2000	2001	2002
Official Crime Rate	248,567	264,391	237,801	228,212	187,391	165,758	179,803
Total Crime Rate from Surveys	1,801,093	983,505	1,382,437	911,348	806,717	1,048,066	1,219,999
Ratio	7.2	3.7	5.8	4.0	4.3	6.3	6.8

Sources: INEGI, *Anuario estadístico del Distrito Federal,* and Procuraduría General de Justicia del Distrito Federal, http://www.pgjdf.gob.mx/estadisticas/resumen_ng.asp.

The authorities would have apprehended and prosecuted an average of 2.2 percent of the total estimated number of alleged criminals over the past decade.

Conclusions

To conclude, let us consider the short-term forecast. Figure 11.11 shows the evolution (in percentages) of crime in the Federal District, based on official figures. It is interesting to note the cyclical evolution of upward and downward trends in reported crimes. Particularly in recent years (1998 to 2002), the curve is comparable to the trends observed in the crime victim surveys, and shows a recent increase in crime prevalence. The same is true of the victimization trends in the preceding figures (which show a proportionately greater increase). This could indicate that crime prevalence is cyclical, and that there may be a slight increase in the crime rate in coming years, if the

Figure 11.11. Evolution of crime and population growth in Mexico City, 1989–2002 (annual incidence of crime per 100,000 population).

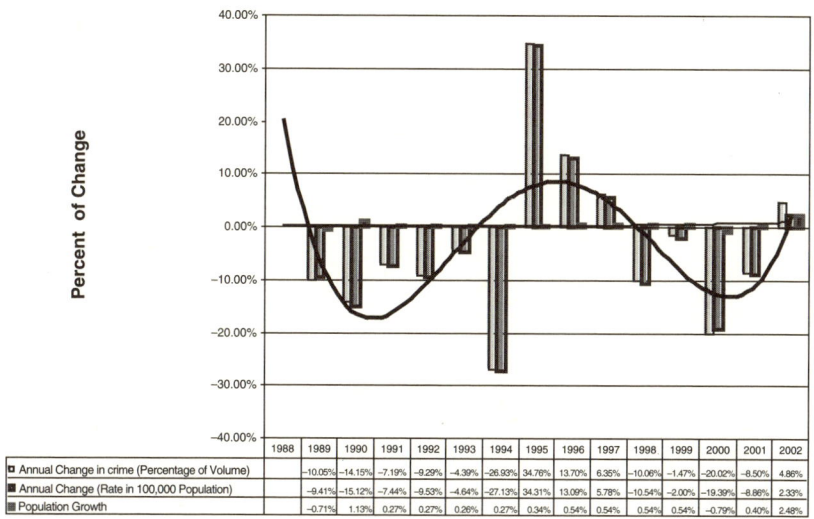

Sources: INEGI, *Censo general de población y vivienda,* 2000, http://www.inegi.gob.mx/difusion/espanol/poblacion/definitivos/iter/INITER09.PDF, and INEGI, *Indicadores sociodemográficos de México, 1930–2002,* http://www.inegi.gob.mx/di.

rest of the variables associated with the phenomenon remain constant (employment, income distribution, public security policy, public spending, etc.).

From 1995 to 1999, metropolitan area residents were anxious about public safety issues. Residents suffered a historically unprecedented crime wave, characterized by high levels of violence, impunity, and government inability to deal with the problem. One terrible conclusion that can be drawn from this situation is that Mexico City residents form part of a society that has become accustomed to accepting victimization: they experience it, but are not sure that attempts are made to try and fix it. Crime rates in the Mexico City metropolitan area have declined over the past five years, with the exception of 2002 estimates, which indicate an upward trend. The increase in the 2002 rates might reflect a seasonal adjustment, a temporary effect, or a more rigid upward trend in criminal activity. Some crimes have increased, such as assaults on passers-by or in the streets (which continue to be a "no man's land"); the same is true for all types of kidnapping. But the other categories of assault, robbery, and homicide appear to be on the decline. The maps in Figures 11.3 and 11.4 reveal these trends. Since 1999 the mortality rate caused by accidents has declined, and the homicide rate has fallen consistently. Based on a comparison of Figures 11.10 and 11.11, it is possible to predict a relative increase in criminal activity in the entire Mexico City metropolitan area that may be the result of a cycle whose causes have yet to be identified.

This chapter presents the distribution of the phenomenon in the metropolitan area, providing a different and more complete view of criminal activity. It also offers an initial estimate of crime, a measurement that is not found in any official statistics or previous studies, and should be used as a point of departure for an analysis of crime. The data provided here can serve as a starting point to reflect more systematically on several hypotheses that could be posed about crime in the capital in the early twenty-first century.

Some Notes on Violence and Crime in Mexico City

In conclusion, what can be said about the reliability of official data or official crime rate trends? There are two important conclusions to draw from the official data. On the one hand, official data cover about only one of every four alleged crimes. On the other, these data demonstrate what the government is able and willing to work toward or achieve with regard to fighting criminal activity in the city.

Official data are not straightforward figures of real crime trends but rather reflections of the government's ability and intention to fight crime. It is obvious that crime has increased during the last twenty years. Data show what authorities consider to be crime and are interested in fighting and regulating. It is said that citizens tend not to report crime because they do not trust the authorities or because they think reporting will not lead to recovery of the stolen goods or compensation for damages. The latter belief is correct. But authorities do receive more criminal reports than the ones they report. It appears that there is a strong discrepancy between the official reports and what are believed to be the "actual" trends. This difference is partially a result of the way the authorities define and process crimes, according to their discretionary understanding of the law. Within this context, it is clear that people tend to report more crimes against property than any other type of crime. As a result, this situation shows a strong trend of property crimes, more than any other type of criminal behavior. But if this is the case, then there is a question as to how people's interests in reporting crimes might be explained. This might also mean that people are challenging the way in which the authoritarian structure of property rights, inherently inequitable, has traditionally protected only the wealthy and privileged.

People perceive the criminal justice system to be weak and inefficient; impunity or lawlessness is still a big issue. The government has a limited capacity to fight crime; it works in effect on only one-quarter of "real crime." The reasons for this limitation are several. First, there is an incomplete, inconsistent, and erroneous integration of crime data by the government. This is due to lack of legislation, and incorrect or incomplete definitions of some types of crime. An example here is the "secuestro express": there is no legal definition for this crime. Thus, the proxies used are a combination of kidnapping and aggravated assault, but prosecutors have no authority to link these two crimes when filing charges. There are no legal or institutional means to collect data and investigate the evolution of crime. One example is the growth in retail sales of illegal drugs. Police and prosecutors have no capacity to prevent and investigate drug-related crimes. Claims persist that sometimes both are part of the problem. Having such a wide range of laws and regulations produces confusion and difficulties in prosecuting crime by police or other authorities. There is no coordination among various police forces, or among institutions, such as the Public Security Ministry of Mexico City and the PGJ. Political cooperation problems are exacerbated further when Mexico City agencies attempt to cooperate with counterparts in other states.

What can we say about overall crime? What do the trends manifest? There are many hypotheses regarding crime trends. One is related to the deterioration of the capital, and more specifically, to the decline of the "old city" and the emergence of the megacity. Another approach is based on demographic trends. Yet another is directly associated with the economic crisis, and still another is related to the unraveling of the political control of police and crime syndicates. There is also the hypothesis that inequality lies at the base of crime development in the country (Fajnzylber et al. 2001).

The first hypothesis is supported by the data and Figures 11.3 and 11.4. Crime tends to concentrate in the central "old" city as well as places where major growth has taken place in recent years (periphery of the capital). This pattern has been consistent since 1994. But this hypothesis does not explain the occurrence of different types of crimes from one of these locales to another.

Another approach is based on demographic trends. During the years when crime rates spiked, there was a concurrent demographic transition, in which a large number of young people "went on the market" and have not been able to obtain a sustainable job in the formal economy. The major increase in the population was among people aged fourteen to thirty, which is also the age group that tended to be more involved in crime. As a result, a significant proportion of this population finds a way to survive in the informal economy, either as vendors, producers, or distributors of goods and services outside the legal market, where stolen, counterfeit, and unlicensed products are sold. By working in this market, people integrate their lives with other illegal activities, such as drug selling. Both the surveys and the official crime statistics indicate that a major proportion of perpetrators belong to that group. Between 1997 and 2002, a large proportion of convicted criminals were part of that subset of the population.

An additional interpretation is related to the unraveling of the political control of police and crime groups such as gangs. During the period observed, Mexicans underwent two major transformations—a political and institutional reform, and an electoral transition in the city. In 1997, Cuauhtémoc Cardenas, leader of the Party of the Democratic Revolution (PRD), won the mayoralty of Mexico City in the first democratic election in almost 70 years. Changes in the administration of the government, inexperience, relocation, *ajustes de cuentas* inside the political apparatus, and a controversy between the military and police bosses produced a partial loss of control of police forces. This conflict within the police force bureaucracy and the military was underway before the new coalition had access to government. Between 1995 and 1997, the Mexico City government faced an important political confrontation inside the police corps, precisely at the same time that crime rates were escalating. Some argue that in this period major gangs also attempted a coup d'etat in order to obtain control of criminal activities throughout the city, with or without an agreement with government. As a result of this situation, both federal and local government officials called the military into public security offices in attempt to contain what seemed to be an irresistible increase in crime at all levels, and former military personnel took charge of the security administration of the Federal District in the middle of this crisis. This political situation suggests that economic crisis notwithstanding, there was an unraveling of the police corps and criminal gangs; this disentanglement produced the end of a pattern of traditional political control over the police rank and file that undergirded the inefficacy, ineffectiveness, inaction, omission, and even corruption and crime of police officers.

A major economic crisis hit the country in 1994 that exacerbated unemployment. Inflation, recession, and unemployment contributed in part to the crime wave against property.

There is also an explanation of the crime wave related to the increase in poverty during this period. However, there is no strong empirical evidence for this hypothesis. Even though most of these interpretations provide explanations for the patterns of crime and its increase since 1994, the fact that the homicide rate varied so little during the period demands more scrutiny and a better set of hypotheses.

Between 1994 and 2003, Mexico experienced a combination of economic, social, and political transformations that occurred at the same time as the most significant increase in crime in contemporary history. The causes of this "peak" are related to both conjunctural and structural patterns. Economic crisis, unemployment, and demographic changes contributed to the increase of property crimes as well as crimes against persons. But a more feasible explanation of this period requires a model that combines economic crises, demographic trends, and political changes, and more specifically, changes in political control of the police and the judiciary that acted as "detonators" of the rising crime wave.

Notes

I am grateful to Alejandro Moreno from Reforma-Investigación and Faviola Tavare Rodríguez for providing me with the data from the *Reforma* surveys. The analysis of the results is my sole responsibility.

1. This chapter analyzes crime trends in the Mexico City metropolitan area, which is comprised of thirty-five municipalities (similar to counties in the United States) in México State and the Federal District, which consists of sixteen political districts. The population of these two geopolitical units totals about 18 million. In this chapter, the "capital" refers to Mexico City or the Federal District, and "metropolitan area" refers to entire urban area of México State, Hidalgo State, and the Federal District combined, unless otherwise specified.

2. Three state and federal security programs were operating in the metropolitan area in 1999.

3. Federal offenses are defined in the Federal Penal Code, such as "offenses against health," which encompass the production, consumption, commercialization, or traffic of illegal drugs; firearms violations; federal electoral offenses; damage to archaeological, artistic, or historical patrimony; attacks on public communications facilities; and violations of privacy. Recently, there has been discussion of making kidnapping a federal offense. I did not have access to complete data sets for Hidalgo State for the time period discussed here; thus, Hidalgo is not included in most of the statistical analyses.

4. Note that the figures for the metropolitan area reveal a slight difference in crime rates per 100,000 inhabitants due to differences in the population estimates used for each

figure—for instance, in 1999, 2,078 versus 2,067. The last figure estimated the total municipal population.

5. It should be noted that the densely populated urban area of México State accounted for 76.5 percent of all crime in the state. By selected categories, the breakdown is 82.8 percent of robberies, 70.4 percent of assault and battery incidents, 66.86 percent of homicides, 73.99 percent of rapes, and 74 percent of other offenses. Crime is concentrated in these municipalities, which account for 69 percent of the state's population.

6. Official data on homicides must be examined carefully. For example, in the first report of the Fox administration in September 2001, reference is made to 35,000 "possible" homicides in 1997, compared to the 13,558 registered by INEGI (2001). This notion of "possible" homicides runs counter to the legal definitions of homicide or attempted homicide. Further, this figure contradicts other public sources, such as the Health Ministry. (From Vicente Fox Quesada, "Primer Informe de Gobierno del Presidente Constitucional de los Estados Unidos Mexicanos," Mexico City, September 2001, 339.) Another problem is the inconsistency in official data sets. Arroyo and Cervantes (1999), Ramírez Ducoing (1999), Figueroa Campos (1998), and Lozano et al. (1997) have documented differences in mortality rates due to external causes from the Health Ministry, and discrepancies between these figures and those provided by the National Public Security System.

7. INEGI, Encuesta Nacional de Violencia Intrafamiliar en el Área Metropolitana de la Ciudad de México, *Encuesta 1999*, 8 April 2003, http://dgcnesyp.inegi.gob.mx/cgi-win/sisesim.exe.

8. Consolidating these crimes is complicated and difficult to reconcile because their definition varies in the criminal code in each jurisdiction. In 1997, in the Federal District this category included breach of trust, plunder, illegal imprisonment, kidnapping, firearms violations, and attacks on federal communications installations, threats, and damage to property. Plunder (*despojo, plagio*) may be understood as looting of intellectual property and tangible goods.

9. In 1997, the following crimes were included in the statistical database of México State: abduction (1995 and before), illegal imprisonment, kidnapping, abandonment of family members, statutory rape, cattle rustling, property damage, and driving under the influence of alcohol. The Federal District includes illegal imprisonment, kidnapping, carrying an illegal weapon, attacks on communications facilities, threats, and property damage. In 1999, the same offenses were included, in addition to cattle rustling.

10. "Real crime" is defined as the sum of reported and unreported crime.

11. CDHDF, *Quinto informe anual,* http://www.cdhdf.org.mx.

12. CDHDF, *Annual Report,* revised, 27 January 2004, http://www.cdhdf.org.mx/index.php?id=informes.

13. See Comisión Estatal de Derechos Humanos del Estado de México (1998).

14. For a more detailed analysis of the problem of police abuse, see Silva (2003).

15. Torture usually takes place after arbitrary or prolonged detentions, when authorities detain a suspect without a warrant or other valid justification or when they hold a detainee in excess of legally allowable limits. In the CNDH cases analyzed here, police detentions ranging from four days to a week were standard practice. On 19 November 1990, for instance, Federal Judicial Police officers detained Martín Arroyo Luna and José Brito Navarro for possession of illegal arms and other alleged crimes. The detention itself did not violate the law, since the detainees were caught in flagrante. However,

police proceeded to hold them far beyond the allowed time before turning them over to prosecutors, and tortured them in the meantime. Three days after their arrest, the victims confessed before the regional PJF commander under duress. The case file contains multiple records of medical exams confirming that they had been tortured. According to the CNDH, eleven officials were eventually fired, but none appeared to have been prosecuted" (Human Rights Watch 1999).

16. Arzt also mentions that the PGR has only 1,800 police officers and 800 prosecutors (*ministerios públicos federales*) in the whole country to undertake the enormous task of fighting organized crime and a number of other federal crimes included in the Federal Criminal Code, the Federal Act against Organized Crime, the Federal Act against Health Crimes, and other related laws.

17. *Reforma* has conducted surveys of Mexico City residents' perceptions of crime and victimization. In 1997, the random sample included 786 individuals aged 18 years and older (one per household) who resided in eighty *colonias* of the Federal District. The sample was adjusted for electoral preferences, gender, and age. The survey's margin of error was 3 percent. In 1998, a random sample of Mexico City's electoral districts was comprised of 799 persons aged 18 years and older (one per household). The sample was adjusted for age and gender. The margin of error was 3 percent. In 1999, the random sample was increased to 1,118 cases (one person aged 18 years and older per household). In 2000, the sample size was 1,037. In 2001 and 2002, the surveys had the same characteristics of the survey in 2000.

18. These figures do not include data on homicide, suicide, drug trafficking, kidnapping and abduction, extortion, and crimes committed by government officials.

19. In *Reforma*'s survey of 8 June 1998, 47 percent of those surveyed felt that the Public Ministry agents were corrupt.

Bibliography

Alvarado, Arturo. Forthcoming. *Criminalidad y estado de derecho en la Ciudad de México.* Mexico City: El Colegio de México.
———, ed. 1998. *Desafíos a la consolidación de la democracia en México: Seguridad y estado de derecho.* Mexico City: El Colegio de México, 2001.
———. 2000. "Seguridad pública en la Ciudad de México." In *La Ciudad de México en el fin del segundo milenio,* edited by Gustavo Garza. Mexico City: El Colegio de México and Gobierno del Distrito Federal.
Alvarado, Arturo, and Diane Davis. 1999. "Descent into Chaos? Liberalization, Public Insecurity, and Deteriorating Rule of Law in Mexico City." *Working Papers in Local Governance and Democracy* 1: 95–107.
Alvarado, Arturo, and Diane Davis, with Mario Arroyo. 1999. *Institutions, Organization, and Activities on Public Security in México City.* Project "Police Impunity, Public Insecurity, and Deteriorating Rule of Law in México City." Chicago: John D. and Catherine T. MacArthur Foundation.
Arroyo Juárez, Mario. 2004. *Rendición de cuentas en la Procuraduría General de la República.* México, Derechos Humanos y Seguridad A.C.
Arroyo, Mario, and Arturo Cervantes. 1999. *Análisis sobre defunciones por homicidio en la Zona Metropolitana de la Ciudad de México, 1993–1997.* Mexico City: Secretaría

de Salud. (Cited in Asesores en Servicios de Salud (ASISA). *Diagnóstico nacional de la mortalidad por causas externas, 1995–1997.* Mexico City: ASISA-Secretaría de Salud, 1999.)

Arzt, Sigrid. 2002. "Combating Organized Crime in México: Mission (Im)Possible?" In *Transnational Crime and Public Security: Challenges to Mexico and the United States,* edited by J. Bailey and J. Chabat. La Jolla, CA: Center for U.S.-Mexican Studies, University of California-San Diego.

———. 2003. *La militarización de la Procuraduría General de la Republica Mexicana: Riesgos para la democracia mexicana.* Working Paper Series. Originally presented at Reforming the Administration of Justice in Mexico Conference, Center of U.S.-Mexican Studies, May 15–17. La Jolla, CA: Center for U.S.-Mexican Studies, University of California-San Diego.

Arzt, Sigrid, and Mario Arroyo. 2006. *Estudio de seguridad pública en cuatro entidades de la República Mexicana.* World Bank Report, México, May 2006.

Asamblea Legislativa del Distrito Federal. 1996. *Cifras comparativas sobre incidencia delictiva en grandes ciudades del mundo y el Distrito Federal.* Mexico City: Asamblea.

Bailey, J., and J. Chabat, eds. 2002. *Transnational Crime and Public Security: Challenges to Mexico and the United States.* La Jolla, CA: Center for U.S.-Mexican Studies, University of California-San Diego.

Cárdenas, Cuauhtémoc. 1998. *Primer informe de gobierno.* Mexico City: Gobierno del Distrito Federal, 17 September.

Comisión de Derechos Humanos del Distrito Federal (CDHDF). 1999. *Quinto informe anual, octubre 1997–septiembre 1998.* Mexico City: CDHDF. http://www.cdhdf.org.mx.

Comisiones de Seguridad Pública y de Administración y Procuración de Justicia de la Primero Asamblea Legislativa del Distrito Federal. 1998. *Algunas consideraciones sobre la estadística sobre incidencia delictiva durante los primeros meses de 1998.* Mexico City: Asamblea Legislativa del Distrito Federal.

Comisión Estatal de Derechos Humanos del Estado de México (CEDHEM). 1998. *Primer lustro de actividades, 1993–1998.* Mexico City: Comisión.

Comisión Mexicana para la Defensa y Promoción de los Derechos Humanos AC (CMDPDHAC). 1998. [Various reports.] Mexico City: CMDPDHAC. http://www.laneta.apc.org/cmdpdh.

Coordinación de Seguridad Pública. 1999. *Estadísticas sobre asaltos bancarios.* Mexico City: Asociación Nacional de Banqueros.

Debernardi, Rodolfo. 1987. "Seguridad pública en el Distrito Federal." In Gustavo Garza, et al., compilers. *Atlas de la Ciudad de México,* 221–224. México City: Departamento del Distrito Federal/El Colegio de México A.C.

Dueñas, Agustín, Leonardo Vite, Larissa Camarillo, Aurora Moncayo, and Martín Flores. 1998. *México bajo el signo de Caín. Resultados de un estudio comparativo sobre el homicidio doloso en México y el Mundo.* N.p.

Fajnzylber, Pablo, Daniel Lederman, and Norman Loayza. 2001. *Crimen y violencia en América Latina.* Washington, DC: World Bank; Mexico City: Alfaomega.

Figueroa Campos, Beatriz. 1998. "El registro extemporáneo de los nacimientos. una fuente de información desatendida." *Demos: Carta Demográfica sobre México* 11.

Gobierno del Distrito Federal, 1997. *Informes de auto evaluación de las delegaciones políticas, segundo semestre de 1993.* Mexico City: Secretaría de Seguridad Pública, Dirección de Logística y Operación, May.

———. 1999. *Informe de gobierno*. Mexico City: Gobierno, April 29. http://www.ddf.gob.mx/sedeco/justicia/delinsen.html.
González Ruíz, Samuel, Ernesto López Portillo, and José Arturo Yañez. 1994. *Seguridad pública en México: Problemas, perspectivas y propuestas*. Mexico City: Universidad Nacional Autónoma de México.
Human Rights Watch. 1999. *Systemic Injustice: Torture, "Disappearance," and Extrajudicial Execution in Mexico*. New York: Human Rights Watch, January.
Instituto Nacional de Estadística, Geografía e Informatica (INEGI). 1989–1999, 2001. *Anuario estadístico del Distrito Federal*. Mexico City: INEGI.
———. 1990–1998. *Anuario estadístico del Estado de México*. Mexico City: INEGI.
———. 1997. *Cuadernos de estadísticas judiciales*. Mexico City: INEGI.
———. 1998. *Cuaderno de estadísticas judiciales No. 5*. Mexico City: INEGI.
———. 1999. *Indicadores demográficos de México*. Mexico City: INEGI.
———. 2000. *Censo de población y vivienda*. Mexico City: INEGI. http://www.inegi.gob.mx-difusion-espanol-definitivos-iter-INITER09.pdf.
———. 2002. *Censo de población y vivienda de los Estados Unidos Mexicanos, 2000: Resultados preliminares*. Mexico City: INEGI.
Instituto Nacional de Estadística, Geografía e Informatica/Secretaría de Salud (INEGI/SSA). 2002. *Dirección general de información y evaluación del desempeño*. Mexico City: INEGI/SSA, 10 November. http://www.salud.gob.mx/index.html.
Ipsos Bimsa Consulting Company. 1997. *Encuesta sobre seguridad en el Distrito Federal*. Mexico City, January. http://www.bimsa.com.mx.
Lozano, Rafael, Martha Hijar, and José Luis Torres. 1997. "Violencia, seguridad pública y salud." In *Observatorio de la salud: Necesidades, servicios, políticas*, edited by Fundación Mexicana para la Salud (Funsalud). Mexico City: Funsalud.
Partido Acción Nacional (PAN). 1997. *Diagnóstico de plataforma de campaña electoral para la Jefatura de Gobierno del Distrito Federal*. Mexico City: PAN.
Procuraduría General Justicia del Distrito Federal (PGJDF). 1996. *Cifras comparativas sobre incidencia delictiva en grandes ciudades del mundo y el Distrito Federal*. Mexico City: PGJDF.
———. 1998. *Estadísticas sobre incidencia delictiva en el D.F.* Mexico City: PGDJF.
———. 2002. *Resumen ejecutivo de las actividades de la PGJDF, y estadística delictiva*. Mexico City: PGJDF. http://www.pgjdf.gov.mx/estadisticas/resumen_ej.asp.
Ramírez Ducoing, Karla. 1999. "La violencia en México: Una estimación de su costo a nivel nacional y en siete estados." Graduate thesis, Universidad Nacional Autónoma de México.
Ratinoff, L. 1996. "Delincuencia y paz ciudadana." In *Hacia un enfoque integrado del desarrollo: Ética, violencia y seguridad ciudadana*. Washington, DC: Inter-American Development Bank.
Ruíz Harrell, Rafael. 1998. *Criminalidad y mal gobierno*. Mexico City: Sansores y Aljure.
Sarre, Miguel. 1999. "Seguridad ciudadana y justicia penal frente a la democracia, la división de poderes y el federalismo." Paper presented at colloquium Desafíos a la Consolidación de la Democracia en México: Seguridad, Cambio Institucional y Federalismo, El Colegio de México, Mexico, January.
Secretaría de Salud (SSA). 1999, 2001. *Estadísticas vitales*. Mexico City: SSA.
Silva, Carlos. 2003. *Abuso policial en la Ciudad de México*. 2003–2004 Working Papers Series. Originally presented at Reforming the Administration of Justice in México

Conference, 15–17 May. La Jolla, CA: Center of U.S.-Mexican Studies, University of California-San Diego.

Sistema Nacional de Seguridad Pública (SNSP). 1997. *Incidencia delictiva del fuero común y fuero federal.* Mexico City: SNSP, Secretaría de Gobernación.

———. 2000, 2002. *Estadística delictiva.* Mexico City: SNSP, Secretaría de Gobernación.

Zepeda Lecuona, Guillermo. 2002. "Inefficiency at the Service of Impunity: Criminal Justice Organizations in Mexico." In *Transnational Crime and Public Security: Challenges to Mexico and the United States,* edited by J. Bailey and J. Chabat. La Jolla, CA: Center for U.S.-Mexican Studies, University of California-San Diego.

———. 2004. *Crimen sin castigo: Procuración de Justicia Penal y Ministerio Público en México.* Mexico City: Fondo de Cultura Económica.

Part III

Conclusions and Recommendations

Chapter 12

Conclusion: Security and the Rule of Law in a Democratic Society

Joseph S. Tulchin and Meg Ruthenburg

Even before September 11, 2001, security had become a major issue throughout Latin America. While terrorism itself was not of foremost concern to most, the vast majority of Latin Americans were deeply concerned about security—namely, their safety and the safety of their loved ones. Crime and violence had become one of the critical issues in public discussion from Mexico to the Southern Cone, whether in the media, in government, or in private social gatherings. In this sense, the deep anxiety prompted by crime and violence is an intensely personal and local phenomenon; it involves bad things that happen to you and your family or friends in your neighborhood. This is the sense of security that has dominated public policy debate in the hemisphere. People want to feel more secure and to the extent that they call on their governments to make them more secure, it is a hot public policy question. However, the response by the state to this demand—sometimes inchoate and sometimes highly focused and organized—is not so simple. The state's response to popular demands for greater security is formulated in the context of a wide range of issues that must take into account relations with neighboring countries; with other nations in the hemisphere, the role of the armed forces in matters of internal security; the recent history in some countries of the police and the armed forces being the causes of citizen insecurity, not the protectors of the people; and the fact that in many countries impunity, corruption, and the lack of effectiveness of the police and the judiciary exacerbate the problem.

Citizen security and national security were once considered distinct realms. During the Cold War under the rule of authoritarian regimes, the distinction was blurred as the armed forces assumed responsibility for internal security. One of the features of the transition to democracy in countries such as Argentina, Brazil, and Chile, was to build a firewall between the armed forces, which were responsible for external security, and the police, which along with the judicial system was responsible for internal law and order. In a post–September 11 world this dichotomy between internal and external security can no longer be sustained. Even before September 11, criminal activity, most notoriously drug trafficking, crossed the line between domestic and international security. Compounding this problem was the fact that the United States used its armed forces as the chosen instrument in the war on drugs, in effect ignoring the anxieties in Latin America about getting the armed forces involved in domestic crime fighting. Quite naturally, the U.S. armed forces turned to counterparts in the region for collaboration in the struggle to end the production and trafficking of drugs in the region. The fact that civilian control over the armed forces in the United States was not always replicated in the region did not seem to disturb the U.S. government. As a matter of fact, in some of the smaller countries the drug traffickers literally could outgun the local forces of law and order, so militarizing the struggle to prevent crime seemed to have a certain logic.

Today, security threats at the national and individual levels merge and are linked in ways that are complex and often hard to understand. While the citizen's demand for greater security may be highly local and may be precipitated by local events such as robberies or kidnappings, criminal acts today are rarely, if ever, strictly local. Increasingly, criminality is related to international traffic in drugs, stolen automobiles, small arms, and even, in some cases, people, and to money laundering. In addition, these illicit activities often are interrelated. In the smallest of states, as in Central America and the Caribbean, criminal activity literally does threaten national security. Even in Brazil, the largest nation in the region, there are obvious connections between local criminal activity in places like São Paulo and international criminal organizations. In both São Paulo and Mexico City, and elsewhere, there are areas in which the state has no authority and the territory is ruled by drug lords or, in the case of Colombia, by guerrillas or paramilitary groups. In Mexico and in several nations of Central America and the Caribbean, due to prisoner repatriation by the United States, armed gangs are assembled and armed in the slums of Los Angeles and other U.S. cities and then exported back to the region, a peculiar and perverse internationalization of violent crime. Is the appropriate response to call in the armed forces? Or, should the responses be multilateral and international? How are the civilian institutions of law and order to be buttressed so as to protect citizen security and enhance the nation's capacity to defend its own security?

To understand the dilemma of citizen security, we must first understand that security exists on five distinct, often interconnected, levels, and the appropriate response to any threat depends on how the threat plays out at each different level. A security threat can be global, as in the case of terrorism; it can be hemispheric, as in the case of an attack on the hemisphere by some power or group outside the hemisphere; it can be regional, as in some criminal activity, such as auto theft or small arms sales, that affects a contiguous set of countries within a geographically defined area; it can be national, as in the case in which one state threatens or attacks another; and, it can be domestic, as in the cases of criminal activity with no known or demonstrable international linkages; or, it might be some combination of these various levels, as is the case with regard to drug trafficking. In all cases, the state response should respect the institutions of the society or societies in question, it should seek to maximize the civil rights of the citizens involved, and should seek to promote the rule of law. Taking the five levels of security into account, increasing security requires robust institutions at the national and international levels, institutions that respect the rights of citizens and that seek to improve the relationship between citizens and the forces of law and order. If nothing else, September 11 and the resulting war on terrorism have brought this fact into bold relief: democracy and security are complementary—not contradictory—objectives. Moreover, to maximize both, it is necessary to strengthen the links between the citizens and the forces of law and order. In a democracy, the people and police must work together and both must be supported by a professional, efficient, incorruptible judiciary.

The preceding chapters have led us to this conclusion; they also point the way to an effective, operational approach to the future. We propose an approach to citizen security that focuses specifically on strengthening democratic governance and security through increasing citizen participation in local communities. As has been demonstrated throughout this volume, a lack of communication between the forces of law and order and the communities they serve is a crucial barrier to decreasing perceptions of insecurity and to the adoption and implementation of successful measures to diminish crime. In addition to efforts to improve policing and judicial effectiveness, improving citizen security requires measures that enhance accountability and citizen participation. These measures, in turn, reinforce the very institutions of democracy. Therefore, while some erroneously believe that security in Latin America can only be achieved with the iron-fist policies typical of the region's past dictatorships, we argue that it is not only possible to achieve security in a democratic society but that security, the rule of law, and democracy are actually complementary and self-reinforcing objectives.

In order to test this hypothesis and reduce the inflated perception of insecurity, we propose an action-research project aimed at empowering citizens at the local level and reducing the distance between the forces of law and order and the community they serve. This action-research project would accomplish three major goals. The first would be to share the knowledge that has been gained through recent research on citizen security in the region, including the research assembled here and in our previous volume *Crime and Violence in Latin America: Citizen Security, Democracy, and the State* (2003). The public is largely unaware of the potential impact of citizen participation on security, on their perception of insecurity, and on the governance of their society. Therefore, the first step in fomenting a more engaged citizenry is educating the citizens about these critical issues. It is important to emphasize that we are not talking about private policing or vigilantism. Neither of these contributes to democratic governance. In fact, the proliferation of walled communities protected by private security companies, which in Latin America are largely unregulated, contributes to social exclusion and actually makes the work of a professional police force more difficult.

The second goal of this project would be to provide a forum for discussion of security issues at the local level, so that people can put their newly acquired concepts to work and gain skills and experience in active community participation. Fomenting citizen participation is particularly important in Latin America, where patronage and clientelism remain strong. In dealing with citizen security, as in dealing with other social problems, it is important to build for the future while dealing with the immediate problem. It is important to create mechanisms or institutions through which citizens can articulate their needs and their interests. This is as vital at the local level as at the regional or national level.[1] It is essential to establish such mechanisms in order to express citizen needs; otherwise, popular outcry often becomes anomic and antidemocratic.

The third goal would be to have citizens use what they have learned by engaging the forces of law and order in dialogue in their communities. Citizen participation is an essential component of any successful public security initiative, including structural police reform. Accordingly, one result of this kind of research would be a set of guidelines regarding the role of citizen participation in these reforms in order for them to be successful at reducing crime and reinforcing democratic institutions.

In seeking this set of goals, the initiative we propose would test three basic assumptions. The first is that educating the citizenry increases their interest in citizen security issues and, in a democratic society, opens the way to greater public discussions of these issues. The second assumption is that bringing the community and the police forces together will increase the community's perception of security. While the notion that excessive distance between the citizens and the forces of law and order heightens the sense of citizen insecurity is one of the most important conclusions of this volume, the proposed project would evaluate the relative importance of this compared to other factors that affect the exaggerated perception of insecurity and the rates of criminality.

The last assumption is that citizen participation in police reforms is vital to obtain the desired results, that is, a series of reforms that will lead to a decrease in crime while promoting a robust democracy. We believe it is precisely this kind of engaged research that will help bring about greater security and better governance, beginning at the local level and reverberating throughout the various levels of security—global, hemispheric, regional, international, and domestic.

Note

1. See, for example, Philip Oxhorn, Joseph S. Tulchin, and Andrew D. Selee, eds., *Decentralization, Democratic Governance, and Civil Society in Comparative Perspective: Africa, Asia, and Latin America* (Washington, DC: Woodrow Wilson Center Press and Johns Hopkins University Press, 2004), and Joseph S. Tulchin and Meg Ruthenburg, eds., *Citizenship in Latin America* (forthcoming from Lynne Rienner Publishers).

About the Contributors

Editors

Joseph S. Tulchin is a senior scholar and former director of the Latin American Program of the Woodrow Wilson International Center for Scholars. His areas of expertise include U.S. foreign policy, inter-American relations, contemporary Latin America, strategic planning, and social science research methodology. Previously, Tulchin was professor of history and director of international programs at the University of North Carolina at Chapel Hill, where he edited the *Latin American Research Review*.

Meg Ruthenburg is former program associate in the Latin American Program at the Woodrow Wilson International Center for Scholars. Her areas of study include the Andes, social movements, and Quichua language and culture. Ruthenburg has conducted research in Ecuador on civil society organizations. She is currently a writer and translator living in Ann Arbor, Michigan.

Contributors

Arturo Alvarado Mendoza is a sociologist and professor of sociology at the Center for Sociological Studies at the College of Mexico, Pedregal. His recent work focuses on issues of justice, security, human rights, and policing in Mexico (monitoring and regulation of police corruption, fiscal limitations of police organizations, wage and benefits structure, systems of training, among others). Alvarado Mendoza's most recent project will contribute to the diagnosis of police organization in Mexico, as well as the mapping of law enforcement agencies and special units at the federal, state, and local levels.

Carlos Basombrío Iglesias is a researcher and consultant on issues of security, democracy, and human rights. He writes a biweekly political column in *Peru21,* a Peruvian newspaper. Basombrío is the former director and longtime member of the Institute of Legal Defense (Instituto de Defensa Legal), a non-governmental organization in Lima, Peru. He previously served as vice-minister of the interior of Peru, where he had a leading role in the process of police reform that took place between 2002 and 2004. He is the author of several books and essays.

Claudio C. Beato F., a sociologist, is director of the Center of Crime and Public Safety Studies (CRISP) at the Federal University of Minas Gerais. He has published more than thirty articles and book chapters about crime and violence in Brazil and Latin America. Currently, he is a visiting professor at Oxford University in the Center for Brazilian Studies. He works as a consultant for governments on citizen security in Brazil and Latin America.

Alberto Föhrig is adjunct visiting professor of political science at the Universidad de San Andrés in Buenos Aires, Argentina. His areas of expertise include contemporary Latin America, focusing on political participation, citizenship, and the quality of democracy in the region. Föhrig has written on the modernization of the public administration system and civil society in Argentina. Föhrig is coeditor of the *Journal of Latin American Affairs.*

Hugo Frühling is director of ALTUS, a global alliance working across continents to improve public safety and justice. He is also a professor at the Institute of Public Affairs of the University of Chile and director of the Center for the Study of Public Safety of the University of Chile. He has written extensively on judicial and police reform in Latin America.

Claudio A. Fuentes is the academic coordinator at the Latin American Faculty of Social Science (FLACSO) in Chile. Fuentes received the 2003 Best Dissertation Award by the Human Rights Section of the American Political Science Association (APSA). His focus includes comparative institutions and observing issues of political and social accountability in the political process.

Cecilia Gortari is the under-secretary of security of the province of Corrientes, Argentina. Previously, she coordinated the Corrientes government citizen security program and worked for the ministry of the interior of Argentina in urban crime prevention. Gortari was the crime prevention advisor to the public ministry of Paraguay and worked with Amnesty International Paraguay to coordinate an arms control campaign. Gortari is a member of the Paraguayan Society of Criminology (Sociedad Paraguaya de Criminología).

James K. Hammitt is professor of economics and decision sciences at Harvard University's School of Public Health and director of the Harvard Center for Risk Analysis. Hammitt's areas of research include development and application of quantitative methods to health and environmental policy. He has previously written on the economic value of reducing health risk in Mexico City.

Paulo de Mesquita Neto is a senior researcher at the Center for the Study of Violence at the University of São Paulo and is executive secretary of the Institute São Paulo against Violence in Brazil. His areas of research include democratic transition and consolidation, human rights, violence, police reform, and community policing. De Mesquita Neto will publish a book on police accountability in new democracies, focusing on the forces that promote and sustain democratic institutions in Latin America.

Andrew Morrison is a lead economist in the gender and development group of the World Bank, where he works in the areas of international migration, labor markets, violence prevention and the economic empowerment of women. Morrison has published numerous works on violence, crime, and social development in Latin America and the Caribbean. He previously worked at the Inter-American Development Bank, where he served as social development specialist.

Julia S. Pomares is the policy coordinator of the office of electoral affairs for the government of the city of Buenos Aires. Previously, she worked at the Office of the Deputy Prime Minister of the United Kingdom and was an advisor to the minister of the interior of Argentina. In that capacity, she coordinated the technical team for the national plan for crime prevention. Pomares has led conferences and written several articles on monitoring and evaluating crime and violence programs in Latin America.

Catalina Smulovitz is the director of the department of political science and international relations at the Universidad Torcuato Di Tella in Buenos Aires, and researcher at Consejo Nacional de Investigaciones Científicas y Tecnológicas (CONICET). She has written on accountability and citizen security in Latin America and on human rights and access to justice. Her publications include "Citizen Insecurity and Fear: Public and Private Responses in the Case of Argentina" in Joseph S. Tulchin, H. Hugo Frühling, and Heather Golding, eds., *Crime and Violence in Latin America: Citizen Security, Democracy, and the State* (Baltimore: John Hopkins University, 2003).

Graciela Teruel is professor and researcher at the department of economics at Mexico's Universidad Iberoamericana in Mexico City. Teruel's areas of expertise include dynamics, spending, saving, and economic crises. Teruel was the codirector of a census conducted in Mexico (2002–2005) to measure the levels of social welfare and social well being (Mexican Family Life Survey). She is the co-author (with Renato Villoro) of "The Social Costs of Crime: Is there an Impact on the Income Distribution?" (Inter-American Development Bank Project, October 2000).

Renata Villoro, an economist, is professor in the master's program in economics at the Universidad Iberoamericana in Mexico City. Villoro is interested in the trends and causes of delinquency in Mexico. She has written on the social impact of crime in Mexico and coauthored a study related to delinquency in Mexico City for the World Bank.

Heather H. Ward was the coordinator for the Vera Institute of Justice's program to survey systems of police accountability in democratic societies around the world with funding from the Ford Foundation. She is the coauthor (with Christopher E. Stone) of "Democratic Policing: A Framework for Action" (*Policing and Society*). She is consultant to the Woodrow Wilson Presidential Library and Museum.

Index

Page numbers in italics refer to tables and figures.

abuses of power, 58; discretionary powers of police, 207–8, 244
academics: Brazil, 175–76, 179; center for police research, 179; Chile, 197; community policing, 20; on democratic policing, 172–73; military justice system, 85n34; partnerships with, 199–200, 200–201; Peru reform, 278; Peru survey, 265; relationship with police, 117; relationship with policymakers, 118; torture in Mexico City, 297
accountability: advocacy networks and, 6; establishing mechanisms, 81; horizontal accountability, 83n7; improving mechanisms, 60; police abuses, 55, 59–60; police attitudes, 36; public debate, 20, 21; rule of law and, 3; training, 24; transparency debate, 65; vertical accountability, 83n7
accounting methodology, 127, 128–29
action-research proposal, 322–23
ACTIVA project, 20
actors in police reform, 197–202; Argentina, 209, 214, 256; human rights advocacy groups, 61; paths to police reform summarized, 7; Peru, 264–65, 275; principal actors, 8; three types summarized, 154

adversarial criminal justice system, 15
Advisory Commission for the Implementation of Community Policing, 28, 29
advocacy coalition approach, 6, 56
advocacy networks: case-by-case strategy, 81; defined, 57; influence of, 59; role of, 55, 56, 80; when influential, 80–81. *See also* human rights advocacy networks
alcoholic beverages, laws controlling sale of, 30, 43, 114, 115
Alianza coalition, 72–73, 75, 184
alliances: local and international, 67–70, 80; recommended, 82
alternative sentencing options, 274
Applying Preventive Citizen Security program, 228–31
Araya Moya, Jorge, 225, 226
arbitrary detention, 297–98
Argentina: block reform attempts, 76; community policing, 208–17; federal structure, 83n9, 249; human rights advocacy groups, 64; neighborhood groups, 217; penal codes, 60; police abuses, 61; police reform, 163–64; police role, 4; police viewed, 4; political parties, 72–73, 75, 184, 187; reform catalysts, 16; security programs in provinces, 209, 210.

329

Argentina (*continued*)
See also Buenos Aires Provincial Police; City of Buenos Aires; National Crime Prevention Plan (PNPD)
Argentine Federal Police, 9, 244, 246, 250, 258, 259n5
Aristide, Jean-Bertrand, 156
armed forces: Carabineros link, 189–90; crime-fighting efforts, 279; Guatemala, 157; Peru, 262; police force ties, 172; preferred to police, 2; United States, 320
armed robbery, 109, 110. See also Belo Horizonte, Brazil
arrest authority, 274
arrest quotas, 283
arrest on suspicion clause, 79
Arslanián, León, 67, 73, 74, 84n29, 85n44, 85n49
Asociación de Mutuales Israelitas de Argentina (AMIA), 163, 235n3
assault and battery, 285, 288–89
Associação de Proteção e Assistência ao Condenado (APAC) program, 97
Assunção, Renato, 176
attitudes of police personnel, 36
attitudes of residents: Argentina, 211–12, 260n13; Peru, 272–73, 276; quality of service, 43
authoritarian regimes: Fujimori, 9–10, 261, 262; human rights abuses under, 165; human rights advocacy in, 81; legacies of military control, 167; police abuses, 18; police reform after, 155; traditional police role, 4. See also military regimes
auto theft, 222
Aylwin, Patricio, 85n34, 162, 225

Bachelet, Michelle, 202n23
Bahia, 18–19
Beato F., Claudio C., 90, 175, 176, 177, 178, 180
Belo Horizonte, Brazil: community policing, 32–33, 178; homicide clusters, 105–8, *106*, *107*; officer attitudes, 36; problem-solving training, 49; property crimes trends, 109
Binder, Alberto, 67, 84n29, 85n43
Bogotá, Colombia: community policing programs, 31–32; community relations, 40; cost and coverage, 34–35; other entities and, 41–42
Bolivia, gender equity, 95
Bolsa Família, 97, *98*
Bonaerense (police force), 181–89
bounded rationality concept, 104, 116
Box-Cox transformation, 141–45
Brazil: citizen participation, 217–23; intervention strategies, 33, 96–97, 99; judicial reforms, 165, 166; Minas Gerais police reform, 174–81; police abuses, 18–19; police reform, 163, 164–65; slums, 105–7; urban crime rates, 105. See also Belo Horizonte, Brazil; community policing in Brazil; Minas Gerais; São Paulo
breach of trust, fraud, swindling, and plunder, 285, 289–90
Brizola, Leonel, 220
broken windows theory, 109
Buenos Aires Province: citizen participation, 210; Iron Fist policy, 244; lessons for Chile, 197; neighborhood groups, 217; police reform, 163–64, 181–89; public security law, 212; reform plan, 183–86, 209
Buenos Aires Provincial Police (BAPP), 61, 72–73
Bulacio, Walter, 61, 68, 83n11
burden-of-disease studies, 129
bureaucratic blockage, 74
Bush (George W.) administration, international civil society, 4
business management concepts, 18, 22

Cabezas, José Luis, 72, 163, 182, 235n3
California (USA), 96
Canada, training changes, 24, 33
Canadian Royal Mounted Police, 24
Carabineros, 25–27, 161–62; characterized, 5; citizen security committees,

230; community participation, 228; efficiency criteria, 228; historical link to military, 189–90; strategic plan, 15–16; trust levels, 224. *See also* Plan Cuadrante
Cárdenas, Cuauhtémoc, 283, 310
Castelar Sur (Buenos Aires), 212–13
Catholic Church, 62, 83n6. *See also* Viciarate for Solidarity
causal mechanisms, 101
Center for Justice and International Law (CEJIL), 68
Center for Legal and Social Studies (CELS), 61–62, 64–65, 67–68, 75, 187; challenges, 81–82; legal experts, 84n29; seminar on police, 72, 73
Center for Studies of Crime and Public Safety (CRISP), 8, 36, 40, 119n5; Minas Gerais project, 173–81
Central America: hedonic model use, 141; pilot programs, 29
centralization: administrative structures, 42; decision making, 37
CGPs, 251–54, 260n15
change: resistance to, 22, 24–25, 35–36; bureaucratic behavior, 74, 172; community policing, 219; corruption, 269; defensiveness, 180; electoral strategy, 74–76; institutional obstacles, 33–38; modest changes and, 180; "old guard," 179; police-led reforms, 198; pro-order coalition, 73–76; purges of police, 268; restructuring or public relations, 233; societal reasons for refusing, 71–72; studies showing, 51n14; three types of, 277
child mortality, 107
Chile: citizen participation, 223–31; decentralization, 21; government leadership in police reform, 161–62; human rights groups, 62; lower class attitudes, 19; Neighborhood Citizen Security Committees, 26–27; penal codes, 60; political influence, 16; political parties, 62–63. *See also* "detention on suspicion" clause

Chilean Committee for Human Rights (CHCHR), 63
citizen control, principle of, 29
citizen oversight, 60, 251, 257, 269
citizen participation: access to information, 251; analyzed, 8–9; Argentina, 208–17; assumptions about, 11; Brazil, 217–23; Chile, 223–31; community policing programs, 49–50, 207; computer "lynchings," 217; consultative, 250, 257; crime prevention program, 250–54; dark side of, 253; in decision making, 250–51, 257; defining, 210–11; encouraging, 273; executive functions, 251, 257; follow-up on problems presented, 50; fomenting, 322; forms of participation, 252; government responsibility for, 49; guidelines, 250; initial discourse, 253; mixed programs, 40; patterns of, 49–50; problem of sustaining, 234–35; reasons for lack, 234–35; recommendations, 321–23; risks of process, 253; roles of citizens, 253–54, 322; selection bias, 252; self-management of, 224–25; testing basic assumptions, 322–23; trust, 232–33, 258; user representatives, 264, 265
Citizen Peace Foundation, 223, 224, 225, 226, 227, 240n59
citizen-police relations, contributing factors, 4–5
citizen protection committees, 225–26
citizen rights: competing coalitions, resources, and strategies, 59
citizens: contributions of, 174; mechanisms for involvement, 199
citizen security: assessment, 270; new policies in Peru, 270–74; summarized, 10–11
Citizen Security in Central America project, 29
citizen security committees, 225–26, local and provincial, 273–74
citizen security policy, Bogotá, 41

citizen security programs: Argentina, 30, 209; Chile, 21; local resident control, 215–17; state agency participation, 210–15
Citizen Security Schools, 32, 40, 42
citizenship, quality of, 2
Citizens' Review Board, 80
City of Buenos Aires: crime and violence prevention councils, 211; National Crime Prevention Plan (PNPD), 243, 246–56
Ciudadela (Argentina), 217, 237n20
civilian killings by police forces, 71, 84n27, 188, 258n4. *See also* police abuses
Civilian National Police, 157
Civil Police, 179
civil rights: Argentina, 244–45; arrest authority and, 274; personal safety trade-off, 56–57, 81; pro-order coalitions, 58
civil rights coalition, 57, 58, 75, 78
civil society: Argentina, 209–10, 257; Chile, 197; judicial reforms, 162–63; organization and mobilization, 167; participatory aspects, 257; police reform, 162–63, 199–200
civil society organizations: citizen participation, 252; combating corruption, 269; leadership in police reform, 154; police abuses, 55; role of, 6, 7–8; technical assistance, 225
clientelism, 254, 322
Código de Faltas, 60
collective efficacy, 108
Colombia: Constitution (1991), 159, 160; government leadership in police reform, 159–60; insider-outsider tension, 63–64, 68; reform catalysts, 16; youth crime prevention, 98–99. *See also* Bogotá, Colombia; DESEPAZ crime prevention program
commanders, 188, 198
community: police relationship with, 38–41; training citizens, 40
Community Councils, 113; evaluation, 40

community groups, contributions of, 174
community intervention, 10
community organizations, links with community policing programs, 49–50
Community Police Department, 218
community policing: academics, 20; Argentina, 208–17; Brazil, 165, 176, 178; case studies summarized, 27, 208; central role of street officers, 34; Chile, 196; citizen participation summarized, 8–9; citizen perceptions of, 220; community needs, 9; conditions for implementation, 207; crime reduction and, 6; definitional issues, 231–32; in developed nations, 46; implementation, 9, 47, 48, 207; initial definitions, 207–8; Latin America, 24–25; North American model, 5, 23–24; officer attitudes, 36–37; ongoing consultation with community, 23; organizational changes, 23–24, 222–23; paradigm behind, 46; planning for future, 46–49; police abuses, 23; police stations, 272; relations with nonpolice bureaucratic agencies, 234; role of community, 23; role of, 17; São Paulo, 218–20; skepticism about, 46; support for, 20; theoretical aspects of training, 48; trust, 232–33
Community Policing Advisory Commission, 38–39
community policing: in Belo Horizonte, Brazil, 32–33; in Mendoza, Argentina, 15; goals announced, 15; São Paulo program, 27–29
community policing programs: Bogotá, Colombia, 31–32; comparison, 5, 231; dark side of, 253; implementation, 47; links with community organizations, 49–50; planning issues, 47; preliminary inferences, 45; projects summarized, 208; range of citizen participation, 207; response to perceptions of insecurity, 206; restructuring police agencies, 233, 258; results of, 42–45;

setting objectives, 47–48; as strategy, 21; sustaining citizen participation, 234–35; Villa Nueva, Guatemala, 29–31
Community Prevention Councils, 246–47
community relations: planning for future, 46–49
Community Relations and Crime Analysis office, 195
Community Security Councils, 29, 32, 39
community service sentences, 274
comparative approach, 3
complaints against police, 82n1, 84n26; hotline, 183
computer "lynchings," 217
computer technology, 177
conceptual discussions, 92–93
Concertación coalition, 62–63
confidence in police, 45; Argentina, 182–83; Guatemala, 43; Peru, 272–73
conflict resolution, 95, 114
conservatives, 172
contingent valuation (CV) analysis, 7, 126, 132–33, 140
controls on police conduct, 19
cooperative planning, 236n15
Coordinator Against Police Repression (CORREPI), 61, 64, 67–68, 80–81
Coordinator of Public Security Councils, 29
Copacabana (Brazil) community policing program, 221–22, 238n34
Corporación por la Defensa de los Derechos del Pueblo (CODEPU), 63, 65
Corporación por la Defensa de los Derechos Juveniles (CODEJU), 63, 69
Corporation for Legal Assistance, 85n34
corruption: Argentina, 85n42, 181, 182, 183, 185; guiding principles, 266; internal controls and efforts to combat, 268–70; Office for the Control of Corruption and Official Abuse, 185; Peru, 262, 263
Costa, Gino, 264, 268, 276
cost-benefit analysis (CBA), 130
cost-benefit ratio calculations, 96, 97, 102

costs of crime and violence, 99–100, 100t, 126–27, 133–39; monetary and nonmonetary, 146n2
country club–type communities, 245
Covas, Mário, 165
crime control programs and policies, 91–92
crime prevention: Argentina, 214, 217, 254–56; citizen groups, 199; efficiency emphases, 55; integrated prevention, 254–56; relations with nonpolice bureaucratic agencies, 234
crime rates: Argentina, 208–9, 216t, 243–44; Buenos Aires Province, 181, 182; as catalyst for reform, 16; Chile, 190, 191, 192, 223, 238n38; City of Buenos Aires, 246; community policing impact, 46; comparative analysis for Mexico City, 300–306; hypotheses on Mexico City, 309–11; as implosion, 104–5; measuring, 201; Mexico City, 280, 283–86, 300–306, 307–8; Minas Gerais, 176; New York City, 55; official data analyzed, 308; pressures on police, 18; readiness to cooperate with police, 41; São Paulo, 44–45; São Paulo State, 28; sensationalist media coverage, 6; soaring, 1; theoretical approaches, 117; think tanks and, 17–18; trends, 20, 45, 90, 126, 171
crime reduction: community policing and, 6; crime control demands, 18; Duhalde reforms, 189; socioeconomic factors, 171; tough approach, 187
crimes against persons, 104–8
crimes against property, 108–11; City of Buenos Aires, 246; Mexico City, 288, 302, 308–9; reporting, 308–9; specific strategies, 116; underreporting, 102
crimes by police against citizens, Mexico City, 296–98
Crime and Violence Prevention Councils, 209, 211, 236n9
criminality: international nature, 320
criminology studies, 101

DALY. *See* disability-adjusted life year (DALY) calculations
D'Angelo, Amadeo, 76
decentralization: Argentina, 249, 251; Bonaerense, 183–84, 186; effect on police, 21; Plan Cuadrante, 238n28; state reform, 21–22, 45
decision making: centralization in, 37; citizen participation, 250–51, 257; reforms, 79, 80
Delegados Departamentales de Investigaciones, 186
delinquent minors, 110
demands on police by citizens, 173
democratic police service, 172–73
democratic system: citizen confidence in, 1; critics from right and left, 153–54; police and judicial reforms, 167; police and legal institutions, 153; recommendations, 321
democratic transitions: armed forces/police split, 319–20; Chile, 224; crime rates and, 2; human rights and, 163; transformations with, 172
democratization: as catalyst for reform, 16, 17; police abuses criticized, 18
demographic trends, 309–10
Department for Community Policing and Human Rights, 165, 219
DESEPAZ crime prevention program, 111–15
"detention on suspicion" clause, 60, 68–69, 76–79
deterrence theory, 91
Development, Security, and Peace Program (DESEPAZ), 111–15
Diadema, 165, 218
dichotomous-choice questions, 133, 146n6
disability-adjusted life year (DALY) calculations, 127, 129–30
disciplinary systems, 188
discretionary powers of police, 207–8, 244
Domestic Security Council, 245, 259n10

domestic violence, 93–95, 100, 113, 119n2; health impacts, 130
drug-related activities, Brazil, 105, 108; Mexico City, 309, 310
drug trafficking, 31, 111–12, 182, 320
Duhalde, Eduardo, 72–73, 74–75, 85n56, 164, 181, 183, 187

economic crises: civil rights-public safety trade-off, 57, 81; Mexico City, 310–11
EDUPAR course, 113–14
effectiveness: measuring, 201
El Salvador: peace agreement, 15; reform catalysts, 16
ENIGH survey (Encuesta Nacional de Ingreso—Gasto de los Hogares), 134–39
Entre Ríos Province (Argentina), 214–16
environmental issues: hedonic models, 131; situational factors, 93
equity promotion, 114
Espinosa Villarreal, Oscar, 283
evaluation: Carabineros, 228; City of Buenos Aires, 211; community policing, 208, 222, 231; DESEPAZ program, 115; factors to include, 208; individual performance, 195; lack of, 116; measuring impact of reforms, 200–202; Policing with Results program, 178; promotions, determining, 272; quantitative targets, 240n56; range of variables, 201; violence prevention programs, 95
extortion, 298

Favela-Barrio project, 221
fear of crime: Chile, 191
Federal Attorney General's Office (PGR), 299–300
Federal Council for the Protection of Children, 65
Federal University of Minas Gerais, 174, 175, 179
Fernandes, Rubem César, 222

Fica Vivo program, 97, *98*
foot patrols, 34, 35, 221
FORJA, 228–31
formal economy, 294
Forum in Defense of Life, 44
Foundation for Consensus for a Federal Security Plan, 245–46
Foundation for Democratic Change, 212, 236n12
free riders, 58, 82n4, 235
FREPASO (Front for the Country in Solidarity), 72, 73, 75, 84n29, 184
Fujimori, Alberto, 160–61, 261, 262
Fundação João Pinheiro, 175, 179
funding: for equipment and databases, 42; for personnel, 34, 271; program implementation, 48

gangs: Brazilian prevention programs, 97; causes, 95–96; Colombia, 114; as economically driven businesses, 96; Mexico City, 310; social rehabilitation, 31
García, Alan, 160
Garotinho, Anthony, 176
gated communities, 245, 322
gender stereotypes, 95
geographic information systems, 103
governments: challenges of security issue, 245; leadership in police reform, 154, 158–62; police as political tools, 16; role in security policy, 234. *See also* municipal governments; state reform
grassroots voluntary groups, 221. *See also* civil society
Gualeguaychú (Argentina), 214–16, 236n14
Guatemala: community policing programs, 29–31; funding for personnel, 34; peace process, 15, 30, 156–58; reform catalysts, 16. *See also* Villa Nueva, Guatemala
Guerrero, Rodrigo, 112
guerrillas: Colombia, 114; Guatemala, 156–57

Haiti, 156
health economics, 131
health losses, 128
hedonic housing methodology, 7, 126, 131–32, 133–39, 140–41, 146n4; details of price estimation, 141–45
Hidalgo State, 281
hierarchy, 37
higher education for police, 178–79
homicide: loss of healthy life, 130; theoretical approaches, 117
homicide clusters, 105–8, *106, 107*
homicide rates: Brazil, 1, 102, 105, 222; Colombia, 1, 112, 114; as criminality indicator, 102; land prices, 132; Mexico City, 134, 135, 136, 139, 140, 285, 286–88, 312n6; São Paulo, 28, 218; socioeconomic variables, 106–7, *107*; trends, 20, 90, *91,* 171
horizontal accountability, 83n7
housing prices, 146–47n8
housing rents: elasticity of, 137, *139*
human rights: accountability, 36; Argentina, 165–66; Brazil, 28, 166; Chilean Committee for Human Rights (CHCHR), 63; Colombia, 31; after democratic transitions, 163; Haiti, 156; Mexico City police violations, 296–98, 300; military regimes, 62; National Program for Human Rights, 166
human rights advocacy groups, 59–61; as actors, 61; Chile cooperation lacking, 80; collecting information, 64–67; influence of, 56; past human rights violations, 68; police abuses, 78, 79; policy experts, collaboration with, 68; policy influence, 70–71; public opinion, 81; torture in Mexico City, 297
human rights advocacy networks: local and international alliances, 67–70, 80
Human Rights Ombudsman, 160
Hungary, 171

Iberoamerican Institute of Penal Law, 67
ILANUD (United Nations Latin American Institute for the Prevention of

ILANUD (*continued*)
  Crime and Treatment of Offenders), 219–20
impunity (lawlessness), 274, 287, 288; Mexico City, 294–95, 296, 309
incommunicado detentions, 78–79
informal economy, 294
information on crime: access to and citizen participation, 251; addressing deficiencies, 117; Argentina, 80, 81–82, 245, 257; Chile, 194–95; creating data and indicators, 7; crime analysis techniques, 180; data banks/bases, 92, 117, 177; data-gathering programs, 92; importance of, 101–3; information and survey system, 115; Mexico City, 309; strategies for action plans, 112–13; types of, 103. *See also* mapping, computer
insecurity: inflated perceptions of, ix, 1–2, 4, 171; action-research proposal, 322–23; addressing effectively, 11; Argentina, 209, 213–14, 216, 244; Brazil, 44, 220; Chile, 191, 225, 226, 230; citizen participation, 235; community policing, 220, 231; distance between citizens and police, 323; effect on civil liberties, 5; as impetus for reform, 199; Mexico City, 280, 300, 313n17; personal and local nature, 319; police reform response, 206; policies summarized, 206; preliminary inferences, 45; punitive response, 206, 207; state response, 319, 321
insiders: working within system (Chile), 63
Institute for Crime and Security Policy, 184, 185, 187
Institute of Criminal Policy and Public Safety, 73
institutionalized violence, 19
institutional traditionalists, 277
integrated intervention structure, 93
integrated policing, 238n34
integrated prevention, 254–56
intelligence directorate, 186

interagency approach, 245, 248, 256, 257–58
Inter-American Court of Justice, 68
Inter-American Development Bank (IDB), violence control programs, *94*
Interim Public Security Force, 156
Internal Affairs Office, 269
international actor leadership in reform, 154, 155–58
international civil society organizations, 4
internationalization of violent crime, 320
interpersonal crime, 104–8
interrogation by police as evidence, 75
intervention programs, 96
intrafamily violence, 93–95
iron fist electoral discourse/policy, 74, 244

Jardim Ângela, 218, 219
judicial reforms, 165–66; accountability, 60; approaches to crime reduction, 171; Argentina, 164, 165–66; Brazil, 165, 166; Chile, 162; civil society, 162–63; Colombia, 160; complexity of, 167–68; Guatemala, 157–58; Haiti, 156; Peru, 161
judiciary: role in Colombia, 7
Juntas Locales de Seguridad, 157
juveniles, 63, 69, 110, 245; alternative sentencing, 274; police killings of, 258n4. *See also* youth

kernel density approach, 119n7
kidnapping, 281, 285, 294, 307, 309, 311n3

Law on the Rights of Arrested Persons (1998), 19
leadership: in reform process, 200; three types, 154
legislative debates: monitoring, 82
life expectancies, 129–30
literacy rates, 107
Local Citizen Security Committees, 277–78
Local Security Fronts, 32, 40, 42

lower class: attitudes in Chile, 19; police relations with, 45
Maier, Julio, 67, 84n29
Management and Participation Centers, 211, 236n9, 247
mapping: computer, 103, 177, 195. *See also* information on crime; spatial distribution of crime
media campaigns, 113, 269–70, 272–73, 275
Mexico City crime trends, 133–39
Mexico City Metropolitan Area (MCMA), 133–34, 135; crime and violence described, 283–86; institutional framework, 282; mortality rates, 286–87; myriad of laws governing, 281; notes on violence and crime, 308–11; organized crime, 294, 298–300; prosecutor's office, 282–83
México State, 281, 286t, 311–12n5
militarized police forces, 16–17. *See also* military police
military courts, 60
military regimes: civil rights-public safety trade-off, 57, 81; human rights activism, 56, 62; past human rights violations, 62, 63, 165. *See also* authoritarian regimes
Minas Gerais: civil society-police collaboration, 8, 39; funding for police, 42; police reform, 174–81
Minas Gerais Military Police, 32–33, 174–81
Ministerio Público (Mexico), 282, 290
Minister of Justice and Security, 181, 185
Ministry of the Interior (Peru), 276–77
Miñones, Emilio, 62
minor offenses, 274
minors. *See* juveniles
Miranda-type rights, 70, 76, 77, 79, 85n38; accountability, 60–61
Mission Bogotá program, 41–42
Model Penal Code for Latin America, 67

models of public administration and management, 16; business management criteria, 18
Modernization Commission, 266, 270
monitoring police behavior, 82, 281–89
Montesinos, Vladimiro, 262
Morales, María Soledad, 235n3
motivation for crime, 104
muggings, 108–9, 223, 239n41
multiagency approach. *See* interagency approach
multisectoral boards, 260n16
Municipal Citizen Security Council, 30, 38, 41
Municipal Defenders of Security, 185, 187
municipal governments: Argentine federal structure, 249; citizen participation viewed by, 226; citizen security role, 49, 227; crime prevention, 114, 116; local security solutions, 191
Municipal Security Council, 113
mutual distrust: citizen-police, 232–33

National Citizen Security Council, 273
National Civil Police: Guatemala, 30–31
National Crime Prevention Plan (PNPD): citizen participation, 250–54; City of Buenos Aires, 246–56; complementary objectives, 247; effects of clientelism, 254; implementation, 252, 257; integrated crime prevention, 254–56; main objectives, 247; organizational structure, 248–50; regional and general coordination teams, 249–50, 256; security as priority, 243–46; summarized, 9; where implemented, 243
National Institute of Justice, 118
National Intelligence Center (Peru), 263
National Intelligence System (SIN), 160, 262, 263
National Police: Colombia, 22, 159–60; hierarchy, 267; Institutional Strategic Plan, 160

National Police: Peru, 22, 161; commission for restructuring, 264–66; militarization, 262; overview, 10, 50n2; principles of reform, 266–67; public security crisis, 160–61; purges, 267–68; reform, 263
National Program for Human Rights, 166
national security, 319–20
Neighborhood Citizen Security Committees, 26–27
Neighborhood Community Security Councils, 209, 212
Neighborhood Councils, 273
Neighborhood Crime and Violence Prevention Councils, 247
neighborhood movements: Argentina, 209–10, 215–17
neighborhood organizations: patrol activity, 40
Neighborhood Policing program, 220–21
Neighbors United Group, 237n17
Neuquén Province (Argentina), 243
new managerialism, 46
New York City: crime rates, 55
Niños Amigos de Paz (Children Friends of Peace), 113
North American model of community policing, 5, 23–24

Office of Citizen Participation (DIRPACI), 273
Office for the Control of Corruption and Official Abuse, 185, 187
Office of the Inspector General of the Police, 269
Office of Internal Affairs, 277
Office of the Police Ombudsman, 277
Ombudsman's Office, 83n8, 160
open-ended questions, 133
operating capacity of police forces, 295
opportunity reduction programs, 116. *See also* situational-environmental prevention
oral trials, 15
Organic Law of the National Police in Peru (1999), 161

Organic Law of the Police of Buenos Aires (1998), 164
organizational changes: Argentina, 209; Chile, 193–94; community policing, 23–24, 222–23; crime prevention plan, 248–50; guiding principles, 267; legislation required, 184; Peru, 277; professionalism, 25; relations among social agencies, 116; restructuring (community policing), 233, 116
organizational paradigms, 46
organized crime, 153; guiding principles, 267; international, 320; Mexico City, 294, 298–300; street crime versus, 270
outsider groups, 63–64

Pact of San José, Costa Rica, 259n7
Paixão, Antonio Luiz, 175, 179
Palma, Raúl (torture incident), 78, 79
paramilitary groups: Guatemala, 30
PARCES program, 114
Pardo Rueda, Rafael, 159
partnerships with other official entities, 248–50
Pastoral de la Favela, 220
patrol activity: Argentina, 237n19; Guatemala, 43; neighborhood organizations, 40; Patti, Luis, 65
Paz nas Escolas program, 97, *98*
Peace Houses (Casas de Paz), 113
peace processes, 15, 30, 155
penal codes, 60, 76, 311n3; Mexico City catalogue of crimes, 282
Peñalosa, Enrique, 41
Peronist (Justicialista) party, 7, 73, 74–75, 85n45, 184
personnel: funding for, 34; movement of, 35; rotation of, 186; training subordinates, 37
Peru: government leadership in police reform, 160–61
Pettigani, Eduardo, 65
pilot programs: selection of, 48–49
Plan Alert, 215–16, 237n18
Plan Cuadrante, 25–27, 189–97; analyzed, 196–97; citizen participation,

227–28; citizen security committees, 230; decentralization, 238n28; deployment by cuadrantes, 193; expansion of, 202n23; factors leading to reform, 190–92; information management and performance measurement, 194–95; major features, 192–95; outcome, 196–97; resource management, 193–94; three elements, 190

Plan for General Reorganization of the Integral System for Security and Investigation of Crime of Buenos Aires Province (1997), 183–86

Plan for Integrated Neighborhood Security and the National Plan for Dissemination of Preventive Police Activities. *See* Plan Cuadrante

plunder, 285, 289–90, 312n8

PNPD. *See* National Crime Prevention Plan

police abuses: Argentina, 61, 181, 258n4; Chilean trends, 65–66; citizen contact, 5; citizen fear of, 71; community policing, 23, 45–46; ethics and behavior guidelines, 186; homicide rates, 218; human rights advocacy groups, 78; improving accountability, 55; minority perceptions, 23; Policing with Results program, 180; political factors, 81; problem of proof, 59; protecting vulnerable groups, 58; São Paulo, 19; three reasons, 19; tough measures against crime, 55; when advocacy networks matter, 59–61. *See also* civilian killings by police forces

police brutality, 176

police-community relations: three models, 38

police culture: culture-dependent skepticism, 46; guiding principles, 266; hierarchy, 37; management concepts, 22. *See also* change, resistance to

Police Ethics Tribunal, 187

police forces: as actor in reform, 264, 275; advantages over civil society groups, 58–59; code of loyalty, 59; community policing support, 41; community relationship with, 38–41; democratic police service, 172–73; employee benefits, 275–76; operating capacity of, 295; peer loyalty, 59; purges, 267–68; relations with other entities, 41–42; salaries and compensation, 283; similarities, 16; traditional model, 16–17

Police Movement (MOPOL), 73–74

police reform: after democratic transitions, 172; agenda setting in Argentina, 64–65; Argentina, 163–64, 258; Brazil, 163, 164–65; Buenos Aires Province, 163–64; catalysts for, 16; civil society, 162–63, 199–200; complexity of, 167–68; conceptual discussions, 93; current trend, 80; different paths and results, 200; exclusion of police from, 188–89; expectations of police, 153; government-led reforms, 198–99; impetus for, 173; implementation, 59; incentives, 8; listed by country, 84n28; major actors summarized, 7; model of, 200; obstacles in Peru, 278–79; origins of, 17–22; Peru, 263, 278–79; police-led, 198; purges, 267–68; range analyzed, 25; response to perceptions of insecurity, 206; São Paulo State, 163, 164–65; three paths summarized, 154; through political agreement, 162–65; time factor, 173; types of, 6. *See also* change, resistance to

police stations: importance of, 271–72; proximity of, 44

police violence: catalyst for reform, 16

Policía de Investigaciones, 161, 191

"Policing with Results" program, 176–79

policy experts, and advocacy groups, 68–69

policy recommendations, summarized, 2

political socialization, 251

politician-led reform, 8, 199, 257

politicians, distrust of, 275

politicians: and mutability of reforms, 219; time pressures, 199
poverty, 311. *See also* socioeconomic divisions
Presidente Perón (Buenos Aires), 213
presidential power, 268
prevention programs: Argentina, 244; at-risk youth, 98
prevention of violence programs, 94–95
primary prevention, 255
private security industry, 183, 191, 322
problem solving: preventive programs, 41; training, 36
ProÉtica, 269
professionalism: levels differing, 16; organizational changes, 25; police-led reforms, 198; two positions, 20
professional police, rule of law and, 3
Programa Uerê, 97, *98*
pro-order coalitions, 57–58, 58–59, 67, 69–70, 71–72; comparative advantage of, 81; electoral strategy, 74–76; framing public safety, 82; resisting change, 73–76; verification of identity clause, 77, 79
property crimes. *See* crimes against property
prosecutor-police relationship, 69
Provincial Public Security Law (1998) provisions, 184–86
public administration, new concepts, 22, 46
Public Defender's Office, 160
public good, 140; citizen participation, 235; defined, 82n3
public image of police, 208
public opinion, human rights advocacy groups, 81
public policies: academia and, 118; conceptual definition, 92–93; design of information systems, 101–2
Public Prosecutor's Office (Colombia), 160
public safety: civil rights trade-off, 56–57, 81, 82; as a public service, 58
public security crises, 159–62

Quadrant Plan. *See* Plan Cuadrante

Rancagua Comuna, 230
rape, 285, 289
rational choice theories, 235
reactive police activities, 37, 42
reporting of crime, 193
repressive measures, 206, 207; tough approach, 55, 96, 187
repressive policies: perceptions of insecurity, 5
reputation of police, 208, 209, 233
Research Center on Public Security (CRISP), 8, 36, 40, 119n5
resistance to change. *See* change, resistance to
results-based policing, 32
reveal preference approach, 127–28, 131
rich and poor communities, access of, 191–92, 193
Rico, Aldo, 75, 85n57, 164, 181, 187
Rio de Janeiro, 220–23
risk factors, 93, 112, 114, 119n1
robbery: Brazil, 222; Mexico City, 109, 285, 288, 295; state of São Paulo, 28; taxis, 180; trends, 20
Rodley, Nigel, 65
Rospigliosi, Fernando, 263, 264, 267, 268
Ruckauf, Carlos, 74–75, 85n56, 164, 181, 187
rule of law: democratic solutions versus repression, 4; elements of, 3–4; public's role, 10

Saavedra (Argentina), 215–16, 216t, 237nn20&22
Safe Commune Plan—Commitment 100, 27, 196
Saín, Marcelo, 85n44
Santa Fe Province (Argentina), 209
São Paulo: changes attempted, 35; community policing, 218–20; community policing programs, 27–29; crime rates, 44–45; opinion polls, 44; police

abuses, 19; police-community relations model, 38–39
São Paulo Military Police, 27–29, 35, 39, 51n16, 218
São Paulo State, police reform, 164–65
school dropout rates, 98
Secretariat of Security, 29
security: five levels of, 321; national expenditures on, 128
security councils, 27
September 11, 2001, attacks, 320, 321
serenazgo patrols, 111, 262
Serrano, Rosso José, 159–60
Service Volunteered for All (SERVOL) program, 99
sex crimes, 286
shantytowns, 220, 221
Shining Path movement, 10, 262
Silva Neto, Severo Augusto da, 177
situational prevention, 110–11; 254–56
slums, 105–7; shantytowns, 220, 221
social capital, 90, 99–100, 108, 112
social class divisions, 19
social cleansing, Bogotá police participation, 31
social compact, 1
social control, weakness of, 108
social prevention, 254–56
social protection buffer index, 107
social violence, 93
socioeconomic divisions: access to services, 191–92, 193; approaches to crime reduction, 171; crime rates and, 90–91; homicide rates, 106–7, *107*; inequality and criminal activity, 294; predictors, 103–4; youth crime, 245
solidarity, reconstruction of, 100
Solís, Zenaída, 264
South Africa, 171
spatial distribution of crime: Brazil, 103–8; Mexico City, 291, *292*. *See also* mapping, computer
spatial logic of crime, Mexico City, 292–94
Special Areas Policing Group (GPAE), 222

Special Commission for Restructuring the National Police, 22, 264–66; guiding principles for change, 266–67; internal controls and efforts to combat corruption, 268–70; mistakes made, 274–76
stakeholders, dialogue among, 3
Stange, Rodolfo, 161, 192
stated preference approaches, 127, 132
state reform, 18; decentralization, 21–22
strategic action planning, 41
street crimes, 108–11
street population, 109, 258n3
strikes, 176
student protesters, handling of, 182
Sussekind, Elizabeth, 222
sustainability of programs, 49
surveys, confidence in police, 20

taxi robberies, 180
technological innovations, 267; tools needed, 271. *See also* information on crime; mapping, computer
terrorism, political use of label, 263
tertiary prevention, 255
thefts, 223
thefts in commercial buildings, 110
think tanks, crime rates and, 17–18
three strikes sentencing policy, 119n4
time restrictions for detentions, 77
Toledo administration, 9–10, 278
torture: Chile, 65, 66; as a crime, 77; Mexico City, 297–98, 312–13n15; Palma case, 78
traffic accidents, mortality from, 286–87
training: accountability, 24; Brazil, 32–33, 177–78; Canada, 24, 33; citizen preventive activities, 225; citizen security programs, 229–30; citizens in crime prevention, 50; command level as facilitators, 33; community policing in Colombia, 31–32; higher education for police, 178–79; internal setting of objectives, 47–48; Ontario police, 24; Peru, 266–67; problem solving, 36; professional commissaries, 272;

training (*continued*)
  technology, 177–78; theoretical aspects, 48; traditional police model, 16–17
Trinidad and Tobago, 99
trust issues, 8, 224, 232–33, 258
turnover rates, 35
two for one law, 259n7

Ugarte, Manuel, 192
underreporting: Argentina, 243–44, 260n13; Chile, 223–24; crimes against property, 102; explanations for, 308; Mexico City, 300, 303–6
unemployment: crime related, 100–101, 309–10; high population densities, 139, 147n12; youth, 259n8
Unión Cívica Radical (UCR), 72, 184
United Nations, missions, 156, 157–58
United Nations Commission on Human Rights, 68
United States, war on drugs, 320
units of service/vigilance equivalents, 191–92, 193, 194
Urban Guard, 31
user representatives, 264

Vecinos Unidos por la Seguridad ¡Asaltados!, 217
Venezuela, decentralization, 21
"verification of identity" detentions, 70, 77, 78, 79, 85n41
vertical accountability, 83n7
Viciarate of Solidarity, 62, 63, 83n14.
victimization: Chile, 191, 223–24; Mexico City, 306, 307; small community police stations, 45; trends, 20; views of police activity (Argentina), 214
victimization surveys, 42–43, 103, 108–9, 244, 300–306

Villa Alonso, 237n22
Villa Nueva: Guatemala, 29–31, 34, 35; citizen surveys, 43–44; other entities and, 41; police-community relations model, 38; victimization surveys, 42–43
Villarán, Susana, 264
violence: against women, 130; community policing impact, 46; conceptual discussions, 93; costs of different types, 127; drug-related activities, 111–12; economic and social costs, 99–100, 100t, 126–27, 133–39; estimating costs of, 126–27; loss of healthy life, 130; macroeconomic effects, 90; prevention programs, 94–95; property crimes trends, 109; as public health problem, 130; trends, 126; violence control programs, *94*. *See also* domestic violence
violent crime: Brazil, 33; strategies, 45
Viva Rio movement, 221–22

weapons: civilian possession of, 245; controls on, 114; homicides in Mexico City, 288; sentencing, 259nn6&9
willingness-to-pay (WTP) methodologies, 7, 127–28, 130–33, 139–40, 146n3
Woodman, Arturo, 264
Woodrow Wilson International Center for Scholars, 2–3, 265

youth: at-risk prevention, 98–99; unemployment, 259n8. *See also* gangs; juveniles
youth development centers, 98–99

Zaffaroni, Raúl, 67, 84n29
zero tolerance security rhetoric, 67, 224